General Doctrines and Private Law

Friedrich Julius Stahl

THE PHILOSOPHY OF LAW

VOLUME I: *The History of Legal Philosophy*

1A: *The Rise and Fall of Natural Law*

1B: *The Recovery of Historical Law*

VOLUME II: *The Doctrine of Law and State on the Basis of the Christian World-View*

PART I: *General Doctrines and Private Law*

BOOK I: *Philosophical Presuppositions*

BOOK II: *Principles of Law*

BOOK III: *Private Law*

PART II: *The Doctrine of State and the Principles of State Law*

BOOK IV

THE PHILOSOPHY OF LAW

Volume II: The Doctrine of Law and State on the Basis of the Christian Worldview

Books I-III

General Doctrines and Private Law

Friedrich Julius Stahl

Translated, edited, and prefaced by
Ruben Alvarado

WordBridge
PUBLISHING
εν αρχη ην ο λογος
AALTEN, THE NETHERLANDS

WORDBRIDGE PUBLISHING
Aalten, the Netherlands
www.wordbridge.net
info@wordbridge.net

German original: Friedrich Julius Stahl, *Rechts- und Staatslehre auf der Grundlage christlicher Weltanschauung: Erste Abtheilung, enthaltend die allgemeinen Lehren und das Privatrecht.* Fifth unchanged edition. Tübingen and Leipzig: J. C. B. Mohr, 1878.

ISBN 978–90–76660–82–0

COVER ILLUSTRATION: "Moses on Mount Sinai" by Jean-Léon Gérôme (1895). This reproduction is courtesy of Wikimedia Commons and is in the public domain.

NOTE ON THIS EDITION

Books I–III of Vol. II, previously published separately as paperback books, are here included one after the other in their original form. Page numbering, tables of contents, and indices are unchanged.

Philosophical Foundations

TABLE OF CONTENTS

PREFACE

The ostensible purpose of this book is to introduce the reader to the philosophy of law. But it is much more than such an introduction. Unsurprisingly, it was also published as a stand-alone volume in 1846, entitled *Foundations of a Christian Philosophy,* which sums up its content admirably. Indeed, even given the 175 years since that publication, one would be hard-pressed to find a better introduction to Christian philosophy. As Stahl put it in his foreword (which can be perused on pp. xxiff. below), "The request of friends led me to provide this special edition under the consideration that a large number of those for whom these 'philosophical foundations' are likely to be of interest, namely theologians and theology students, cannot or will not seek them out in a work on legal philosophy." And that is the point. Although it provides the framework within which legal philosophy should be pursued, this book also does the same for the other disciplines, not only theology but economics, natural science, business administration, the humanities. For it provides the metaphysical and ethical basis to pursue these other disciplines. What is needed in our ethically challenged day and age is precisely a metaphysical and ethical orientation that slashes a way through the wilderness of ideologies and power-craving opinions that threaten to overwhelm civilization, as indeed they already have overcome the universities.

In this respect, not much has changed in the intervening 175 years, and in fact what we are living through now is the inevitable harvest of the *Bildung* that began shaping public and private opinion in the Enlightenment, if not before. What was then in the minds of men (dead white males!) is now in the streets and in the halls of representative assemblies, in corporate boardrooms and at the desks of bureaucratic "public servants" (who long ago lost the notion of servanthood in favor of unaccountable dictatorship – ah yes, for the greater good, of course), in classrooms high and low. And what was in the minds of men was radical subjectivism. As I wrote in the preface to *The Rise and Fall of Natural Law,* "There is no overarching standard that transcends individuals and what they, each in and for themselves, determine to be right and wrong, good and evil, worthy of praise or of opprobrium. As a result, there is no shared set of values by which individual self-determination can be guided or restrained; instead, what passes for a shared set of values is simply the aggregation of individual legislations pitted against similarly aggregated yet opposed legislations, whereby the winners impose their aggregated mass of particular interests on the entirety" (p. xi).

The root of this subjectivism is the notion that there is no personal God. And Stahl stakes his ground precisely here, at the "polar opposition" of God or no God. "Every philosophical science must begin with the supreme principle of things, the 'absolute.' To do so, it must decide on the polar opposition that has come to clear awareness in our time, as to whether this supreme principle is the personal, otherworldly, revelatory God, or an impersonal power inhering in the world itself – *pantheism*" (p. 5 below). Everything boils down to personal theism or pantheism, for radical subjectivism is nothing other than the equalization of God and man, Creator and creature, eliminating the distinction between them, whereby everyone is a god; for "each individual has become a legislating god pronouncing his or her 'LET THERE BE ...' and woe to whoever stands in the way of every particular 'AND THERE WAS ...' ."[1] Stahl elaborates on this in the preface to the second edition: "The fact that I once again put the doctrine of the personality and freedom of God at the forefront is self-explanatory. In itself it is the supreme, decisive doctrine for every philosophical conception, influential especially in the entire ethical-political sphere – the current manner of treatment has no inkling of this – and in particular is the cardinal question of the present. What impels this in its innermost being is the struggle between theism and pantheism; it is nearly the same thing, at least in terms of result, as the struggle between Christianity and the de-Christianization of the civilized world" (p. xxxix).

But whence cometh the right to postulate the living God as the principle of knowledge? It is a simple *requirement of philosophy.* How so? Consider this: "The course of all scientific investigation in fact is not, as one commonly assumes, to proceed from given data with logical consistency to conclusions with regard to the uncertain, but instead to ascribe something as-yet unknown, a hypothesis, to known phenomena in order to see if it explains them" (p. 148). This being the case, "according to philosophy's own law – not to ignore anything that

---

[1] *The Rise and Fall of Natural Law,* p. xvi.

exists – it is requisite to make such a use, as hypothesis, of revelation, which makes the claim itself to be the supreme knowledge" (p. 149). In this way, philosophy is to test "the worldview of the doctrine of revelation as *solution key* in its sphere and put... such to the test *according to its own laws"* (p. 148). In so doing, "the meaning which revelation attributes to itself is preserved, while without it the true worldview would not be capable of discovery"; nevertheless, "this does not eliminate the independence of philosophy, for it takes on that foundation *not in faith, but only as, and to the degree that, it is tested"* (p. 149).

Scientific integrity is preserved while the unavoidable reality – the existence of the personal, revealing God – is no longer assumed away but rather made available to the investigative mind. And why should this not be the case? Why is it *scientific* to assume that God does not exist?

> If there were a God and He created the world, should that not be accepted because it is unscientific? If reason really did not carry the world in itself and could not find the world out by itself, would it nevertheless have to remove the world from itself, because that alone would be scientific? One might just as well require on the basis of science that man should not be born but rather should exist from eternity; or that man should feed himself from himself without food; or that the eye should see of itself, without objects and their impressions from outside. Scientificness demands that you be gods, but the fact is that you are only human – do you have to comply with scientificness? Indeed, if philosophy really showed in terms of scientific laws that the world is the result of logical necessity, and how it is so, and then someone came along and wished to impose on it the opposite from faith and the Bible, then philosophy would have reason to complain about a violation of its independence. But it did not show this, but only assumed it; the reverse is the case, the edifice of knowledge which it founded on this premise, turns out – precisely according to scientific evidence – to be insufficient to explain the world, and to be inconceivable in itself. Not only religious belief, but all empirical science – natural, historical, and legal science – has set up the most zealous guard against it, through their most outstanding representatives! (p. xxxiv).

It is the heighth of presumptuousness to maintain this façade as if it were the only possible way of looking at things scientifically. But this façade is ripped away when the presumption is laid bare.

> Now should science be so independent that it does not have to inquire into the facts of reality and the laws of truth? Is it the trick to explain the world without God, in and for itself, regardless of whether the explanation is sufficient – is this the essence and the glory of the scientific character? It is no subjection of science to authority if one expects of it that its knowledge should correspond to the object. No natural scientist will want to avoid the fact that his teaching must pass the test of the phenomena of nature – and yet the philosopher should have the privilege of his teaching merely being seen as logically consistent in order to be considered true, even if contradicted by all the facts, even if it leaves the great object it is supposed to solve untouched! (p. xxxiv).

Indeed, the entire enterprise is exposed as the ramshackle illusion it in fact is, supported only by the will to believe it, the desire to be free of this God, to appropriate divinity to oneself. Pantheism was supposed to be scientifically established and personal theism scientifically refuted, but that was only a convenient illusion.

> Now there are those who say that scientific research necessarily leads to pantheism, and we close ourselves off to it only because our hearts cannot accept it. In fact, the reverse is true. Even if the God in which religion believes cannot be demonstrated mathematically, scientific research comes down decisively against the pantheistic assumption; and one adheres to it only because of the impulse of the heart, by the force of a deep temptation with which our times are encumbered, similar to the polytheistic temptation of the ancient world, or the ascetic temptation of the Middle Ages (p. 6).

There is more to it than just facts, there is the interpretation of those facts. Ever since Kant it has become clear that the mind puts its own "spin" on the data it receives. As a result, we have what we call worldviews. "The apprehension of things in their all-encompassing interconnection according to their highest cause and their final goal is what we term worldview" (p. 2). And no philosophy is free of worldview.

> Every philosophical system of whatever name in the final analysis rests on a foundational presupposition that is nothing more than faith, no matter what claim it may make to so-called scientific certainty. Even unbelief is a faith – one cannot reason from naked doubt.... It only depends on which basic assumption takes hold of the full inward person with the impression of unmistakable truth. The error of many lies in the fact that the basic assumption of the philosophical system that sweeps them along is not clear to them in its pure, sharp form and in its full meaning; and to display the opposing world views – of philosophy and of Christianity – against each other in their basic assumption with such clarity and sharpness, and with the complete consistency to which they must proceed, is therefore not only the sole but also the immense service that science is capable of providing for ultimate and supreme convictions (pp. xxi–xxii).

Christianity's worldview begins and ends with the sovereign creator God who acts in history to redeem a fallen world. This thesis explains what no other hypothesis can. For it is in the triad creation-fall-redemption that the peculiar condition of earthly life can be understood. By taking on the Christian revelation as a working hypothesis, philosophy – lo and behold! – comes to discover

> that the Christian revelation is the solution of the riddle – that it gives the explanation of all phenomena for which philosophy has no explanation – that it explains the dichotomy of human existence, shows and resolves the contradiction of reason and will, of spirit and flesh, of confidence and despondency in their origin – that it allows us to recognize a plan and purpose in world history, which plays out confusedly and purposelessly before our natural eye, in the economy of redemption and the kingdom of God, which mysteriously permeates them as a determining power – that it reveals the moral order in a perfection and eternal harmony, such as we never ourselves could discover, but which our whole innermost man recognizes as the clarity of its premonition, as the image of its primal memory, as its own eternal being – that a majesty of the divine arises in it which can only be the splendor of the true God (p. xxxiii).

And so Stahl gets to work, fleshing out the details of this "working hypothesis" in the areas of metaphysics and ethics. Stahl's metaphysics focuses on personality, first God's, then man's, and consequent on this, the inclination of the entire creation towards personality. "If the cause of the world is personal, then personality is also the archetype manifested in its formations, and it has the drive and the goal to be elevated thereto. This cause is not logical (ontological) determinations as such; rather, these are themselves only an abstraction from the person, his being and his creations. What we esteem in nature or in the realm of thought, organism, system, etc., is only an afterimage along the lines of the character of personality" (p. 17).

Personality entails a series of positions each of which is mutually reinforcing. The one that most forcefully impresses us is freedom, as opposed to the necessity ordained by impersonalism. What exists does not exist of necessity but by virtue of an absolutely free, creative act, an "*absolute beginning.*" For "only in this way is the world a creation of God and not just His elucidation or emanation, be it physical, be it logical. 'God calls into being that which is not' applies not only to the existence, but also to the essence of things" (p. 22). This is creative freedom as opposed to ethical freedom, in which a (theoretical) choice between good and evil is posed; it is the freedom to act without predetermination. Impersonalism, by contrast, entails determinism. Being persons, human beings participate in this freedom at their respective level. This also yields the proper understanding of the totality of occurrences which we call providence. Our acts are free and yet they are all brought to cohere under a guidance by which all things are led to the final end. "The absolute coherence which we require over and above the series of individual causes and effects, if it at the same time is to be in harmony with them, cannot lie anywhere else than in divine providence. Only a personal spirit is able to combine the myriad of individual causes into one result, and to set in motion the intermediate real means to achieve the representation of an ideal conception. This is the only way to explain both the subservience of physical results for spiritual ends, and the often likewise artistic significance of these ends themselves" (p. 33).

How is this possible? How can our acts and our destinies be ends in themselves yet at the same time serve a higher end? It is an impenetrable mystery rooted in the fact that God lives in an eternal present, and for Him there is no before and after. We see this in the case of the creation of this world:

> Although for God there is no past and future, the possibility of another is for Him as it is for us subsequent to an act that has already taken place, which excludes the same. We can therefore assert the possibility of another world only in the relative and ideal meaning that the definite world is not just given by the divine being, but is the work of free act, insofar as another was possible; on the other hand, we cannot assert the possibility of another world in an absolute or real sense, because God has really decided on this world, and according to the eternity of divine relations, we cannot set a point in time at which He would not have decided on it. But now we have no idea of the state of an eternal present; indeed, it is contradictory to us that the divine counsel of creation, which is an act, and therefore occurs in time, should nevertheless be an eternal one. We are therefore absolutely incapable of thinking how possibility relates to reality and necessity in God (p. 30).

Yet this freedom is not arbitrary; it is balanced by that other position, the divine will, which is wholly good and cannot choose evil. Indeed, the essence of the will *is* the good; and the conflict among the medieval schoolmen as to whether the good determined God's will or God's will determined the good is hereby rendered moot.

> The divine will in its substance is infinite love, mercy, patience, truthfulness, loyalty, justice, spirituality, etc., everything in its totality and its concentration on the innermost being of God which we characterize as the *holiness of God.* The holiness of God therefore as little precedes the divine will (the scholastics' *sanctitas antecedens voluntatem*) than follows it; instead, it is this will itself. Or, the good is just as little a law for the divine will (that God wanted it because it was already good in itself) than it is a creation of the divine will (that it only came into being because and after being willed by God); but it is just the primordial will of God from eternity to eternity (pp. 65–66).

So what then of the capacity to choose between good and evil? For God, it is theoretically but not actually possible. For man, the same held true until he fell, at which point came a rupture between his essence as person ("the good is nothing other than the essence of the person," p. 66) and his will. "In the condition of man whereby he stands apart from God and at the same time under the power of evil, the ought and the will are not merely differentiated but are separable and in conflict. There is a will in man that contradicts his ought. At the same time... the ethic, which as its own original will would be of infinite intensity and capacity for improvement, becomes, as an external power opposed to the will, a delimited rule. The good in this form, on the one hand as an external power that can be separated from one's own will, on the other hand as a delimited rule, is the ethical law" (p. 77). We arrive at the familiar condition of having a standard over us telling us what to do, when originally we knew from ourselves what to do.

This not only holds true for people individually, but collectively. There is not only individual morality but also an ethic for the common human condition, expressed in the institutions of law and the state. This is the result not only of the twofold nature of the ethical world, but also of sin. "In the empirical condition, subjective ethical behavior, *morality*, and objective ethical behavior, *law*, are *heterogeneous* and *separate*. Morality has the character of *accidental fulfillment*, law has the character of *externality* and *limited* (only *negative) content*. So, the former has forfeited certainty of fulfillment, the latter inwardness and with it real ethical behavior. And the law in many cases allows and sanctions what morality forbids. This is not just the unfolding of the ethical world on both sides in the spheres of the individual and of the whole, in line with its nature (§. 25), but rather a division and laceration of it" (pp. 111–112). This collective order of things is known as the civil order (§§. 48ff.).

At this point we have arrived at the starting point for the consideration of the legal order, which is the purport of *The Doctrine of Law and State on the Basis of the Christian Worldview*. The civil order, while an expression of the ethical kingdom, is specifically geared to the condition of sin. "The civil order... is an ethical kingdom insofar as it is realized in the actions of personal beings, but it is nevertheless a kingdom of external law, ultimately supported and maintained by physical power and consummated in external actions and conditions" (p. 114). But because of this origin, it can be turned to evil ends: "But what is specific about it... is the potential for evil, the constant possibility that it itself may fall away from the law which it has the task of enforcing – unjust laws and unjust rulers" (p. 114). For this reason the civil order ought to incorporate countervailing powers to ensure that despotism is not established. The realization that our condition is fallen should put us on our guard. Such a realization will ensure that "we harbor no meaningless expectations of a perfect political situation vouchsafing the salvation of the peoples, no more than a philosophy that will penetrate us with new discoveries or mathematical certainty about eternal things or satisfy the longing of the human heart. It will also maintain the sobriety whereby politics acknowledges 'the measure of given conditions.' Above all, it will oppose the unlimited power of the prince no less than the unlimited power of the people, but rather make them inclined to the condition in which manifold human positions are secured and manifold organs are open to power and influence on the public, so that each force placed in the community by God finds its free development, by which the temptation inherent in every human position finds its moderation in the strength of the other positions" (p. 114).

The book concludes with a discussion of the ideas of justice and atonement. Stahl restricts himself to a discussion of civil justice without exploring other spheres of application as would later legal philosophers such as Herman Dooyeweerd (e.g., justice within non-state, private associations), not to mention what is known as "social justice." But he does pave the way for those discussions by propounding a twofold concept of justice, *retributive* and *protective,* roughly corresponding with the Aristotelian categories of distributive and commutative (although Stahl is critical of that categorization – see §. 55). Retributive justice establishes the rule of the ethical kingdom, whether divine or human, and in the state, it is the standard of the rule of the civil magistrate in affairs of criminality. It is the justice by which threats to the majesty of the law and the magistrate are put down. Protective justice, on the other hand, maintains the entitlements of persons; it upholds them in their rights and their competencies. For its part, atonement is not a function of the civil order at all but of something greater, the eternal kingdom. It is the process whereby the threat to the majesty of God's rule is dealt with while the violators of that rule are restored. As such, it is the fulfillment of justice while also the means of redemption of the violators thereof, and it is accomplished by the Son of God, Jesus Christ.

The appendix contains an interesting and revealing discussion of the relationship between theology and philosophy, which lays bare Stahl's distinctly Lutheran framework for understanding this relationship. This understanding revolves around the, in Stahl's view, restricted nature of revelation. For instance, Stahl argues earlier in the book that revelation does not inform as to how to arrange the civil order: "revelation provides regulations governing man's behavior in relation to the existing order, but it does not give instructions about the formation of this order. No divine image of the civil order is given, because the way it is, is not of God" (p. 115). This typically Lutheran understanding of revelation is further explained in the appendix as having to do with the purpose thereof, which is to reveal the relationship of God to man and His plan to restore that relationship. "In terms of the aspect of absolute knowledge, which theology represents, man is *supported by a divine revelation* which is lacking to him in terms of the other aspect thereof, represented by philosophy. For example, we have a revelation regarding the divine *redemption plan* but not one of the divine *world plan.* Likewise secular knowledge here below consists in *discursive thinking,* analogous to the externality of the state, while religious knowledge consists in *intuition,* at least to a certain degree, through that real union with God" (p. 145). But these two forms of knowledge are not divorced, as they ultimately deal with the same reality; and in fact, it turns out that revelation can be put to the service of philosophy, in the manner discussed (pp. viiiff. above). So we end up with a robust, albeit indirect argument in favor of the application of revelation and theology to public life, one indeed far more robust than contemporary Christian "political theology" even attempts.

This summary description of the contents of this book is intended to do some justice to those contents. Of course, it by no means exhausts that content. What is clear is that Stahl provides the first coherent, comprehensive exploration of the direct application of the distinctive Christian worldview to public affairs in a scientific manner. Previous treatments did not scratch the surface of what a Christian worldview entails. This not only scratches the surface but sets a standard which even today is rarely met.

As such, it is disgraceful that Stahl's immense contribution to Christian-worldview understanding has not been recognized. Histories of worldviews such as that put forward by Naugle[2] contain no mention of Stahl, despite Stahl's pioneering efforts. In his day he was recognized as such. One such admirer was the Dutch antirevolutionary statesman Guillaume Groen van Prinsterer, who

---

[2] Naugle, *Worldview: The History of a Concept.*

spoke of his "singular yet lamentable career"[3] – lamentable precisely because misunderstood, especially by those who should have been kindred spirits.

> But why was Stahl, the outstanding defender of Christian truth, not infrequently the target of sharp and vehement polemic even by many faithful Christians, even those whose merits and character I highly value? Because they do not see the identity of the struggle in religion and politics. Because they fail to notice that this struggle, in principle, is waged, beyond all distinctions of polity and creed, over submission or resistance to the ordinances of God. Because, often orthodox and free-thinking at the same time, they overlook the Revolution in its proper character and therefore regard the aspiration of the antirevolutionary party as a stubborn adherence to all that is old, as an obstinate rejection of all that is modern.[4]

Is this not the reason for Stahl's oblivion, from which he still has not been restored? Is it not because of Christians – those who claim to promote Christ's kingdom but in fact yield to the spirit of the age and end up promoting the very liberalism and neutral state that lie at the heart of the Revolution? They promote stopgaps while blindly allowing the motive force to remain in place. Typical of blinkered conservatism, they think only to slow the progress of the disease, instead of striking it at the root.

> We do not imagine that the Revolution, because it was defeated, is ended. Even now we sit atop a volcano; though the fire does not break out at this moment, it smolders; and we know not how long the period may be that we are allowed. I ask: how do you stop that volcano? Many answer: by liberal concessions.... Others argue that powerful reaction is required.... Finally it is said that the Revolution does not end except by satisfying the need for German nationality. Come now, do you not know that in France for a long time neither unity of representation nor centralization of national power was missing? But there, too, one

---

[3] *Ter Nagedachtenis van Stahl* [In Memory of Stahl], p. 8. A translation of this book will *Deo volente* be published soon.

[4] *Ter Nagedachtenis van Stahl*, p. 37.

> stands before the Revolution as before a gaping abyss. No! the evil lies deeper. Only when one works from the inside out, can it be healed. Concessions, reaction, nationality, can all be good in their place; they do not exclude the Revolution. The Revolution in Europe is ended only by *Christianity and the Christian state and the Christian school.* For this reason I bid you improve the constitution on this point; restore the bond between church and state, between church and school.[5]

Indeed: restore the bond between church and state, between church and school. Not much has changed in 175 years.

---

[5] Stahl, "Speech on the Separation of Church and State [1849]," in *Siebzehn parlamentarische Reden* [Seventeen Parliamentary Speeches], pp. 106–107.

NOTES ON THE TRANSLATION

Square brackets [like this] are used either to show the original text in cases in which the translation is not straightforward or unambiguous, or to provide interpolations for better understanding, or to provide supplementary material.

A key term used by Stahl is *Anschauung,* from *anschauen,* which means to view, to envision, to contemplate. *Anschauen* is used to describe human cognition in its fullest sense. It is the immediate pre-analytical (intuitive) apprehension of things. It is made possible by the way in which we are created: We are so made as to apprehend directly, and only then to analyze and deduct. Discursive reasoning follows along, making understandable that which is already immediately apparent, but also opening the way to understanding things that are not immediately apparent. Nevertheless, in our separation from God, discursive reasoning is disconnected from this vision and becomes totalitarian, pursuing its independent wrongheaded course. Stahl explains this in detail in Part I, ch. 6, "Human Cognition." I have usually translated *anschauen* as "envision," *Anschauung* as "vision."

Stemming from this is worldview – *Weltanschauung,* vision of the world. Here we use the conventional translation of "view" rather than "vision," as it would be futile to attempt to introduce such an alternate usage. The notion of worldview took wing when, in the face of the rationalism which was predominant in the 18th century, speculative philosophy began to postulate the primacy of prerational vision, the presuppositional framework on the basis of which reason operates. This had the effect of making explicit the subjectivism which was already rampant but lay hidden behind the guise of rational objectivity. Worldview-ism certainly is a product of that turn; worldview could be and has been abused in terms of subjectivism, but the abuse does not negate the use. Stahl demonstrates as much as he outlines here the Christian worldview in its philosophical and scientific application.

AUTHOR'S FOREWORD TO THE SPECIAL EDITION

What I present to the public under the title *Foundations of a Christian Philosophy* is an unchanged copy of the greater portion of the first book of my *Philosophy of Law*. The request of friends led me to provide this special edition under the consideration that a large number of those for whom these "philosophical foundations" are likely to be of interest, namely theologians and theology students, cannot or will not seek them out in a work on legal philosophy. I have added a chapter on "Justice and Punishment," a chapter on "Atonement" (an attempt at a more satisfactory presentation of the doctrine of satisfaction), and finally an appendix "On the Relationship between Philosophy and Theology," which likewise is a discussion of the theological standpoints of Hegel and Schleiermacher. The first is for the most part put together from later parts of my work on legal philosophy. The other two are properly worked out. Through these additions, the work, in its separation from the work on legal philosophy and especially for the readership for which it is intended, forms a whole that encompasses a range of related scientific problems.

I chose the title *Foundations of a Christian Philosophy* because the text not only is not a complete system of philosophy but is not even the outline of one. Natural philosophy is completely absent from it, and regarding logic only the metaphysical elements are provided. Of the parts of philosophy which it covers, metaphysics and ethics, only those which seemed decisive for the cardinal questions of human belief and knowledge are dealt with. So the object is nothing other than the most basic foundations upon which a Christian philosophy is to be conducted. Nevertheless, the character of such, its entire structure and position, is definitively predetermined thereby.

The *problem* of the philosophical doctrines given here, even in their original elaboration, which at the same time was intended to support a specific part of philosophy – the philosophy of law – is an independent one: *the scientific confirmation of the Christian worldview*. To wit, the apprehension of things in their all-encompassing interconnection according to their highest cause and their final goal is what we term worldview. Every philosophical system is such a worldview. Every religion, and particularly the Christian, contains such a worldview, though not always with the same degree of realization. We base the doctrine of law and state upon the Christian religion. But that scientific confirmation of the Christian worldview cannot extend so far as to make faith optional for its acceptance. Science can only make room for faith, it cannot render faith superfluous. Only keep this in mind, that such is no less the case with every other worldview as well, even those schools of current philosophy that oppose Christianity. Every philosophical system of whatever name in the final analysis rests on a foundational presupposition that is nothing more than faith, no matter what claim it may make to so-called scientific certainty. Even unbelief is a faith – one cannot reason from naked doubt. We have no immediate or homogeneous view of the highest principles of things and thus no absolute certainty; therefore for philosophical systems a purely objective knowledge independent of all personal judgment, as in the manner of mathematics, the natural sciences, or even the positive sciences, is ruled out (see below, §. 21). It only depends on which basic assumption takes hold of the full inward person with the impression of unmistakable truth. The error of many lies in the fact that the basic assumption of the philosophical system that sweeps them along is not clear to them in its pure, sharp form and in its full meaning; and to display the opposing world views – of philosophy and of Christianity – against each other in their basic assumption with such clarity and sharpness, and with the complete consistency to which they must proceed, is therefore not only the sole but also the immense service that science is capable of providing for ultimate and supreme convictions. That is the aim of my presentation.

It is therefore also at the same time a discussion of the philosophical development from Descartes and Grotius up to Hegel. I hope this will not cause it to lose its value and interest; indeed, it conducts such a discussion in a *positive* way, as the first volume of my legal philosophy did in a negative way. If it answers to the task set for it, it shows, on the one hand, the untenability and impracticability of the assumptions of this philosophical development not only in itself but in relation to what I assert as positive truth, and on the other hand not only shows what is wrong with the concepts which produced it but also the true motive and true component contained therein, which must be appropriated to our worldview, and indeed which constitute an advancement and expansion thereof for all time.

Hopefully I do not have to defend myself against the idea that I wanted to found a new philosophical system in the sense that is usually associated with it. It does not occur to me to undertake this myself, nor do I believe that anyone more capable than I am can or should do so. Fortunately, the time of philosophical systems is over. The wisdom of the world has lost its impressive prestige, one is no longer amazed at new, unheard-of knowledge that no one dreamed of before. What I designate as Christian philosophy is only the scientific order and more succinct exposition of the concepts of which the entire consciousness of our time and especially the Christian consciousness is filled, not some new principle, a new way of thinking contrary to the general way of thinking of men, nor any other higher knowledge which in its nature has gone beyond the limits of previous human knowledge. Rationalistic and speculative philosophy are opposed to general and natural thinking and recognize themselves as such; mine strives for nothing else than to promote the self-consciousness and vividness of general and natural thinking in its own way.

Berlin, February 1846

AUTHOR'S PREFACE TO THE THIRD EDITION

Upon publication of this third edition, I find myself in the favorable position of not having to change or withdraw anything of the essential content of principles and treatment. Nevertheless, through my continued lectures on the subject, through the experiences of my parliamentary activity, and through the lessons which have been taught us by the powerful events of the times, I believe that I have made progress in scientific substantiation and conception as well as in practical insight; and this progress I must not withhold from the book.

Thus, Part I of Volume II has seen considerable expansions and, I hope, improvements. The first chapter of Book II [*Principles of Law*], "The Concept of Law and its Relationship to Morality," has been reworked. My earlier teaching on this is by no means abandoned but only more deeply grounded and more precisely defined, and I place special emphasis on the new presentation of this basic concept of legal theory, which I believe has been brought closer to its clear and secure determination. As a result, the following two chapters, "Positive Law, Natural Law, Revealed Law" and "The Origin and Sources of Law," had to be revised in many cases. The foundation of property is significantly expanded (Book III [*Private Law*], Part II, Chapter I), something which the movements of the times demanded. Newly added chapters (except the chapter on "Atonement" which was taken over from a late "special" printout of the philosophical presuppositions) are the following: the popular character of law – freedom and equality – protection of acquired rights – the principle of humanity – Communist-Socialist repudiation of property – concerning mixed marriages – freedom of instruction. In addition, many particulars have been expanded upon.

It is a source of particular satisfaction to me that the new edition of my work offers the opportunity to furnish it with a higher degree of perfection. Already upon initial publication of the first volume, this work fully embodied the serious opposition to the direction of the times which has attracted extensive hostility to me all my life and which recently, in turn, has earned for me gratifying approval and recognition. My lecture "What is the Revolution?" which expresses this contrast in a concentrated form, and which my opponents interpreted as a speech calculated to defend a contemporary political party, is only the popular translation of what was given there on a detailed and strictly scientific basis. The principles of my political career were already laid down in that first volume and were developed in what followed in the later edition. It is the starting point and center of my public activity; it will also one day be the lecture in defense thereof, for which reason I cannot do enough to bring it to full truth and lucid representation.

In particular, when the first volume of this work [*The History of Legal Philosophy*] initially appeared, it already constituted a call to the "turnaround of science." The occasional cursory mention of this was received with indignation, straightaway as a denigration of science – until recently. Now my weak voice of 25 years ago is being echoed by the thunderous voice of world events.

In 1829–1830, human wisdom, which had put itself in the place of the divine, was yet at the zenith of its power. It filled the professorial chairs with its devotees, the bookstores with its findings. It sat in judgment of the manifestations of the entirety of literature and believed that it ruled the kingdom of minds in all of that kingdom's impulses and future developments. But now, regard for philosophy has fallen to a level never before seen among civilized peoples. The memory of it has virtually faded away. There is scarcely a mention of the most renowned philosophers in the daily press, in social interactions, in the works of positive science, in the great proceedings of church and state. No book appears any longer in the form of the dialectic method, which then was held to be the indispensable stamp of scientificness. Should a chair of philosophy fall vacant, no one any longer asks by whom it will be filled.

A well-earned judgment has been passed on philosophy. The ecclesiastical movement at the start of the 1840s, and the political movement at the end of it, revealed twice to the entire world that the manner of thinking pertaining to the entirety of the more recent (pantheistic-rationalistic) philosophy had at its core the *denial of the living God,* and that the destruction in church and state was only the final factual fulfillment of the philosophical doctrine which had been admired for so long.

From the time of Christian Wolff until our day, the enlightened world has ever received with disgust the accusation which religious faith has been compelled to raise against philosophy, denying it as untrue and unfounded. It was in vain that we provided the most thorough scientific evidence for this, that later works confirmed it, that later disciples betrayed the secret doctrine. But since the seed has borne fruit, the doctrine of the professorial chairs has become a worldwide happening; indignation is still possible, but denial is not.

From whence came the alleged new reformers in Catholicism, Protestantism, and Judaism, the heralds of the friendship of light of all confessions and all gradations of their doctrine, than from that philosophy, in accordance with the degree of sophistication of their systems, and even if their popular form and lack of talent differentiated them from the masters, who could demonstrate a difference in terms of the content of their doctrine? What else was it than the basic idea of celebrated philosophers, indeed celebrated Protestant theologians, which could be read on wall notices in the summer of 1848, when a well-known democratic leader informed the people that he had refused the judicial oath on the ground that he "did not believe in an individual, that is, a personal God." And what, in its core, was the antagonistic opposition against the ever-so-moderate enterprise to restore Christianity and the church in their right, which prior to this latest catastrophe was raised in the periodical press, in pamphlets, in protests, in solemn speeches, accompanied by slogans about the struggle for spiritual freedom, other than the struggle for the God of philosophy against the God of Holy Scripture? Or who could still deny that the overthrows of the state in 1789 and 1848 were the basic implementation of the legal-philosophical doctrine cultivated and developed from Grotius up until Rousseau, Kant, and Fichte, which indeed Hegel in many ways countered with political truth in a highly honorable manner, but who stood in equally stark opposition to religious truth, and therefore was incapable of keeping even his own pupils from defection, much less of erecting a dam against the destruction of the public mind?

For such a long time, philosophy had taught rational religion, deism, and pantheism, had declared the facts of Christian revelation to be untrue and impossible; how could it keep from finally elevating deism and pantheism to the level of popular religion? For a century and a half, philosophy founded civil government, marriage, and property, not on the basis of God's ordinance and disposition but on the will and agreement of men; and now the peoples were obeying their doctrine in that they raised themselves above their civil governments and all historically established orders, finally also above the right of existing property. Against this, philosophy had no cure to offer, it at a later stage having proclaimed the majesty and sanctity of the concept in place of the sovereignty of human will. For who is afraid of this concept and who respects this concept which, according to its devotees' own statements, hears no prayer and punishes no outrage, which like the mute idols of paganism is itself a work of the hands of men?

So then, by 1848 the natural law of Grotius, of Kant, of Rousseau had twice upended the ancient ordinances and put the world at its feet, and twice it showed itself impotent to establish and maintain order, even for the shortest time. And during this great catastrophe of the world spirit, the philosophy of Hegel (as such, apart from the personal loyalty maintained by a few of its followers) stood mute and idle, without a word to teach or to turn to; it did not raise a flag or fight under its motto, while the old positive belief and the old allegiance sent its standards into the field against the positive historical ordinances of its masses and led the struggle for the intellectual goods, thus also for science and philosophy, by which it was so little cherished, against the onset of barbarism.

The philosophy of the earlier natural law doctors spread that profane and immoral conception of marriage from which the corresponding marriage legislation emerged; and when the attempt was made to purify this, opposition came especially from disciples of the latest philosophical system (I leave to one side whether this was done in faithfulness to the master [Hegel] or not).

Finally, philosophy accomplished the vaunted labor of thought which converted the hereafter into the here and now, that is, denying continuity and the kingdom of God after this life, a doctrine which likewise has penetrated the masses, both the learned and the unlearned; and those masses now say, in compliance with the inevitable psychological law that the Apostle laid down: "let us eat and drink, for tomorrow we die!"

What began in the spirit of elevated science ended in the flesh of widespread materialism. Above all, there is now a strange generation, unknown to previous history, which says: "we ourselves are the god revealed in philosophy," which in the dichotomy between its divinity and its capitulation to the flesh and to demonic powers, consumes without profit its flickering little light, and ends in pale weariness – "a tale, told by an idiot, full of sound and fury, signifying nothing."

In France, the National Convention decreed: there is no God! In Germany, it was science that abolished God. In all the philosophical literature that I have come across, including legal philosophy, the word "God" no longer appears, when this characterization of the deceased Lord of the world is not allegorically given to the absolute of philosophy. But while in France Christianity was openly opposed, in Germany the pantheistic doctrine was wrapped in the robe of Christianity, and the half-educated masses were filled with such a confusion and sanctimoniousness of thoughts that they scarcely understood anymore the difference between belief and unbelief.

Ever since these world events took place in all their ferocity, the memory of that philosophy has virtually vanished; but the destruction of the public mind that it effectuated remains. Now then, human doctrine can change the human will, but it cannot change the natural laws of human society. For this reason, we are confronted with the unnatural conflict and struggle between doctrine and society. Doctrine takes shape against the natural and historical construct of society – against princely, aristocratic, corporative, even domestic power, against the church and the Christian state – and the powers of society react to this doctrine in terms of the laws of self-preservation. Doctrine has emancipated itself and the peoples from the requisite obedience to the authorities, and the authorities have emancipated themselves from the requisite respect for doctrine. If another spiritual power did not intervene, the original bond of ethical and real powers would have to split apart into a disintegrating doctrine and a mindless power.

Now that science has traversed this course to the bitter end, in systematic development and in factual implementation, is there not justification to call for a *turnaround?*

In judging their doctrine, I do not pass judgment over the men themselves. The times upon which they exercised such a powerful influence in turn influenced them greatly and even determined them beforehand. Because they were not aware of the erroneous nature of their point of departure, they operated in terms of the consistency which itself is a duty of the practitioner of science. And they at least achieved everything that is possible apart from Christian faith for the solemnity of the ethical law, in glorious opposition to what in France was called philosophy. Neither do I lump the master himself and his faithful followers together with the later school. The former sought science and in it, truth; and the denial of the revealed, finally the personal God, was only an unforeseen result which they could not resist. The latter look for this denial from the start for its own sake, it is their goal and their joy, and they are full of zeal to turn this into the peoples' way of thinking. Nor even do I deny the value of their achievements. In the way that thought here is made the object of thought, its laws, operations, primordial concepts, and relations to the object are developed, and how likewise such a correction of the instruments of our cognition renders cognition itself more secure, more clear, and gives it sharper outlines, indeed to the degree that actual characteristics of the world conjuncture are incorporated into our thought, and the purified instrument even reflects a beam back onto the object – all of this, even though it is permeated through and through with the error of the standpoint, still ever remains an enrichment and deepening of human learning. For this reason, I would like to ban from the pantheon neither these thinkers nor their serious labor, for which I, on one side, am thankful enough. It is only the *rationalist-pantheist basic vision,* with its consequences for the religious, ethical, and political areas, and thereby certainly that scientific method as well that only stems from it and is indissolubly connected with it, to which the call for the turnaround of science is directed.

Accordingly, it has never occurred to me to wish to *eradicate philosophy.* I do not share the contemporary dominant one-sidedness which only accepts positive, historical knowledge or practical proficiency and considers philosophical investigation to be vain; in fact, I lament it. Disregard for itself is not the least evil that philosophy has been guilty of in recent centuries. The investigation by which the attempt is made to understand things in the final ground of all existence, and above all to understand oneself, such as was once awakened in the motherland of youthful splendor and courage but made its most dignified appearance, not with the claim to a closed world system and a finalized wisdom, but precisely as "love of wisdom" – this investigation still remains a vocation of the human spirit, an essential component in the culture of a people. The end of learning cannot dispense with what the beginning possessed. Philosophy must not cease while wealth and not poverty is the commandment of peoples. But even in the contemporary struggle of world principles, philosophy cannot be absent; rather, true philosophy must be sought. It is true that the victory of truth is not based only, or even mainly, on scientific conviction and, above all, on the systematic form, but rather on the power of faith and historical tradition and the example of deeds and painful conversion through the iron blows of necessity and hardship. But there is certainly also a power in philosophical doctrine; this is precisely what the current establishment of rational concepts at the heart of our time's learning proves. And we wish for such a power to be left entirely to the enemy, on the day of the battle for which the two armies are preparing! Should theology not, in addition to its even more urgent tasks, also have the task, from the viewpoint of Christian knowledge, of sifting through and rectifying that wealth of concepts which philosophy has developed, in order for it to be changed from bitter water to fresh by the staff of God which has been given to you? In recent times a science of Christianity has often been provided from the standpoint of reason; it should be time to provide a science of reason (which has human knowledge as its object) from the standpoint of Christianity. If theology were to conquer the field of philosophy, it would provide the most certain security that philosophy would not keep trying to reconquer its field. Or should legal science, in addition to its other important tasks, not have the spare time and vocation to defend the supreme concepts of law in order to protect them from the rush to annihilate them, which is based everywhere on science? Should one simply leave the question "what is property?" to the Proudhons of this world? Should popular sovereignty and equality, or the concept unfolding in the constitution, be discoverable by the science of the philosophical system, while authority by the grace of God and legitimacy and acquired rights and the Christian state are left to the area of facts, and fall prey to violence and *vis inertiae*? I do not wish to fend off philosophical research; rather, I wish to stimulate it to the highest degree. If we could only maintain a philosophical and in particular a legal-philosophical literary movement of the kind we see in the time of Kant, Fichte, Feuerbach!

But this kind of philosophy has come to an end, and had to come to an end; the kind which sees as its task the derivation of the natural and moral world from human reason, from the processes and determinations of thought (*a priori*), which claims to have sole possession of its own purpose and measure while bestowing purpose and measure on everything else; which sets itself up as the final, supreme stage above religion and crows that in this, it is only the handmaid of theology (*serva theologiae*) in that it presents theology with light, a light which, as has been shown, is only a will-o'-the-wisp; which ensconces itself in the temple of God in order itself to be the cult of the nations. This philosophy has come to an end. Faith has recognized it and rejected it, and unbelief no longer believes in it either.

This call for the turnaround of science had already risen powerfully in the church, no less so in the positive sciences; my book only carried it into the heart of philosophy and, in particular, legal philosophy. But for that very reason, at least regarding my intention, it was not just a call, but also a *guidebook* for the turnaround of science. Philosophy must give up the first lie: the explicit or tacit assumption that the world exists from eternity according to logical laws; it must acknowledge the simple fact that God created the world according to His free counsel. Then it will no longer presume to draw its knowledge from logical laws (from reason) but will see that it knows nothing but what it finds in the object itself from experience. It will no longer proclaim with its eyes closed, as if from within, what it has just learned externally; rather, it will open wide its physical and spiritual eyes to take in what God has created and accomplished. It will cultivate the exploration of reason (the human cognitive faculty) as a valuable science alongside others, instead of as science *per se,* standing above all sciences; it will no longer imagine that the knowledge of the world-cause and the world-conjuncture can be had simply through the knowledge of the laws of thought. It will not refuse to penetrate beyond the material laws and phenomena of nature into its creative thoughts, beyond the facts and human motives of history into its artistic and providential plan; but it will not find the means to do this in a formula that has already been established in advance (taken from the laws of thought); instead, it will do so by submerging itself even more deeply into the object, and putting itself into the totality of the object (nature, history, human spirit and God's revelation), through which a light falls on every side of it. And as a result, it will expect no more than an approximating, preparatory knowledge, as the often-tentative revelation of individual features of the great mystery. It will not presume to present a natural philosophy and philosophy of history as a certain and closed science, like logic. That would be nothing less than the science of God's plan in the creation of the world and God's councils and judgments in guiding the peoples, regarding which nobody knows but God alone; should this be a science similar to that of our own reason, the laws and activities of which we constantly observe?

Because of this, that which philosophy, not content with the laws in nature and the motives in history, has taught up to now as a (logical) law about nature and about history – this construction of nature and construction of history – has been shown to be, not a science and solid knowledge, but an empty game and foolishness. Above all, philosophy will admit to itself that regarding God, it on its own perceives only weak and uncertain features, only the hollow forms of His existence, and would therefore eagerly receive the radiant knowledge of Christian revelation, not from authority – otherwise this could refer to Mohammedanism as well – nor from reason – because this only shows that Christianity is only one possibility among an infinite number of other possibilities, rather than that it is reality – but from *testing against the object*,[6] because it finds that the Christian revelation is the solution of the riddle – that it gives the explanation of all phenomena for which philosophy has no explanation – that it explains the dichotomy of human existence, shows and resolves the contradiction of reason and will, of spirit and flesh, of confidence and despondency in their origin – that it allows us to recognize a plan and purpose in world history, which plays out confusedly and purposelessly before our natural eye, in the economy of redemption and the kingdom of God, which mysteriously permeates them as a determining power – that it reveals the moral order in a perfection and eternal harmony, such as we never ourselves could discover, but which our whole innermost man recognizes as the clarity of its premonition, as the image of its primal memory, as its own eternal being – that a majesty of the divine arises in it which can only be the splendor of the true God.

Admittedly, such a philosophy renounces the high position of the present one; it has a more modest task; it cannot achieve a uniform system that encompasses the universe; its solution is only piecemeal. It therefore will not arrogate to itself its being its own end, but rather find exaltation in its likewise being a means for the glorification of God, for the proclamation of His wisdom and justice, and His profundity, unfathomable even to it. It will not lay claim to being the most holy of holies, but joyfully serve at the sanctuary with every other science and art, indeed even serve in the forecourt, in the hope that one day, when the piecemeal ceases, it also will receive the full, pure light for its knowledge of the world, of which only a ray is granted to man on earth, for the knowledge of the way to salvation. It will not undertake to establish the ordinances of the peoples on its own, but cultivate reverence for all ordinances and authorities that God has set over them, and of all conditions and rights that have come about under His disposition. It will be a guardian for the goods of the human soul and the foundations of human society, which until now philosophy

---

[6] [Cf. p. 147 below.]

has more or less had a go at destroying.

A baseless objection that is raised against this is that it violates the independence and dignity of philosophy – that it is unscientific.

It is clear from the outset that there can be no talk of scientificness or unscientificness when it comes to basic facts. If there were a God and He created the world, should that not be accepted because it is unscientific? If reason really did not carry the world in itself and could not find the world out by itself, would it nevertheless have to remove the world from itself, because that alone would be scientific? One might just as well require on the basis of science that man should not be born but rather should exist from eternity; or that man should feed himself from himself without food; or that the eye should see of itself, without objects and their impressions from outside. Scientificness demands that you be gods, but the fact is that you are only human – do you have to comply with scientificness? Indeed, if philosophy really showed in terms of scientific laws that the world is the result of logical necessity, and how it is so, and then someone came along and wished to impose on it the opposite from faith and the Bible, then philosophy would have reason to complain about a violation of its independence. But it did not show this, but only assumed it; the reverse is the case, the edifice of knowledge which it founded on this premise, turns out – precisely according to scientific evidence – to be insufficient to explain the world, and to be inconceivable in itself. Not only religious belief, but all empirical science – natural, historical, and legal science – has set up the most zealous guard against it, through their most outstanding representatives!

Now should science be so independent that it does not have to inquire into the facts of reality and the laws of truth? Is it the trick to explain the world without God, in and for itself, regardless of whether the explanation is sufficient – is this the essence and the glory of the scientific character? It is no subjection of science to authority if one expects of it that its knowledge should correspond to the object. No natural scientist will want to avoid the fact that his teaching must pass the test of the phenomena of nature – and yet the philosopher should have the privilege of his teaching merely being seen as logically consistent in order to be considered true, even if contradicted by all the facts, even if it leaves the great object it is supposed to solve untouched! And how are things with this logical consistency, with that which reason really derives from itself? Each of the once admired systems has been irrefutably proven by its successor to be based on gross logical errors at the most crucial point. With regard to the latest of these, however, I have – of this I am certain – proven irrefutably that, among other things, the dialectic on which in its entirety it is built is nothing other than a sophistical, thus illogical play with the different meanings of contradiction.[7] Indeed, Kant himself already showed the inconceivability of his successors' point of view, as they then did with his. It reminds us of the fable of the lions, who in their hunger so ate each other that nothing was left of them. I ask of every trained and honest philosopher, whether there is still one system standing of all them, whether any yet had a foundation that has not been scientifically destroyed? Truly, with my call to a turnaround I do not oppose the scientific character of philosophy but rather its unscientific character. I deny it not because of scientific rigor and regularity, but because of scientific arbitrariness and violence. Although I argue *from* faith, I do not do so by means of faith; I do not issue a decree against it from revelation but have shown that it itself made vain decrees against faith, from the beginning until now.

In addition to this scientific proof, I also reproached philosophy for its effect on religion and morals and civic order; only the most extreme human arrogance can complain that this runs against the dignity of science, the purpose and standard of which [it is said] lie not in its effects, but only in itself. It is true that every activity in the realm of the mind, even the smallest, is its own purpose; how should this be denied to science that penetrates the depths? But every activity, even the highest, has a purpose outside of itself, to wit, the glorification of God and the fulfillment of its own vocation. It is not, as the newest school proclaims, that philosophy is the ultimate goal of God; it is God that is the ultimate goal, yes even of philosophy. Even through the most contemplative knowledge, a ray of love must go to Him whose essence and work is alone worth knowing, and the astonishment which according to Plato is the sentiment (πάθος) of the philosopher, must at the same time be laud and praise, it must be a psalm to the riches and the wisdom and the mercy of God, with which one's own soul and all the world are to be filled. Even the most contemplative knowledge, while it gathers people in the eternal origin of their existence, must at the same time give them light and strength for their knowledge of the temporal and their acts in time. If philosophy is the entry of knowledge into the dead sea of the absolute

---

[7] Vol. I, pp. 438, 446 [*The Recovery of Historical Law,* pp. 86, 91ff.]

or the world substance, then admittedly it may politely say: how does life concern me? But if philosophy is the retreat of knowledge into the living personal God, it must necessarily give heightened impulses and powers of knowledge and will to fulfill God's commandments and the positions in which He has placed us.

Genuine philosophy must conduce to that end in all positive science, in theology, law, and medicine, and must conduce in every profession and every duty. Wisdom is more than just science, it is attitude. That is why philosophy only testifies against itself when it stiffens coldly and thoughtlessly in the architectonic of the determinations of reason; and the public apostasy from religious belief and, in consequence, the rebellion against the authorities and the dissolution of society which have followed the grand course of philosophy, while they may not in themselves be a refutation of philosophy, are a reminder that it should reflect on whether it has performed the calculation correctly, the proof of which leaves so much to be desired.

To expect science to adapt to the existing religious system or the existing political system is far from my intention. But Christianity is not an existing religious system, and government by the grace of God is not an existing political system. The eternal truth, the ordinance of God is not an existing system. This is precisely the fundamental error: as if philosophy now occupies a similar position vis-à-vis Christianity that it did in the states of classical antiquity vis-à-vis paganism, as if it were set against an accidental positive national institution. If this were the case, contemporary philosophy could as little be reproached for contradicting Christian revelation as Plato could be reproached for not bringing his doctrine in line with the legend of the gods.

The relation of philosophy to public religion is now entirely the opposite of what it was then. At that time, public religion was a profound aberration of the human race, and philosophy, at least in comparison with it, had a far more worthy knowledge of God, a far more noble moral teaching. Nowadays, public religion is eternal truth itself, of a majesty of the knowledge of God and a sanctity of morality such as the human spirit could not of itself discern; and therefore philosophy, like all human wisdom, falls far short of it. What are those meager abstractions of philosophy about the absolute, about the indifference of the real and the ideal, about pure being, by comparison with the knowledge of the almighty Father, Creator of heaven and earth, with the mystery of the incarnation of God and the atonement of all sin through the obedience of the Son of God until death on the cross; what are these moral doctrines of the categorical imperative, of acting according to a maxim which, if followed by everyone, does not annul itself, of the merging of the particular into the universal, etc., by comparison with God's command: "Thou shalt not, for I am the Lord," with the Sermon on the Mount and the high priestly prayer and the hymn of love in the letter to the Corinthians? What are all the achievements of philosophy when it comes to understanding our own existence, by comparison with the Pauline "I do not do what I want, but what I do not want, I do"? In antiquity, therefore, philosophy wrought *wise men*, behind whom those brought up in public religion might perhaps shelter in the trials of life. In Christianity, the patterns of self-denial, of purity of soul, of a holy lifestyle, proceeded from the church; philosophy has only wrought famous *thinkers*. Plato could once rightly say that the states would only be good if they were ruled by philosophers, and Frederick II could just as well say that if he wanted to punish a province, he would let it be ruled by philosophers. By philosophers Plato understood, in accordance with the ancient view, wise men who have the eternal over the transitory in mind; Frederick II understood by philosophers, in accordance with the contemporary view, the founders or followers of a certain system who believe they have the key to things in their formula. Then, philosophy was at least partly a yearning for the truth from error; now, it is disdain for the truth presented.

Once the divine wisdom has been proclaimed, human wisdom can no longer exist without receiving from it. Since public religion itself has become the truth, philosophy can only be a national good if it is in harmony with public religion, if it is in the service of the church. How public faith and public education, theology and philosophy were manifested in undisturbed unity in Thomas Aquinas! And how these powers now struggle with one another in enmity, with the result that conflict and discord run through our entire public condition! A rebirth of philosophy which, after the enrichment and sifting in all areas of knowledge and especially the great achievements in philosophy itself, and after the deepening of religion and the elimination of all pagan elements from it, summarizes all the moments from within, is reconciled with faith, reconciles also the divisions of faith, establishes and guarantees the moral concepts, the foundations of the civil order in faith and education, and establishes a work of knowledge and doctrine that for our time is what the *Summa theologiae* once meant for the Middle Ages – that is the turnaround of science that I have in mind.

Berlin, March 1854

FROM THE AUTHOR'S PREFACE TO THE SECOND EDITION

The fact that I once again put the doctrine of the personality and freedom of God at the forefront is self-explanatory. In itself it is the supreme, decisive doctrine for every philosophical conception, influential especially in the entire ethical-political sphere – the current manner of treatment has no inkling of this – and in particular is the cardinal question of the present. What impels this in its innermost being is the struggle between theism and pantheism; it is nearly the same thing, at least in terms of result, as the struggle between Christianity and the de-Christianization of the civilized world. For an abstract theism, the doctrine of a personal God capable of revelation who nevertheless does not reveal Himself, a Creator who does not reside in His world but discharges it out of Himself like a machine, is now, according to the state of philosophy itself, at least scientifically, downright impossible. For this reason, there is everywhere a pressing forward to a momentous decision. Public manifestations are emerging with increasing energy in one direction and the other, and a limp, *merely* theistic center, as filled the world in the most recent period, no longer has any power in the realm of spirits.

That the agent of a philosophical-ethical discipline has the moral vocation to testify to this, and the scientific one of justifying it, does not need any proof. Regarding the doctrine of the freedom and personality of God, I do not represent a scientific standpoint peculiar to myself, but the general or at least still predominant faith of humanity. From me is only the characterization of freedom as "unending creative choice." Even this I could not sacrifice to the shallow and unworthy polemic which was apparently waged against it, but actually against that doctrine itself; rather, I hope it here will only be made more secure and more well-founded. But though this characterization of such a difficult concept may be inadequate – and who could adequately represent the power of the true living God, not a mere self-made God? – the innermost core of it, the perception of creative freedom as opposed to the mere legalistically necessary explication, is incontrovertible truth, and it is this alone that matters, it is this alone of which I will make further applications.

Yet I could by no means fail to deal in detail with the general scientific point of view, and still more with ethics, according to their supreme principles, even though this should be of no interest to some legal scholars in the field. Since Kant there has been no legal philosophy which has not formed an integral link in a clear and explicit coherence with a system of philosophy as a whole. A new philosophy of law, which in no way breaks with the previous one, setting aside the knowledge gained thereby, but which nevertheless is contrary to it in principle and standpoint, cannot possibly assert itself scientifically if it stands alone without any such background. Since I do not profess any of the existing systems of philosophy, I have been forced to contrive and advance even the most basic features of the full scientific view on which my doctrine of law rests. After all, Pufendorf already observed a similar procedure, and even Hegel, who in his logic and encyclopedia had sufficient philosophical background, nevertheless included in his legal philosophy these general spheres which do not belong specifically to legal theory. If I here and there have gone further than seems necessary to this purpose, it must be remembered that the guarantee of my concepts could only be achieved through a more abundant implementation, which both removed the apparent difficulties and demonstrated their positive force in solving the problems. I therefore had to provide this implementation on all sides and independently, even if it were not at all a matter of law and the state. Admittedly, I had to abandon the phalanx of a system conducted through all areas of knowledge, in particular through logic and natural philosophy. But for this purpose the antecedent philosophical foundations do not contain a particular system of thought contrary to the way of thinking of all other human beings, but on the contrary precisely that generally human, and in the relevant points Christian, way of thinking; the former opposes the latter only in scientific argumentation and in scientific analysis.

Berlin, January 1845

INTRODUCTION

§. 1. The standards of law and the institutions of the state differ across different countries and times and being the work of man, everywhere and of necessity contain bad as well as good. There is indeed however something higher, something universal, at work in all creations of law and the state, which purposes to be consummated in all of these, the consummation or lack thereof amounting to the superiority or poverty of the same; and that is the inward unchanging essence of law and state.

Now jurisprudence is the science of law and state as it exists in a particular time under a particular people. From this arises the demand for a higher science, having as its object this inner unchanging essence of law and state. It may be called the *doctrine of law and state.*

Its task is firstly that deeper scientific knowledge itself. In consequence, however, it also serves practical ends, the purer application of law, the recognition of existing legal institutions, the standard for their development.

§. 2. Law and state rest on the one hand on natural laws, the external conditions of human existence; from this perspective the doctrine of law and state is a *natural doctrine of the state.* On the other hand, law and state rest on ethical demands, and from this perspective the doctrine of law and state forms part of ethics, the character of which is completely opposite to the natural sciences. Ethics has to do with laws found only in the will; the given material – law and state in their factual existence as they have developed through human choice – is not, as with the natural sciences, the unconditional standard and archetype thereof; in part it is concerned with material that is not even extant, with law and state as people ought to shape it, as history is going to shape it.[8] The source of knowledge of this ethical dimension is however a dual one: external to us, the actual legal structures and their historical development in which that nature of

---

[8] For this reason, a natural science of the state is warranted which restricts itself to illuminate only one aspect of the state and precisely the lesser, and not law and state as a whole (Leo).

law necessarily must manifest itself, and internal to us, the ethical standard.

§. 3. The doctrine of law and state is not separate from positive legal science. Much rather, the latter cannot truly scientifically be pursued without becoming the doctrine of law in one degree or another, i.e., without penetrating into the inner universal nature of legal institutions, while the former cannot recognize the inner universal nature of legal institutions apart from determinate positive, albeit varying, legal institutions. To the degree that the doctrine of law and state is obligated to take its cue from positive legal institutions, it may make use of this or that particular example as the basis and goal of its considerations; and it has the authorization and in fact the vocation to select its own times and its own country for this purpose.

§. 4. The inquiry into the essence of law and state may set itself the goal of a greater or lesser degree of penetration. If it goes as far as to bring law and state into connection with the highest cause and the final goal of all existence, it is legal philosophy. The doctrine of law and state is not usually considered to have to venture this deeply; there is thus a doctrine of law and state as a science over and above positive jurisprudence which for all that is free of all philosophical admixture.[9] On the other hand, legal philosophy cannot be of the sort that derives its entire content from those highest relations. There is much too much human freedom and earthly contingency – perhaps, one dare add, divine positivity – keeping us from fathoming the borderlines and connections between reality and eternal principles. The highest that human science may hope to achieve is therefore simply a doctrine of law and state on the basis of philosophy.

§. 5. The apprehension of things in their all-encompassing interconnection according to their highest cause and their final goal is what we term worldview. Every philosophical system is such a worldview. Every religion, and particularly the Christian, contains such a worldview, though not always with the same degree of realization. We base the doctrine of law and state upon the Christian religion. Right from the start we are justified in this by the external legitimation

[9] Examples include Savigny's *Vom Beruf unsrer Zeit für Gesetzgebung und Rechtswissenschaft* [On the Vocation of Our Time for Legislation and Legal Science] as legal science, and Burke's, Genz's, and Dahlmann's political writings as political science.

that nearly all European states, and especially Germany, have this religion as their factual foundation, and that the majority of persons, even those having rejected the Christian confession, still have not broken in any way with the Christian worldview. The inner justification, however, the one that tips the scales of scientific proof, will be provided, we hope, by this presentation. The scientific confirmation of the Christian worldview cannot extend so far, however, as to make faith optional for its acceptance. Science can only make room for faith, it cannot render faith superfluous. Only keep this in mind, that such is no less the case with every other worldview as well, even those schools of current philosophy that oppose Christianity. Every philosophical system of whatever name in the final analysis rests on a foundational presupposition that is nothing more than faith, no matter what claim it may make to so-called scientific certainty. Even unbelief is a faith – one cannot reason from naked doubt. We have no immediate or homogeneous view of the highest principles of things and thus no absolute certainty; therefore for philosophical systems a purely objective knowledge independent of all personal judgment, such as mathematics, the natural sciences, or even the positive sciences, is ruled out (see below, §. 21).

Accordingly, I cannot refute the charge that the philosophical foundations contained in Book I below will in part remain unacceptable to those who categorically reject the Christian revelation; I may however respond in the same way regarding every other philosophical exposition. But with regard to the subsequent exposition of the doctrine of law and state, in that it deals with immediately present, observable things, I do make a claim to the objectivity that renders its results scientifically certain through the internally consistent elucidation of the subject matter.

PART I: THE SCIENTIFIC STANDPOINT

Chapter 1: The Personality of God as Principle of the World

§. 1. Every philosophical science must begin with the supreme principle of things, the "absolute." To do so, it must decide on the polar opposition that has come to clear awareness in our time, as to whether this supreme principle is the personal, otherworldly, revelatory God, or an impersonal power inhering in the world itself – *pantheism*. This opposition is not overcome if the philosophical and theological system which pantheism represents dismisses this characterization as empty "talk" on the part of its opponents. For in that case it forces upon those opponents a concept of pantheism which no one connects with that description, namely, the one in which God is "all," i.e., a colorful aggregate of the particulars of finite things or the entirety of these things.[10] This, however, should not be called pantheism but rather a potentiated fetishism. Instead, as is evident from the opposition above, we place the essence of pantheism simply in God not being a personality, having no self-consciousness, or, as one might say, not being a He [der Gott] but an it [das Gott], which alone is of practical interest. For whether the One, here called God, coincides with the world or is distinguished from the world, whether it is its law or the totality of its manifestations, may be of great importance for the scientific mastery of the system, but it lies entirely outside the vital questions which fill the human mind when one inquires into the existence of God.

For this reason, we do distinguish between the various forms of pantheism, namely the Spinozan and the Hegelian. The former finds the crude and undeveloped God in undifferentiated inert substance in which individual things are subsumed, while the latter finds Him in a movement of thought, of logical differentiation and unification of opposites, realizing itself as an ordered world. And yet, in the latter we can only recognize a scientific development of the Spinozan basic vision [Grundanschauung], not a basic vision of another sort. For

[10] Hegel, *Vorlesungen über die Philosophie der Religion* [Lectures on the Philosophy of Religion], vol. I, p. 94; *Encyclopädie* (1840), p. xviii.

here as well, there is no essential difference in God being substance, per Spinoza, and God being "not only substance but also determined in Himself as subject,"[11] per Hegel, for Hegel likewise holds God to have no existence separate from the world, but is a subject, gains self-consciousness, only in His realization as man. At bottom Spinoza did not deny this; at most, he would have disclaimed the manner of expression as shocking.[12]

Now there are those who say that scientific research necessarily leads to pantheism, and we close ourselves off to it only because our hearts cannot accept it. In fact, the reverse is true. Even if the God in which religion believes cannot be demonstrated mathematically, scientific research comes down decisively against the pantheistic assumption; and one adheres to it only because of the impulse of the heart, by the force of a deep temptation with which our times are encumbered, similar to the polytheistic temptation of the ancient world, or the ascetic temptation of the Middle Ages. This becomes clear from the opposition of motives:

§. 2. From Spinoza to Strauss,[13] the main difficulty raised against the personality of God has been: Personality is the distinction of self from others. If God is personal, He has opposite Himself an existence, the world, which is not Himself. This signifies a restriction, making Him finite. But God or Absolute Being must be infinite, thus unrestricted. For the same reason, God as God (the One Being) is consistently denied any determinacy, since any determinacy entails a limit, and thus a negation outside the limits (*omnis determinatio est negatio).*[14]

Nevertheless, if there is *created* being outside of God, this by no means constitutes a restriction which could contradict the basic vision of absolute single

[11] Hegel, *Vorlesungen über die Philosophie der Religion,* vol. I, p. 93.

[12] For this reason we cannot at all admit that Spinozism is not *atheism* but only "*acosmism*" (Hegel, *Vorlesungen über die Geschichte der Philosophie* [Lectures on the History of Philosophy], vol. III, p. 373), God for him not being subsumed in the world but the world being subsumed in God. For if there is no God, then the world cannot be subsumed in Him; in fact, for him the world is not subsumed in God but rather the developed world is subsumed in the one undifferentiated substance of the world.

[13] *Die christliche Glaubenslehre in ihrer geschichtlichen Entwicklung* [The Christian Doctrine of Faith in its Historical Development], vol. II, p. 504.

[14] *Ethics,* Part I, Prop. 8, Scholium 1; Epist. 50.

being outside of which nothing else can exist. For created beings are always only in and through God. It is for this reason that substance or the power of being remains in them. Therefore, absolute being is not abolished thereby but only conceived of as creative, and for it not to be so would in fact constitute a *petitio principii*. Our own consciousness provides an analogous vision, in that we are restricted against our own thoughts and are not the same as the epitome of these thoughts, even though we are their absolute general being. Why should God not likewise restrict Himself through His thoughts, to which He gives reality, through the world, and nevertheless remain the One and All? Indeed, the same difficulty holds true for Hegel's pantheism. For when God is not "All" but only "the general, substantial, lifted out of the particular," the essence of things, the "ideality" of the manifold in space, time, and matter, then God is restricted where this particular, spatial, material, coincidental begins, and therefore is no longer the absolute. For the absolute is only the entirety. One erroneously concludes from this that only God and the world as inseparably one can be called absolute. For if the world is not a part (modality [Affektion], determination) of God but a creation of His, then this unity is not one of God and the world but of God as the entirety. For this reason, we rightly say that the absolute of man is not his spirit [or mind: "Geist"] alone, but the entire man, spirit and body. But if man should have the power to lay down his body and pick it up again, if the body is only the creation of the spirit, then we would have to say that the absolute of man is solely his spirit.

Another, recent objection against the personality of God is the one asserted by proponents of "speculative theology," to wit, that for the personal God, thus the God prior to and beyond the world, no content of self-consciousness and will, which everywhere can only be derived from the objects of a world, can be conceivable, and yet without this there can be no personality. If we were to yield to this objection, we would be left not with the nonpersonality of God but with the eternity of the world. For if God from eternity bears within Himself the thoughts of the world, a world which we of necessity concede to be the actual world, as content of His consciousness, then nothing hinders us from assuming that He nevertheless distinguishes Himself from these thoughts of His as an I, which sets them in motion and contemplates them. But by no means can we accede to this objection, for it is based simply on the false operation of declaring everything to be impossible which lies outside our vision. For what is it that justifies the assertion that the divine being as such is not a sufficient object and content of consciousness, or that divine power, love, wisdom, holiness do not exist in themselves but only in their effect on objects outside God, only as formative principle for the world, or that an absolutely spontaneous creative understanding rather than a merely receptive one is impossible? The motive for such an assertion is certainly none other than that human consciousness, the only one which we can envision, does not exist without relation to a given world before it. Those who raise this objection with such a claim to infallibility would certainly also assert, if they had never seen light, that it is impossible for such to exist in itself, but can only be thought of as that which gives color to the bodies outside of it.

§. 3. By contrast, the pantheistic assumption encounters entirely insurmountable difficulties:

One such is the impossibility of demonstrating a law according to which individual things emerge from the world substance precisely as they are. Spinoza maintains that things exist out of divine necessity (*ex divina necessitate*), but he does not even try to demonstrate this necessity. Philosophy undertakes this demonstration from Fichte to Hegel; but the undertaking is like using a net to scoop liquids, as we have shown everywhere in the first volume [*The History of Legal Philosophy*].

But then that assumption forfeits the *unity of the universe* which its most essential motive is to preserve. If we grasp God as static substance, or as an eternal process of movement, as an unfolding concept, unity is always lacking. For what is the unity in all the modalities by which the substance remains the same? If substance as such is nowhere, but only in certain modalities, then the universe is only all those modalities taken together. Likewise, what is the unity of that eternal process, that rotation that proceeds from itself and returns to itself, such that that which rotates (i.e., undergoes the process) remains itself? Where is the "spirit that remains with itself," or what is it that is rotating when the rotation itself is the rotating subject?

This is not disposed of by saying that the final result, that is, the concept that has passed through world history and has come to its consciousness in philosophy, is precisely the power which evokes all earlier moments, and hence also their unity. For it is not possible to see how this result (the final form of things and their knowledge) could effectuate anything, let alone the entire previous course, without the real power of a personality; nor can a unity be found in this result itself, a center that would be something in itself, just as the person is one who, if he distinguishes the whole determinateness of his being and action from himself, nevertheless remains an existence and reality as an I, and by virtue of this, then also concentrates the totality in himself. On the contrary, according to that view, everything falls apart in the periphery, and the center is merely apparent, a mere abstraction of the thinker.

Add to this that the assumption of Christianity contains at the same time both the basis for the explanation and the basis for the justification as to why it is unable to solve the difficulties that always remain; and it finds this in the real distance of man from God. By contrast, the pantheistic assumption must logically pose the requirement of the complete solution of the world problem to itself. To be sure, Spinoza still contented himself with the fact that, as a mere part of God, he could not grasp the entire understanding that lies in God; Hegel's pantheism, however, wishes to go beyond Spinoza's precisely in that it specifies God not as substance but as consciousness, i.e., as the consciousness existing in his world, that is, man and philosophy; then he must postulate, really postulate, that God comes to complete consciousness in philosophy, which is to say, no problem can remain as something that cannot be known to man.

§. 4. Personality alone is *true being*, concrete and spiritual at the same time. The philosophy which does not recognize personality as original, namely the Hegelian, can therefore only find the spiritual in the abstract (the universal determinations of thought), and this only becomes concrete for it through the material-sensual (nature); hence, spirit ultimately is for it the redissolving of the material into the abstract (into the legal forms of life and the philosophical system); and so it is an eternal oscillation: if it becomes concrete, it becomes material, if it returns to itself as spirit, it becomes abstract. Personality, on the other hand, is originally the most spiritual and originally the most concrete thing of which we can think, and everything else concrete and spiritual can therefore only have its source in personality and its creative faculties. Just as personality is *primal being*, so also is it the *primal concept*. Hence it cannot be defined or constructed, but only directly envisioned [angeschaut].

Personality alone is *substance* in the true sense, which remains the same in all accidents and yet is different from them. Only it is the unity, the one unchangeable subject remaining with itself, in the multiplicity of its attributes and in the sequence of its actions, or the change of its states. The unity of the concept is merely of a formal kind; it is limited to abstract characteristics; it does not include the whole of particular things. The unity of the work of art (e.g., the statue) is only ideal, it consists only in the creative thought, and therefore leaves all real material outside of it. The unity of the organism is only essential [wesenheitlicher], not actual [aktueller Art], and is therefore only the unity of the members in the totality of the organism, not of each other. But personality is *absolute* unity. The properties, powers, and relationships of the person are not only together the one person, but the whole person is in each of these individually, that is, all the other properties, powers, and relationships of the person are present and active therein. In the same way, with every single act of will, there is the entire full I, the fullness of its being and self-consciousness – not, as Hegel constructs the will, the abstract I – that produces it; and the more that is the case, the higher that personality, right up to the absolute personality of God.

Personality is therefore *from the outset the fullness of being*, the subject of the most diverse forces and qualities: self-consciousness, will, understanding, power, or, as we term the divine qualities, omniscience, omnipotence, immutability, justice, holiness, loyalty, love, mercy, blessedness, eternity, etc., and these attributes stand especially in reciprocal condition and interaction as a totality, so that the one cannot be derived from the other as preceding or following, neither in terms of time nor of concept. All are equally original, and each presupposes the other, just as, conversely, the other is presupposed by it, for example, consciousness the will, the will consciousness. None of them can be active without the cooperation of the others, thus all having a share in the product, and none can exist apart from personality, which in itself comprehends them all indissolubly.[15] A scientific system that confesses a personal, transcendent God

---

[15] Therefore, every investigation must show none of these properties to be conceivable, defined, or determined in their purest and highest form without all the others, and this is doubtless what Plato intended with his dialectic and with the structure of his conversations, in which the attempt to comprehend a single property, e.g., piety, bravery for itself, always ends unsuccessfully. But this dialectic only befits the essentialities of God, not His free action, not creation and history: neither does Plato ever apply it to these.

must therefore accept this from the outset as a totality, as, e.g., Christian dogmatics has done at all times. On the other hand, on the basis of this confession it is not consistent to wish to construct God from potencies which (even if only according to the concept) are supposed to emerge one from the other, making the beginning into a "being" or "possible being" or "blind being," instead of the full eternally existing God, in whom there is no before ("prius") and no after.[16]

The being of personality, however, is *act*, continual inner act, for it is only as will, and depending on the decision, external act, that it has an effect outside of it. If this effect is an existence that now exists in itself, the act is *creation*, and this pertains only to the divine personality. But *every* act, including human acts, generically is no different than creation. The act, as belonging to the essence of personality, like the latter itself cannot be defined or constructed, but only envisioned. The same is true of creation, but we as creatures have no vision of it.

§. 5. Fichte was the first to express the great thought that there is only self-consciousness, and that there is no being apart from this, that everything unconscious is only there for the conscious. But Fichte's saying is by no means the whole truth. For the self-consciousness that Fichte makes the solely existing, as it emerged from Kant's formal unity of apperception, is merely the formalism of personality, the abstraction of its activity; therefore with him there is no possibility of differentiating between divine and human personality. The I posits itself in terms of personality, in that it thinks; and with thinking as such, apart from all content, degree and other forces, the I is finished. But personality is not originally merely abstract self-consciousness any more than it is abstract being; rather, it is conscious of itself as something very definite and fully abundant. God is conscious of Himself, not as an abstract I, but as God, as Almighty, as infinite love and so on, man as well in his way. One cannot, therefore, assume this abstract form of its activity ("pure I") as something preceding first, prior to that full content. Fichte's I no more characterizes a real I than Hegel's being does

---

And it is quite inappropriate for Hegel's philosophy to intend to develop nature and history dialectically.

[16] Cf. Vol. I of this work, 2nd ed., p. 495 [*The Recovery of Historical Law,* p. 134].

real being.[17] This lack in Fichte's doctrine is probably the reason that what was true of it was given up again by the successors. In the first beginnings of Schelling's doctrine, and above all in Hegel's doctrine, being is not ascribed to individual material things, but a god is assumed who has as little self-consciousness as these things, i.e., supreme being itself is made into something lacking self-consciousness.

Of course, this is not conceded everywhere. For the concept which Hegel makes God is not for him a "concept that is in itself," one that is still unconscious; but only insofar as it becomes "for itself," i.e., arrives at its consciousness, namely, sets a natural existence opposite itself, and, in thinking, cancels that again, takes that back into itself, hence in human consciousness in general, but especially in religious and philosophical consciousness. Thus, in terms of the process of Fichte's individual I, a self-consciousness of the All-being, the world substance, is artificially formed. We might say that Hegel's entire worldview is the futile attempt to do without the supernatural God and therefore to form an artificial personality in the universe and in world history. But against this doctrine of Hegel's one can first of all appeal to the view from which the first author, Fichte, indeed alone appeals. Fichte could demand that everyone should only look at himself, his own I, in order to find the theory confirmed. By contrast, no one has a view of the concept that comes to *its* consciousness in people, and Hegel himself only extorts this view, or rather the illusion of it. But even when examined in discursive thinking, Hegel's doctrine is refuted by the fact that the unity of the two moments "in itself" and "for itself" is missing. For that which in the sphere of logic and nature is "in itself" is quite different from that *for which* it is, in man and in religion or philosophy. The concept that with the former was in itself, in philosophy did not become for *itself* but for *me*. That is also why Hegel's "for itself" (consciousness) has an infinitely smaller scope than the "in itself." The concept in itself is the whole universe and all of history; the concept for itself is only in man, with his existence that is so limited in time and power (and in only a few people to boot). Shouldn't there also be a for-itself (consciousness) in which the concept would become as great for itself as it is in itself? Shouldn't the subject, which in itself embraces the entire universe, also be

[17] The same conception of the I is also implemented by Schelling in his "transcendental idealism."

that which is conscious of itself?

According to this false and forced conception of self-consciousness, personality in Hegel always has a substrate that is before it and alone gives it some content; but personality itself is merely something negative, namely, the ability to abstract from this substrate, this antecedent content, the ability to negate it. Personality is the same as the faculty of abstraction, and the faculty of suicide (as the most extreme abstraction from antecedent being) is therefore the culmination of personality and an attribute of the same which, according to the concept, is eternally necessary.[18] The truth, however, is that personality is what is original and positive; it contains the power, not to negate the given, but to posit something new, the power of act and creation, as will be shown in more detail below.

No less, however, must we reject Schelling's recently published teaching that "God, in order to be personal, must have a reason for His existence that is not Himself as God (viewed absolutely or in so far as He exists)," which is just "nature in God" which, "although belonging to Himself, is different from Him," according to which the "will of love" in God as the will of God according to His true absolute existence, and the "will of the ground" as mere nature in God, are two different wills, each of which is for itself, and the will of love "allows" the will of the ground "to work."[19] Because thereby something would be posited in God that is not pure divinity, a being with which He is encumbered, that has effects on Him – drives, longings, even if they are eternally overcome by Him – which cause God to create, similar to the working of desires in people.[20] This is not merely the transfer of our view of personality to God, to which we are fully entitled, but the transfer of our view of the limited personality of man raised from matter to God. The main motive for this, however, is nothing else than the reluctance to accept true creation, of which we have to admit no vision, and

[18] Cf. Hegel's *Grundlinien der Philosophie des Rechts* [Outlines of the Philosophy of Law] §. 5, addition. Hegel is so far from postulating a personal God that, should he do so, he would be forced to attribute to Him the possibility of committing suicide.

[19] *Philosophische Untersuchungen über das Wesen der menschlichen Freiheit* [Philosophical Investigations into the Essence of Human Freedom].

[20] "It is not a will that is conscious or joined to reflection, albeit not a completely unconscious will either, one that moves according to blind mechanical necessity; rather, it is intermediate nature, like desire and lust" (pp. 481, 482).

therefore the intention to extract some *matter* in God from which the world and men are made, so that the way in which they are in God (immanence) and yet separate from God Himself as God, can be understood. For this purpose, that ground in God is postulated, and a will different from God is assigned to it, which God only in His "independence allows to work" (p. 458). The "ground" is then the substance of the creature, and God as God only the shape-giver. This doctrine is not pantheistic, like the doctrine of Hegel, because it does not deny God His own separate consciousness, allowing divine and human consciousness to coincide; on the contrary, it expressly vindicates God's providence, the counsel preceding creation. And yet it erases the complete independence of God. According to it, God and man receive a common basis of being which is something independent, which stands over against God as much as man. Accordingly, man belongs essentially to the existence of God because he is the very existence of the ground (of nature) in God, and God feels the deeds and fates of man in a suffering way; indeed, as Schelling expressly explains, God cannot even do away with evil (this effect of the ground in man) without doing away with His own ground, hence His own personality (p. 492).[21] We too have to postulate a real being (omnipotence, love) for God as the ground (object) of His self-consciousness, but not something that is different from God, with its own will; we can only postulate an effectuation of God in pure spontaneity, pure love, justice, and so on, not "a stimulus of God according to His nature"; and we only lay down in God a power of the absolute production of that which is not Him, not a being in Him that is not Himself.[22]

---

[21] The relation of Schelling's most recent teaching to this can only be stated when it has been published in an authentic way (written in 1854).

[22] When Schelling (*op. cit.*, p. 455) asserts that everyone must admit "that desire, which constitutes the basis of every particular natural life, and the urge to maintain oneself not only in general, but in this particular existence, was not added to the already created creature, but instead was itself the creator," I only admit the former, that it was not added to the creature, but not the latter, that it was the creator (which would make God into nature, nature into God); rather, they themselves are also the creature, and indeed in the form of a free work of divine creation. That the ground which belongs to the divine existence, or the primordial will in God Himself, has the desire and pleasure

In this manner there is a worldview which is based on the personality of God that almost everywhere is the opposite of the pantheistic one. Its most essential elements are the inclination of creation towards personality – freedom in the creation, and with it the absolute value of everything positive and individual – providence – the possibility of a transformation of creation in its basic conditions for the establishment of a glorious kingdom.

---

which now fills the animal, that the animal's pleasure and sensation are the pleasure of that ground, and that it is only through this that the animal came into existence – I deny it absolutely. In so doing I am not denying principles existing in creation that run through a necessary process, but I do deny that these principles are already set in God Himself in the same quality. Accordingly, I do not find the unity of the real and the intellectual sides in God in an "indifference," an "unground" which is neither, like Schelling does, but antecedently in the totality of divine personality, which is both.

Chapter 2: The Inclination of the Creation toward Personality

§. 6. If the cause of the world is personal, then personality is also the archetype manifested in its formations, and it has the drive and the goal to be elevated thereto. This cause is not logical (ontological) determinations as such; rather, these are themselves only an abstraction from the person, his being and his creations. What we esteem in nature or in the realm of thought, organism, system, etc., is only an afterimage along the lines of the character of personality. There where the life of the whole body is contained in every part, is organism; there where all knowledge is present in every part, is system, and not just pattern [Schema]. The natural creation ascends to the personal existence of man, and every man who has come into existence is to be preserved forever as the particular person who he is. But the task of man is to be a true and perfect person, to put his whole existence, his whole personality into every action, into every thought; therein consist presence of mind, energy, concentration, and indeed his personality according to its true innermost determination, as it is in God. This is true systematic action by contrast with mere formalistic systematic action, i.e., acting according to "general maxims" which Kant sets up as a moral ideal.

Ultimately, the goal of all creation, the highest good, is that the divine personality should be fully present in every human being, that it should fill him, and do so as a person, hence fill him with the whole content of its being and spirit (its ideas). This is the Christian view, to be realized first by the church, that it be the body of Christ, then in the final manner in the kingdom of God. According to the Christian view, the kingdom of God is not just a kingdom (rulership) of the personal God, but itself again to a certain extent a personality in a way that exceeds our present imagination, in that men only know themselves in God and shall take part in Him in the fullness of His glory. In any case, in terms of this view, the unity of God and man is not, as is asserted by "speculative theologians," an impersonal thing that as such stands above both but is nothing other than the personality of God itself and its effectuation.

By contrast, Kant's and Fichte's highest ideal is a "realm of ends," a "moral world order," in short, a union of rational beings through a higher law of reason, a moral republic. But this always remains an incomplete union; it is not a real penetration of all by all, of each by the full concrete totality. For Schelling at his earlier stage, the work of art is the pinnacle; Hegel already criticizes this,[23] but for Hegel himself, the pinnacle, even more inadequately, is the concept (the logical categories) which realizes itself in human social institutions and understands itself in the human spirit, above all philosophy – in the technical parlance, "the absolute spirit."

"Speculative theology" has sought partly to set this vision of the absolute spirit in opposition to the Christian view of the kingdom of God, and partly to attribute it to that. But it is diametrically opposed thereto and falls far short of it. According to this vision, the individual personality (man) would know the spirit, or more properly speaking, the meaning of the whole (the ethical world), but the whole would not know the spirit of the individual personality. Accordingly, man understands the world spirit, but the world spirit does not understand man, for it does not understand anything at all. This is therefore no real "kingdom of the spirit," for it lacks the transfiguration and transparency of the mutual self-understanding of the whole and the members. As far as the doctrine that "the highest can only be something impersonal" is concerned, it is thus a shallow excuse when it is said that this impersonal, as the whole of the ethical world, contains personality (people) as moment and part, thus making it more "super-personal" than "sub-personal."

§. 7. Legal institutions are also subject to the general inclination towards the personal. They should first of all have an organic character, because the organic is the afterimage, the type of personality in the impersonal. Then they should be elevated to the character of the personal, each according to its relation, partly to bring the personality of man to full revelation, partly to bring human community to the manner of the person, i.e., to a totality which is ruled by a will in accordance with a law (specific determination of the will). Their appropriate further development is no less along the lines of personality, hence conscious free design just as much as uninterrupted unity, historical continuity. Usually only one of these is taken into account as the essence of personality or of the self-conscious spirit, free reform, and not the other, continuity, but both necessarily belong to it. Above all, the latest philosophical school finds the essence of the "self-conscious mind" (to which, in terms of what has already been said,

[23] Hegel, *Vorlesungen über die Geschichte der Philosophie*, vol. III, p. 660.

Hegel certainly gave rise) only in the negation of matter, the possibility of abstraction; therefore freedom and spirit consist in breaking away from everything that has been passed down, the antecedent (*a priori)* beginnings of conditions. It regards what is encountered as the material to be negated, and therefore considers the destruction thereof to be the most sublime expression of the spirit, and considers the constitution based on historical development, and so the true quality of the spirit, the continuous identity with itself, to be something menial.

"The inclination of creation is to pursue the personal" is the same as "the inclination of creation is to pursue the spiritual." Creation strives after the stage of the divine, and God is spirit and is person, and is the one only because He is the other. But it is the peculiar aberration of our time not to regard spirit and person as the same, to find the character of the spiritual not in personal actuality but in the abstract determinations of thought. During the period of French philosophy, the inclination towards the spiritual had to be asserted; during the period of Hegelian philosophy, it is the inclination towards the personal that has to be asserted. But these are one and the same truth.

Chapter 3: Freedom in the Creation

§. 8. The assumption of the personality of God is also inseparable from that of His *freedom* or His *creative faculties*, just as, on the other hand, the pantheistic assumption only admits necessity and regularity. *Either* the relation of the primordial power (of primordial being) to all derived existence is one in which the latter is already posited exactly as it really is with the former and in the former, that is, by necessity – *pantheism*. *Or else* the derived existence is something really different from the primordial power. In that case, it is impossible to derive the individual, actual specificity of what exists from the nature (the natural, logical, or moral essential determinations) of the primordial power, and to assume such to be already posited in it (even if merely conceptually). Instead, this is the *work of its act,* which means nothing else than that it posits every single existence, both according to the existence and to the specific determinateness thereof (as far as this goes) as an *absolute beginning*. Only in this way is the world a creation of God and not just His elucidation or emanation, be it physical, be it logical. "God calls into being that which is not" applies not only to the existence, but also to the essence of things.

§. 9. This creative freedom, since it evokes something that is not already posited in the essence of the Creator, to this extent has no necessarily determined object to produce; and with everything that it brings about, it is accompanied by the awareness of the infinite possibility of the other. For this reason, it can be called choice, namely, *primordial choice* or *infinite choice.*

Nevertheless, note the following:

First, we are talking here only of *creative* freedom whereby that which is specific to what is created is the result of absolute choice (i.e., the absolute beginning), not of *ethical* freedom whereby there is the choice between good and bad. Rather, the good belongs to the original essential determination of the person (§. 10), which he can never give up. Yet the world did not emerge merely from the ethical qualities (holiness) of God, but from His creative spirit. In the same way, the life of man is not merely the result of ethical necessity, but also of free creative power.[24]

Second, creative freedom is not even remotely related to *empirical choice*, i.e., selection and combination from among what already exists, but is a primordial choice, a choice that precedes the objects and first creates them. Precisely for this reason it is also infinite choice, while empirical choice is limited by range of objects among which it chooses. As such, it is purely active choice; no object can have a determinative effect on it; while in empirical selection, each of the objects determines us, for which reason the principle applies: "He who chooses, loses" [Wer die Wahl hat, hat die Qual].[25] In this alone lies the difference between creation and emanation or development. The latter presupposes a limited content that can be exhausted, and then, when all has been developed, it no longer has any power of production. But freedom as the infinite choice, as the power of absolute creation, has no limit.

The concept of infinite choice in no way involves a vision of that which is not chosen (created), but instead is excluded by what is created; for that which is not chosen, it not being called into being either in terms of its essence or its existence, for that very reason has no shape that could be viewed. It is merely the abyss of infinite possibility.

I am speaking here of divine things in a human way, but I am also aware that I am not speaking adequately, but only approximately. The approximate insight into the essence of divine creation, which is granted to us, cannot be derived

---

[24] Regarding ethical freedom, see §. 39 below. Ethical freedom is that of one's own being, the other is freedom of production. What is true for the one does not thereby apply to the other. According to Hegel, however, the will comes into consideration only from the ethical side (as the realization of the good), not from the creative side; for with him, creation, nature, precedes volition and is the consequence of logical emanation. Similarly with Kant: *Metaphysik der Sitten*, p. 36.

[25] In his review of my *Philosophy of Law* in the *Jahrbüchern für wissenschaftliche Kritik* [Almanacs of Scientific Criticism] of 1835, Feuerbach tried, with great but entirely superfluous wit and sagacity, to demonstrate against me that one does not place freedom in choice (selection), and such a selection may not be ascribed to God. Although at that time I protested just as decisively as I do now against this confusion of infinite choice, which precedes objects, with finite choice, this did not in the least disconcert his polemical stratagem.

from any other source than from the contemplation of the creations of the human spirit.

§. 10. Now then, creative freedom is by no means to be seen for itself as the fullness of the divine personality. Instead, it is but one of the attributes of the same, inseparable from the other attributes, both of the unchangeable divine being (love, justice, wisdom, etc.) and of divine purpose and providence, and in this lies *necessity*, which is no less a characteristic of creation than is freedom.

For it is just as unthinkable for personality to be without a definite essence and will as without creative freedom, and all activity of the person, divine or human, is a reproduction of its own being, a revelation of itself, albeit in a creative way, i.e., newly beginning, newly positing. Everything that is necessary and lawful, indeed, the concept of necessity and the law itself, stems ultimately from this. The unchangeable faithfulness of God to Himself and consequently the unchangeability of the ideas which He has posited for the creation according to His essence, and the determinateness which He has given to every creature, is the original concept and is the embodiment of what is necessary in creation. For the laws in nature and in the moral world are nothing other than the specific essentialities of creatures. What is called natural law is only the specific essence of natural objects or substances, and moral law is only the true essence of man. We thereby predicate of God above all the ethical necessity of justice, love, mercy, which are the eternal content of the divine will, but then no less an intellectual necessity which lies in the eternal content (substance) of divine wisdom – this, however, is not a system of categories or abstract ontological determinations, which the school calls "reason," but an abundance of concrete, definite visions (ideas) – finally also an artistic necessity, in that God maintains unchangeably in the essentiality once given to it, what He freely creates on that eternally necessary basis. A (positive) necessity of any other kind cannot be asserted for absolute power. Logical (metaphysical) necessity is not a positively determining principle; it contains only the negative, the limit of the possible, and physical necessity, i.e., that which lies in the specific effectuality of natural forces, can as such only apply to the created, not to the act of creation itself, and is therefore not in creation as an original principle, but merely as a product, which itself can only have its cause in that partly intellectual, partly artistic necessity.[26]

---

[26] Regarding the laws of nature (and these are also the laws of history, insofar as they are something else than ethical requirements) we demand something even higher, i.e., a law (apart from any purpose) for the sake of which these laws, or, as we say, these specific substantialities of things exist; for example, why fire, light, water, etc., exist in just the qualities that they do. Hegel finds this higher law in the logical categories, e.g., "*fire* is *being for itself*, not the indifference of rigidity but the unrest of *individuality* that is for itself, and air *in itself* is fire and in fire it is posited as *negative universality*, or *negativity related to itself*" (*Encyclopädie*, §. 283). But with these determinations of "in itself" and "for itself," "negative versus other," "to itself," that which is specific to fire is not designated, much less the reason for which it is fire. The same is true for the way in which another philosopher puts it, that water is fire brought to rest.

I posit this higher law in the eternal concrete relationships of the divine being, which are put forward by God in a definite (free) conception as archetypes (ideas) of creation, but into which we have no insight because we know God only from His ethical side (justice, love), according to which He is present to us in conscience, but not from His creative and intellectual side (power, wisdom). I therefore do not withdraw my earlier assertion that earthly things bear an analogy to the divine relationships (relationships of the divine essence) in themselves; but I admit that the desire to demonstrate such an analogy is untenable and, precisely from this point of view, foolish, since we lack the vision of any, in fact the main, object of comparison. I by no means thereby rule out that "God created things according to concepts that we must recognize as divine and at the same time as eternal," but I do deny that these eternal divine concepts exist in categories or in potencies instead of concrete visions, and I deny that any human being has discovered or can discover them. Accordingly, I establish a natural philosophy based on the augmentation and spiritualization of natural science, not a natural philosophy in the now usual sense. The human spirit does not penetrate beyond the laws inherent in nature itself. The logical provisions and laws that we recognize, however, are not the laws for and above the laws of nature. Finally, with regard to legal philosophy, which indeed may already presuppose natural philosophy as far as its sphere extends, I am completely content to recognize the determination of human life conditions and legal institutions, marriage, property, the state and so on, as given, i.e., not through positive law but through the institution of nature (God). The question, however, as to why

In the same way, intention and providence are inseparable from our view of personality. Act and creation, if they really are that, which is to say, if they really proceed from the person, are related to a conscious purpose, and this all the more, and all the more consistently, to the degree that the originator truly is a person. In the absolute personality of God, we cannot think of any creation or counsel that is not related to the absolute purpose of the entire world plan. "Known unto God are all his works from the beginning of the world" [Acts 15:18].

In this arrangement, in terms of which freedom is only one of the powers that determine creation, freedom is distinguished from arbitrariness and randomness, which after all contradict our basic view of the Godhead. For the opposite of arbitrariness is the determinateness and consequently the necessity of divine being, and the opposite of randomness is intention and providence.[27]

§. 11. But this in no way means that freedom is withdrawn again and dissolved into necessity. For the *individuality of the act or creation, or the determinate*

---

reproduction is arranged in this way by nature, why human existence has been tied to the needs of food and clothing, etc., or above all the proof of the mathematical necessity that nothing could be otherwise and can be otherwise for eternity, I exclude from the field of my scientific research.

[27] Against this argument, Feuerbach (*op. cit.*) remarks 1) I owe the necessity of the divine being, according to which the possibility of evil, of ungodliness, is excluded from God, not to my philosophical standpoint, but to some catechism that has fallen into my hands (p. 6)! 2) The determinacy of being, to which I take refuge in desperation, is just as applicable to animals, trees, and stones as to personality, so that one suddenly finds oneself displaced to the field of mineralogy and the like – albeit with this difference: a purely physical determinacy for the former, an ethical determinacy for the latter. 3) Once I have declared the freedom or choice of God to be the principle of the world, the essence of God itself is nothing other than arbitrariness, "for what, if we ask more closely, is the determinacy of God? nothing else than absolute choice or arbitrariness, which, as the essence of freedom, is the essence of God?" (p. 13) – as if the power to reveal one's own essence (love, wisdom) in a creative way, or with infinite choice and freedom in the manner of revelation, would be the same as having as essence choice itself and only choice.

conception of ideas, is not given in any way either with that essential determinateness of the person, or with this intention and calculation of purposes. One must say of every divine work that it is a revelation of the divine being and that it intervenes as a supplementary member in the divine world plan, but one cannot say that it follows *precisely as it does* from the nature of God or from its ultimate end. There is nothing that does not have its reason and purpose, but nothing is already completely determined and characterized by its reason and purpose. The ongoing individuation which creation actually undeniably contains, from its great groupings, indeed from the conception of its ideas, down to the smallest individual entity specifically determined in all things, cannot be explained in any other way than *from freedom*, from a force to begin absolutely (for no reason) in this relation with each and every individual; because from law and rule (necessity) only the same follows. This creative freedom can therefore also be called the *power of infinite individuation*, i.e., precisely the power to posit something specific, which as such has no law, no rule, no reason in anything antecedent. Freedom is therefore a principle of creation which is completely different from necessity but is not separate from it; these are cooperating, interpenetrating principles. But to what degree the ideas of creation are the eternal content of divine wisdom or to what degree they are God's free artistic conception, is beyond our knowledge.

Certainly, Feuerbach asserts against me that all diversity and individuality are precisely what is flawed in creation, and he does so because the object does not adequately express the idea – that the true and perfect is by its nature a ἅπαξ λεγόμενον [i.e., unique].[28] I admit that with regard to the ideas of God, being

[28] " – as if the word of God were the world, not a ἅπαξ λεγόμενον, as if God is not God precisely because what He creates is absolutely as it should be, i.e., absolutely equal to and in accordance with the idea, and therefore where there is an absolute identity between the concept and the object, between the idea and the product or being, all possibility of being different, consequently all choice and diversity, is excluded. Diversity owes its origin only to the misery, the hardship of material existence. The multiplicity of human individualities only arises from the fact that no single individual, because of his limitation, is the adequate expression of the idea, of the species, and therefore nature seeks to supplement the lack of one existence by the creation of another being in order to use this multiplicity to represent the unity of being in existence." *Op. cit.*, pp. 4, 5, 6.

eternally identical with themselves, they are only once, uniquely, thought and expressed, but I do not admit this with regard to His creatures. The creature *should* be independent and therefore determinate, and as such is not supposed to "adequately," i.e., *exhaustively* express the idea. In this lies the joy and vitality of creating. The eternal theme of the divine idea *should* have its infinite variation in creation, the light eternally identical with itself *should* have its manifestation in the infinite free play of colors, these should indeed be transfigured into light, but never cease to be color; the eternal Word of God is only uttered once, uniquely, but the sermon *should* expand its inexhaustible riches forever in infinite variety and individuality. So also the human being who is Himself the divine Logos is the only begotten (*unigenitus*); but all other human beings who are not God *should* eternally be individualities and thereby different from one another, diverse. God's infinite wealth of production, His infinite creative freedom, consists in this: that He is able to call forth these individualities, not merely posit His own idea eternally.[29]

---

[29] If the work of art is an imitation of nature in the right sense, i.e., not imitation of its finished forms but of the spirit that informs it, then the conclusion backwards from the mode of the work of art to the mode of the spirit ruling in creation is justified. Now necessity in a work of art does not exclude creative freedom but rather requires it as another potency that, as it were, comes before. If for example we take the highest work of art, drama, it consists first of all in the characters being the expression of ideas, that is, determined by them, who remain unchanged once they have been determined. But that precisely these ideas are expressed, and are expressed in this connection, and that precisely these individualities were used for them, is a matter of free conception and creative production. Lessing possessed that aspect of necessity in high degree, and yet he did not consider himself a dramatic poet. Then there is still another necessity in the dramatic work of art: that the characters, while acting only according to their own determination, nevertheless fulfill the one higher intention of the whole precisely in that way. Even through this necessity, corresponding not to legalism but to providence, the individual forms are by no means absolutely determined; for if the poet were to establish a character merely for his ultimate purpose, that is, if he were to use its determinateness merely as a means, we would blame him for lack of poetic power and unnaturalness (i.e., inconsistency with the spirit that determines life). Rather, the individual characters are

§. 12. Now the threefold character of creation – necessity, purposiveness, and reciprocal suitability [Aufeinanderberechnung] – and infinite free individuation are *completely* dissolved by *the latest philosophy* into *necessity*, and indeed into mere *metaphysical necessity*. Both teleology and particularization are, according to Hegel himself, only the results of dialectical, that is, logically more necessary, development. Even Leibniz in his *Theodicy* definitely traces creation back to accordance with law (*ratio sufficiens*). He does not find this in metaphysical necessity, which he correctly limits to the negative, but in purposiveness. But by not accepting that principle of creative freedom, purposiveness becomes an absolutely determining factor for him – because of His perfection, God had to choose precisely this world from the store of possible ones, because it is the most purposive – bringing his entire doctrine into contradiction because it makes the quality of things, on which their suitability for purposes depends, a first and determining factor for the Creator, who bestows these on them. According to this point of view, however, philosophy cannot explain where this specific determinateness of things comes from. Spinoza does not even pose the question. In his *Monadology,* Leibniz explains this from the fact that the emanations of God, through which the monads arise, work differently depending on the greater or lesser receptivity of the creature. Hereby, however, a receptivity, i.e., a property of the creature would be assumed which should determine its creation before its being created. Hegel replaces the living Creator with his "concept," that is, the logical unity of the universal, the particular, and the individual. Instead of a personality evoking the individual through acts, it should rather be a logical law that the universal is necessarily also the particular and the individual. And if one wished to admit that, it would only explain the category of particularity and individuation, but by no means the particular, the individual itself – that A and B are precisely this or that particular.

On this, however, is based the mighty contrast between our conception and

---

presupposed to be independent, absolutely (indeterminately [Zwecklos]) present, and artistic perfection consists precisely in their being joined to the plan of the whole regardless of their independence, their indeterminate existence. But how it happens that what is absolutely independent, only determined from and for itself, at the same time is also a means for the whole, that is, determined by it – this is inexplicable and inscrutable to us even with human works of art; how much the more with divine creation.

the current philosophical conception in practical application. If everything that is individual is only a consequence of the necessary process of what is universal-abstract, then only this universal-abstract, or the law of its process, is what actually is, the truth in everything concrete, for example, not the individual determinate human being but the idea of the human being and the idea of particularity. Likewise with regard to natural entities, legal institutions, historical events. In that case, the effort of our masters of the positive, which stops at the mere shadow and is no longer needed once those philosophical laws have been discovered, is wasted. If, on the other hand, the individual is a work of freedom, then its concrete, positive, individual determinateness is of just as infinite absolute value as the aspect of universality (the "idea") in it. The same is true in the area of ethics: the denial of the principle of creative freedom leads consistently to the puritanical standpoint of only tolerating what is absolutely required in the ethical community of people, but condemning everything else that might be done without or done differently (such as, for example, images, embellishment of worship, folding of hands, hierarchy of power, finally art and science). To accept such creative freedom, we are not moved by idle contemplation. We do not get into our heads the desire to explain the essence of God and the process in God when He created the world. This is an unavoidable problem for the pantheistic point of view, an inadmissible one for us, but it impels us to the practical need: to save the value of the positive, the concrete, the individual, the value of the facts.[30] On the other hand, it by no means deprives logical development (e.g., the consequences contained in the principle of a legal institute) of its value, but only directs its right use. For this can only consist in recognizing or factually clarifying the specific essence of a thing (e.g., a legal institution) as a given object, not in revealing the reason and necessity of its existence itself.[31]

---

[30] I therefore put no weight at all on the *expression* "choice" [Wahl], innocuous as it is in terms of my more specific determinations, but only on the *matter* as discussed here and already in the first edition, in opposition to the current philosophy.

[31] If finally the question is raised here of whether, by virtue of God's creative freedom, a world other than the one that actually exists was possible, as dealt with by Leibniz, Spinoza, Schelling and others, it goes without saying from what has been said that an unjust, unwise, etc., world was impossible because its wisdom and righteousness follow

from God's being. But when Leibniz further concludes in this way that the "*most perfect*" world follows from the being of God, he is thereby presupposing a standard, that of perfection, for things which cannot be applied to them. Which is more perfect, the smell of a rose or a carnation, the beauty of Apollo or Adonis, the state of the Greeks or the Romans? The principle of creative freedom involves precisely an individuality of things which excludes any comparison and thus any measure of higher perfection. It is therefore not a question of the possibility of a world of opposing moral characters, but only that of a world of a different individuality, a different specific determination of conception, and by our principle this possibility seems to have to be accepted. Before any answer, however, the question itself must first be clarified. With possibility, we always think of an act as still imminent, which, if the future shows that not it but something else has happened, it is no longer possible. So then, all possibility rests on the fact that something else was valid before rather than after. But now with God everything is eternal presence, so there can be no possibility for Him in this sense. Although for God there is no past and future, the possibility of another is for Him as it is for us subsequent to an act that has already taken place, which excludes the same. We can therefore assert the possibility of another world only in the relative and ideal meaning that the definite world is not just given by the divine being, but is the work of free act, insofar as another was possible; on the other hand, we cannot assert the possibility of another world in an absolute or real sense, because God has really decided on this world, and according to the eternity of divine relations, we cannot set a point in time at which He would not have decided on it. But now we have no idea of the state of an eternal present; indeed, it is contradictory to us that the divine counsel of creation, which is an act, and therefore occurs in time, should nevertheless be an eternal one. We are therefore absolutely incapable of thinking how possibility relates to reality and necessity in God, *and thus incapable of actually and positively answering that question.* But only by virtue of our God-consciousness can we *negatively* exclude the erroneous ideas, on the one hand possibility in the human sense, therefore God's consultation and a state according to which God would have to say to Himself: at that time I still had the possibility of another world, but now it is too late; and on the other hand a necessity, be it an inward one, according to which the entire determinateness of the world, apart from any divine act, would already be posited with the divine being. The pantheistic axiom that in God there is pure *actus* and nothing of mere *potentia* might signify that former truth, but it does not; it signifies this latter error, that all real things as such are given with the essence of God.

Chapter 4: Providence

§. 13. If creation is the work of personality, then purposiveness [Zweckmäßigkeit] is not just the form in which things appear (as in Hegel's system), but the real cause of their existence. They are created in terms of purpose and intention. Everything that is there is not only homogeneous in its foundation, based on uniform law, but also appropriate in its reciprocal effect, and also present for the sake of this effect. This is what we call *providence*, in which we find the most genuine and exclusive attribution of personality. Yet purposiveness is not in itself the principle of creation, any more than freedom; rather, it presupposes free production as well as that partly ethical, partly artistic necessity (§. 10). This removes the objection that absolute power needs no means and cannot depend on the usefulness thereof to attain its goal – that the notion of providence, as opposed to absolutely necessary effectuation, is a notion that is unworthy of God. For God, to be sure, the perfection of His works is not a mere means, nor is there any restriction of usefulness other than the essentiality which He himself bestows on things. But the providence at which we marvel is this: what is evoked for its own sake, according to the essentiality given to it, at the same time serves the plan of the whole.

§. 14. Speculative philosophy rejects the entire empirical causal nexus, i.e., that things have their real foundation in the causes which experience shows us. The innumerable causes by which any particular thing or event arises – e.g., the French Revolution through the despotism of Louis XIV, the immorality of Louis XV, the weakness of Louis XVI, the arrogance of the nobility, the financial hardship brought about by the American war, centralization, the affair of the diamond necklace, etc. – have no connection with one another and are each based in turn on innumerable causes which in themselves have no relation to this event (the Revolution). But what is the cause of this coincidence of all the causes? Because if this has no cause, the final result, the event itself, is a coincidence!

For this reason, speculative philosophy postulates an absolute coherence above the empirical causal nexus, but it finds it in the logical law or process – Schelling in the process of its two potencies, Hegel in the dialectical development of the concept. So, for example, the French Revolution is nothing else than the concept of the will which in the course of its world-historical development enters at the moment, purely as will, as the notion of the will, more specifically as abstract will, to subjugate the external (objective) world.

The holy of holies of speculative philosophy is precisely that it should delineate the standpoint of speculation by contrast with the standpoint of mere reflection, and upon this is based in particular the construction of world history, through which it lays claim to hitherto unheard-of achievements. Granted, the deeper historical conception which is peculiar to our time explains the spiritual achievements of a nation together as a whole from one principle, namely the inherent sense of this nation, e.g., Greek art, science, custom, state constitution from the sense of beauty. But speculative philosophy does much more than this. From the one principle, it also explains nothing less than the external conditions and happenings of the nation. That the Greeks were partial to beautiful embodiment, that they split up into several ancestral states so that they could represent a diverse and yet harmonious whole, that they had just enough fortune in arms to maintain their independence yet not enough to make conquests, which kept the self-contained form of the work of art from becoming discombobulated, that Alexander died as a youth because he represented this people of youth, etc., all of this, according to the speculative view, is no less a necessary result of the idea of beauty and the work of art than the Lycurgian constitution, the Attic tragedy, etc. This Greek principle of beauty is itself a result of the dialectical process of the will. The substantial will (universality, higher objective power over man) sets up the subjective will (the right and act of the individual) as its opposite, but both, not yet put asunder (as in the Roman world), but maintained in ideal unity (mutual permeation), are precisely this realm of beauty. Thus did the dialectical process of the will, as the absolute and sole reason, determine both the inward spiritual direction and the outward composition, conditions, and fate of the Greek people.

But since all processes are based on the causal nexus, one must demand from speculative philosophy an explanation as to how the logical development of the idea has an effect on this causal nexus. Even if one were to acquiesce in that logical operation according to which the category of cause and effect, as well as the end, of itself and as such dissolves into that higher one of absolute coherence, that is to say, turns out to be mere appearance in itself, still this would not explain how a particular idea effected these particular individual causes, e.g., how beauty, as the idea of Greek life, effected the wind which was favorable to the

Greek fleet one moment and unfavorable the next, or the fever that killed Alexander. Certainly, the explanation will be proffered that all these circumstances exist of themselves with the idea as their integrating part, since this is precisely the unity of concept and object, or of spiritual thought and its bodily realization. But such is thinkable and comprehensible only where the corporeal is an immediate and necessary expression of something spiritual, not where, in itself coincidentally, it serves the thought merely as an external means; for that wind or that fever is certainly not a direct expression of the idea of beauty.

§. 15. The absolute coherence which we require over and above the series of individual causes and effects, if it at the same time is to be in harmony with them, cannot lie anywhere else than in divine providence. Only a personal spirit is able to combine the myriad of individual causes into one result, and to set in motion the intermediate real means to achieve the representation of an ideal conception. This is the only way to explain both the subservience of physical results for spiritual ends, and the often likewise artistic significance of these ends themselves. For such artistic explanations as that of Alexander's early death, because he, like Achilles, represents the people of youth, or consumption, of which Spinoza had to die because, according to his doctrine, the individual things disappear in God[32] – the correctness of which in these examples I put to one side – is by no means peculiar to speculative philosophy. It has always been current with the Christian way of thinking, under the name of the typological interpretation, although manifesting itself not as the primary end, the way in which, as here, the real art form of the type does, but only as a secondary end. Theologians have always interpreted Moses' death before entering the promised land to mean that he is the representative of the law, but the law does not enter the kingdom of God, whereas Joshua leads into the promised land because, as his name shows, he is the example of Jesus, even though the actual and primary cause of Moses'

---

[32] Hegel, *Vorlesungen über die Geschichte der Philosophie*, vol. III, p. 370: "Spinoza died on the 21st of February, 1677, in the forty-fourth year of his age, from consumption, of which he had long been a sufferer, in harmony with his system, in terms of which all particularity and individuality vanishes into the one substance." Similarly on p. 378: "For it is rigid immobility, the only activity of which is to cast everything into the abyss of substance, in which everything vanishes, all life perishes in itself; Spinoza himself died of consumption."

death, his unbelief, is not put aside. Similar interpretations can be found in the sacred documents themselves. Such attainment of the manifold purposes and forms in the one great, primary course of events, which this mode of explanation presupposes, is plainly and simply the work of the personal, foreseeing Spirit.

From this providential standpoint, world history appears as a means to an end beyond its own end, the kingdom of God (§. 17), and at the same time as an end, a perfect whole in itself; and in terms of the latter relation, it is characterized with indisputable truth as a work of art.[33] It is a work of art according to the way it proceeds, in that all individuals act according to their nature and freedom, and yet, regardless of human resistance, even by means of it, fulfill the higher thought; and it is a work of art in terms of its content, as a harmoniously developed portrayal and succession of divine ideas. Every people and every age therefore has its own special vocation in it; each is the bearer of a divine thought and a divine task in the development of the human race, and such is its world-historical principle. The peculiarity of their being stems from this; that is, their valuation of life and their dispositions stem from this, no less, by virtue of divine providence, their conditions (outward form, places of residence, clan relations, etc.) and their destinies, and this explains the agreement and coherence of that inward and this outward, where no direct effect of the one on the other takes place. This artistic conception and providence is the higher ground above the empirical causal nexus which speculative philosophy rightly postulates, but wrongly locates in a logical process. Also, because it is itself a real acting power, it is not in opposition to the causal nexus but is of a similar nature and in the closest connection with it. Divine love as the supreme cause (motive) and the kingdom of God as the ultimate goal also surrounds and permeates the artistic conception of the world-plan. But this artistic and providential connection, as a work of divine freedom, can only be recognized in a few rays, by way of presentiment, not exhaustively demonstrated in a rational system – as if it were the totality of the divine world plan.[34]

---

[33] Schelling, *Vorlesungen über die Methode des akademischen Studiums* [Lectures on the Method of Academic Study], Lecture XI.

[34] This in no way contests the great achievement of speculative philosophy, whereby it observes principles (laws) which pertain to nature or history or larger sections of it as a whole, not individual things, classes or people, and to a course (process) which answers

The unfathomable depth of everything created rests upon infinite creative individualizing freedom, then upon the infinite intensity of the divine being, finally upon providence, which brings the infinite wealth of independent data into unity; and is itself, insofar as it is understood, eternally accompanied by the impression of veneration. The dictum of the poet[35]: "No created spirit penetrates the interior of nature," Hegel considers to be maladroit since nature has no interior at all but is precisely the exterior of logical determinations. If that really were the case, then surely nature would not be unfathomable, would run no deeper than the law of the triangle, and its powerful poetic effect would be inexplicable. But since behind nature there is a personality, a spirit, the poet is absolutely right.

---

to its own nature and thus is necessary, by which phenomena are explained which cannot be resolved from the nature of the individual structures, people, peoples. In this way, one can speak of a mythological process. In this way, the principle of beautiful humanity, to which the Greek world is traced (which, by the way, was viewed in this way not solely by philosophers), is a concrete and true principle, without having to admit the allegedly still higher law from which this itself came about, the course of the will (concept) in terms of its substantial and subjective moments. To have presentiment of such principles in terms of their process and rhythm is the gift of the philosophical artist which Schelling possesses in such a high degree, and which Hegel, though less well endowed with it, applied across a greater expanse. For these reasons, Hegel's philosophy of history is to be preferred over the works of the historians, in that they usually do not penetrate to the general principles governing the epoch, but only have in mind what moves people, and therefore do not understand reality with the same intellectuality. Certainly, Hegel is supported thereby by his athletic treatment of the categories. On the other hand, however, Hegel's philosophy of history has a continuous trait of affectation which causes it to fall short of those simple historical works, in that it asserts the false ground of the logical process over these revealed concrete principles, and thus dissolves the living phenomena into the abstract form of thought, which in truth is alien and external to them, and moreover does violence to their real character.

35 [Albrecht von Haller]

Chapter 5: The Temporality of Earthly Constraints

§. 16. The assumption of the personality and freedom of God, and consequently also of man, first makes *history* in the true sense possible. The history of the world is then undoubtedly a work of the act, of divine disposal and of human action. But this does not rule out at least the possibility that the basic terms of the human condition setting the course of world history were the result of an act of people, which thus occurred before there were or would be others.

According to the Christian revelation, man was in a primitive state of innocence in God ("paradise"); through the *act* of people, there came about the present (world-historical) state with its conditions: isolation from God, and in the wake of this, the power of evil with natural evil (death, pain, etc.). By means of the divine act of redemption the original bond to God is restored for man in his innermost life. Finally, however, through the act of God, an eternal state of ethical and natural perfection ("the kingdom of God") is supposed to be re-established – the latter of yet another, higher sort than in that primitive state, namely one in which the material basis of human existence is transfigured into the spiritual, the immediacy of the first state being elevated to the most penetrating knowledge ("to know as I am known") and, to the exclusion of all possibility of apostasy, the innermost self of man being immediately filled and permeated by God ("that God be all in all").

This is the simple, grand vision of Christianity. If it finds its possibility in the presupposition of the personal God, then it finds its confirmation to a high degree in the actual situation. For human existence contains contradictions for which there is no explanation, except in that act of diremption through which the moral world came out of joint. Likewise, the inner state of the person, the longing and the presentiment, the contradiction between demand and fulfillment, as well as the outer shape of the moral world, the injustice of earthly fortunes (Kant), the never-decided battle of the truth with lies, etc., even the actual social institutions, e.g., the indestructible presence of a church alongside the state, point to that promised state of perfection. It is the idea to which all threads of the moral world lead.

Speculative philosophy could not shut itself off from the depth of this Christian revelation of the world. But what for the latter is act and history, becomes for the former eternally existing logical relation. Just as for it the world is not a fact but is the particular already posited in the universal simply according to the concept, so also is the fall into sin not a fact for it, but is entailed in the concept that subjectivity must deepen to the extreme opposition to the substantial in order for the latter thereby to come to full consciousness, or that there is a personality (a "for himself") who as such opposes the universal, so that for it, consciousness as such is sin.[36] The resurrection is not a fact which occurred eighteen hundred years ago and will repeat itself someday, but is that which happens at all times, in every moment, when the human being in his consciousness surrenders himself to substance, and so continues by the fact that the rational world continues (since he no longer wants to be an I). The kingdom of God is not the future world beyond earthly conditions, but the ever-existing institution of the state in its architectonic of rational determinations.[37]

Along these lines, the conditions of the present earthly condition are eternal. Things will never be other than that man is born in sin, and the imagination of man's heart is evil from his youth [Genesis 8:21], never other than that pain fills his life and death brings it to an end. The consciousness of all peoples, the tradition throughout the entire history of the human race, points to a lost paradise and to a promised future in the beyond. A pain and a hope fill human life in its depth. Here, hope is removed while the only remedy offered for the pain is to rise above it in thought. What is the scientific motive for denying that assumption of religious belief, i.e., not to explain it as unproven (which goes without saying), but as untrue, impossible? None other than that initial presupposition

---

[36] Hegel, *Grundlinien der Philosophie des Rechts,* §. 139; *Encyclopädie* (1840), p. 55 [§. 24, addition 3]; *Vorlesungen über die Philosophie der Religion,* vol. III, pp. 259, 260.

[37] Hegel, *Grundlinien der Philosophie des Rechts,* §§. 258 (p. 313), 270, 360; *Vorlesungen über die Geschichte der Philosophie,* vol. III, p. 133; *Vorlesungen über die Philosophie der Religion,* vol. II, p. 250ff. Hegel's own utterances are indeed not as undisguised as those of his newer school, but are not for that reason the less unequivocal. For his part, Fichte occupies a similar position to Hegel with regard to the promise of the eternal kingdom. For he also finds eternity and bliss only in the here and now, and indeed in the suprasensorial and therefore supratemporal nature of the I (personality) and the suprasensorial and therefore supratemporal meaning of moral action, while Hegel finds them in the external formations of earthly life.

whereby there is no personal God who can create and change, whereby everything is logically necessary, thus equally eternal, according to which the contradictions in the world can only be resolved logically. But the contradictions in the world are not mere logical contradictions, but real conflicts for which there is no logical necessity whereby they could or should be in harmony, which find their solution not in a logical agreement, a rich concept, but only in a real change. In particular, the unification of the substantial and individual will, which Hegel himself regards as a postulate of reason, is never really imparted by the state, as he assumes. Because the individual will, which needs to be backed up by the military and police power in order for it to fulfill the substantial will, is not truly united in the state. Only the kingdom of God, in which the human will is inwardly permeated by the divine, contains this unity.

§. 17. Pursuant to this, then, *world history* occupies the space of earthly existence. Its task is to elevate the undeveloped state of humanity to that of full development. As a result of man's fall, however, this development does not take place *in* God, but *outside* of Him. It is therefore also *mere* development, not at the same time a continued new creation, not an increase in innermost being and ability through the influx of new divine forces, not real progress. Accordingly, world history certainly embodies a steady increase in self-consciousness (reflection, speculation), rule over individual intellectual forces, thereby superiority over nature (technology), rule over united forces and thus over the common condition (state mechanism of modern times) – in this respect, world history shows a constant *perfectibility*. But through this development the developed substance itself, the human mind and spirit, is in no way improved or enhanced. Therefore, neither the ethical nature nor the creative (artistic) power of man are augmented, nor does philosophical insight into the eternal foundations gain a generic expansion in history. Moreover, evil, which now also pertains to the human being, unfolds in the same measure with its train of evils and everywhere permeates the increase in spiritual powers. Innocence, naturalness, and the simple enjoyment of life diminish with culture. Indeed, augmented culture often gives birth to states of unculture, dullness, and narrowness, precisely through this proliferation of evil.[38]

Locked within these limits, then, world history can never lead to a generically higher condition of the human race; it is never a progression, a series which at its end would by itself lead to a state of perfection.[39] Rather, this can only take place through an act of God, which abolishes the basic conditions of the earthly state.

Now then, for the relationship of man to God, religion, God intervenes directly in this state of alienation from Him in order to restore the sundered bond and to eradicate evil, sin – *revelation* and *redemption*. Throughout the course of world history as the realm of natural development, the divine economy of redemption runs as an invisibly visible supernatural realm, an intervention of the eternal world of the beyond into the world of the here and now, which in itself has no connection to it, in order to conduct that world to it. At its innermost, the activity of this supernatural realm is of a different sort, the directly personal act of God, which essentially changes the position of man towards God and elevates man above the basic conditions of his nature – *revelation*, *grace*, *miracle*. Assuming the personality of God, miracles are precisely His natural mode of operation, and it is unnatural (the simple consequence of human guilt) that God should withdraw or hide His immediate personal act, that He allows nature such as it is to go its own way in its inadequacy, merely according to its own powers. It is true that this revelation and redemption also have an indirect effect on that natural development, since religion exerts a necessary influence on morality and education; but their supernatural power is limited to religion, the innermost bond with God. The conditions of men are not freed from the character of temporality by them, nor is theoretical knowledge expanded beyond its limits. This is misunderstood if one expects from Christianity and the condi-

---

[38] Some of Hegel's school deduce from the fact that God directs world history the conclusion that what is contemporary, what is latest, must always be the best, hence modern times are absolutely better than the Middle Ages or the times of the early church, the Prussian land law is the most perfect legislation, French conditions are better than English, modern unbelief is better than ancient belief. One could have argued like this under the Byzantine emperors and ten years prior to Luther. If God really was only Hegel's "world spirit," the conclusion would be correct.

[39] This constitutes a major objection to Rothe's doctrine of church and state.

tions of the New Covenant the supersession of monarchy, indeed of civil authorities generally, the abolition of the death penalty (Schleiermacher) and the like. Likewise, when one lays claim to a philosophical knowledge of a completely new kind (e.g., as a result of being born again). God is only revealed to us from the ethical side (justice, love, holiness), not also from the creative and intellectual side (power, wisdom, plan of creation). When the apostolic saying that the Spirit reveals the depths of God [1 Corinthians 2:10] is invoked in order to justify the enterprise of speculative philosophy, it is based on this mistaken identity.

§. 18. If, accordingly, the fact of original human guilt is an indispensable factor in explaining the temporal condition, this destructive act must by no means be regarded as a *positive* and *constitutive cause* of it. Evil is not creative; it does not generate ideas but can only cloud and alter them. Therefore, in terms of their idea, law and the state cannot be derived from the sin or the sinfulness of man; only their temporal nature (the externality of law and the state's separation from God) can be derived from it. Likewise, in terms of its idea, world history must not be viewed as a consequence of the fall. In terms of the eternal divine idea, the primitive state of man (paradise), as the church herself believes, required development to become the perfect kingdom of God. The fact that this development takes place outside of God – it is this which is a consequence of apostasy. The ethical world therefore has its absolute character, which necessarily pertains to it in all stages and under all conditions, and the stage of the earthly condition does not fall outside the whole of the world plan. Eternal relations are present in it, even if in a tarnished and disturbed way, and even the state of perfection is already present and active in it, as germ and power, even if it remains hidden to the empirical person who only allows himself to be affected by the present. To this extent, certainly, it is not just a hereafter, that is, it is not a pure antithesis of this world; yet its true realization is not given in the here and now but can only be expected in the beyond.

To contemplate this nearness and presence of the higher realm in the temporal is practically the aspiration of religion, but no less theoretically the task of genuine speculation.

One of the characteristics of the earthly condition is the fragmentation of the moments which are indeed distinct in the eternal condition but indissolubly permeate each other. Thus, above all God and man, thus law and morality, state and church, philosophy and theology, etc. The task is therefore to hold onto the deeper unity of these moments just as much as the necessity of their continued separation in earthly existence. Speculative philosophy contains a deep truth in its presupposition of the unity of these opposites (more correctly these moments) and seeks to demonstrate it. But it is mistaken when it also believes them to be one in their empirical form and seeks a unity they ought to have in this form. An example of this is when we consider church and state in their empirical form to be one, and then pursue their unity by granting them equal status, with the same supreme head (Marheineke).

Chapter 6: Human Cognition

§. 19. Since God as a person is just as originally real being and real power (will, act, love, creative power), both in indissoluble unity, as He is intelligence, and consequently everything created is originally just as real as it is rationally determined, so is all knowledge (divine or human) not the dissolution of the real (object) into thought-determinations but the reception thereof as something specific and at the same time primordial, eternally distinct from thought-determinations; this is *vision* [Anschauung]. It is by no means necessarily of a sensorial nature, for the action of spirit can only be recognized through vision. If on the other hand we grasp all reality only as a *logical* emanation, like Hegel (or Fichte already before him), then cognition [das Erkennen] consists in "removing the sensorial from an object and turning it into a thought."[40] But as every example shows, that is incorrect. With this dissolution of the object into thought-determinations, there is always something left that is not necessarily of a sensorial nature, and that something is precisely the most important thing, the thing itself.[41] Our cognition of the individual is only explained by the fact that all cognition is ultimately vision. This would not be possible merely from the universal, which is what the thought-determinations are, for there remains a gap between these and the particular that cannot be filled. But vision as that which corresponds to personality and act, is from the start a reception of the universal and the particular, both as equally primordial. The concrete consists in this: that even the slightest *sensorial vision* is granted the preference over abstract speculation (the dissolution into thought-determinations), a preference which, of course, pertains to spiritual vision in a much higher way. How this is possible, and what it means to envision a reality, to receive it in thinking, cannot be further defined, cannot be proven (i.e., made comprehensible from something else). Like personality that consists in doing and envisioning, it is the most primordial that

---

[40] Hegel, *Grundlinien,* §. 4, p. 33. Further developed in the *Encyclopädie,* §. 223ff.

[41] So for example when Hegel (*Encyclopädie*, §. 283), "turns into thought" water, air, and fire, in that fire is nothing else than the "unrest of individuality that is for itself" and the like; in this way one entertains many things that can be said of water, air, and fire, but not water, air, and fire themselves.

there is. The unity of this real and the vision of it (the "ideal") does exist, but it does not lie in the fact that the real itself would be pure *reason* (thought), but in *personality*, which and which alone is such a unity.

Accordingly, however, all cognition presupposes an object and its immediate presence which cognition envisions. Now it is the character of human cognition that man, as he, in terms of his existence, is first elevated to personality from the foundation of nature, so also first comes to consciousness through objects outside of himself, nature, before he himself becomes an object of consciousness (Locke); for this reason, *sensorial* vision forms the basis of all his cognition, and further, his cognition of things outside himself is purely receptive. We say the opposite of this in both respects of God when we confess him as "Creator." For in accordance with this, He is a person and therefore conscious of Himself before He had objects outside him, and His thoughts are not the effect of things but their cause, just as Kant describes spontaneity as the difference between divine and human cognition. What then remains as the object of divine cognition knowledge is simply God's own being and act. The "how" of such spontaneous vision is beyond our comprehension.[42]

§. 20. The problem of human consciousness of external things involves a twofold question. For one: how is it possible that two existences (the object and the I) affect each other? and for another: how can, in particular, a physical thing produce an intellectual effect (representation)? It is solved by the existences being just as fully independent as they are filled and enclosed by the one substance of

[42] Philosophy (Spinoza, Hegel) rightly asserts that in God, thought and object (more correctly, vision and act) are one and co-existing, but it erroneously conceives both not as acts but as determinations of God, and (at least in the case of Hegel) divine thoughts not as the vision of concrete objects but as mere categories. Certainly, the latter would make it clear how there are thoughts in God that precede things as a *prius*, not in terms of time, but in terms of the concept as their cause (the entire Hegelian logic), while the Christian vision encounters the difficulty of what God thought before He created the world. The truth of the matter is, however, that things could never have arisen from *these* thoughts, i.e., categories. On the contrary, the categories or ontological determinations, insofar as they refer to creation and not to God himself, in no way precede creation; they are the effect of one and the same act which posits creation really and ideally.

the universe, and by all the effect of independent existences, including that of the body on us, being, in terms of its innermost essence, *act*, and thus real-intelligible effect.

Since Kant and Fichte, the question has simply been posed as follows: How can a thing generate intellectual representations? But there is a question that precedes this one: how can one act on the other at all, hence likewise, how can one rational being act on another, like one thing acts on another? Leibniz's investigation deals with this preliminary question and ends with the result that one existence simply cannot affect the other. Leibniz does not, like Fichte, take umbrage with the heterogeneity of matter and spirit, since he "intellectualizes the whole world" from the start; rather, he takes umbrage with the absolute unity of every existence ("substance"). But it is the act, and only the act, in which there is the possibility of all reciprocal action. The act is the "window" that Leibniz cannot find, through which the monads come out of themselves, and he does not find it because he conceives of existences as "substance" (self-contained being) and not as personality. Even material things, just as their being at its innermost is nothing other than will,[43] so also, and in the same sense, is their effect nothing other than act. Because of this and only because of this, "motion," according to Trendelenburg's expression, "is the basic phenomenon of all nature," so for example "when the stone is at rest, gravity moves it ceaselessly to the center of the earth." The doctrine that we can include objects in our thinking because they are themselves intelligible (that is, because the same reason that is in us is likewise the substance of things), does not make cognition comprehensible; for according to it we would only ever receive what is intelligible about them, the rational form and limitation, as knowledge, but not their specific, real element, which constitutes their innermost existence. Our cognition can only be explained by the fact that things are also produced in terms of this specific reality and are the permanent effect of a personality, act, and, conversely, cognition is a reception of the real as such (§. 19).[44]

---

[43] Schelling, *Philosophische Untersuchungen ueber das Wesen der menschlichen Freiheit*, i.e., the reality in material things, the resistance engendered in them, etc., is not their will but the will of the principle of the whole of nature.

[44] In accordance with this, it is an important step, putting philosophy on the right path,

The presupposition of all cognition is of course the immanence of God in us as in things; without the one world substance, of course, no coming together would be possible. But this does not mean that it is God who recognizes things in us (He recognizes them in a completely different way than we do), but rather that by virtue of the independence of the creature we recognize them simply as ourselves. What seems quite natural to the impartial person, that things are outside of us and as such affect our representations, becomes incomprehensible to incipient reflection. Indeed, since no representation follows without conscious activity in its own right, there is even a doubt: is it not just my imagination that does all of this? Do I have proof that everything is not just the world of my

---

by which Trendelenburg (*Logische Untersuchungen* [Logical Investigations]) bases logic on a *real* principle, *motion*, from which both the sensorial perceptions of space and time and the categories are genetically brought forth. But this does not seem to have brought philosophy to its goal. For in itself, movement is not original; it is only an effect or an attribute of the act. The act is what is original. It is only from the identity of the person and the act that "the continuous coherence which is the essence of movement" (p. 185) befits movement. The poet [Goethe] says, "In the beginning was the act." If this really is the principle of being, then it is also necessarily the principle of knowing. It is, as Trendelenburg postulates, that which is "common" to being and thinking, it is that which is "recognizable from itself, originates from itself" (for movement originates from it or is abstracted from it), "which allows itself only to be created, not dismantled;" it is "the simple" if one understands "simple" not as the opposite of abundant, multifaceted, but only of composite. The principle of action would engender those genetically generated categories even more satisfactorily than that of movement (for example, in the same way that Trendelenburg on p. 132 genetically derives infinity from movement, I do so from acts, in volume I, p. 506 of the 2nd edition of the *Philosophy of Law* [*The Recovery of Historical Law*, p. 134]). This would vouchsafe the sought-after unity between the category of cause and the category of end, and no less between the categories of modality (which presuppose active cognition) and the categories of external objects. With this I am not disputing Trendelenburg's theory of logic; rather, I am on the same ground with it, but only maintain that it could be reduced to an even deeper center, while it lacks the copestone for an overall system of philosophy. If this were to be accomplished in the solid and exhaustive way of these "logical investigations," then, in my opinion, the science of logic would be established for all time.

consciousness, but really an external world? This doubt is quite natural. The true condition would be, that the world would actually be just as much in us, and indeed really and not just ideally in us, as outside of us. For if man were in God as he should be, then he would see the creation as he does his own act.

§. 21. Accordingly, our knowledge of the highest object (God and the universe in God) can, in terms of its true nature, only be vision ("view" [Schauen]). Namely, just as personality as a totality is present in each of its relations, forces, acts (see above §. 5), true spiritual cognition is also a vision of the totality in every particular, or every existing being [Seyenden] in the whole of existing being,[45] and ultimately in its original ground, in God. This is the "view" of Holy Scripture.

But such a vision is not possible in a state of alienation from God, because such an object (God and His activity in the universe) is not present to us; but without the presence of the object, as has just been shown, there is no vision. In this condition, therefore, we only view the individual created objects as particulars, but we cannot envision the total spiritual coherence of them, which is precisely in and through God. However, through isolated relations (abstraction and combination) and through mediation from the envisioned particulars (conclusions) we look for the coherence, initially only of the particular to the particular, then also, with great effort and limited success, of the whole – this is discursive

---

[45] This alone is true system. In the Kantian period, which consciously and honestly professed formalism, the system was found in the complete and reliable mapping of the forms of thought, i.e., that the forms are all shown within which all possible knowledge must move (table of categories). From Fichte to Hegel, on the other hand, the system is found in *methodical generation*, whereby all knowledge is gained from an initial assumption without composition and without taking anything in from the outside, just as the vessels of the Jewish temple had to be of embossed work. But this system has two deficiencies, that of a purely logical and that of a purely sequential character. Uniform genetic production is certainly a true requirement of the system, but this must be real production, not just a logical process, the initial producer (God) being not simple but a fullness of being, and production generally everywhere coining a wealth of relationships, in terms of which merely sequential order manifests itself to be untrue, even in logic.

thinking (Kant).

What therefore remains for human cognition in this condition is:

1. The vision of the mere abstract form of the world as a whole and of world relations (of unity, of development, etc.) detached from their content – this is "*reason*"[46] with its forms of thought. This includes what Kant called "ideas or principles of pure reason," e.g., the totality of the conditioned must have an unconditioned as cause, the totality of the world must have a quantity, a limit, and so on. Likewise, Aristotle's proposition that there must be something unmoved over what is moved, likewise the ontological proof, etc. Kant's categories, axioms, and rational ideas are not in the least the mere means of bringing the object [Objekt] to unity in our apperception, which is how he presents it; rather, they are the relations of the object [des Objekts] itself and its unity. This element of our cognition is the object [Gegenstand] of all logic and dialectic.

2. *Active* but only *discursive* thinking, which becomes proficient in the visions [Anschauungen] (first of all the sensorial, then also the spiritual ones mentioned under 3.) and seeks results here through abstraction and combination, and especially through induction and analogy. To this belong, e.g., the Aristotelian: "Nature strives for perfection," likewise Jacobi's: "The dead, unconscious, cannot have produced the living, conscious," likewise the proof of God which Kant calls the "physico-theological" as well as the higher intellectual activity in all empirical sciences.

3. Finally, however, a remnant of the content of that *lost vision* of God and the relations of our being and of the universe to Him. For this is so necessary to the essence of man that, if it were completely absent, his concept itself would cease. This includes the Platonic "*anamnesis*," the "*ideas*" or "*reason*" of Jacobi. The entirety of our ethical knowledge is based only on this intuition; we can neither observe with our senses the good, love, etc., nor draw them (as in §. 29 below) from the above-mentioned two sources of knowledge. In conscience there is also the unique presence of God, and the good is a reality which, by virtue of our indestructible nature as human beings, forms our own being, and is therefore a direct vision of ourselves. But even our theoretical knowledge of God and suprasensorial things has its center and foundation in this remnant of

---

[46] According to the terminology of philosophy, which in *this* regard is the same from Kant to Hegel.

an immediate spiritual vision.

These three elements of our cognition, individually or even in their union, are nevertheless not in any position to attain the true knowledge of suprasensorial things, i.e., to take the place of vision. "Reason" in the above sense by itself necessarily leads to error, since it provides the adumbration of the content, and even if used correctly provides only the lowliest part of knowledge. The understanding active in objects, with its inferences and analogies, etc., leads with things beyond experience always only to a probability. The remainder of that original spiritual vision, however, is only a dark, nebulous picture, a mere dim presentiment, comparable to the face of a wizened old man. The Deity Himself makes Himself known to this noblest organ through revelation, and therefore here is the center for the cognition of divine things. But revelation has only a limited scope for a specific practical purpose (salvation of the soul), and even with it the object (God) is not immediately and constantly present, but always remains in the beyond, crossing over only in exceptional moments. Both completeness (self-containedness) and immediacy and certainty are lacking; these are only given by vision itself. That is why there can never be a demonstration and mathematical certainty of *divine things* (theology, philosophy, morals); for this certainty rests, even in the mathematical sciences, as Kant has shown, not on logical necessity, but on sensorial vision. There is, of course, a subjective certainty here through the real (practical) union of man with God in faith. Here the object of knowledge itself approaches him; but this is only subjective for the believer and must be attained by constantly overcoming the presence of the sensorial ("the kingdom of heaven suffers violence"), and is never, like vision, a quiet possession. Accordingly, all philosophical sciences can only be brought to a greater inner verisimilitude through mutual connection in the application of those elements of cognition, but never to indisputable objective cognitive necessity, as the empirical sciences are.

§. 22. The entire rationalistic development from Descartes to Hegel is limited to the first and ignores the last most important element of our knowledge, that of suprasensorial things, and nevertheless desires to have knowledge of them, even with mathematical certainty. Hence it also happens that between it and religion there is no medium of understanding at all, since the organ of cognition is no longer shared.

Spinoza's philosophical insight is nothing else than the vision of the form of the world as a whole mentioned under 1. above. That is why he is filled with the idea of the unity of the universe, which he expresses as the unity of substance. This vision is in fact only the silhouette of the universe, in that it makes the inner connection of the existing, the living production of things (modalities) by God (substance) vanish in the darkness. Furthermore Kant, in that he stakes out the area of our cognitive faculty, divides it into two factors, sensorial perception and the form of reason; a third, the remnant of intellectual vision, he ignores. But if it were really absent, not only would we not *have* any cognition of suprasensory things (Kant's result), we would not even *inquire* about suprasensory things.

Kant's successors undertook to supplement this third point. On this rests the *intellectual vision* (distinguished from sensorial vision and ready-made categories), which, beginning with Fichte's doctrine, received its fullest development through Schelling, as well as Hegel's *speculation*. Both, however, are far from being real intuition (which Kant also understands as intellectual vision, which he ascribes to divine intelligence), but is merely the observation of our inner thought-determinations or thought function, which is then wrongly passed off as an objective world-forming function. Both are therefore only abstract vision, a further (and questionable as to whether true or erroneous) formation of the element mentioned under 1. above. In addition, there is something even worse here, that this so-called "intellectual vision" or "speculation" is given out as that power to see the absolute regarding which Kant at least admits that reason does not possess.[47] It is Jacobi's great merit that, in opposition to the final systems of rationalism, he vindicated this organ which they ignored.

Just as the error of the human will is twofold: falling for the external objects

---

[47] Schelling's much-discussed intellectual vision leaves no doubt about his own clear explanations (e.g., *System des transcendentalen Idealismus,* p. 50). It is the vision of what we ourselves are producing, what is our own act, whereby for this reason producing and produced, thinking and envisioning, are one. This view therefore presupposes the world being the product of our (or at least likewise completely immanent in us) reason, while the pure spontaneity which Kant only grants to the divine is attributed to human cognition, which Kant grounds in receptivity. That Kant is right in this respect regardless of the other advances in philosophy since Fichte, must be evident to any impartial observer. The same is true regarding Hegel's speculation.

of the world (sensuality), or satisfaction in and withdrawal into one's own I (arrogance), so is that of human cognition. These are the two paths: *empiricism* (ultimately *materialism*) and *rationalism*, in which philosophy has been divided since Descartes.[48] The human spirit had to turn in these two directions when, in its investigation, it gave up the higher bond to God which the external power of the Catholic church and for a short while the young evangelical faith had contained until then. The final result of the former direction is the *Système de la Nature*, the French sensual, materialistic atheism, while that of the latter is the newer school of Hegel, logical pantheism.[49] For the higher unity of empiricism and rationalism which speculative philosophy comprises is an imagined higher unity and reconciliation, with which it is encumbered in other respects as well. In reality, it merely dissolves empiricism itself into rationalism, which is no combination of the two under a higher unity.

§. 23. Finally, as regards the mediation of all our knowledge through the perception of time (on the faultiness, i.e., mere subjectivity of which the entirety of Kant's philosophy is built), the objectivity thereof is by no means to be denied. As Kant rightly asserts, one cannot ascribe to time either a *subsisting* existence or an *inherent* existence in individual things and processes; nevertheless, it does have an inherent existence in the totality of creation and history. These are not, like individual things in time, surrounded by time; the converse is true, time is only in them as their attribute, i.e., they have the attribute of *successivity*. Just as eternity is the attribute of personality (in the eminent sense), so time is the *attribute of act and effect*. Denying the objectivity of time therefore means to deny the objectivity of cause and effect, the objectivity of the act. The limitation of our knowledge in the state of temporality lies only in the fact that our

---

[48] From this parallelization of the theoretical aberration with the practical one it does not follow, as goes without saying, that the one produced the other, let alone that they are connected to one another in the person who entertains them.

[49] In his history of modern philosophy, Erdmann has excellently shown that the materialism of the French is only the consistent outworking of Locke's standpoint; I believe that in the first volume of my *Philosophy of Law*, especially in the revision of the 2nd edition [*The Rise and Fall of Natural Law*], I have shown that Hegel's system is the consistent outworking of the Cartesian standpoint.

observation happens (successively) in time, but not in the fact that we observe things as in time, i.e., as successive. So for example prophecy, which rises above the limitation of time, views events in time, i.e., in successive coherence, even though it itself is *above* time. But a cognition which, like the divine, sees things in succession even while an eternal presence without any succession, of this we can have no idea, precisely because we are temporal; and this is the most decisive limitation of human cognition, the reason for the insolubility of a number of problems, e.g., the incompatibility of divine prescience and human freedom. For if God knew beforehand man's action from its determining reasons, it would abolish human freedom; rather, He knew it directly as in the present, because for Him there is no before and after. But we have no insight into how this is possible.

PART II: ETHICS[50]

Chapter 1: Construction of the Ethical Sphere

§. 24. Starting from the personal God and the conception of creation, we see two supreme relations: the *world-creating* and the *world-enveloping* activity of God. God created the world and especially the pinnacle of it, man, in order for him to be perfected in Himself, i.e., in order for the divine being to be revealed in him (§. 10). God envelops the world and especially man so that he can only be through, in, and to Him. This is the vision of creation – creatures are independent in themselves and yet eternally referenced to God. The two ethical spheres are distinguished accordingly: *ethical behavior* (morality) and *religion.*

Ethical behavior is the perfection of man in himself (of course here in terms of the aspect of his will) or the revelation of the divine being in him. Man is in the image of God, therefore God-like in his nature, perfect in himself,[51] and

---

[50] By ethics I mean the laws regarding the requirements on the human will, hence religion, morality, law. With this concept, the will of man is manifested as the subject to which the requirement is directed, and which fulfills that requirement. For Hegel as well, ethics is the domain of the will, but in a different sense, not because the living (human) will is the referenced subject, but because according to him the concept of will itself is what is to be fulfilled, the ethical object. The concept of will contains the ethical requirements and, even more so, the ethical life relations. The concept of will requires that there be marriage, parental authority, that there be classes [Stände], trades, states, and it is also the concept of will that realizes itself, that is, that has fulfilled the ethic [Ethos]. More on this in the other books of this series, especially in the first chapter of the second book [*Principles of Law*].

[51] Certainly perfection, as Kant (*Metaphysik der Sitten* [Metaphysics of Morals]) objects, is an indefinite concept which first awaits its further definition. This will be given in the next chapter; here it is only a question of delimiting morality from religion. Wolff certainly did no disservice to ethics with his conception of morality as the "perfection of man." Nevertheless, when I consider morality to be the perfection of man in himself,

Godlikeness is the goal and commandment (Matthew 5:45). Religion, on the other hand, is man's bond with God, whereby he only ever knows and wills himself in God, and relates himself to Him everywhere – hence, complete devotion [Hingebung], personal union with God. So, for example love of neighbor, courage, spirituality (non-sensorial) are possibly purely moral traits, whereas faith and love of God are purely religious. The courage of the Napoleonic Guard is a moral virtue (the quality of will in man himself), while Luther's courage is a religious one (a force from the bond with God). Accordingly, religion is first a *sphere of its own*, with a content differentiated from that of morality, a content in faith, the confession of faith, love of God, contrition (which is something quite different from the mere moral position vis-à-vis one's own unethical behavior); and second, it is its own motive as obedience to the person of God, differentiated from the moral motive of obedience to the moral law in its manifestation to man as his own perfect being.[52]

---

religion to be the unification of man with God, I have no mind to renew Wolff's notion. For Wolff set up this determination once and for all without any regard for religion, yes, ignoring it, and yet as the epitome of the entire ethic. As such, what matters is in what this perfection consists. To me it consists in the concrete substance of the divine will, but for Wolff, rationalistically, it consists in the richest order, i.e., that which has the most rules, and order is for him the conformity of the manifold in the sequence thereof, upon and beside one another (*Metaphysik*, p. 60). Finally, Wolff regards perfection in morality not as the end of God who wants His works to be perfect, but as the end (the motive) of morally acting people themselves, so that for him, bliss also consists in the joy of man's own perfection (instead of the possession of God and the beauty of the ethical world).

[52] I have already given this definition of religion and morality in the first edition of this work (vol. II, p. 59). It was carried out in a clearer and more developed way by Rothe, *Die Anfänge der christlichen Kirche und ihrer Verfassung* [The Beginnings of the Christian Church and its Constitution], although deviating from my view. On this, see my *Die Kirchenverfassung nach Lehre und Recht der Protestanten* [The Church Constitution in accordance with the Doctrine and Law of the Protestants], pp. 270ff. The main reason for our divergence is that Rothe, in line with Schleiermacher, places the concept of the moral in the conquest of nature through reason, according to which everything

Not only do both relationships permeate each other in their results; in themselves, in terms of their true nature, although always distinguishable, they are yet inseparable. Just as it is the state of perfection that the creature, regardless of its independence, nevertheless is thoroughly in the Creator, so it is necessary that morality should be thoroughly the outflow of religion and relation to God – that religion should completely absorb it. According to Christian doctrine, that which is apportioned to God is therefore only religion, as the innermost principle in which morality (like the creature in the Creator) is rooted; indeed, Christianity, since it only presents us with the image of the perfect, absolute ethic, nowhere separates religion and morality (fear of God and Godlikeness), and from this standpoint the distinction has no practical interest with regard to one's actions, but only for evaluating conditions outside of Christianity. Only in the empirical condition, in which neither relation is manifested in its perfection, can they be separated from each other. Religiosity is never found without morality, but often with a lesser degree of it, while morality is found with little or no religiosity at all. Of course, the former is not true piety, the latter is not true (absolute) ethical behavior.

The task is to bring every sphere, every relation of human existence to full development. That is why morality had to be separated from religion, with which it initially was merged without distinction. In order to fulfill this task, Grotius took the mighty step of saying that there is a *jus naturale* (i.e., an ethical and civil law) even if there is no God. But the statement as formulated is erroneous. Apart from the internal contradiction that the content of the ethic would be the same regardless of whether the highest world cause is God or some natural power, and that the final ultimate sanction of the same should not lie in the highest world cause (regarding which see §§. 28ff. below), this statement not only distinguishes the moral sphere from the religious one and develops it independently, which is Grotius' achievement, but rather separates it completely and tears it away. Later successors asserted this with even greater emphasis, as for

---

that expresses itself as action is attributed to the moral sphere; religion is left only with the inward, in opposition to its outward expression; so that even the cultus should pertain to morality, not to religion, because it subjects natural means to itself. According to this, religion and morality manifest themselves only in the relation of faith and works, as already conceived by Möhler, and not as two distinct spheres.

example Wolff, who argues on the most ad hoc basis that the atheist, if he is consistent, must and will act just as morally as the theist or the Christian.[53] From this point of view, Grotius' enterprise is the first germ of the renunciation of religion, which unfolds in Kant as ignorance and in the most recent school as denial of God. In this entire period of the development of ethics, the true distinction between the religious and the moral realm is lacking. The earlier (subjectively rationalistic) ethics, since it derives everything from human reason, either comes to the inconsistent result of considering religion (duties to God) itself to be an outflow of morality, e.g., Pufendorf, according to which religion ultimately dissolves into morality and only differs from other moral precepts by the object, or it virtually abolishes religion from the outset. So, for example, Kant's "religion within the limits of pure reason" is nothing other than morality. Likewise with Fichte, the "church" or "community of saints" is only a community of morality (that is, mutually by way of conviction to bring each other to the place that man makes nature into a means for reason and not the other way around), and the religion he adds to this is only belief in the eternal meaning of moral action, and so not really religion. But even according to Hegel's objectively rationalistic standpoint, these two ethical areas cannot be clearly distinguished, since God (the absolute, and precisely so here in the determination of the ethical world) is nothing other than the epitome (the mutual interaction) of the ethical order and the human personality. Hegel does not understand religion as that other *ethical* sphere as opposed to morality; but merely as the other sphere of *cognition* as opposed to philosophy, namely as knowledge of the absolute in its indistinctness and rudimentariness as opposed to its development into nature and the ethical world, and therefore also as knowledge of it in feeling and imagination instead of in thought.[54] Conversely, Schleiermacher places religion

---

[53] In fairness, it should not be held against sincere Christians such as Francke that they took offense at a morality that is completely detached from all fear of God.

[54] Recently, one of the most recognized supporters of the Hegelian system, Vatke (*Die menschliche Freiheit in ihrem Verhältnisz zur Sünde und zur göttlichen Gnade* [Human Freedom in its Relation to Sin and Divine Grace]), provided a very similar definition of religion and morality, and carried it out in a scientifically conclusive manner, in the same way as we have presented it in correspondence with the Christian standpoint. But

this has a different meaning for him, and in this meaning is simply not tenable. In its "universal" which must "particularize" itself, speculative philosophy apparently, but only apparently, has two data such like the Christian consciousness has in Creator and creature. From this, Hegel (already in the *Philosophische Propädeutik* [Introduction to Philosophy], §. 71) derived the two modes of cognition, the religious, which recognizes the universal without the particular, and the philosophical, which recognizes the latter in the former. Similarly, Vatke now has two ethical spheres: Morality has particularity, the development of the ethical idea as a legal ethical community with its "formations" (family, civil society, etc.) as its content, while religion has the universal, the "absolute point of unity" (p. 10) from which this development proceeds, and indeed following from it, going back to it. So, while we draw a contrast between the ethical world created by God, and the Lord and Master who is supreme over it, Vatke contrasts the ethical world as developed and as undeveloped principle. Therefore, according to us, religion is also the higher, for it has the higher, the highest object; for Vatke, on the other hand, morality and philosophy must logically be higher, for they have the developed as object, into which the undeveloped must yet merge.

But this universal as such, distinguished from its particularity as ethical world, is here necessarily empty, abstract, nothing in itself, only the "absolute reflection from all reality in simple identity, the *form* of the absolute goal." According to this, then, religion truly has no content, no requirements. What ostensibly should be its content, the love of God, is immediately determined more precisely to the effect that it is only the unity of the subjective and objective moments of will, that is, the unity of law and human disposition (p. 211), and indeed, by Vatke's own explanation, an entirely general abstract disposition which only receives its particularity and therefore its concrete content in love of neighbor, namely only "the general form of love" which is still lacking "specific" content (p. 215). Accordingly, religion does not manifest itself as an ethical sphere of its own, but merely as the motive or impulse of morality. But even in this character it cannot maintain itself, but instead coincides entirely with the moral motive or impulse. Love for something general which is nothing apart from the particular is nothing other than love for that particular. The religious motive or the alleged love of God is nothing other than love for the ethical world order, the ethical forms of love of neighbor, friendship, family, state, etc., and that again is the moral motive; for since Vatke himself will not maintain that the moral motive consists only in the love of these figures in the sphere of bare reality, in the feeling of dependence, in order to separate it from morality as subjection of nature to reason. But even with this, the spheres are not separated in terms of their truth. Both are based as much on feeling (real power) as on cognition, and it is only the different relations among subjects (personalities) that distinguish them.

§. 25. In the divine world plan, however, man is not provided for as an individual for the sake of isolation, but rather as the human race as a whole, as a unity. Therefore, besides the two relations of the religious and the moral, the ethical realm has two relations in terms of another aspect, namely the *archetype of man as an individual* and *God's plan for the human race,* which people in their common life are to fulfill as a unity.

The archetype of man undergirds the *virtues:* love, humility, heroism, temperance (spirituality), faith, patience. Their epitome is *sanctification.* God's plan for the human race undergirds the structure of human life relations and the ethical notions inherent in them: requirement for goods and property – duality of the sexes and marriage – division of occupation and classes [Stände] – national community and state – religious community and church. Their epitome is *God's world order.* By this world order of God, the human race by nature consists in reciprocal need, thus a community of both natural and spiritual substance. For there is a natural community through descent, first in the nations, and then higher up, as the doctrine of religion presupposes, in the entire human race,[55]

---

individually and not in their totality and unity, how should what Vatke calls love for the "divine will" differ from the "ethical archetype," which he describes as a form different from religion (p. 437)? If the point of unity of the ethical world is not a personal God separate from it, there is no religion different from morality.

[55] Even in the first man, according to the divine intention and vision, the whole of humanity is contained as one species [Gattung], and this is its supreme unity. But God allows the races [die Geschlechter] to be generated from man himself, because he created him as an independent being; and therefore, the previously created individuality should itself be a determining factor in the newly-to-be-created individuality, even though such is always a new beginning (§. 8). The physical and spiritual constitution of the human being is a reciprocal permeation of divine and human production and a reciprocal permeation of independent individuality and common substance. The human

and a common spiritual ethical consciousness everywhere fills the whole, and indeed in terms of the earthly division of peoples and times, which does not arise through the composition of individual cognition and will, but precedes them as something higher and original, determining them even if determined in retrograde fashion by them.[56] All of this is already given by nature. But *common existence as such also entails ethical requirements* which are to be fulfilled

---

race as a whole and in its national grouping thus has a unity not only in higher dominion, but a unity in its essentiality, and indeed not merely by means of the divine idea but at the same time through its own real causal connection. For this reason, the denial of descent from a couple is a humanity-degrading notion. For humanity would lose the innermost essential unity which is the character of spiritual personal existence. This essential unity explains shared family and national sentiment according to which the joy and pain, honor and disgrace which affect the family or the nation as a whole are felt by each of its members as his own, as well as the reckoning by which families, dynasties, peoples as a whole, meet the nemesis which unmistakably holds sway over their fates. But this also explains the two greatest facts of history in which humanity appears as a unity: original sin and redemption. For although Adam is humanity's original matter, Christ is humanity's original idea in God, both of which live and in person. In them, humanity is one, for which reason the sin of one man became the sin of all, and the sacrifice of one man for all became atonement. Every leaf of a tree can turn green or wither on its own; but each one suffers from the disease of the root, and recovers from its healing.

The more superficial a person is, the more everything will appear to him to be isolated; because on the surface, everything is separated. In mankind, in the nation, even in the family itself, he will see only individuals whereby the act of one has no connection with that of another. But the deeper one goes, the more these inner relations of unity that emanate from the center intrude on him. Indeed, love of neighbor is itself only the deep sensibility of this unity; because only with whom one recognizes and feels oneself to be one, does one love, and Christian morality commands nothing other than the love of God and of neighbor. What Christian love of neighbor is for the temperament, the unity of the human race is for cognition.

[56] In this lies the explanation of how the law arises from the popular consciousness, how every age, every nation has a peculiar ethic, a peculiar ethical-spiritual determination – the basic vision of the Historical School of Jurisprudence.

through the will and action of people; and only through this does that world order come to fruition. In addition to the ethic of the individual, then, there is also an *ethic of common human existence.*

This, too, is now necessarily subject to that double relationship (§. 24). The human community should be united to God and also should be perfected in itself. In the former respect it is the *church of God* (ἐκκλησία τοῦ Θεοῦ), in the latter respect we may call it the "*ethical world.*" The church of God consists in men being united in a community and institution in order to glorify God and to bind the individual to God; for its part, the ethical world consists in the divine (ethical) ideas being realized in the human community's own life relations, and these in their formation reveal their own ethically reasonable will (e.g., maintenance of justice, maintenance of discipline and mores, care for the common good). Those life conditions of the human community, however, as just touched upon, are already given by nature as reciprocal need, reproduction, descent, etc., but their pure order is the human ethic. The ethical world therefore has absolutely a natural arrangement as its basis.

What I call the ethical *world,* then, is not merely an ethical *community,* i.e., shared cultivation of individual morality (like Fichte's moral community), but rather a realm of ethical configurations [Gestaltungen] that pertain only to the existence of the community as such. In the same way, the church of God not only consists in the shared cultivation of the piety of the individual, but at the same time in the pooling of their various gifts to a single ministry and in the power of edification and mediation, which is only committed to them as a unity.

§. 26. The perfection of human common existence, through which it becomes the ethical world, is now necessarily the requirement of *both the individual and the community,* each in its own way. The community has to maintain the ethical ideas of life relations which form the common existence as the universal, continuously necessary, and therefore *external existence* of life. The individual, for his part, must internalize them and realize them as a constant free *act,* and therefore also individualize them and intensively augment them.

Thus, through the archetype of common existence, the *ethic of the individual* is expanded. It thereby has a double sphere, on the one hand the ethical will of man according to his constitution in himself and his relationships to other individuals (e.g., truthfulness, charity, friendship) and on the other the ethical will of the same in relation to the institutions of common human existence (conjugal love, loyalty, filial piety, civil obedience, love of country).

But an ethic of a different kind, dealing with completely different subjects, is added on top of this: the *ethic of human community as such*, whereby it realizes the ethical formation of common existence through *its*, that is, through *common action*. The latter can be called the *ethical formation of the world* or also the *objective ethic* as opposed to everything that is the requirement and ethical will of the individual, the *subjective ethic* or "*morality*." But as far as they impinge on each other, both have their higher unity in the archetype of common existence which is realized in both at the same time.[57]

§. 27. Just as in terms of their true nature and in the state of perfection the ethical relations of the individual – religion and morality – are only different but not separable (§. 24), so are the ethical relationships of common existence. In the kingdom of God (βασιλεία τοῦ Θεοῦ), which is the expectation of the Christian faith, the divine community (ἐκκλησία τοῦ Θεοῦ) must be in complete unity and reciprocal permeation with the ethical world, just as the objective, ethical formation of life must be so with the ethical will of the individual, and the order maintained by human community, if it persists, with the order given by God

---

[57] Therefore, by "objective ethic" I do not understand the archetype of common human life or the ethical world in its entirety, but only the ethical world to the extent that it is also fulfilled by the community (not the individual), as it is to be realized in a permanent, objective formation of life. For example, I count monogamy as part of the objective ethic, whereas the practice of conjugal love is part of the subjective ethic or "morality." Hence, with this terminology I look to the *fulfilling subject*. It can be done differently. Thus, Hegel understands by his concept of "ethical behavior" the image of the institutions of the family, the state, etc., without distinguishing between the external formation of life, which is the task of the community, and the demands on the individual. I choose the former terminology because of its better practical use. For the fulfilling subject is the decisive consideration for the delimitation of the field of law. Along these lines, the concept of objective ethic therefore corresponds with that of law. Hence, the two viewpoints are not to be confused; on the one hand there are the archetype of man and the archetype of human communal existence, and on the other the requirements for the individual and requirements for the community; although these do not coincide, they intersect.

Himself. Because if God is "all in all," then the perfection of human common existence eternally proceeds from God and refers back to Him, and the common will and all objective forms of life are completely pervaded by Him in the same way as the individual will. This is the absolute divine archetype of common existence, just as the "image of God" is the archetype of the individual human being.

But in the empirical condition, whereby man finds himself outside of God, these spheres have also deviated from their unifying center and so are manifested in their separation. This determines their character in reality. The assembly of God [Gottesgemeinde], separable from the sanctification of the individual and leaning on a non-homogeneous life condition, is merely the *church*, and the ethical formation of the world separated from individual morality is merely the *civil order*, that is, *law and the state* (see below, chap. 5). In these conditions, church and state are independent of one another; each has its own center within itself.

Accordingly, the relationship between the civil order (law and the state) and the church is similar to that between morality and religion.[58] The former aims at the perfection of the human race in itself, the latter in its union with God. The civil order is therefore also a bond and a unification of the human race in itself. The individual sustains the whole, the whole sustains the individual; reproduction is inherent in it. And in its existence and in terms of its content it is its own work. It exists as a consequence of the common will, and it is sustained by the legislative authority thereof (the state). It posits itself. On the other hand, the church is not a coherence of humanity in itself, but in God and through the relation of each to God; and if it is not to cease being the church, its foundation is a work of God and determined in its content by God; for in specifically ecclesiastical matters, it has no power of legislation, but only of protection and

---

[58] Rothe not only makes the state parallel with ethical behavior, but furnishes it with ethical behavior as its concept. That would be correct in one respect, if the ethically objective life formation was the only thing understood thereby. But Rothe does not distinguish it from subjective ethical behavior and – this is the main point – ignores the quite heterogeneous character of the former in our actual condition, leading every impartial observer (e.g., the reviewer in the *Evangelische Kirchen-Zeitung* [Protestant Church Daily]) to object as a matter of course that the essence of the state is not ethical behavior but law.

witness.

At the same time, however, it is evident that church and state, and furthermore the civil order and individual morality, although inseparably permeating each other in terms of their idea and perfection, must always remain independent and separate on earth. But regardless of this, they will, by virtue of that original destiny toward unity, remain in one bond, just as they cannot actually fail to practice the most powerful interaction.[59]

---

[59] "Culture" [Kultur], that is, the development of the physical and intellectual powers of man, is entirely different than the ethic. In this we include science, art, social customs, gymnastics, etc. This is another object of the ethic, as is self-preservation and the like. For as renunciation [Entäußerung] for the benefit of one's neighbor or a cause pertains to the truly perfected willing of man, so also does willingness to pursue one's own bodily and spiritual perfection.

Chapter 2: The Ethical Content

§. 28. Both the *content* and the *sanction* of the ethical can only proceed from the absolute cause, which according to our assumption (§§. 1ff.) means from the *personal God*. He is the *ethical archetype* and the *ethical primordial power*. The essence of the ethic then is not a relation of two potencies or moments – "the subjective and the objective," "the ideal and the real," "reason and nature" – with the former ruling over the latter (Fichte, Hegel, Schleiermacher); this is only its expression. Rather, the essence of the ethic is the relation between two personal wills, the divine and the created, and the inclusion of the former in the latter, by which is meant both submission under the majesty thereof and filledness with the character thereof.[60]

§. 29. The original concept of the good is the will of God in its substance, i.e., considered in Himself, not in what it brings forth outside Himself (creative will).[61] But the divine will in its substance is infinite love, mercy, patience, truthfulness, loyalty, justice, spirituality, etc., everything in its totality and its concentration on the innermost being of God which we characterize as the *holiness of God*.[62] The holiness of God therefore as little precedes the divine will (the

[60] That the content of the ethic should be the same "even if there were no God, although there is a God," as Grotius asserts, is a contradiction in itself. If there really is a God, then the ethical must ultimately have its root in His essence and be something else than what is merely derived from human relations. The commandments of Christian ethics therefore everywhere differ from, e.g., the Spinozist, Kantian, Hegelian. Not to speak of Spinoza's crass ethics, which reject humility and repentance as unreasonable, the Hegelian, for example, diverges from the Christian in that it regards the reserve which the Christian ethic obliges with regard to human knowledge to be absolute sin; similarly, for it love of neighbor is the lesser, vanishing thing, while the fulfillment of civic duties is the complete good and straightaway eternal, etc.

[61] Perhaps this is how Christ's saying: "Do not call me good, God alone is good" should be understood: namely, even the Son of God is good only through and in the Father. The good, like being, can have its source only in the Creator.

[62] One cannot take this content of the ethic to be reason overcoming nature, etc.; for in

scholastics' *sanctitas antecedens voluntatem*) than follows it; instead, it is this will itself. Or, the good is just as little a law for the divine will (that God wanted it because it was already good in itself) than it is a creation of the divine will (that it only came into being because and after being willed by God); but it is just the primordial will of God from eternity to eternity. Accordingly, however, the good as the substance of the divine will is something specific, independent, eternally distinct from the divine intelligence (or above all, the logical determinations, "reason") and divine omnipotence, although no less primordial; and it arises purely from the will (initially the divine, and likewise, in a derivative way, the human, as shall be shown); even so, it does not arise from the abstraction of the will (Kant's abstract concept of self-legislation, Fichte's abstraction of pure self-activity) or the formalism of its function (Hegel's development of the ethic from the moments of the function of the will), but rather from the eternal *positive content* of the will.

Generally speaking, the good is nothing other than the essence of the person. One could therefore attempt to derive the concepts which we recognize as qualities of God and as virtues of man from the basic concept of personality. In the essence of personality lies spirituality, which resists being lost in external objects and sensory impressions, and only this, nothing else, was scientifically demonstrated by Kantian-Fichtean ethics. Furthermore, in the essence of personality lies the immutability of the will, which, in relation to the ethical world order, is justice, is selflessness, absence of need, absolute freedom, love for other personalities, especially their productions [Geschöpfen]; because pure love, which continuously proceeds from itself and desires the salvation of the other person, is nothing less than the thought of the *purus actus*, which the older philosophy already expressed regarding God as spirit and person. Finally, in the essence of the person there is the retro-relation and concentration of all these qualities and activities in the innermost center of the person, and thereby the impenetrability by anything external and alien – holiness. But even this mere conceptual

---

God (and in eternally perfect man) there is no nature that first has to be overcome, and our concepts or correct views of love, etc., neither involve a nature that first has to be overcome, nor do they contain a submission of something real to something ideal (law of thought), but rather are themselves primordial realities, which as such are not to be overcome but rather preserved.

deduction is insufficient, like any other. It is not the concept of personality but the concretely determined personality of God from which the ethic follows, and not the characters obtained through such deduction, but rather the very concrete properties of "love, justice, holiness," as these are only envisioned, not defined. These properties, as they are the primordial determinations of the primordial person (God), are absolutely and immediately the good, and a further communication as to why they are, is not merely unnecessary but downright untrue.

Accordingly, the ethical is thoroughly concrete, specific, full of content and yet purely spiritual, and is absolute plain and simple, primordial, consisting as little in logical laws and determinations as in external goals. One arrives at this result if one accepts primordial being as personal. This is not the case with the newer ethics. Of the two directions into which the latter divides, the *eudaimonistic* resolves the good into *enjoyment* (good) and expediency for enjoyment (this is the case with the English moral philosophers, then Thomasius et al.) while the *rationalistic* resolves it into *correctness of thought*, the realization of logical determinations. It is in fact so already with Wolff, since he finds the perfection which he makes the principle of morality ultimately in orderliness (cf. *Metaphysik* [Metaphysics], §. 68.), and quite definitely Kant. For him the ethical law is a consequence of the law of thought, and he expressly explains that the concept of the good must be derived from a preceding law, namely the general law of thought or non-contradiction.[63] Likewise, according to Fichte the good consists in the fact that the I (which is bare intellectual, cognitive activity) precedes the object and determines it, as it conversely is determined by the object in cognition, by which apriorism, absolute causality of thinking prior to the empirical, also is the good.

At bottom, Hegel has the same view as Fichte.[64] Logic posits itself first as the object (nature, etc.), then as subjectivity with the drive to convey itself (thus, again logic) to the object, to be realized in it. According to Hegel, therefore, the good is nothing other than the realization of the law of thought. The only difference is that he establishes a different law of thought (logic) than the earlier one. For Kant, the supreme law of thought is the principle of non-contradiction, so the good consists in acting according to a universal (i.e., non-contradictory)

---

[63] *Critik der praktischen Vernunft*, 4th ed., p. 101.

[64] *Encyclopädie*, §§. 232, 233.

maxim. For Hegel, the supreme law of thought is the distinction and re-unification of the logical moments of the universal and the particular; therefore, the good consists in the fact that a universal (general will, i.e., law) and a particular (human will or human existence) stand opposite each other in various groupings; finally in a formation (family, state) according to which the universal (the state) durably exists only through the particular (people) and in it. That which is good in the family and the state, the absolute basis and purpose of everything ethical, is therefore nothing other than the logical unity of the universal and the particular.[65]

Even according to Schleiermacher, the ethic consists only in the subjection of a nature to reason (thought), and accordingly, ethics is derived from the relation between knowledge and being.[66] The rationalistic ethical doctrine cannot consistently come to any content, except for the formal: "Act consistently, act according to a (one does not know which) maxim, which could become the universal one!" Or (with Hegel) "there shall be an (objective) order of life (one does not know which) realizing itself through people and in them!" If Hegel nevertheless arrives at a content, it only happens through his oft-criticized usurpation by which he takes up into his abstract moments the ethical relations (marriage, state) found in experience.

That which Kant so emphatically emphasizes is certain: the good cannot consist in suitability for an end outside of it, for this would abolish the dignity of the good; regarding this, every ethical consciousness gives direct testimony. But it is no less certain that the good cannot consist in mere agreement with some logical law, and that the ethical law and the law of thought (or the

---

[65] By contrast, we say that the good is the divine (or the true human) will itself in its determinate and given content, which is primordial and does not follow from any law of thought. That there be love, righteousness, etc., is the absolute reason and purpose, above which there is none higher. This is why I cannot agree with a spirited representative of a positivist orientation who derives ethics from the concept of purpose, so that the knowledge of the divine purpose is wisdom, the act of devotion springing from it is love, and so on. For what is the basis and content of the divine purpose if love is only agreement with it as something that precedes that love? Rather, love, wisdom, etc. are themselves the content and motive of the divine purpose.

[66] *Grundriß der philosophischen Ethik*, §§. 1–80.

substance of thought) are eternally distinct, the former being just as absolute as the latter; and every ethical consciousness testifies no less to this. Love, mercy, generosity do not follow from the laws of thought but are in themselves the eternal law, i.e., the eternal quality of the will, and there is nothing more wrong than, e.g., deriving the commandment of love from a preceding higher law (principle of non-contradiction) or a preceding logical development (moment of the universal and the particular).[67]

Contrary to our "theological" principle of ethics, Kant[68] raised the objection that the derivation of human morality from divine perfection, since we in turn derive the latter only from human perfection, is circular. This is based on his

---

[67] For the prevailing conception of our time, nothing is more certain than that it is precisely "*reason*" which gives us the ethical precepts (their content and their sanction). All that matters is to nail down the expression precisely. With this assertion, the prevailing conception takes "*reason*" right from the start in the sense of *ethical knowledge* itself. Our insight into good and evil – good being love, sacrifice, continence, etc., the opposite being bad – this is what it calls reason. A similar use of language can also be found among the philosophers of ancient times, of the Middle Ages, with Melanchthon; even Grotius and Pufendorf often designate reason (*ratio*) to be that which distinguishes humans from animals, i.e., thought and mores, conscience, all taken together. In this sense there is nothing to be said against asserting that reason (that is, our ethical knowledge) teaches us the content of the good. But that is not the sense in which modern philosophy claims it. For it, "*reason*" is merely the *law of thought* (or the epitome of logical determinations), and the assertion at issue here is that the ethical law, both in terms of content and the existence of an ethical law generally, is to be derived from the law of thought. This also shows what is meant by the opposition of a positive philosophy to the negative rationalist one: it is nothing else than that we accept reality as something original, not something that flows from the laws of thought. Our positivism does not consist in our considering love to be ethical only because it is commanded in the Bible (instead, we would not consider the Bible to be the Word of God if it did not command love), but rather because we do not derive personality and love from any further ground, and consider no necessity of thought to be the substance and purpose of the world. They are this substance and purpose because of what they are in themselves [Sie ist dieß, weil sie es ist].

[68] *Grundlegung zur Metaphysik der Sitten* [Metaphysics of Morals], p. 92.

purely formal notion of morality. If the ethic consisted in the logical law, as Kant assumes, then it would of course be superfluous to first take the higher logical law, common to God and to man, from us and relocate it in God, to then take it back again from Him. But if the ethic is something concrete, specific, a real quality of the will, then the higher real power from which the human will takes its origin must be its principle. As surely as in earthly conditions our self-knowledge is the starting point for the knowledge of God (*initium cognoscendi*), just as surely must we, by contrast, acknowledge God's character as the real principle of our being (*principium essendi*).

But lately this objection has emerged in a much more glaring way and with the more consistent intention of denying God and religion, since in fact the alternative cannot be avoided: either no God, or a theological principle of ethics. The entire belief in God is represented as a mere projection of human imagination, by means of which man projects his own ethical being out of himself and turns it into a god, which is why every epoch, every people has a different one, in accordance with its own ethical character. Why is such a wise, good, just God necessary, since it is sufficient that wisdom, goodness, justice as such exist and manifest themselves in the universe and especially in man? As such, the erroneous nature of this is psychologically demonstrable, and the proof is provided by the entire history of religion.[69] Against this, it can already be noted: in what consists the certainty of this argument? Supposing things stand the way religion teaches, then should not goodness and righteousness also be in us at the same time, even though they are completely so only in God, and should the human being who is really like God (filled by Him) not be capable of envisioning His true being? How can the fact that justice, goodness, etc., are also in man, justify

---

[69] Feuerbach, *Das Wesen des Christenthums* [The Essence of Christianity]. The triviality of this way of looking at things can, however, serve as a desirable foil for the old-school Hegelians. At least for Hegel, belief in God is abandoned in favor of a great scientific concept: the idea, this primordial power of the universe, is to expose its true rich content according to its individual moments in the history of religion. Here, on the other hand, this content of world history is merely the result of accidental human error, and science is a narrative of mental illnesses and the psychological means of curing them. The resonance which this writing has found among a section of the public demonstrates that the age of Bahrdt and Nicolai never dies out.

the assertion that they cannot have their source in God? With what right can one pass off this psychological explanation, which at most (even if it does not contradict itself) could only be regarded as a ground for skepticism, as positive proof of denial? Hence, the doctrine of religion still has an independent positive weight in the fact that the fundamental vision in us (or also "reason") positively postulates the unity of the real and the ethical primordial power. This unity exists when the real Almighty is at the same time the archetype of the ethic, the completed personality. On the other hand, according to the former assumption, real power is in the universe and in the events and results of history, while ethical power is merely internal in man, with no connection one to the other; ethical power has no real strength, as a rule succumbs, while real power has no functionality in terms of ethical principles.

§. 30. Man as a person and in relation to other persons has his archetype in the *idea of completed personality*, hence *directly* in the being, i.e., the holiness of God,[70] modified in terms of the creaturely position of humans, from which stem the requirements of love, truthfulness, etc. The same is not true for common human existence in its articulated form, God's world order for the human race. This has its archetype from the free – albeit answering to His holiness – *counsel of God* in the *free, divine world economy.* Marital love and faithfulness, or patriotism, *cannot* be derived from the essence of God or man's image of God, and even less so the institutions of the family, property, the state; for in God Himself there is nothing of any of this. The institutions and bonds, the entire structure of the ethical world with regard to the civil order and its ethical principles and commandments are a direct outflow not of divine holiness but of God's free creative intelligence, with this holiness as basis (for nature as well in an analogous

[70] "You shall be holy, for I am holy" [Leviticus 11:45]. A similar acknowledgement can be found in Cicero, *The Laws,* I. 8: "Est autem virtus nihil aliud, quam in se perfecta et ad summum perducta natura, est igitur hominis cum Deo similitudo" ['This virtue is nothing else than a nature perfect in itself, and wrought up to the most consummate excellence. There exists, therefore, a similitude between God and man.' From *The Treatises of M. T. Cicero...*, trans. C. D. Yonge (London: Henry G. Bohn, 1853), p. 409].

way); they therefore have an artistic character on an ethical basis.[71] Love, justice, truthfulness, etc. are thus the original and eternal good. On the other hand, conjugal love, recognition of property, etc. find that good in relation to institutions the eternity of which is not established. Nevertheless, the idea of the completed personality and this world economy, because the former is always the basis of the latter, stand in the closest connection, even though we do not everywhere recognize it.[72] Accordingly, the ethic has its content everywhere through the holiness of God, but is specifically determined for man through the divine arrangement as it emerges from the intelligence and the free (creative) will of God, in greater or lesser degree depending on whether it concerns the objective ethical world or subjective morality. In this way the venerable question is to be decided as to whether the *lex naturae* [law of nature] is based on the *sanctitas* [holiness] or on the *libera voluntas Dei* [free will of God]. But it is completely erroneous to deny both, as Pufendorf does,[73] and establish as a principle some mechanical necessity (that God cannot preserve human beings other than through benevolence and so on).

Accordingly, the content of the ethic has a twofold principle: the idea of completed personality and the plan of the ethical world. But this in no way results in two separate systems; rather, both stand in mutual interpenetration, in which they cannot be separated from each other. The institutions of the ethical world (marriage, the state) derive their content from the idea of completed personality (spiritual purity, justice), and the content of the idea of completed personality is determined for man by the requirements of the institutions of the ethical world (conjugal fidelity, civil obedience). Yet each must be held onto as an independent principle. The objective ethical world is not to be derived from

---

[71] Herein lies the last and deepest reason for the *positivity of law* in relation to its content. Just as from the beginning the construction of the ethical world is a free (positive) act of God based on divine holiness, so also is its formation, which pertains to mankind independently, a matter of free (positive) arrangement based on its necessary ideas. Cf. Book II [*Principles of Law*], §. 6 and §§. 8ff.

[72] In particular, the perfect formation of the latter, the "kingdom of God," is also the most perfect revelation of personality and has the perfection of all personalities as its content. See above, §. 6 and §. 27.

[73] *Jus nat.*, lib. II, cap. 2. §. 5.

the mere nature of the individual (Kant), and personality must not be treated as an empty vessel into which the ethic is first poured from the formations of the ethical world (Hegel).

The continuous and distinctive character trait of subjective morality is *devotion, renunciation*, be it in thoughts, things, people. In absolute terms this lies in the fact that *selflessness* (absence of need) is a necessary correlate of completed personality, and that the flourishing of morality, love, includes positive devotion.[74] In relation to people, however, it is further given by his being a creature and belonging to a whole, to which he is to devote himself as a member.

For this reason alone, the earlier (subjectively rationalistic) ethics, which derived its entire content from the nature of the individual, is incapable of finding not only the objectively ethical world, but also even the content of subjective morality, because the latter, as shown above, is given together with the former. Speculative philosophy – first Schelling, then Hegel and Schleiermacher – brought the idea of the objective ethic, that is, of an ethical world, to scientific consciousness. But thus far only in a more or less pantheistic way. It is not the way we see it – the divine personality, which, in itself already a substantial, concrete, holy will, has established man in its image and an ethical world according to its plan; rather, it is the absolute ("reason," "spirit"), which, in itself without content, dichotomizes itself into the opposites of human personality and external common form of life and consists in the reciprocal condition of both, so that its expansion and contraction at the same time result in individual morality and the structure of the ethical world, like a large tapestry.

As a result, first, the human being is no longer truly the subject of the ethic; this subject is rather the impersonal world-reason which only needs man as its instrument in order to realize its logical figures or its essentiality in some other manner. Thus, according to Hegel, reason (substantial will) is realized in that it posits personality (subjective will) as its negation and then annuls it again, and it is the same way even in Schleiermacher's philosophical doctrine of ethics, in

---

[74] Even the divine will – although God, as the center, must necessarily refer the world to Himself – can, from the aspect of infinite love, have devotion to and renunciation regarding man attributed to it. The Christian church in particular praises God for *giving up* His Son, and has in God incarnate the model of self-renunciation and sacrifice that exceeds all human standards.

which reason can only assimilate nature in the form of personality.[75]

Second, the idea of completed personality is no longer the supreme or even an independent principle for the content of the ethic; instead, the architectonic of the ethical world is the original and sole ethical content, from which then the content of subjective morality emerges exclusively. It is true to a large extent that which Hegel asserts against the earlier "ethics," that subjective morality ("the good") derives its content first from "law and morality," i.e., from the relations of legal matters, the family, civil society, and the state. But on the other hand, he likewise surrenders the moral content that really has its independent source and fulfillment in the individual, in man's likeness to God, e.g., love, truthfulness. In particular, he allots only a subordinate moral level to love of neighbor, under the designation "well-being" [Wohls]; it is not yet truly good.[76] Since for him the ethical world emerges from the play of the two moments of the substantial and subjective will, the former has no content apart from the latter, and the latter has no content apart from the former. For Hegel, therefore, a perfect personality consisting in something other than the fulfillment of familial and civic duties is not even conceivable, and God, if there was one, could only be good because of this. From this it follows once again that there is no room for God in Hegel's system except insofar as He is conceived as a mere law, as world order.

§. 31. But the content of the ethical is partly universal, partly individual. It is universal according to the unchangeable essence of those virtues and the unchangeable ethical meaning of life relations; and it is individual in two respects,

---

[75] This is not to be lumped together with the Christian worldview, according to which the divine world plan is likewise fulfilled by people, because with the latter, God does not need people to posit Himself, and the architectonic of His kingdom is not an end for which people serve as a mere means; rather, the personal completion of each individual in himself is no less an absolute end as such.

[76] Hegel, *Grundlinien*, §§. 123, 124. Now Christ was hardly concerned with what Hegel calls ethical behavior – family ties, business activity, state citizenship. The "well-being" that Hegel disregarded was the predominant mode of His activity. Hegel admits this himself, but he helps himself out by saying that this is only the polemical side with which the new religion first had to appear, which has lost its validity with the resurrection of Christ because "love for all people, not simply for a few particular individuals, is an empty sprawl" (*Vorlesungen über die Philosophie der Religion*, II, pp. 289 and 292).

on the one hand in that man (e.g., people, epoch), who as such is supposed to fulfill the ethic as personality, is also to meet its universal requirements as an individual in accordance with his individuality, and on the other, in that the divine will, which is itself the ethic, also requires from us something particular, determinate in every situation of life in which it places us, on the basis of the universal-ethical. The latter, however, since it is based on devotion to God and not on the nature of man's will in himself, no longer pertains to the purely moral sphere, but impinges on the religious. The purely moral man acts only according to universal ethical principles and according to his individuality; the religious man seeks at the same time, within the limits of what is predetermined by the universal ethical law and his own individuality, also to become certain of God's will for the individual case.

Schleiermacher's ethics gained the true principle of human individuality as the basis of determination for ethical action. On the other hand, Hegel deserves no less merit for asserting the sanctity of the law and its objective and unchangeable content against the false individualization of the ethical, by which the latter is drawn into subjective intention and conviction.

Chapter 3: Ethical Power and Ethical Motive

§. 32. Just as the good has its *content* from the divine will, so also does it have its *binding regard*. The good is an ought, it is an obligation for man just by virtue of his dependence on God as Creator and Lord. But in terms of the independence of the creature (vision of creation), the ethic (both religion and morality) is not merely a required condition from God, but at the same time the creature's own essence and will. As such, morality and religion have a twofold side, that they determine human beings first as divine will and then no less as one's own will – as true human nature – so that from the outset they are just as much an ought, a requirement, as a will, a being, and a quality of man. The former lies in the creatureliness, the latter in the personality of the person, by necessity.

Schleiermacher wrongly removes the ought from ethics, postulating that reason solves its problem (the mastery of nature, which is where he locates the ethic) on its own as it were, it being a process and not an ought. This is due to the pantheistic foundation, something of which, as is known, Schleiermacher's point of view is not free. By contrast, just as God and man remain different, so does the ethic always remain an ought, even if a condition should arrive in which man always and necessarily desires and fulfills it. Just as Schleiermacher banishes the ought from the idea of the good, so at the other extreme does Hegel teach that the idea of the good (subjective morality) is the sole and eternal ought. The opposition of the subjective (particular) to the objective (universal) is precisely morality, and a state of unity between the two, in which "subjectivity could no longer increase to evil," for him falls outside the realm of conceivability.

§. 33. But in the condition of man whereby he stands apart from God and at the same time under the power of evil, the ought and the will are not merely differentiated but are separable and in conflict. There is a will in man that contradicts his ought. At the same time, that flow of ethical forces which emanates from the primordial ethical power is cut off, and the ethic, which as its own original will would be of infinite intensity and capacity for improvement, becomes, as an external power opposed to the will, a delimited rule. The good in this form, on the one hand as an external power that can be separated from one's own will, on the other hand as a delimited rule, is the ethical law. Man stands under the ethical law insofar as he is not elevated to a freer and higher position, in individual spheres through natural, moral gifts and powers (inspiration), and in the entirety through divine transformation of his entire being. That this higher position does not abolish the content of the ethical law, but is precisely a greater, an increased fulfillment, is particularly evident from the Sermon on the Mount, where the Mosaic ethical law (not, e.g., the ceremonial law) and the Christian union of the human will with the divine are set in opposition to one another.

Since, therefore, divine and human volition are by no means inseparable in our condition, we sharply distinguish the two relations. Insofar as the good binds us as the will of God, it is the *ethical law* and *ethical duty* (namely, the commandment is the act of God as ethical primordial power, duty is the effect of the same on the ethically dependent); insofar as it really forms the quality of human will, it is *virtue*. Another distinction based on the essence of the person should not be mixed up with this, namely the distinction between *good attitudes* or *qualities of will* and *good acts*. Rather, both distinctions are to be combined; good attitudes are as much duties as they are virtues, and good acts fall just as much under the purview of virtuous acts as of duties.[77]

---

[77] Schleiermacher's division of "virtues and duties" is intended to express nothing else than the last-mentioned distinction between the disposition (constant inner will-direction or willingness of will) and individual acts as an expression thereof upon conditions. But the concepts of virtue and duty signify at the same time yet another opposition: the former describes the good as an existing good quality of man, the latter describes it as a higher requirement and constraint. Schleiermacher ignores this meaning because he does not accept any ought at all in ethical science, while the language usage of the word duty may not be separated from the significance of ought. But it certainly does not gybe to view the disposition of human beings merely as virtue and not also as duty, and individual acts merely as duties, not also as expressions of virtue. Is not, e.g., the disposition of love not every bit as much duty as the individual act of love? Incidentally, if Schleiermacher realizes the highest good only in duties (individual acts) and not also in virtues (convictions), this is because for him the virtues as reason of the individual coincide with universal reason the existence of which resides precisely in each such individual, and therefore manifests itself merely as the realizer of the highest good, not as the realized highest good. In truth, however, God, who stands above the virtues (of reason) of

§. 34. If, in the true condition, the good is a product and a postulate of divine requirement and of human will at the same time, the original *sanction* and the specifics of the *law* and of *obligation* lie only in the former. Insofar as the ethic is our own will, it is not law except in the sense of the laws of nature. An ought, an ethical law, necessarily presupposes a higher will to which ours is bound, and if it is to be a truly ethical, i.e., internally and absolutely binding law, then it must be *that* will which we likewise recognize as our own (physical and ethical) substance (i.e., as the immanent cause of our existence and the quality of our will). This also eliminates Kant's objection[78] that the derivation of the good in terms of content and sanction from the divine will establishes "*heteronomy*" for the latter (control by an external power). On the contrary, the bare *law of thought* (reason) could only have an ethically binding power for us, and count as the autonomy of our will, if our substance really were (as is taught) a mere thought-determination. But we are real beings, and therefore a real personal power is our substance and the source of the ethic.

This is recognized almost unanimously by the earlier writers. Hobbes[79] recognizes that all the rules of *ratio* would be mere *conclusiones* and not laws if it were not for someone higher, namely God, dictating them. Likewise Pufendorf [80]: there can be no moral command without an *impositio* by someone higher. According to both, indeed, the content of the ethic is quite independent of God, but they derive the binding force of it only from His sanction. Wolff [81] is the first to completely abstract from God; the atheist must act just as morally as the theist. But he still demands a *real "motive"* for the concept of "obligation," recognizing that without such there is no obligation. Now then, he finds this real motive in physical nature rather than in God. So, e.g., "nature imposes on us the obligation to marry because it connects cohabitation with a tender pleasure." Incidentally, it is evident that this eliminates the specificity of the ethic, as

---

the individual as standing over that which is created by Him, is the realizer, and the highest good is realized just as much in the attitudes ("virtues") as in the acts ("duties").

[78] *Grundlegung zur Metaphysik der Sitten*, pp. 89–92; *Critik der praktischen Vernunft,* pp. 68ff.

[79] *De cive,* lib. I. cap. 3. §. 32.

[80] *De officio homini et civ.* lib. I. cap. 2. §§. 4–6; cap. 3. §. 10.

[81] *Vernünfftige gedancken von der menschen thun und lassen*, ch. 1.

well as its sanctity. Kant is the first to posit the real obligating power in thought (reason) itself, which is the fulfillment of the rationalistic principle. The purely logical laws of universality and non-contradiction which pertain to us as intelligible beings should have such a real power even over our natural instincts (e.g. self-satisfaction, etc.) – the "imperative." But we do not have to prove that this is completely incomprehensible and inexplicable, since Kant himself expressly admits it.[82] With Hegel (as with Fichte) it is indeed completely consistent that logic is the sanctioning power of the ethic just as it is the source thereof, because according to this system all reality, even nature, is the result of logical determinations, in other words, because logic is our substance. But the truth of the latter must once and for all be disputed, for on this assumption we must also ascribe our infringement to this substance, and therefore also consider it legitimate, as Spinoza more consistently teaches. If logic and not a personality is the substance of the world, then it is by no means possible to foresee how evil, i.e., the opposition to the good, which then necessarily also belongs to the logical emanation, should be worse than the good. The relationship between the pious and the villain is instead no different from that of two good actors, one of whom plays Heinrich Richmond, the other Richard III.[83] Those writers, on the other hand, who in this period fully represent the theological principle of ethics and who base the content and regard of the good on God, such as Selden and Crusius,[84] limit themselves too exclusively to man's external relationship of dependence on

[82] *Grundlegung zur Metaphysik der Sitten,* p. 124: "How it is, however, that pure reason without other motive forces, from wherever they may have been taken, be practical for itself, i.e., how the mere principle of the universal validity of all its maxims as laws (which, of course, would be the form of a purely practical reason) without any matter (object) of the will, in which one would take any interest in advance, would provide a motive force for itself, and an interest which would be called purely moral, or in other words: *how pure reason can be practical* – all human reason is *completely incapable* of *explaining* this, and all effort and labor to look for an explanation is thrown away."

[83] On the other hand, do not come with the objection that God as nature causes evil but God as an idea excludes it, because where then is the unity between God as nature and God as idea? And beyond that, it is not just God as nature, but God unfolding according to intellectual law, who works evil and posits Himself as evil.

[84] Seldenus *de jure natur. juxta discipl. Ebraeor.* lib. I. cap. 7 et 8. Crusius, *Ethik.*

God, without properly entering into the fact that the good is at the same time the inner substance of man himself.

§. 35. But since God personally hides Himself in our temporal state, the unifying force which He alone gives to true human nature and the structure of the ethical world can appear to be original and simply inherent therein, and from this emerges the *specifically moral motive force* in distinction to the religious one. Man's own ethical nature (as opposed to his arbitrary volition) and the ethic of the conditions in which man finds himself (marriage, childhood, status, state) are initially set as ethical power opposite to him, and also assert themselves as such even should he have broken away from the deeper power from which alone they derive theirs, from God. In absolute obedience he submits to the ethical law (content) that he finds contained in his own nature and in social relations. But true insight only ever sees the derivative in the original source at the same time. In particular, our own ethical being, which we perceive as an ethical power over ourselves as *conscience*, is only this power because it has its root in that higher substance, in God; otherwise, our condition between good and evil would only be a dispute of inclinations, not a dispute of ought versus a contrary inclination.

Conscience is not the mere power of the subjective and of inwardness in opposition to religion as external power, as Hegel[85] depicts it; rather, conscience is a primarily objective power which at the same time works in us as the power of our own nature. It is the point at which the divine and the human will interpenetrate and form the ethical nature of man, which is created and independent at the same time.

§. 36. In accordance with that twofold relationship of man – his creaturely nature and his independent personality – the *ethical motive* is then also twofold. It is the subjection, submission to the higher ethical power, and the particular, freely willed character of its content, i.e., *obedience* and *love*. In true and complete ethical fulfillment, the two are united. Since the former relation precedes the latter and is its root, obedience is also the first and indispensable ethical

---

[85] *Grundlinien*, §. 136. Incidentally, the opposition of conscience to religion cannot be admitted, if only because conscience is at least as much a religious as a moral principle.

motive, the foundation of all that is ethical; and love can only arise on it and from it; and only by including obedience in itself can love spring up.[86] But love, while it rests on the basis of obedience, is a higher mode of fulfillment than mere obedience. Consummate religiosity not only includes obedience to God but also the love of God; consummate ethical behavior acts not only out of duty, but also out of love of one's neighbor, love of truth, joy in spiritual freedom, love of the fatherland.[87] In obedience and loyalty to duty, man is completely a creature; in love, he is godlike. However, the aspiration of man need only be the former; the latter is an effect which is linked to it of itself through higher assistance, and which in any case lies entirely outside of his responsibility.

But the highest ethical motive, just like the highest ethical virtue itself, is *love for the person*. Because the original concept of love is for the person to find his own satisfaction in the satisfaction of the other person. All other love is borne by this.

It is a deep thought, first expressed by Geulincs,[88] that virtue does not consist in the love stemming from well-being (*amor benevolentiae*), nor even in the love stemming from emotion (*amor affectionis*), but in the love stemming from obedience (*amor obedientiae*), namely, as he further develops it, obedience to reason as the law of God. The epoch which Kant forms in ethics is based only on the complete implementation of this thought, namely, that morality consists not in "pathological love,"[89] nor in the pursuit of happiness, whether one's own or someone else's, but in respect for the law. This conception of the ethical motive is one-sided (apart, of course, from the fact that Kant turns the content of the law, as shown above, into a complete abstraction). The truth of the matter is only that obedience is the first, the indispensable basis of ethical life, without which love really is always only pathological and therefore accidental, applied only to

---

[86] Therefore, in education it is also wrong first to wish to have obedience freely generated out of love, instead of necessarily having obedience precede love as a basis.

[87] Christ performed His work out of obedience to God, and out of love and mercy toward man.

[88] *Ethica,* initial chapters.

[89] [pathological: "2. Relating to the feelings or emotions." In: "pathological, adj. and n." OED Online, Oxford University Press, September 2020, www.oed.com/view/ Entry/138800. Accessed 11 November 2020.]

this or that object of ethical requirement,[90] and therefore only a sort of fine natural ethical life, not remotely true ethical life, since love for the content of ethical life *in its totality* arises only on the basis of obedience. On the other hand, it is erroneous to regard the permeation of feeling by the ethical will, and the love of the whole concrete content of the ethic and, finally, the love of the person, as something beyond the ethical, or even, like Kant,[91] as opposed to the ethical. On the contrary, this is precisely the fruit of dutifulness. Those who do good with an inclination toward, and love for, their neighbor are one step above those who do it with the constant exercise of willpower.

For Hegel as well, the moral motive is merely dutifulness, not love. By contrast, with the current "speculative theology" the religious motive appears to be the love of God, but conceived as the unity of the subjective (human) will and the objective, i.e., impersonal will, similar to Spinoza's love of God who Himself is incapable of love. On the other hand, philosophy, by rightly striving to keep mere *pathological* love distanced from the realm of ethics, posits a purely *abstract* love. Here too, however, the truth about the abstract and the sensorial is at the same time *the personal.* When love is stripped of all sensorial admixture, what remains is by no means abstract devotion to the universal or even to the ethical world order, but *love of the person*, and this is not material or pathological, but precisely the most spiritual, the act of will, in which it has its highest freedom.[92]

---

[90] As Geulincs (*Ethica Tract.* II, §. 1) quite rightly notes, whoever is polite but not chaste does not have the virtue of politeness either; for, as is evident from this, he does not have it from obedience. Therefore, virtue is only one.

[91] *Grundlegung zur Metaphysik der Sitten*, p. 89: "Therefore I should, e.g., seek to promote the happiness of others, not as if I were interested in their existence (be it through direct inclination or some pleasure, be it indirectly through reason); but only because the maxim that excludes it cannot be grasped in one and the same will, as a general law." The same applies at pp. 58–61. Conversely, in the first stage of Schelling's philosophy, in accordance with the spirit of the period of genius which existed at that time, only free enthusiasm manifests itself as ethical behavior, in actuality oneness with God in a pantheistic way according to which our actions are the highest culmination of divine action itself, without any prerequisite of obedience, self-denial, etc.

[92] But a distinguishing mark of the true, i.e., personal love of God from that merely

Incidentally, when we speak of the motive of morality, we must distinguish between the objective and subjective end, i.e., the divine goal and the human motive. The former is the perfection of the creature, while the latter is the higher law, the well-being of one's neighbor, and so on. God demands love from us, not because it is the means for Him to achieve the welfare of others, but because love is good and perfect, hence for our sake; on the other hand, we should love, not so that we know ourselves as perfect, but from those motives. That is why it is a blatant confusion and destruction of any true ethic when Wolff at the beginning of his ethics characterizes the ethical motive as the aspiration to be perfect, and salvation as the joy of one's own perfection.

§. 37. If the good does not consist in a law separate from the real being of the person, but if it is precisely the will of the person himself – in an absolute way for the divine person, in a derivative way for the human – then it must, since personality is necessarily an end in itself and a center, also include the *real satisfaction of the person*. So, we ascribe not only absolute holiness to God Himself, but also absolute *bliss* [Seligkeit]. For man as well, the highest good only consists in both at the same time. To be sure, bliss conceived as a reward outside of ethics and sanctification, and as the satisfaction of various sensory and selfish instincts, would constitute the abolition of true ethics and sanctification. But in the first place, the fulfillment of duty, or beyond that pure love, already contains in itself a satisfaction of the person, and this is a no less essential aspect of the highest good than the fulfillment of duty for its own sake. A good in which the subjects would not personally find their full satisfaction is unthinkable [ein Ungedanke].[93] Secondly, the highest good, since the source of the ethic is personal, does not consist in a mere quality in accordance with it (fulfillment of its

---

abstract love of God is the discretionary *act* [die in der Mitte liegende That]. The love of God on the part of the religious mind is deepened not only in being bound to the person of God but also in the acts of God: redemption, suffering, daily conduct of life, etc.

[93] This is the deep secret of the ethical world: that self-renunciation (love, ecstasy) is at the same time the highest self-satisfaction. Renunciation, however, is a self-acting cessation of self, which as such presupposes the *continuation of one's own personality*, not a cessation of the creature in God, as Johannes Angelus and others imagine.

requirements), but in a real union with it, which is necessarily reciprocal, and which grants the highest, absolute satisfaction. The highest good is not only man's love for God, but also God's love for man, and precisely this, which contains no human action and fulfillment, is absolutely blissful. So, while sanctification and bliss are by no means the same thing, they are in an inseparable unity. That is why the desire for bliss is a true ethical motive. It is not selfishness for man to desire his genuine satisfaction – expressed more purely, his peace – which consists in freedom of the spirit, in pure love for God and his neighbor, and in being loved by God and his neighbor; it is the eternal nature of personality, and it is unnatural to assert that man should only have the love of God and not a desire for his own happiness.[94] Christian revelation thus sanctions this motive of bliss. In doing so, it does not refer bliss *merely* to a hereafter, to which the Christian life on earth would relate as a torment by which it is earned. On the contrary, the requirement is to find satisfaction here below in sanctification and only in it, despite all sensorial external suffering. But it never recognizes perfect bliss in a state in which man is not ever completely free from sin, in which he suffers from the power of nature as from the power of evil, and above all in which the absolute moment of bliss, God's love for man, is not revealed in its fullness. It is therefore only promised in the coming kingdom. Fichte's polemic[95] against Christian ethics – which, among other things, is the most radical thing ever written against Christianity – as if it only wanted the good for the sake of reward, turns out to be completely unfounded and unjust; it would only fit with the Mohammedan heaven. But it corresponds entirely to Fichte's standpoint, the denial of the real aspect in all being. On the other hand, Kant recognizes the truth and depth of Christian ethics in contrast to the Stoic ethics precisely in the fact that it also wants the highest level of human satisfaction.[96] The

---

[94] Fenelon's doctrine does not consist in the exclusion of the motive of bliss, but only in the true assertion that the motive of love of God must be the absolute, independent, first motive of bliss, and not a mere means to that end.

[95] *J. G. Fichte's... Appellation an das Publikum über die durch ein Kurf. Sächs. Confiscationsrescript ihm beigemessenen atheistischen Aeusserungen* [Fichte's Appeal to the Public regarding the Atheistic Expressions attributed to him in the Elector of Saxony's Rescript of Confiscation], pp. 62–73.

[96] *Critik der praktischen Vernunft*, p. 229.

pantheistic view, of course, needs no bliss in its system because it is only reason (world spirit), and not man himself, which through him accomplishes good, realizes itself, and is already satisfied by positing good. Hegel therefore treats bliss as a merely alternate expression for well-being, happiness, etc., from the point of view of the lower level of good, where it still manifests itself as the satisfaction of subjectivity, but which must give way, i.e., disappear as a delusion, where the good is recognized in its true form, which consists in the realization of the objective institutes (civil society, state).[97]

§. 38. If afterwards in the perfected state the fulfillment of the ethic (sanctification) and satisfaction permeate each other in indissoluble unity, this is by no means the case in the empirical state. Apart from the corruption attendant to it, here the human being is grounded on a material substrate to which his satisfaction must also extend, and the human condition in which he has his calling is not everywhere and directly related to the highest good (God). Here there is therefore a satisfaction that pertains to natural existence, that is to say, not evil and yet found independently of the fulfillment of the ethic. This is the concept of "*earthly goods*" in distinction to the virtues and duties. So health, prosperity, good reputation, convenience, comfort of life, etc. They are only relatively good, namely a satisfaction of the person for certain conditions thereof, which as such do not pertain to his eternal essence. These goods, however, stand in a manifold relation to the ethic. They are gifts of divine love, received as such and therefore outflows of the highest good, which, however, evidently always presupposes that the satisfaction they grant must be a good in and of themselves because otherwise they would not be gifts. According to the same presupposition, they are the object of the duty of others to us and vice versa, and a task of the human community. In many cases they are a precondition for the fulfillment of ethics, e.g., concern for health, and to that degree they are our own duty. Finally, even where they are not directly connected with any ethical purpose, they are natural real satisfaction, and to that extent they form the *sphere of the ethically permissible.* The concept of *what is permissible* rests precisely on the fact that satisfaction is just as absolute an end, founded in the essence of the person, as is ethical fulfillment; therefore, in the condition in which the two diverge, it has its independent sanction from the original ethical power in the ethical world. What is

[97] *Grundlinien,* §. 124.

permitted is therefore not the result of an *ethical command* (requirement), because this can only command or forbid; but neither is it something ethically indifferent, merely natural. Rather, it is the outflow of *ethical power*, the same from which the ethical command itself also proceeds. But the condition in which ethical fulfillment and satisfaction are separated from each other is an imperfect one, which therefore must increasingly be overcome. The steady diminution of the sphere of what is merely permissible, i.e., what is indifferent to ethical fulfillment, constitutes advancement (progress of sanctification), whereby satisfaction is sought in what likewise constitutes ethical fulfillment (act of love, etc.). But this always remains a mere approximation. This is why one should never stint on this natural satisfaction (the permitted enjoyments) to the less developed (especially the youth); nevertheless, those who observe higher requirements (above all the ministers of the church) must not halt at what is commonly permitted.[98]

[98] The superficiality of the Pietistic as well as the Puritan view draws a strict line here, allowing one thing to the Christian but not another. They thus prohibit things that no longer suit a certain level of Christian advancement and therefore are already shed from within, but which by no means are sinful in themselves and therefore incompatible with Christianity in general; and on the other hand they consider things permissible that a condition of spiritual advancement would find repellent; likewise they do not distinguish between individuals, e.g., whether it is not less harmful for A or for B to find satisfaction at the theater rather than with one's own eloquence.

Chapter 4: The Will and Ethical Freedom

§. 39. The *will* and the activity of the will, the *decision*, are the essential attribute of the person. With the decision, something is newly posited which in no way existed before, nor yet was hidden (*implicite*) in the existence of the person like the plant in the seed. The will is therefore a force of *absolute beginning*, of *absolute causality*. Precisely because of this, the decision is at the same time the active exclusion of the infinite possibility of something else, whether this is something possible in terms of act or, like evil for the holy will, only possible in terms of thought; in other words, whether it be entirely or only physically, not morally possible. The will is therefore also a *power of choice*, even if depending on its place [je nach seinem Orte] it is a necessary choice.[99]

Even so, as an attribute of the person, the will includes the full quality of the person. The will is therefore primarily based on the *consciousness* in which the decision is made. Furthermore, the will rests on a *determinate ethical being* of the person, disposition, character, which is revealed in the decision, albeit in a free (i.e., newly creating or newly affirming) manner; for without such there is no person. Now then, this ethical essence of the person is itself nothing else than will, it is by no means stationary, finished, but rather the uninterrupted series of acts of will (decisions), yet nevertheless, in this *continuity and identity* with itself, it is again something that is extant, distinct from the *particular act of will*, with which it stands in reciprocal interaction. It is determinative of the decision as it itself is determined by the decision. This and only this is the real concept of *self-determination*. Finally, the will rests on a center of the person, the *innermost*

---

[99] The will therefore has an infinite content of mere *potentia* which does not become an *actus;* on the contrary, this is effectively excluded. The fundamental proposition of pantheism is the reverse, that in God everything that is *potentia* must also be *actus*. Spinoza, who made this proposition, consequently asserts that God has no will (*voluntas*). On the other hand, Hegel's pantheism, although he adheres to the same proposition that in God everything that is potential must also be activity (or actually already in action), nevertheless predicates "will" of God. That is an inversion of language. Human language does not understand by will the realization of the three moments of the concept of will, any more than it understands by God the absolute of Hegel.

self, from which the ultimate decision proceeds and to which it refers back, namely, which finds *its satisfaction* or, in the purest sense of the word, its "*peace*," in all its decisions, either in a wrong way in selfish appropriation, or in a true way precisely in the renunciation of self. The whole person is therefore present and active in every decision, the totality of his definite content-rich being and his relations to the outside world and his inmost self, the focal point of his being and willing.

The absolute causality of the decision, the infinite possibility of another, the consciousness, the self-determination in which the mind of the person generates the decision and the decision generates the mind, finally the constant reciprocal action of the decision on the person, that he finds in it his satisfaction (his purpose) – these are the moments which together in their indissoluble unity, like the nature of the will, also form its *freedom*. *Freedom of the will* does not exist in any of these individually, but *only in their totality*.[100] That is why freedom and will also coincide completely in their original concept; the will is free, and nothing other than will is free.[101]

---

[100] Thus Kant places the essence of freedom simply in absolute causality, Spinoza simply in being determined merely by one's own nature, which is why he nevertheless strangely ascribes absolute freedom to his God to whom he denies understanding and will, Hegel simply in the positing and cancellation of his contradiction, etc.

[101] This is the case with the Protestant dogmatists (Gerhard): "Liberum et voluntarium sunt synonyma, ac voluntatem non liberam dicere, est perinde ac si quis dicere velit calidum absque calore" [The will and freedom are synonymous, and to say that they are not is like saying heat is without hotness] (Harleß, *Christliche Ethik* [Christian Ethics], p. 44). Hegel pronounced this thought even more emphatically, *Grundlinien*, §. 4 addendum. On the other hand, we must decisively reject Hegel's construction of the concept of will (*ibid.*, §. 5ff.). For him, like everything, it results from the diremtion of the moments of universality and particularity and their union. The will is namely: 1) *Universality* [Allgemeinheit], the "I" capable of abstraction from any particular content, motive, drive, etc., but also completely without content and indeterminate. 2) *Particularity* [Besonderheit], the particular inclinations, drives, purposes that challenge the I. 3) *Individuality* [Einzelnheit], the grasping of such a drive, purpose, etc. by the I, which still as consciousness remains the universal I, that is, capable of grasping or of not

§. 40. Freedom of the will in the true and perfect sense is however nothing but *ethical freedom*, i.e., the *immutable and self-assured willing of the good.* For the essence of the person, the divine and the truly human, is the good. Only in the pure ethical will does the innermost essence of the person (the substance of the will) determine the act of will, and the act of will determine the essence of the person in mutual presupposition and causality (identity) – equally as the harmony of an eternal chord. But here then the person is causal in the totality of his being, thus free; every relation in him is just as much determining as determined, thus here alone is there true continuous self-determination. In this manner, the divine will is eternally determined by justice, love, and wisdom as its substance, and justice, love, and wisdom in turn exist as the eternal act of the divine will. The divine will is just as much eternal existence as uninterrupted beginning, eternal condition and eternal activity. It is analogous with man: the

---

grasping. It is only in the last moment that the I is a specific empirical I (person). The objection to this, however, is that if the I, which remains within itself in all its particular decisions, is merely an emptiness, "pure indeterminacy," then it is impossible to foresee how this indeterminate taken together with these particular drives can ever come to a definite decision. Rather, the I is already something very definite in itself, from which it cannot abstract. It is a definite being (one cannot abstract oneself from one's conscience even if one does not follow it), and even as I it is striving after satisfaction and as such is itself the primordial drive, the primordial motive, without which all the particular instincts and their totality would have no relation to it. This real primordial determinacy of the person simply has no place in the mere system of categories. Here the I is only "pure *thinking* of itself." From the pantheistic point of view it is of course meant quite differently. The I is not here a real I, a person. Rather, the concept (the world principle) posits itself first as a universal possibility, then as a particular drive, purpose, then finally as a decision; only when it does the latter does it become a person, or do people arise. According to this, the concrete self, striving for its satisfaction, would only be sought in the last moment. But this last moment is only a specific individual decision, so the identity of the I (i.e., this personal I of man) in all decisions, and the distinction between the I and the individual decisions, is missing in the construction. The supposition that the (universal) I of the world spirit remains with itself as the same in all decisions of man or by man, simply won't do, since the human I is indisputably something that remains with itself, something identical in itself.

more ethical he is, the more the decision is a pure consequence of character, and character is a pure consequence of the decision. From this point of view, the ethically free will is also an ethically necessary will; it is determined by the necessity of one's own ethical being.[102]

But in our actual condition, the human will does not possess this ethical necessity and immutability; it instead has the *dual power of good and evil*. This, however, is not *ethical freedom* but only *ethical arbitrariness*.[103] Here, too, man's decision is always absolutely causal; nevertheless, his true being is no longer absolutely causal but is suppressed, and this by the causality of his own will. As a result, man is not causal in the totality of his personality.[104] Here man always

---

[102] Ethical freedom is therefore *inseparable* from ethical necessity. It is the necessity of one's own being, according to which the good must always be willed, and evil cannot be willed. But it is not *the same thing* as ethical necessity. For it does not exist in this moment alone, but in all which, according to the above, form the nature of the will. The ethical free will always has the physical power of evil and the consciousness of it, even if it eternally excludes it as will, as for example the holy will: it of course cannot will evil, but it could do so if it wanted to, and is aware that it could. The ethically free will also has this reciprocal causality in which it eternally generates itself and has the nature to find its peace in what is willed. Through all of this, ethical freedom as such forms the opposite of necessity.

Ethical freedom is also something else than creative freedom (§. 9). Their shared higher concept is the general concept of freedom as the faculty of the absolute beginning. With the former, freedom begins with external objects, with the latter with one's own volition. Both are therefore attributes of personality. But they are also connected to one another. Ethical freedom as such is not without creative faculty, in that it never posits the good as something given or finished, but always produces such in infinitely rich individualization and in infinite intensive augmentation, both in its inner will and in its doing. The ethical will is an inexhaustible wellspring which multiplies and increases itself to infinity.

[103] It is Kant's great contribution to the doctrine of free will to have brought the difference between these concepts to scientific insight.

[104] If Kant differentiates between freedom of choice and freedom of the will, and Schelling likewise distinguishes between formal and material freedom, it must also be shown how the two types of freedom result from a higher common concept of freedom.

decides as a person, namely with consciousness and by virtue of his particular being; but this essence of his is itself now no longer in agreement. There is a split in his state of will, a conflict between conscience and inclination, and there is a split between his condition of will and his decision. The righteous stumble, and the wicked feel a human touch.[105] Ethical arbitrariness is therefore not a *lack of freedom* (negative opposite), but rather *unfreedom* (positive opposite). Because we do not describe the positive opposite of a force as the lack thereof, but as its reversal and self-destruction. Freedom, by its nature, consists in the power of a being that is in agreement with itself. When it has broken away from this agreement, it is inverted in itself and continuously destroys itself through its own activity. But it is freedom itself that brings about this inversion. Only in freedom could this ever begin; only through freedom can it be continuously maintained. Unfreedom is also a freedom – just as bad luck [das Unglück] is also luck [ein Glück], a happenstance [ein Ohngefähr], and resentment [Unmuth] is also a courage [Muth] – only a wrong one.

Nevertheless, ethical arbitrariness must never be understood as a choice between good and evil, so that the will itself, as an emptiness-in-between, would relate in the same way to the one that is presented to it as to the other. Because if a person decides to do good, he has not first chosen this, but has acted according to his innermost being, as that which he truly is; on the other hand, if he decides to do evil, he has grasped something that does not belong to his being – he has chosen. The innermost I which decides is indeed neither good nor bad but is the center of individuality, which can just as well be the one as the other. But this I has the root of its existence in the ethical primordial power. With the former decision it remains in the origin of its activity; with the latter, it steps out of it. Herein lies the possibility that arbitrariness will be elevated to ethical freedom and that man will desire it.

That which ought to be is obviously not the choice between good and evil,

---

[105] All arbitrariness has a character of *contingency*, not in opposition to intentionality but to self-assured *being in agreement with itself*. The state of extreme wickedness would certainly be called freedom, namely freedom in evil, if otherwise the person did not have an indelible destiny for good. For this reason, the evil one can never will in complete harmony with himself, and so cannot have peace, and his power of actuality, detached from the primordial power, must ultimately dry up.

but the inner necessity of good. Ethical freedom should therefore be vouchsafed the victory over moral arbitrariness. Now, of course, ethical freedom is augmented through the more conscious and more energetic expulsion of evil, and to this end, in line with the given circumstances of the human condition, *arbitrariness must be preserved.* But such must not be cherished and nurtured as if it were an end in itself, and augmentation in freedom must not be found in the increased fluctuation between good and evil. It is therefore not the task of the individual or of the state to augment the possibility of evil to a higher degree, so as to make the decision about the good all the more free, but only to keep it open to such an extent that the given forces of manifold activity are undiminished, and that the act is a decision, not a mechanical effect. Indeed, the guiding principle in the ethical world is that the possibility of evil is only granted in proportion to the power of good, in order for the latter to overcome it. So, religion commands man not to seek temptation but to flee it where there is not a positive vocation that leads him to it, for which he is promised the strength and assistance to conquer it. So, too, should social institutions above all have the security of public order and mores as their guideline and allow arbitrariness only to the extent that it not overcome them.

§. 41. In its practical interest the *problem of free will* relates to the condition of arbitrariness. The question arises, does the human will have the power to decide on the good, even in the face of all opposing impulses, so that the decision for evil, the non-use of this power, is only caused by it, the will, and nothing else? *We assert this freedom of the will.* The will is not compelled by *material instincts and external stimuli;* it is not a product of physical forces, like the materialistic doctrine of Hommel, Mirabaud, and others contends. For both the real power of conscience (the original ethical being) and the faculty of thought, which illuminates the evil impulses for the former, are so original and so different from all physical forces and elevated above them, that they can never be determined or overpowered by drives according to physical laws.[106] But neither is the will

[106] Ever since idealism (Fichte), materialistic determinism has indeed been contrasted with the nature of the I or spirit in the character of pure actuality, pure self-positing. While this must be fully recognized, it does not get *us* where we need to be, because here the I is conceived as thought, and only thought is ascribed to that nature (by Fichte and

compelled by the *being*, i.e., *the character of man himself*, that is, his own internal relations to external stimuli. For this character, as shown, is not ready-made, given, but rather an unceasing volition, and therefore, even if determined by the particular decision, is itself just as capable of determining that decision. But we also assert freedom not from the individual act of will for itself, nor from the previous character of man for himself alone, but from both in their unity, from the whole person. The reciprocal precondition for change between the two, since it lies in the nature of the will, is found not only in the pure will, but necessarily also in the dishonest will, only in that case not as an eternal reciprocal affirmation, but often as a reciprocal negation, as if in an out-of-tune instrument. If our knowledge were not bound to the limit of temporality, we would look at a person's entire life as *one total act* which would contain all the individual decisions as their members, i.e., interlocking and yet independent, in which the character of the person and all decisions appear together as the one absolute causality.[107]

Hegel); we, on the other hand, assume that the I is something real, which acts according to real motives. *Our* refutation of materialism must therefore be based on the real ethical motives being completely different from everything material.

[107] This is what moves Schelling (*Philosophische Untersuchungen ueber das Wesen der menschlichen Freiheit*) to assume that every person through his own act has already determined his essence from his birth, from eternity (that is, not in the time of birth but out of time), and that hereby all his individual actions, including his subsequent conversion or obduracy, are given with unalterable necessity, according to which only that first act, not subsequent individual decisions, is free and accountable, so that the evil one is "right to say, that it was impossible for him to act otherwise," and yet to him "the irresistible tendency to evil is attributed, just as if every single act had really been in his power." This gainsays the vacuous idea that separates the decision from the person and his particular being. But here the being of man is just as impermissibly understood as something ready-made prior to and outside of individual decisions. It by no means eliminates the difficulty of making an absolutely groundless decision. For even if "the inconsistency of the accidentalness of the individual actions is removed," there arises on the other hand the inconsistency of the accidentalness of that act which determined the essence of men. Accordingly, that Judas betrayed Christ certainly seems necessary, "so

Indeed, the decision is never *groundless.*[108] It has a ground in the good and bad nature of man, his conscience or his desire. But it is *not a necessary* one; he could follow one or the other. There is no further ground for the fact that in a certain case a certain person followed, not his conscience, but his desire as a ground, than simply an act of his will, and precisely because this has no ground, we call it arbitrariness. The arbitrariness in the decision between good and bad is by no means the same as creative freedom, but they do have in common that which is the essence of the act in general: something is posited which is based on the inner determinacy of the person and yet is not given with it but is an absolute beginning. Human nature is a mixture of good and evil; the fact that evil becomes actual, that man determines himself to it, does not follow from that mixture, but is an act that simply begins, that posits something new. This alone explains how something can be the motive for the will, and yet not compel the will; that every decision of the will has all the good and bad impulses in the character of the person and in their relations to the outside world as a presupposition, as a ground, and yet does not emerge from the number and degree of these as if from a physical process according to dynamic laws,[109] something which is already evident from the complete dissimilarity between ethical motives on the one hand and sensual and selfish motives on the other.

But it also follows from this that the human will has *no unlimited freedom*, which would be incompatible with the nature of a created being. This is because the ethical, intellectual nature of the human being forms its limits, and this does not contradict the concept of freedom as absolute causality. For man apprehends the good or evil that is offered to him within these limits by absolute decision, but he cannot apprehend any good or evil beyond them. He decides completely freely which side of his being he wants to reveal, but he cannot reveal something that is not in his being. The good (objectively) that people are

---

that neither he nor any creature could change it"; but that Judas made himself into Judas and not John before his birth, would be groundless, accidental, all the more so as this act would precede being itself as well as consciousness.

[108] Jacobi (*Werke,* VI. 1) especially emphasized the absurdity of a groundless decision of the will.

[109] As Leibniz already stated, undeniably correctly: every decision arises from determinative reasons and yet there is no "nécessité absolue" for it.

capable of is therefore also different in type and degree, according to people [Volk], age, upbringing, even according to individual ethical aptitude, but the ability itself (subjectively) is equal to all people, because it is an absolute. Likewise, it is not a contradiction that, as Christian doctrine asserts, man in the given conditions and by nature is incapable of true good, and yet has the absolute ability to decide between good (i.e., the good still offered to him) and evil (of which the details below).

The main difficulty with the freedom of human will is its contradiction with the *unity and necessity of the world plan*. We cannot regard the world plan, that is, the course of world history, in any other way than as a coherent, artistically necessary conception that serves a total purpose; but if human decisions are free, it is composed of nothing but acts that begin with absolute, that is, nothing but independent, unrelated details. The fact that human freedom moves upon a necessary ground, that no man can go beyond his people, his age, his ethical and spiritual gifts, only diminishes the contradiction in degree, but does not resolve it as such. Proceeding from the unity of the world plan, one consequently arrives at the absolute determination of the will, whether one regards it, depending on one's point of view, as a *material* (Hommel), as *mathematical-logical* (as Spinoza states and Hegel conceals), or as *providential determination*.[110]

Regardless of the apparent contradiction, we must now hold on to *both*, the unity of the world plan and human freedom. We cannot assume that world history is merely the result of human decisions, but neither, conversely, that human decisions are merely the result of the conception [Konception] of world history. This is now certain: the human will is determined by the divine disposition which gives it gifts, insight, and instantaneous influence, up until an innermost point of decision, the yes and no, and only this ultimate, outermost affirmation or negation is actually what is man's own. On the other hand, however, we can probably also assume that such a decision of man again has a reaction on the conception of world history – (i.e., not just on its events, but on the artistic predisposition in the divine spirit) – which by virtue of the divine prescience, as we

---

[110] In his antinomies, Kant shows the inevitability of this consequence, and when Spinoza declares that we only consider our actions to be free because we do not know their causes, it is the unity of the universe that moves him to do so, although on his terms, not as an articulated conception but as the blind necessity of God.

have asserted above, is integrated into the unity and totality of the same. Such a reaction, far from being in conflict with the essence of the deity, seems rather to be called for by it. For if the world plan is not to be a mere mechanism or a logical system, but a personal realm, its harmony can only be built up out of sheer freedom, from sheer absolute beginning, truly causal forces. To establish a Spinozist unity, or, in Hegel's way, to develop the idea into world history according to its logical moments and to let acting people be determined by this development, so that the free act of man as such has no influence on the conception itself in its further course, it always only proceeding from itself – God would not be required for this, any person could also rule the world. In any case, the human being would only become a figure in a puppet show. We postulate such an interaction between divine disposition and human resolution as the activity of two independent personalities which permeate each other at every point, and we must postulate it from our standpoint, although we immediately admit that it is far beyond our insight and perception, and therefore is beyond our ability to verify.

In any case, however, the difficulty is in no way eliminated by the pantheistic view, according to which it is precisely God (the absolute) who realizes Himself as world history and who realizes Himself as individuals, and therefore God's disposition, if you want to call it that, and human resolutions entirely coincide as one and the same undifferentiated act. Rather, this view irredeemably eradicates human freedom. For if God, as world spirit, is to develop world-historical ideas completely, and in accordance with the necessary (dialectical) process, then as the specific individual He cannot want anything else, good and bad, than what is His part in the representation of the idea, and therefore as an individual has no freedom.[111] But free will has no interest in this point of view. So, Hegel

[111] If by virtue of their freedom Robespierre and his comrades had decided on humanity and leniency, then the dialectical element – the subjective will with its abstract equality, which in the deepening into itself as the extreme negation of the objective world structure, up to the highest tension of the antithesis, had to advance to the jealous rage to destroy – would not be realized, and the world spirit would be put to shame. So Robespierre cannot have had the freedom to do so. Or did, for instance, the world spirit just cast up the idea of terrorism, leaving to the freedom of whoever wanted to take action,

actually bypasses the whole problem and passes this off as his solution. What he understands by free will is not the *individual's ability to will*, but the *realization of the concept of will*, that is, not that the particular person in the particular situation has the ability to act in one way or another but that the three moments of the concept of will (universality, particularity, individual item) are found in every act of will and are represented in even more elevated manner in the social institutions (property, family, state) with an external fixed existence through the various (forced) persons. Because in this way the concept of will everywhere posits itself as the universal, posits the particular (the subject, the human being, or particular instincts, etc.) over against itself, and subsumes this again into itself, into the universal, and therefore is truly free.

The problem that exercises mankind is not that the objective will, i.e., the concept of the will arrives at its freedom, but that individual human beings be free.

§. 42. Now then, philosophy views the state of arbitrariness or imperfect freedom in which man finds himself as being something which is eternally necessary, founded in human nature which has never been and never will be different, and therefore also takes the good of which man is capable in it to be the only possible and as such the true good. The Christian religion, on the other hand, teaches that this condition is contrary to nature and the result of the guilt of the first man, and that man does not have the ability to do true good in it but can only gain that ability through a directly divine act, "pardon, rebirth, conversion." The problem of philosophy is therefore freedom of the will in the undifferentiated series of decisions, while the problem of theology lies mainly in this act of rebirth. The doctrine of philosophy, when we here leave uninvestigated its logical correctness and agreement, contradicts the innermost postulate in us according to which evil should not be, not only on the part of the individual, but

---

to take hold of it? Conversely, if, according to the theory of a follower of the Hegelian philosophy, only a little evil is necessary from God (absolute, world spirit), enough for the concept of good to become possible through this opposition, while more of it is merely human arbitrariness, coincidence – then all construction, all scientific understanding of world history vanishes, the dialectic of which is consummated everywhere in these extreme manifestations of evil.

in itself, least of all for eternity, and no less the fact of internal and external experience that man never overcomes the impurity of his inmost will by himself. The doctrine of the church, however, has its own significant scientific difficulties. These are mainly: the initial origin of evil from a purely good nature; the inability to do good together with freedom of the will; freedom of the will together with conversion effected only by God.

Our discussions thus far offer the premises which at least contribute to the elimination of these difficulties:

The emergence of evil in an originally innocent will is explained by the fact that in man the ethical essence and the center of personality are not absolutely one, as with God, but can be separated, the former being the constant effect of divine forces, the latter being only he himself, his own being. This center of his personality, the innermost human I, can therefore possibly be posited simply as such, instead of at the same time with and in the divine from which it is made. To wit, the person in his innermost center has a power of an absolute beginning, but also has a ground and content in the pursuit of satisfaction which is absolutely inseparable from the person. By virtue of that power of the absolute beginning, he can now maintain this in God or he can seek it in himself, detached from God. In this pursuit of satisfaction, then, lies the ground (by no means the necessity) of the first evil; in that absolute free decision of man, his reality. This is the only way to explain the occurrence of a principle that does not belong to divine creation. Evil cannot have its origin in the created being (substance of the will) of the human being, for otherwise it would come from God, but can only have its origin in the absolute causality of the human being; and it cannot have its basis in the individual instincts, desires as such, because these, as created by God, can themselves originally only be thought of as pure and innocent, but only in the universal, innermost pursuit of satisfaction.[112]

---

[112] The objection that evil cannot have its origin in the I separate from certain individual drives and desires, because this I is nothing other than empty form-movement, is based precisely on Hegel's construction of the will, which we were obliged to contest above. The I is not an abstract emptiness; it is the striving for self-satisfaction in its innermost center. There is even empirical confirmation of this. A person can tire of all particular drives (lust, honor), and yet still seek himself, his satisfaction, and despair over the fact

The doctrine whereby, in the absence of such an original act, the human will must unfold continuously from the state of indifference into the difference between good and evil according to the eternal law of its dialectic, such that the good can then be realized through the abolition of evil and indeed not develop merely as the knowledge of evil in opposition to the good but at the same time as the activity thereof, because without such activity that knowledge could not be gained, and God Himself (if there were one) would have to sin in order to become holy – this is based on the dictum that it is absolutely impossible with regard to all conceivable being that evil be recognized and excluded as a mere thought prior to all materialization; and regardless of all the expressions, it does not remove the consequence that the consummation of evil, precisely because it is an integrating element of good, simply is not to be held accountable and punishable.

Furthermore, man's incapacity for true good in his natural condition does not contradict the freedom of will that we assert for all conditions. Because according to our discussion, the will has an absolute but not unlimited causality by virtue of its freedom; it decides with freedom between good and evil only within the limits of its nature. Now good is still in the nature of man, otherwise he would have ceased to be man, but that is only a limited and obscured good, while the true good consists only in the direct bond to God, who paid for man's

---

that he no longer finds a single drive to use as a means for that general drive, which is the end. I by no means deny that in our empirical state, the general urge for satisfaction is not aroused except in certain instincts and inclinations, and whether in the first human sin this innermost detachment of the I for its own satisfaction at the same time generated a certain desire (desire, arrogance, curiosity), as it were as its body, of this I have no knowledge. Accordingly, the fall of man is originally religious, not moral. Man renounced God. As a result, however, he also loses his moral character. After he set himself as the center, his I also revolted against the order of the ethical world, against the love of his neighbor, and his materiality revolted against his spirit. He is by no means able, by virtue of his I, to cope with this I in rebellion against the center, and the material side in rebellion against the spiritual. He could only do this through divine assistance, as long as he remained in God. Accordingly, Christian doctrine is completely consistent when it characterizes the reconnection of man's real bond with God as the restoration of faith.

sin. Accordingly, it is entirely congruous to say that man in this condition is absolutely incapable of true, i.e., God-satisfying good, but that in the sphere of the good which still pertains to his nature, i.e., the sphere of what is humanly right and noble, the will freely apprehends good or evil. Therefore, even among those who are outside Christianity, the distinction between good and bad has not ceased, and the decision for the good in this sphere is also the point of contact for higher divine grace. Accordingly, the proposition that the virtues of the heathen are brilliant vices cannot be accepted in that unconditional manner.[113]

Finally, the fact that the rebirth of man is God's work does not exclude the freedom of the will as it has been described up to now. For only the transformation of the human being, the will substance, is purely God's work. This is not a mere stimulus, but a real influx of divine forces, sacred inclinations, drives, thus already a real transformation of his nature. Without such desire of the holy, with which man has really already become another – has received a different nature – no decision of the same to sanctification, conversion, etc., is possible. In relation to them, though, the will does not behave otherwise than as a "block" or a "statue" according to Luther's expression; for the will absolutely cannot decide in favor of something, it can only long for something that lies outside of its nature. It (the natural will) therefore in no way comes to the rescue itself in order to overcome its own weakness (Melanchthon), but on the contrary, it opposes and must be beaten down (Flacius). Regeneration is a new creation, and man's activity has no part in it, any more than in his first creation or his birth.

On the other hand, man's decision, through which he must now ratify, affirm, hold on to this, his transformed nature – since rebirth, like all creation, is a creation for its own life, that is only completed with the act of its own life – this decision is his deed, hence an affair of his freedom (Harleß). Man has the dual ability to allow the sacred drives that he once again receives to be granted in himself or to be pushed away, and from this, not from a divine predestination and necessity, does it happen that some are converted, others not. All this follows from the nature of the will as we have discussed it, or, to use Strigel's words, from its *modus agendi*, which is exactly the same in natural and reborn man.

Accordingly, man's conversion is by all means likewise his own work. But in

---

[113] In relation to the imputability of original sin, what is said above (§. 25 note) about the unity of the human race should not be disregarded.

terms of that universal nature of the will, such as was discussed above, devotion to the good, therefore in this case to transforming grace, is an activity of a completely different kind than in that other case, resistance to grace, the election of evil. The former is a mere instrumental activity, the latter an original one. Man's causality is not the same for good as for evil. Just as the shadow cast by an opaque body and the light emitted by a transparent body cannot be regarded as the effect of the body in the same way, so the granting of grace and the resistance to it cannot be regarded as the work of man in the same way. In the former, the divine power only grants man what his substance is and what it is or has become again; his doing is therefore absolutely without merit towards God. In the latter, on the other hand, he chooses what is not his essence merely through his own power of the absolute beginning and behaves in no way passively or receptively. His doing is therefore entirely his fault.[114]

---

[114] The deepest religious spirits everywhere have made the foundation of their doctrine the idea that the conversion of man is merely the work of God, to which man should not deserve any credit. So Augustine, Calvin, Luther, and generally the Protestant church. In this thought there is now apparently, but only apparently, the consequence that, conversely, the non-conversion of man, the rejection of grace, must be the work of God, and in order not to give up the thought itself, Augustine, Calvin, even Luther have acknowledged this consequence as well. This is the *doctrine of predestination*.

On the other hand, fear of this consequence has driven us to give up the fundamental principle itself and at the same time to present conversion as an independent work of man under various degrees. Not to mention the Pelagian, semi-Pelagian, as well as the Catholic doctrine, Protestant *synergism* taught only a cooperation of the regenerated will and only a passive ability of the same to allow itself to be determined by divine grace, but it positions itself implicitly on the premise that man (original or born again) carries the good within himself, not as a constant flow of divine forces, as constantly inhabited by God, but as a power belonging to him, although communicated by God to him, but now detached from the act of God, and so ignores the continuous immanence of God in the act of conversion. Hence the simile of the magnetic needle which, when coated with one matter, loses its direction to the north, then when coated with another, regains it again. On the other hand, church doctrine in some provisions, e.g., of the indispensability of a human act of will to bring about conversion, of the manner of human

§. 43. Imputation pertains to the state of arbitrariness or imperfect freedom. Its concept is that the person as a person is the cause of the act or, going deeper, the cause of the decision. But it is this wherever there really is will, that is, freedom of the will in the universal sense. Therefore, where freedom is lacking, imputation is ruled out, but not where there is unfreedom. If a man is materially determined by mechanical force (e.g., falling from a roof, he kills someone), or if he lacks consciousness (e.g., in a state of insanity), he does not act as a person – this is the lack of freedom. On the other hand, if he has succumbed to an evil passion (vindictiveness, lust, pyromania) without resistance, in this case he is always a person and as a person is the cause of the act; he does not lack freedom but is only unfree. But such unfreedom is precisely what is imputed. The lack of freedom has its cause in things outside of man, but unfreedom is the act of his will itself. Without freedom there can be no imputation, for without unfreedom, no sin and no crime can be committed.[115]

The lack of freedom which in accordance with this renders us unaccountable, cannot have its ground in the *nature of the decision,* because the decision is always absolutely causal. Lack of freedom just means that there was no decision

---

volitional activity (*modus agendi*) remaining the same before, during, and after rebirth, should allow itself to be corrected by the synergistic theory. So now, Harleß has taken up synergistic elements in his excellent presentation, in my opinion rightly so. In general, the basic truth and motive of religion in the doctrine of free will is that man must ascribe his sanctification to God's grace only, while his apostasy and resistance must be attributed to himself. The coherent derivation of these apparently contradicting propositions is the problem of theology, and the difficulty of clearing it up has led to the contradictory determinations which divide the denominations, regarding which one is religiously much closer than one scientifically can present.

[115] This principle of imputation has been asserted against the totally wrongheaded theories of medical writers by our important criminalists, for example by Abegg and mainly by Jarcke, *Die Lehre von der Aufhebung der Zurechnung* [The Doctrine of the Cancellation of Imputation]. By distinguishing between "lack of freedom and unfreedom" I already believed in the first edition to have established it in its innermost core. Lately this principle has been carried out again in a creditable way by Berner in his *Grundlinien der criminalistischen Imputationslehre* [Basic Outlines of the Criminalistic Imputation Theory]. I distance myself from the "speculative" additions which this writing contains.

(no act) in the true sense of the word. Furthermore, it cannot have its ground in the *constitution of the ethical being* (character) of man; for this being which he reveals in his act is precisely what is imputed. The lack of freedom can therefore only have its basis in the presupposition apart from which there is no act, which then reveals an ethical being, namely in consciousness. The *lack of consciousness*, and *only this*, is the ground for ruling out imputation.

But the consciousness which is necessary for imputation is the *consciousness of the ethical* (or civil) *significance of the act*. This includes not only the knowledge of the ethical *law* (of ethical law in general, or the law "you shall not murder," etc., in particular), but also the judgment about the *relation of the act* to the law, or more specifically about the intervention of the act in the ethical world order.[116] To this pertains the *possession and use of the mental powers* which make up *general human nature*, whether in a high or in the slightest degree.[117] Where these are absent or there is no ability to use them, there is *mental illness* which excludes imputation, e.g. imbecility, insanity. On the other hand, a wrong use of the same, which leads away from the normal conception of the objective world, but where correct use was not impossible, is not a mental illness and does not remove the imputation, e.g. superstition, mistaken ethical theory (Sand), etc. This is the boundary, for example, between folly or melancholy which are mental illnesses, and folly (e.g., someone imagines that he is the greatest and most deserving man, that all his colleagues are intriguing against him, that he has found the undiscovered key to knowledge, etc.) or melancholy which are not. Mental illnesses differ from one another in two respects, both in the way in which they displace the normal receptivity of the outside world (intellectual, ideal side) and in the way in which they affect the mind of man and arise from a modality of the mind. But all of this is a purely psychological problem. Only

---

[116] The executioner servant Hoppe (cf. Jarcke), who killed his wife, knew that murder was forbidden, but, through no fault of his own, was prevented by madness (demonic manifestations etc.) from properly evaluating the significance of *this particular* murder.

[117] To give a definition or construction of what mind is and what thought is, in order to make the question of imputation depend on it, would be most dangerous. The usual designations of the "subsumption of the particular under the universal" or "rational universality" or even the "dissolution of the sensorial in thought" are neither correct nor fruitful.

the question between the wrong *use* of the power of knowledge which man makes, and the wrong use which is a *condition* of his spiritual functions themselves, is decisive for imputation. This is the principle according to which the requirement of consciousness for imputation is determined. The application is likewise connected to empirical criteria, which still need to be brought to scientific insight.

Moral and *legal* imputation are one and the same concept, the causality of the person as a person. They differ, however, not only, as is commonly assumed, by the *object* of imputation, sin and wicked customs for the former, crime for the latter, but consequently also by their scope. Just as the legal transgression consists only in the violation of the external order by the individual external act, so legal imputation includes only the causality of the person *in the individual decision* to carry out this act at the moment of its perpetration. By contrast, moral transgression consists in inner willing, in the devastation of one's own moral being; moral imputation therefore also and mainly includes the causality of the human being in his entire *constitution of being (of character),* both when this itself is to be morally imputed, and when a single act is to be so.[118] Moral imputation is also about human insight and human vocation.

Since imputation depends on consciousness, and consciousness as a positive force is capable of infinite increase and decrease, so there are also *degrees of imputation*. Moral imputation does this everywhere and in a fluid manner, in that it fully connects to the inner state of ethical consciousness. Legal imputation only does so in certain externally recognizable diminutions of consciousness and in fixed concepts, e.g., age, mental retardation, somnolence.[119]

---

[118] So, e.g., an assassin motivated by religious or political fanaticism legally appears no different than any other criminal. On the other hand, moral imputation would have to examine the entire life process by which he came to this mode of thinking, whether and to what extent liberation from false ethics was in his power.

[119] The majority of the most respected criminalists, e.g., Jarcke, Heffter, deny degrees of imputation. My assertion of the same has recently been countered by Berner (*op. cit.*, p. 37) who asserts that it is based on a confusion between "*levels of criminal will*" and "*levels of imputation.*" I cannot admit this confusion. If there is a reduction in sentence because of youthful age which nevertheless does not exclude imputation, because of insanity

that is not imbecility, etc., then the *ground* for this mitigation or lesser criminal liability is not the lesser degree of "criminal will" but the lesser degree of consciousness, the *lesser ability to appreciate the full ethical* (or civic) *significance of the act*, thus "*diminished responsibility*," as Abegg rightly calls it. With his denial of the possibility of degrees, Berner also gets into difficulties, so that in the end he actually claims that children are *accountable* but not *punishable* (p. 100); in which case one must then ask why they are not punishable and why is childhood still listed by him as a reason for the annulment of imputation? Just as the transition from age of accountability to unaccountability, from complete imbecility to sufficient judgment, from complete somnolence to complete wakefulness in itself is undeniable, so is the gradation of accountability. Another question altogether has to do with the extent to which legislation should address this gradation, and I do not deny that it should not take the reduction of punishment because of diminished imputation too far.

Chapter 5: The Ethical World

§. 44. For morality (the ethic of the individual) we have an ideal, an image of perfection which, even if it should not be attained, is nevertheless everywhere and always the *unconditional norm* of action. But for the common state of human beings – the ethical world – we have no complete and certain ideal, and even to the degree that we have it, it is not an unconditional, indeed not an immediate norm of action. This is because the true form of the ethical world contradicts the conditions of reality, while it necessarily presupposes the ethical purity of all things as well as a quality of the physical state corresponding to this ethical condition. The individual can achieve the highest and best that he knows through the power of his will, and must make no lesser demands on himself. But the common condition, which is the product of innumerable personalities good- and ill-willed, cannot do so, and therefore ought by no means to be established by the premise that it could.

Science cannot resolve this contradiction, but it must understand it, and only by understanding it will it be able to set the limit as to the extent to which requirements for the common condition are to be imposed or rejected. Now the Christian worldview grants the key to explain this in terms of its deeper origin and its full extent. Here, man's stepping away from God is the reason that man's inner nature and the outer conditions of his earthly existence are clouded. For the individual, the pure state is now established through redemption, even if not manifestly and in all external appearances, at least in his innermost being. But for the common condition and its order, this clouded condition remains the case until the end of earthly things. For this reason, while we have a certain and complete view of the true, eternal nature of the individual (sanctification), we do not have that of the true, eternal nature of the community, for such is beyond our ability and beyond our existence. But for the same reason we cannot set the actual shape of the ethical world positively alongside its true shape for comparison, for in that case we would have to envision the latter as well as the former. Nevertheless, certain traits of incongruity to its inherent postulates can be shown in a negative way. For this we have a standard in the deepest basic ethical vision that forms our human essence, which is further supported by the intimations of revelation. We find such traits of the incongruity of the actual common condition with the true shape of the ethical world with regard to its *ethical norms*, with regard to its *actual life relations*, and with regard to its *ruling power*.

§. 45. As far as the ethical norms of the common human condition are concerned, the relationship between the shape of the ethical world (objective ethic) and the ethical behavior of the individual human being, as our innermost basic moral vision attests, is necessarily a relationship of unity, i.e., *homogeneity* and *mutual permeation*. Even though it be common uniform order, the shape of the ethical world should be the product of the free (inward) fulfillment of all individuals, for it is only a truly ethical world if all the individual actions in which it is realized proceed from the ethical volition of the doer.[120] Likewise, the content of both would have to be in agreement and mutual fulfillment, so that the ethical behavior of the individual could only freely individualize, and intensively increase to infinity, those ethical principles which the objective way of life would contain in its more general terms (§. 26). In real life, ethical public opinion already relates in a similar manner to the ethical action of the individual. They are different, the latter is independent, but they interpenetrate without a boundary.

Nevertheless, in the empirical condition, the fulfillment of subjective ethical behavior (morality), contrary to its true idea, is incidental – here it is fulfilled, there not – and therefore the preservation of the objective existence of the ethical world cannot emerge from it, cannot be dependent on it. Instead, in order to maintain itself the ethical world must exercise a power that rests only within itself independently of the will of the individual, indeed in opposition to him, that is, externally compelling him. For the sake of this externality alone, the law of the ethical community (objective ethic) cannot take up the true full requirements of the same in itself, since these refer absolutely to truly ethical, i.e., free fulfillment. In addition, the will of the whole (be it the legal representatives thereof, be it the will of the whole directly) likewise lacks purity, and for this reason the individual must have a sphere of complete independence and separation from it. Therefore, the objective formation of life contains ethical ideas only at their most distant, outlying boundaries (as shown in Book II [*Principles of*

[120] This is not only true of a state of perfection (the promised kingdom of God), in which the limitations of human nature are abolished, but is an absolutely necessary assumption, as is abstracting away evil. Even so, evil cannot be considered by an impartial person to belong to the *eternal idea* of the world.

Law], §. 6, only from their negative side). It not only lets loose individualization, but it has to let loose and sanction that which the ethical law of the individual (morality) forbids: the immoral, the selfish. This shape of the empirical condition is that in which the law [Gesetz] of the ethical community (the objective ethic) – *law* proper [das Recht] – consists.

Through this separation from the inner will of the individual, law itself becomes *external* for the community (which ultimately consists only of individuals). It detaches itself as an independent power (*vis inertiae*) from the common consciousness from which it has emerged. It is therefore not constantly, directly being molded by the common consciousness, but continues of itself even if that consciousness has long since become something else – this is the *external traditional character*[121]; and it dominates the condition not as the constant actual inner valuation of the community, but as an existing abstract rule that often contradicts the inner justice of the individual case – the *formal character*. What can be called the *materiality* of law is this, namely that it is not something that is continuously ruled by the spirit of community, its flow, but something that is rigid, fixed in itself (cf. n. 122 below).

Thus, in the empirical condition, subjective ethical behavior, *morality*, and

---

[121] This is the truth in Mephistopheles' statement:

Law and rights pass on
like an eternal disease;
they drag themselves from generation to generation
and move gently from place to place.
Reason becomes nonsense, benevolence a plague:
Woe to you that you are a grandson!
Of the right with which we are born
Unfortunately, that is never the question.
[Goethe, *Faust,* I, verses 1972ff.]

The brochure [by Bernoulli], *Göttliches Recht und der Menschen Satzung* [Divine Law and Human Statutes], Basel 1839, seeks to liberate law both from its external traditional and its formal character. Although this is the longing of a noble mind, it misunderstands the restrictions of the actual human condition.

objective ethical behavior, *law*, are *heterogeneous* and *separate*. Morality has the character of *accidental fulfillment*, law has the character of *externality* and *limited* (only *negative) content*. So, the former has forfeited certainty of fulfillment, the latter inwardness and with it real ethical behavior. And the law in many cases allows and sanctions what morality forbids. This is not just the unfolding of the ethical world on both sides in the spheres of the individual and of the whole, in line with its nature (§. 25), but rather a division and laceration of it.

§. 46. Furthermore, the actual life relations which are the subject matter of the legal system are also in a clouded state. It is not that the substrate is of the same material nature, for such necessarily has pertained to the earthly condition from the beginning, and it is only from the kingdom of God that the Christian faith expects the transfiguration thereof into spirituality.[122] Rather, as reality shows, these relationships are permeated by evil itself and by its consequences. One of the consequences of this is the curse on labor, accompanied by the glaring chasm between the various classes and, above all, widespread poverty ("pauperism"), conditions which none, our age least of all, can consider to answer to the idea of human communal existence, and which nevertheless no human wisdom is able completely to banish. To this also pertain death and the succession of the generations. Evil itself, however, expresses itself for the common condition as a power in injustice, in crime, in the subjugation of peoples through war, in tyranny and rebellion. How far conditions correspond to reality in their pure form, how far they are only the result of the earthly necessary material base, or how far they are corrupted, alienated from their original purpose, and above all how they would be if that corruption had ceased, are all questions that are as idle as they are insoluble. In the latter respect, however, this power of evil itself must again serve as a substrate in order to manifest the principle of law as an ethical order in a manner that is all the more elevated and victorious. This is the significance of civil punishment, of just war, of heroic greatness.

---

[122] "Material" is by no means to be understood as the physical. The body is not an antithesis to the spirit, but rather its eternally necessary organ. Rather, material is that quality of the physical by which, instead of being a consistently controlled tool of the spirit, it has an existence and a power in itself that is not obedient to the spirit, even strives against that.

§. 47. Finally, the *ruling and unifying power* of the common human condition does not correspond to its idea either. Unification and common rule, without which human community can never realize a common goal, an ethical world, can, according to its idea, be none other than the *absolute ethical power* itself, which at the same time is the substance of man. From the present standpoint of philosophy this should not be denied; the only question that can be asked is whether this power is the world substance or the personal God. If the former is the case, then of course the current state is how it should be and how it will remain forever. If, on the other hand, our above-mentioned justifications are correct, then human community, if it is to be ruled by the primordial ethical power, must be ruled by the personal God, be it directly, be it through organs suffused with God. In that case, *theocracy* is the true condition. In the given condition, however, this rule is represented by human organs in independent power apart from divine influence, be it a prince, an assembly, or the majority of people in general, and the contrary holds true, any alleged theocracy is inadmissible. This is the earthly empirical *state*. The concept of the state describes this purely human rule in contrast to theocracy.

§. 48. The ethical world in this incongruity with its original purpose is the *civil order* (*status civilis*). This is the one expression for *law and state* together. It is not, therefore, that the civil order, law and state are essentially a consequence of sin, but rather that they are essentially the ethical goal, the former the legislation, the latter the governing of the ethical world which are entrusted to human community; only in their empirical form are they the result of sin.[123] The civil order therefore on the one hand forms the opposite of the idea of a *state of nature*, that is, a coexistence without rules and ordinances, while on the other it no less forms the antithesis of the *ethical world in its true condition*, of which it at best is a mere surrogate. The civil order is thus an intermediate stage between the kingdom of nature and the kingdom of God. The former is a purely material kingdom, the

---

[123] Even the rationalistic philosophy of law in the epoch before Hegel deduced the state from sin without being conscious of it. Because people of their own accord do not obey the law of reason, which dictates mutual restriction of freedom, a society is required to force them to do so. But why do rational beings not obey the law of reason of their own accord?

latter a purely ethical personal kingdom (§. 27). The civil order, by contrast, is an ethical kingdom insofar as it is realized in the actions of personal beings, but it is nevertheless a kingdom of external law, ultimately supported and maintained by physical power and consummated in external actions and conditions. But what is specific about it, which distinguishes it from both – in line with its origin – is the potential for evil, the constant possibility that it itself may fall away from the law which it has the task of enforcing – unjust laws and unjust rulers.

The rationalistic philosophy of law wrongly sets off the civil order only against the lower realm of nature, where it appears as the realm of freedom and reason, instead of also against the higher realm, the kingdom of God, which makes it clear how much it falls short of the true kingdom of freedom and reason. In particular, Hegel's mode of conception actually reverses the true relationship in that it regards the expression of ethical laws in external actions and institutions, materialized ethicality as it were, to be higher than that which is inwardly active, i.e., as the personal rule of God and human fulfillment.

Things are similar with the congregation of God as with the ethical world. It is true that in this sphere, according to Christian faith, there is a direct divine influence both for the individual and for the whole. But this divine influence in itself is not fully present, but only shines through a powerful sensorial presence, while its result for the individual is always dependent on his subjective belief; Christ's kingdom is not manifest here below. That is why the congregation of God in the empirical state is without visible divine guidance and subject to the possibility of apostasy, and at the same time maintains itself independently of the actual divine suffusion of its members as an external institution through confession and constitution. The congregation of God in this form is *the church*. The medieval hierarchy wrongly applies this when it asserts the remoteness from the true theocratic state in relation to the earthly state but ignores the fact that this applies no less to the earthly church.

It is precisely for this reason that the ethical world is not exhausted by the civil order, nor the congregation of God exhausted by the church. That is to say, not only are individual mores and individual belief a factor in them apart from what is eternally necessary, but also a community of mores, a community of faith, remains as a spiritual element which does not shade into the objective formations of state and the church, but is always free and spiritual, and for that very reason is also subject to change, which hovers over it.

§. 49. Because of these traits of inconsistency with its purpose and true idea, the civil order can never be perfect, but only a pursuit of perfection, similar to science ("philosophy"). That is why Christian revelation is indifferent to it. This revelation provides regulations governing man's behavior in relation to the existing order, but it does not give instructions about the formation of this order. No divine image of the civil order is given, because the way it is, is not of God. But within the boundary given by those traits, enhancement and approximation is the task.

This realization must therefore by no means make one indifferent to the condition of law and the state constitution, any more than to science, which we also recognize as being "piecemeal," or to temporal life in general. Enthusiasm for the establishment or maintenance of a prosperous state of order and freedom not only is not alien to it but is required. This is the only way for it to ensure that man stands over these endeavors with his eternal existence, and that we harbor no meaningless expectations of a perfect political situation vouchsafing the salvation of the peoples, no more than a philosophy that will penetrate us with new discoveries or mathematical certainty about eternal things or satisfy the longing of the human heart. It will also maintain the sobriety whereby politics acknowledges "the measure of given conditions." Above all, it will oppose the unlimited power of the prince no less than the unlimited power of the people, but rather make them inclined to the condition in which manifold human positions are secured and manifold organs are open to power and influence on the public, so that each force placed in the community by God finds its free development, by which the temptation inherent in every human position finds its moderation in the strength of the other positions.

Therefore, the civil order, like science, is only a fragment of what is to come, and when the perfect is there, then the fragment will cease. But it is our belief that one day this perfect will come about. Then the kingdom will come "when he shall have put down all rule and all authority and power" (1 Cor. 15:24). The great construct of state and church will cease, for God himself will be the state and the church as, according to John, there is no more sun in the heavenly Jerusalem, because God Himself is the sun. The transformation from the earthly state to the eternal one will take place "in a moment, in the twinkling of an eye, at the last trumpet" [1 Corinthians 15:52]. For the most elevated events are acts of God, not mere developments. History contains only a preparatory development for this final transformation, not one that merges into this of itself; for it only brings about the development of human powers, but not their essential purification or elevation (§. 17). It is from this point of view that the further development of social institutions is to be considered and appreciated. Accordingly, it should be a constant approximation whereby the general knowledge of what is right increasingly gains the upper hand over the accidental will of rulers, by their being hemmed in with barriers, by the formation of various organs and institutions, by the purely moral, unwitting but nevertheless formidable power of spiritual communication and community. But there can be no progress where individual people are kept less and less under the discipline of what is right, or where the opinion of the masses determines the authorities directly and externally through the force of the masses. Because the sinful nature of human beings and the mass of human beings always remains unchanged and always requires defensive barriers. These barriers will only fall when the earthly ceases. In the same way, many advances are required which are brought about by increasing population, rapprochement of nations, increase in skills, fluency of communication; but the basic circumstances of the social condition are unchangeable and always require the same care and stance. Therefore, make no mistake about it: as long as man is born in pain and comes helplessly into the world, as long as hunger requires us to eat, illness and suffering wear us down, and death is our inheritance, so long as well will the institution of public life have to pay its toll to *materiality*. So long is it foolish to unsettle the solid ground of landed property for the benefit of economic potential [zum Vortheil der Kapacitäten], to open the boundaried seats of settled residence and mutual sustenance to an unlimited influx. So long is it foolish to exchange the ancient power of royalty for the will or the conviction of the people, to surrender the faith of the church to the accidental opinion of men; so long above all is it foolish to expect purity of morals, the dignity and sanctity of public life from *voluntary fulfillment*.

§. 50. Christian consciousness has always regarded the civil order in the character which it in reality has, as the consequence of the fall of man. Thus above all Augustine, who, however, goes far beyond the boundaries in that he does not recognize in it the divine order which always remains in law and the state regardless of all turbidity, but understands by them the earthly kingdom (*civitas terrena*), to which he opposes the kingdom of God (*civitas Dei*), and alternately understands by it the kingdom of the wicked and the institution of the state, the latter generally referred to as a need and a work of the earthly-minded.[124] This false appraisal of the state found no followers, but the idea that he expresses that all rule and authority among men is the result of sin[125] is found throughout the Middle Ages, even among political writers.[126] It pertains no less to the Protestant church, although the Reformation, in extreme contrast to Augustine, saw as its task the vindication of the worldly authority with the same divine character as that of the spiritual. Luther declared the state to be the "kingdom of sin," i.e., that it exists only as a result of sin and as a means and barrier against it.[127] On

---

[124] Augustine, *De Civitate Dei,* XIV.5; XV.1.

[125] Augustine, *De Civitate Dei,* XIX.15.

[126] e.g. Marsilius of Padua: "In quo (sc. statu innocentiae) siquidem permansisset (Adam), nec sibi nec suae posteritati necessaria fuisset officiorum civilium institutio" [If Adam had remained in the state of innocence, neither he nor his posterity would have needed to institute civil office] (in Goldast, II, 161, 171). Petrus de Andlus (in the introduction to his *Works*): "Omnis vero humani regiminis et superioritatis necessitas ex peccato per venit" [The necessity for all human regiment and superiority came from sin].

[127] Luther (Wittenb.) *Genes.* II. 30: "Politia autem ante peccatum nulla fuit, neque enim ea opus fuit. Est enim Politia remedium necessarium naturae corruptae. Oportet enim cupiditatem constringi vinculis legum et poenis, ne libere vagetur. Ideo Politiam recte dixeris regnum peccati, sicut Paulus Mosen quoque vocat ministrum mortis et peccati. Hoc enim unum et praecipuum agit Politia, ut peccatum arceat. Sicut Paulus dicit: Potestas gerit gladium in vindictam malorum. Sic igitur homines non essent per peccatum mali facti, Politia nihil fuisset opus, sed Adam vixisset cum posteris suis in summa tranquillitate, ac plus effecisset moto uno digito, quam nunc omnes gladii, cruces, secures possunt efficere" [Civil government did not exist before sin, nor was there any need for it. Civil government is the remedy for corrupt nature. Cupidity must be restrained by laws and punishment, not be free to go astray. For this reason, civil government is called the regime of sin, just as Paul called Moses' ministry the ministry of death and sin. Civil government deals with this one most important thing, to restrain sin. As Paul said, the state wields the sword to punish evildoers. If men did not do evil because of sin, there

the other hand, Gerhard, the representative of Lutheran dogmatics, with deeper insight distinguishes between government and subordination in general and in the specific existing form, whereby only the latter is the peculiarity of the fallen state.[128] Even the first founder of today's Enlightenment, Thomasius, examines in a more detailed elaboration than can be approved what the conditions of the paradisiacal state would have been in contrast to the civil state that came about through Adam's fall, and denies as definitely and generally as Luther the state for the first.[129] This consistent Christian appreciation of the civil order has only been lost since the emphatic rule of rationalism; and with the reawakening of the Christian faith in more recent times it has returned and has been scientifically asserted in many cases by Catholic writers, but among Protestants especially by Göschel.

But where there is no Christian consciousness, the deeper minds have not been able to withstand the dissatisfaction with the empirical state and the longing for that true, eternal nature of the common human condition. This, but also only this, explains the motive of so many conceptions of the state drafted with a noble mind which for all that are yet untrue. They recognize the true postulates

---

would be no need of civil government, but Adam would have lived with his posterity in tranquility and accomplish more with the movement of one finger than any number of swords, crosses, or axes today].

[128] Gerhard, *Loci theol.* (Cotta) XIII. 240: "Atque haec argumenta firmiter probant, talem quandam despoticam dominationem et servilem subjectionem, cum repugnantia voluntatis et molestia conjunctam, qualis post lapsum in imperiis politicis adparet, in statu innocentiae locum haud quaquam habuisse; ex eo tamen inferri nequit, omnem omnino ordinem, omnem gubernationem subjectionem ἁπλῶς et late acceptam ab innocentiae statu semotam fuisse" [In addition, this argument firmly proves that such a servile subjection, a kind of despotic dominion, joined with the resistance of the will and vexation, which is provided by political empire after the fall, had no place in the state of innocence; but it cannot be inferred from this that all order, all government was removed from the state of innocence].

[129] Thomasius, *Institut. jurispr. divinae* lib. I. cap. 2. Pufendorf rightly polemicizes against those detailed investigations into whether parental authority would have existed in Paradise, and the like, in his pamphlet against Valentinus Albertus (see appendix to the edition of his *jus nat.*).

in their innermost being: the *complete unification of human beings in an ethical kingdom* and the *complete freedom and self-determination of the individual*, and, since they have no otherworldly realm of perfection before their souls and ignore the depravity of human nature, expect this of the earthly condition, where it is impossible, and of the earthly state, the calling whereof it is not. Thus, Plato's basic idea is the complete unity of the state through the merging of all individual wills in it. His republic is therefore of much greater *ethical* than *political* significance. He depicts the state as such in a manner that is contrary to nature. But a transfiguration hovers over the book: the inkling that the true human condition is only where the individual gives himself completely and without reservation to the harmony of a higher ethical whole; but this ethical whole, in which man should merge with his whole existence, is not the earthly state. Similarly, on the other hand, Rousseau's basic idea is the complete freedom and self-determination of the individual. What he expresses as a problem, a condition in which everyone remains absolutely free, so that when he obeys the community he obeys only himself, is the deep eternal truth; but it is palpable folly to regard the *contrat social* and the rule of the *volonté générale* as the solution to the problem.[130] To obey the *rational* "general will," however, is not a limitation on the individual, for thereby he only obeys his own will, which according to its innermost nature only desires the rational. But *this* "general will," the essence of which is to be formed through the competition of all individual wills, gives as little guarantee of its rationality as the will of an autocrat. Those who do not agree with this general will, which is the result of a numerical majority or energetic party power, can and indeed will for the most part be precisely the entitled and the ethically understanding, and can it be said of them that they only obey themselves because they voted and were outvoted, because they fought and were

---

[130] "Trouver une forme d'association, qui défende et protège de toute la force commune la personne et les biens de chaque associé, et par laquelle chacun *s'unissant à tous, n'obéisse pourtant qu'à lui-même*, et reste aussi libre qu'auparavant? Tel est *le problème* fondamental, dont le *contrat social donne la solution*" [Find a form of association, which defends and protects with the full common power the person and the goods of each associate, and by which each being united with all, nevertheless obeys only himself, and remains also freer than before? This is the fundamental problem, of which the social contract provides the solution]. Rousseau, *du Contr. Social,* lib. I, ch. 6.

defeated, or that they are not subject to anyone (*assujetti à personne*) because they are subject only to the plural or the more energetic and clever? Even with the difference in human conditions, namely the difference between the poor and the rich, is it to be expected from this *volonté générale* that it will satisfy evenly for these different situations, so that everyone, poor and rich, only obeys himself, at least only his interest when he obeys it? The problem whereby the individual by obeying the community obeys only himself cannot be solved otherwise than by the fact that the common will and the individual will want the same *materially*, i.e., by the fact that they both want what is ethically reasonable everywhere, and, as the fact shows and Christian knowledge explains, this will never occur on earth. On the other hand, the merely formal unification of the common will and the individual will, in that the latter is formed through the equal constitutional competition of all, is not only no solution, but not even an approach to the problem. The teaching of Rousseau and the implementation of the revolution are therefore nothing other than a caricature of the freedom which the Christian faith anticipates. The matter is similar regarding the political theories that proceed from the equal distribution of goods. The full satisfaction of life for every person is certainly an eternal postulate of the common condition. But just as Rousseau overlooked *sin* in his calculus, so did he likewise overlook the consequence of sin, *labor*, which lies between man and goods, which can only be set in motion by reference back to the person, to property.

Indeed, the Christian sects or denominations which wish to establish a "reign of the saints" on earth and do not recognize the existing civil order for Christians because it is administered by dishonest people as appointed by succession and property and electoral institutions, and tolerates impurity, are entangled in the same delusion. They recognize the clouding of the earthly condition through sin; but they believe that the grace of redemption extends not only to the individual and the inwardly hidden but also to the external common state, and in such an obvious and visible way that the true constitution is restored or at least made accessible. This deception is a temptation during every turbulent Christian era, as in the early days of the church and in the early days of the Reformation. The apostles oppose it with the statement: "All government is from God," "Honor the king," just as the German reformers do when they emphasize that the civil order (*magistratus politicus*) has God's authorization. Calvin does so in like manner.[131] Even the Catholic hierarchy, as mentioned before, leans, as do these Protestant factions, on the opposite usage, on the erroneous assumption that through a divine miracle, earthly impurity is removed from the church also in terms of its *external earthly side*, its constitution and church government.

Everywhere, then, where a ray of deeper longing has fallen into the soul, there the conflict between the true eternal requirement and reality shows itself. It is a commonly-held error, contrary to pure evangelical knowledge, to believe that this conflict is entirely solvable here on earth; it leads to the temptation to establish false institutions. By contrast, Hegel explains the conflict itself as a delusion; actual conditions correspond to eternal reason. Like Rousseau, he restricts human existence to this world, but he does not place the postulate of the inner moral basic vision (either according to the aspect that Plato conceived, or Rousseau) as a standard for this world, according to which he likewise strives to transform it from the ground up, but the other way round: he makes the actual condition as it is into the measure of the ethical postulate. That the absolutely reasonable is already absolutely realized in reality is the presupposition on which his whole conception and all his results are based. Just as he regards the activity of evil to be an eternally necessary element of the ethical idea, precisely because reality contains it inextricably, so in the two ethical areas, morality and law, he considers precisely the characters that run counter to its idea (§. 45) to be its essence. For him the innermost, eternal concept of morality is "contingency" and the mere, never-fulfilled "ought," that of law (or "ethical behavior") is externality and materialization, that is, the rule which is realized by individuals apart from, indeed often against their will. The architectonic of the state, which presents the idea of a general [will] and the particular as intertwined, is for him the solution to Rousseau's problem. That this general will by no means always desires what is right, that people really only in a poor way find their right in the state and develop their freedom in it, that the great mass is left to their miserable existence, that the state, this "reality of the ethical spirit," has not insignificant forces pushing for control in court cabal and backroom bribery and demagogic agitation, that selfish interests provide not insignificant supports of its maintenance and its equilibrium – none of this is any shortcoming for the deeper philosophical knowledge. Hegel brought to bear a deeper and truer insight into the

---

[131] Cf. Book IV of his *Institutes.*

essence of the state than Rousseau. But the eternal human longing for true liberation that prevails in all those aberrations does not exist for him at all. Hegel's later school has completely returned to Rousseau; it is annoyed by the master's philosophical task of merely grasping life optimistically instead of shaping it according to a higher ideal.

So three standpoints stand out: resignation in the face of the evils and infirmities of reality and of the ordinary, as if these themselves were the eternally reasonable – emotional involvement with regard to the true eternal postulates of human nature, whereby, however, the limits of earthly conditions are misunderstood, are considered to be absolutely realizable, the realization of which is necessarily pursued in the wrong way – insight that these undeniable eternal postulates are to be pursued only approximately in this world and only according to the measure of the given conditions.

Chapter 6: Justice and Punishment

§. 51. The content of the ethical requirements and commandments, and of the ethical ideas, is manifold: love of neighbor, conjugal love and faithfulness, piety, continence, vocational loyalty, civic loyalty, patriotism, and the like. But there is one idea which gives them all the seal of inviolability – the *idea of justice.*

Justice is the idea of the ethical world as such; that is, the idea on which its existence and maintenance are based. For it describes the relation of ethical power and authority (of God and of the state) to the free personalities (human beings) who are under the command thereof. This relation, however, consists in the unalterable maintenance both of *their command* and of the *sphere* of existence and entitlement *vouchsafed to people,* at the same time. For the concept of justice is everywhere none other than the *unbreakable maintenance of a given ethical order*, but the person and their right are themselves an eternal principle of the ethical order, no less than the commandment that is to be fulfilled through it. Justice is therefore expressed in two ways: as a *protective power* that inviolably guarantees the right granted to other people as well as to itself, and as a *retributive power* according to which, depending on fulfillment or transgression – as these lie in human freedom – *reward* or *punishment* is imposed, in order to reveal the eternal rule of the ethical order through both. These two relations and only they, then, necessarily lie in the essence of justice, and indeed in an inseparable unity.

Accordingly, the idea of justice is not limited to the area of law; it belongs to the ethical world in all its spheres and levels; where there is ethical order, there is justice. According to the highest internal sphere of the ethical world, justice is *divine;* it is God's commandment (religion and morality), which is upheld by the eternal judgment of God or by the nemesis, which already rules over earthly fortunes. In the lower, external sphere of the ethical world, justice is *civil;* it is the law and regard of the state, upheld by the civil court. Transgression in the former is sin,[132] in the latter is crime. But everywhere the reward consists not so

---

[132] *Sin* signifies the transgression against a higher *personal* will, as distinct from *transgression of mores* [Unsittlichkeit]. The latter as such is a deplorable bad [üble] quality but does not call for punishment if it is not at the same time a sin. See above, §. 34.

much in special honors than in participation in the ethical order itself. Membership in the kingdom of God and peace of soul are the reward of those who keep God's command, and loyal subjects find their reward in the protection of the law and in the right of, and honor as, a compatriot. The idea of justice is therefore one and the same here and there and has the same effect; it is therefore also an idea entirely common to theology and jurisprudence.

§. 52. Justice has its origin in the supreme personality, who *immutably wills His own holy will* and nonetheless grants the other wills under it their freedom and right in the fullest measure. The wonderful world arrangement whereby violation of the commandment is permitted and yet the commandment is irrevocably sealed, can only be explained from this. Only for this reason does justice move eternally around the two poles by which nothing is forgiven a holy order and yet the right and freedom of man remain unabridged. Justice is also only the attribute of personality. We cannot ascribe justice to the impersonal substance of Spinoza or Hegel; likewise, we ascribe necessity, immutability, but not justice to a law that is inevitably self-fulfilling. In fact, if the supreme world cause were really impersonal, the idea of justice could not exist at all. Accordingly, however, justice is attributed to personality only in its relation as the will of the ruler towards subordinates, namely free subordinates; besides, faithfulness to oneself is not the same as justice. Justice therefore presupposes a kingdom; that is, the rule of a personal will over personalities. We ascribe justice in this original and objective sense only to the higher one who imposes or maintains the law, first to God, then to the prince or other authorities, the legislator, judge, father, etc., but never to the human being, the citizen as such, never to equal versus equal. But justice is used in another, subjective sense, namely as the *steadfast fulfillment of the commandment* on the part of the subordinate, as the former describes the *steadfast maintenance of the commandment* on the part of the ruler. This is especially the biblical usage. Yet as this confirms, everywhere there is the inviolability of a given order which, apart from its content (benevolence, patience, continence), merely as such constitutes the concept of justice.

§. 53. The idea of *protective justice* appears in its clarity and definiteness only in the *Roman world epoch*, because only here does subjective entitlement receive its full recognition. The expression of this is the "suum cuique" in the sense that everyone gets what is *his entitlement*. This expression excludes what is due to a person not as his entitlement, as the granting of his will, but as a *standard of his actions,* to wit, punishment. The *law of the Athenians*, by contrast, is predominantly determined by the idea of retributive justice. It corresponds to their whole principle of life. This is namely by no means exhaustively indicated by the idea of beauty or artistic harmony but is based on a far-reaching view of the ethical world order. What fills them in their innermost being is the thought of *nemesis*, the thought that punishment and ruin unstoppably, inevitably follow upon human guilt according to eternal order. Just as this thought has a moving effect in their poetry, so is retributive justice the principle of their law. That is why the most ancient Athenian legislator had his laws "written in blood," because even the "slightest sacrilege deserves death." That is why they developed like nowhere else a complete system of retaliation, a system of public rewards and punishments. That is why even the administration of civil justice, which by its nature serves protective justice, bears at least the form of retribution with them, namely, with the exception of the diadikasías,[133] there is no suit without ἀδίκημά [misdeed], i.e., not for the sake of the right of the plaintiff, but for the sake of the injustice of the defendant, and the outcome of the lawsuit is τίμημα (penalty). That is why the courts stand as a higher power even over the sovereign people's assembly, not for the protection of acquired rights, but as representatives of the laws and ideas of the state. That is why Plato is unable to grasp the "suum cuique" in any other sense than to allocate rewards and punishments according to merit, namely, to do good to friends and bad to enemies.

§. 54. In terms of its idea, *retributive justice* is the establishment of the empire, i.e., the glory of the ethical power (of God or the state) through the destruction or torment of those who have revolted against it. Through the transgression (sin or crime) the perpetrator makes himself a lord over the order of God or the state; he establishes another kingdom of his own in the ethical world. This is why the

---

[133] ["(διαδικασία; diadikasía). In Athens a judicial procedure aimed at organizing the legal situation without plaintiffs and defendants." Thür, Gerhard (Graz), "Diadikasia", in: *Brill's New Pauly*, Antiquity volumes edited by Hubert Cancik and Helmuth Schneider, English Edition by: Christine F. Salazar, Classical Tradition volumes edited by: Manfred Landfester, English Edition by: Francis G. Gentry. Consulted on 26 November 2020 <http://dx.doi.org/10.1163/1574-9347_bnp_e316330>.]

higher power of God or of the state must prove itself to him, in the external world as in the consciousness both of the human community and the evildoer; it must annihilate him or otherwise let its gravity be felt, overcome his will by depriving him of what he wants as will, satisfaction, and what he does not want, pain, restriction, so that only its kingdom exists and nothing else – this is *punishment.* Such is not supposed to uphold or restore the *law* – that would be impossible, the transgression thereof is irrevocable – but its supremacy [Herrlichkeit]. According to its concept, justice does not demand that there be no violation of the law, it only demands that no unlawful will assert itself and gain the victory in spite of the higher order.

It is the eternal law of righteousness with regard to evil – sin or crime – that punishment inevitably follows; this is expressed by every uninhibited consciousness. But the difficulty for analytical thought is this: how can a restoration of the violated order lie in the infliction of an evil, which the punishment undeniably is, on the violator? The fact that a second evil comes into the world does not remove the incongruity which the first contains. But justice (in the objective sense) does not consist in the fact that no evil comes into the world, but in the fact that the rule of ethical power in the ethical kingdom is inviolably preserved. Every act involves a form of rule; there is an infinite real power in it, an absolute effect. What is inactive, passive, is what obeys; action is rule. If a person acts against the law, he possesses a supremacy in the ethical world against the ethical power to which that world submits, according to which it is to be shaped. It is not the destruction of this act itself, the undoing of it, that justice demands, but the supremacy which lies in the act. If this is broken, the incongruity is resolved. But this supremacy is precisely the supremacy of the perpetrator, so the higher supremacy of ethical power must be validated in him. This can only happen by making him a mere ruled, passive person, someone who does not act but is subject to acting as an object, and this is *suffering* (as the word already says), pain, death. Man wants to exist as a personality, to develop himself, to be satisfied, in himself, in the free use of his existence and his powers, as well as in the effect on the objects outside himself. That is the substance of his will itself (§. 37). He can and should also have such existence and satisfaction in accordance with the ethical power to which he is subject and by which he is. In the same way, however, in accordance with its immutability, he must perceive it as hostile, taking from him existence, free development, and satisfaction, as he steps out of it and makes himself master, detached from it. The rapport between transgression and punishment is precisely the innermost personality itself, this being the author of the act and at the same time a being that demands satisfaction. In the kingdom of personality everything goes back to the person as the center and totality. The act as such has no meaning, but only the personality from which it proceeds, in its whole being, and this comes into consideration entirely as person, as the subject both imposed upon by the ethic and satisfaction-seeking. It must settle up in its entire innermost being: what it owes on the one side, it must atone on the other. Considered more deeply, there lies in the evil which the perpetrator suffers, a real abrogation of the act in terms of its ethical world. The punishment of the offender shows in a real way that the ethical order is the master. Thus, the evil itself, by being pressed to the ground, must serve to glorify ethical power. The execution of civil punishment is a glory of the ethical order, notwithstanding its grave appearance.

Hence punishment is carried out for the sake of justice. The punishment cannot have a mere future end (that no crimes occur in future) and cannot be a mere factual mechanical means; but the accomplished act plain and simple demands punishment for an ethical reason. Where there is justice, punishment must follow upon evil, and conversely there can be no punishment except as a necessary command of justice. This is the specific and general concept of punishment, and if the evil which the criminal suffers at the hands of the state should be something else – deterrence, self-defense – at least it should no longer be called punishment.

But for this reason, punishment is by no means *revenge*. For revenge is based on the infringement of a personality in its subjective satisfaction, while punishment is based on the infringement of a higher ethical will as such, or an ethical order; and revenge seeks the suffering of the offender for the sake of suffering (invests personal feeling in it), whereas God or the state do not punish the violator so that he may suffer, but make him suffer so that he may be punished; revenge has no limit but pleasure in suffering, while punishment is subject to necessity both in measure and in inception. Nor is punishment in general, and the punishment of the state, *retribution in the ordinary sense;* for it does not exist so that the perpetrator can experience again what he has done to others (or to God or the state), but so that his will does not assert its rule against the order which maintains ethical power. It is by no means the same or a similar effect which the perpetrator carries out and which is now being carried out against him, that he "infringed" the order and is now "infringed" again, as Hegel puts it (which is merely a word-game with the different meanings of the word "infringement" [Verletzung]). Its effect on ethical power and order is quite different from the effect of this power and order back onto him; the former does not do injury in the emotions, in the feeling of existence, or in the pursuit for satisfaction, like the latter does, but is rebellion, disobedience, transgression. The relation does not lie in injury and counter-injury, but in presumption of the will and suppression of the will. This also has its consequences for the type and measure of the punishment. If the punishment were retribution in that common sense, then the point of comparison would be the pain itself. That which other people (or that which God's will or the state) suffered through the transgressor, he would have to suffer again; this is the idea underlying the *lex talionis*. According to the true meaning of punishment, however, the point of comparison is the supremacy in the spiritual kingdom which is validated by both acts, transgression and punishment. In this, punishment must be equal to the transgression and surmount it. In the way and to the extent that man has rebelled, he must also be suppressed.

If, accordingly, the essence of punishable justice is the same in the ethical and the legal spheres, its expression is different in these two areas. The violation in the former has the ethical commandments as object, the latter the legal order; in the former it is already accomplished through the inner will, in the latter only through the act performed externally; in the former the punishment consists at the same time in an inward evil, pain of the soul, sensation of divine wrath in the mind, in the latter merely in an outwardly physically inflicted evil. Ethical punishment, punishment in the kingdom of God, is eternal and intensely infinite. For in God all relationships are absolute. Neither can His holiness endure the slightest defilement, nor His righteousness the slightest opposition to His order. There is no transition from less to more between devotion to God on the one hand and detachment from Him and highhandedness on the other. The individual manifestations of human sin are of a finite nature, contain less and more, and the evils which follow them partly through the natural order itself and partly through divine disposition (nemesis) are of a finite nature, and are greater or smaller. But *the* sin of man himself, of which all this is only an expression, is infinite, and so is the punishment that man owes before God's judgment.

By contrast, in the civil order, which presupposes the sinful, imperfect state of the human race, conditions are relative, there is a gradual sequence of crimes and punishments. It is true that here too there is an absolute crime, the completely free (premeditated) murder, as the crime against the most sacred good that the civil order has to protect according to God's command, and there is also an absolute punishment for this, the execution of the criminal. But even the death penalty, seen from the standpoint of eternal power, is only relative and fleeting: relative, for since it affects mortals it only deprives a number of years, and fleeting, for it is a mere instantaneous act of annihilation; but the punishment in the ethical kingdom is the eternal experience of the destructive wrath of God.

§. 55. For Plato, justice consists in the fact that every force and activity (in man or in the state) should retain its proper sphere and not encroach on that of the others. This concept gives one side of justice, namely the inviolability of once established relations, but it lacks precisely what is specific and innermost to justice: the principle of personality, both the respect of the will of the ruler (law) and the right of those who obey.

Medieval Aristotelian ethics differentiates between *justitia universalis* and *particularis*, the former as the epitome of all virtue (similar to the biblical concept of justice), the latter only referring to relations to other people. The latter is again differentiated into *justitia commutativa* and *distributiva*, the former relating to transactions (contracts, compensation), the latter to the allocation of reward and punishment. This theory contains an improper combination of *legality* [Rechtlichkeit] and justice. Fulfilling legality (*commutativa*) rather than protective justice is here contrasted with retributive justice (*distributiva*) as the other member. Moreover, the latter is only indicated in its effects, not in its essence.[134]

---

[134] This also applies to Richter's *Das philosophische Strafrecht* [Philosophical Criminal Law], which finds the essence of justice in the balance between evil [Bösem] and illness [Uebel], good and reward. The balance is only the result of justice. Leibniz's *Theodicy* (Part One, §. 73) in the same way speaks of a "relatio quaedam convenientiae" [relation of appropriateness]..., "Quemadmodum elegans concentus musicus aut egregium opus architectonicum" [like beautiful music or a fine architectural work] etc., which is only

The subjective-rationalistic philosophy of law understands justice simply as the grant or protection of the rights of men. Justice for it is that a thing becomes one's own, not also that the commandment of a higher power is preserved. The administration of criminal justice therefore manifests itself merely as a means of protection against future infringement. This is the essence of *relative criminal law theory*. In the same way, rational theology is unable to enter into the idea of divine justice, which demands the punishment of sin. Even with Schleiermacher this is the weak point at which he did not overcome the standpoint of the culture surrounding him. In his doctrine of belief, he denies *ethical* punishment in terms of its *existence*. He denies that there are evils which are attached to sin by ethical power (God), indeed which only arise as the effect of sin. There is no last judgment in the Christian sense, no otherworldly punishment for sin and hardening in this world.[135] The natural evils of the earthly state (death, illness) did not arise as a result of sin (to think so is an "adventurous idea," I. 499), but are the original natural arrangement ("inevitable imperfection or stimulant for the development of the spirit"), and in themselves are not evil at all, they are only punishment because we, with our weakened consciousness of God, do not accept them with joy as a divine institution, but rather "feel them to be evil" (I. 463–469), and that too not as punishment freely set by God (which implies an idea of divine arbitrariness and vengeance) but as the naturally necessary consequence of sin. This also applies to social evils (reciprocal damages). What God's justice effectuates is merely our "consciousness of *culpability*" and by no means any external consequence (I. 514) – although one would have to ask how the thought of culpability is possible when there is no causal connection between sin and evil either intrinsically or extrinsically. Above all, it is inadmissible for the individual to regard an evil affecting him as a divine judgment (I. 513), since that would presuppose a free ethical disposition of God outside the natural context. This is Schleiermacher's conception of ethical punishment – the most logical implementation of the most unnatural and insubstantial thought. Of

---

a very apt parable and a correct description of the impression of retributive justice, but not a description of its nature. Melanchthon, *Philosophiae Moralis,* p. 69 gives three kinds of explanations of *justitia*, but all three relate to subjective justice; he completely overlooks objective justice.

[135] *Der christliche Glaube*, vol. I, p. 514; vol. II, p. 538.

course, he cannot deny the existence of *civil* punishment, but he denies its significance as punishment. For he sees it merely as a (mechanically indispensable) means of protection for society, which is why he in a strange way detaches the administration of criminal justice from the administration of civil justice, with which it actually belongs as the *other aspect of the idea of justice* (protective versus retributive justice), and combines it with the military as the *other aspect of the defense of the state* (defense against the internal versus the external enemy).[136]

The *absolute theory of punishment*, which accordingly is the true, the inescapable one, can be conceived in different ways. Kant recognized the unconditional requirement of justice as the essence of punishment with an ethical depth and certainty and did not allow himself to be led astray because this did not agree with his overall philosophical standpoint. But his discursive exposition of this demand for justice again suffers from the shortcomings of the latter. For him crime (this must be accepted according to his entire legal theory) is always only a violation of entitlement, that is, the freedom of others, and the essence of justice, which demands punishment, is only the logical law of non-contradiction. Hegel grasped the absolute necessity of punishment more correctly since it also corresponds more closely to his overall system: he recognizes in crime the violation of the objective ethical command (the "general will"). But his exposition of the essence of justice is, as with Kant, only the logical one. Kant deduces the necessity of punishment from the logical law of non-contradiction, Hegel the necessity of both crime and punishment from the logical law of necessary contradiction and its cancellation (dialectic). With Hegel everything becomes a mere conceptual (instead of real) relation; crime is the conceptual negation of law, punishment the conceptual negation of crime. Thus, for Hegel the reality (not just the possibility) of crime is just as necessarily a component of the ethical world as is the reality of law, and punishment has for him no mere *hypothetical* necessity (if crime occurs), but is another *categorical* concept, a higher concept than law (because it contains this and its opposite), and therefore must be arrived at: there is an ethical necessity that crimes exist, so that punishments can. How it is, however, that law is established by the punishment that falls on the

---

[136] See Schleiermacher, "Über die Begriffe der verschiedenen Staatsformen" [Regarding the Concepts of the Various Forms of State]; *Die Lehre vom Staat* [The Doctrine of State].

criminal, Hegel tries to make understandable in this manner: the law as such cannot be infringed at all, because it does not exist externally; the positive existence of crime is therefore only the particular will of the infringer; therefore, the "infringement that happens to the criminal," the cancellation of the crime (*Grundlinien,* §§. 99 and 100), means that the cancellation of the act of the criminal and its outward result is not the point, but rather that restoration take place in the person of the perpetrator. Rightly so! But this does not yet answer the question as to how an "infringement" of the perpetrator as a person is a cancellation or a logical negation of his past criminal decision and act, above all that even a repentant criminal, in whom the crime no longer exists, must or should be punished. Moreover, punishment appears at a stage of his system in which there is still no talk of magistracy and state, of any ethical kingdom. The truth of the matter is, however, that crime has a positive existence not only in the will of the criminal but in the ethical kingdom, the supremacy of which it denies; it puts itself in the place thereof, and continues therein as an act (i.e., not as an outward effect). The real absolute theory of punishment does not start from the law, but from the ethical kingdom and ethical power, and has everywhere to do with real conditions whereby ethical power alone is absolute, all other existence exists only in it and with it, and its will is the only one that counts in the ethical kingdom.

In addition to all of this, Hegel knows no other punishment than civil. Since he has cast off the hereafter as a delusion, God's judgment and punishment no longer have any place. The idea of justice, going more deeply, is not in his system at all, it being incompatible with the impersonal world cause. Rather, there is merely the process of the will, which first posits itself as law, then, according to its own necessity, opposes itself as crime, and returns to itself as punishment.

Chapter 7: Atonement

§. 56. As has been shown, justice demands, equally for both the ethical and the legal sphere, that guilt be followed by punishment; and for the ethical sphere, in accordance with its inwardness, punishment, like guilt itself, is infinite and eternal: it is the eternally unresolved pain, the eternal quarrel of man with the ethical power over him (God), which is necessarily an eternal and felt annihilation of man. But here in the ethical sphere there is also another way to satisfy justice, and if punishment as such is not averted, at least the infinite punishment and infinite discord which are owed are to be – and that is atonement [die Sühne]. Its most general nature, by which it differs from punishment, consists in its effect: the reconciliation by which the ethical power does not merely outwardly assert the rule of its will through the annihilation or suffering of the wrongdoer, but inwardly again unites with him, takes him back into the ethical kingdom. This concept of atonement pertains only to the ethical (not also to the legal) sphere, and this being so, it in the first place has neither clarity nor certainty when considered in the mere finite relations of human life, because the ethical judge and the ethical court are not revealed here below.

Now the existence of such an ethical relation as that of atonement, and certain general features of it, is that to which our ethical consciousness testifies. For we find in the events of world history and in the course of life individual moments which we are inclined to regard as atonement for past guilt. We reproduce this in a transfigured way and feel it again in dramatic artwork. So, for example, one can feel inclined to see in the death of the last noble Constantine in defense of the fatherland an atonement for the horrors of the Byzantine emperors, and in the death of the morally pure, well-meaning Louis XVI an atonement for the sins of his vicious and despotic ancestors. If a pardoned criminal has found death for laudable purposes, it will be taken as an atonement for his earlier guilt. Given the impression of tragedy, which can only rest on our general ethical concepts, we do not hesitate to regard the death of the innocent Antigone as an atonement for the crimes of the house of Laos, Romeo and Juliet also as an atonement in a less clear way for the sinful enmity of the two houses, Mar and Tecla for the ambitious endeavors and entanglements of their fathers.[137]

The ethical effect which we have in mind when we characterize this as "atonement" is the same in all these cases and is clear enough. Everywhere there is presupposed by us an ethical power which has punishment follow guilt in infinite progression, and which now calls a halt thereto, and takes guilt to be redeemed through the death of the innocent, by which it is satisfied. The concept of atonement is therefore the averting of an infinite punishment by accepting a finite suffering. The death of, e.g., Antigone eradicates the punishment which would forever have burdened the house of Laos and the Theban people. But the features which give the act or process the ethical quality of atonement are more fluctuating. They are: *willingness* (acceptance of the suffering or at least consent to it or the fulfillment of ethical requirements with the awareness that suffering is the inevitable consequence) – then *innocence of the atoning party* (even the criminal used as an example is manifested to be innocent after the pardon; if he had died a praiseworthy death before the judgment – thus as the guilty party – he would not have atoned for justice but eluded it) – and therefore for this very reason in by far most examples, hence as a rule, *vicarious* suffering. While according to justice it is in the nature of punishment that it can only be executed on the guilty party, the reverse is the nature of atonement, that it cannot be attained by the guilty party himself, but only by someone else, the innocent, albeit considered to be in some relation to him. So it is with atonement for the family, for the people, for the ancestors on the throne.

Naturally, atonement as a voluntary giving of life cannot be made by one who has forfeited his life. The inability of the guilty to make his own atonement is also expressed in the Greek myth of the gods, according to which, if a hero is guilty of blood, only some god can atone for him with the injured gods. Likewise, in all the cults of antiquity, atonement for the guilty can only be carried out through the consecrated priest. These are the features peculiar to atonement; in each of them lies a part of the atoning power, and we are touched by it, even if we only find them individually, although viewed more deeply they belong together. It is by no means to be asserted that in the cases cited there really

---

[137] [Stahl seems here to be in confusion with regard to Tecla, the saint of the early church. "Mar Takla" is the Arabic form of "Saint Tecla." So, it is not two persons, but one person concerned here, Tecla.]

lies, or can only lie, an atonement (of course always only a relative one), but only that in its impression on us it becomes clear that our ethical consciousness sets as a requirement the existence and the necessity of such atonement. The deeper knowledge of the essence of atonement and thus also the explanation and summary of its individual, scattered features, we only get when we consider atonement in its absolute form, i.e., from the religious realm, the redemption of infinite guilt and the averting of eternal punishment of the whole human race through the perfect and infinite satisfaction of the Son of God, as divine revelation has revealed it to us; and our inmost being confirms its truth. Only in the latter is there truly atonement; in the former, there is only intimation and symbol.

§. 57. The vicarious satisfaction of Christ, which the church rightly maintains as the center of the Christian faith, is satisfaction not through *punishment* but through *atonement* in this specific concept. Its purpose is precisely to prevent punishment. In it, the essence of atonement is revealed in a pure and absolute way. Suffering is taken over by Him who was free from *all* sin. It is taken over not merely as a necessary consequence of ethical fulfillment (Antigone), but *directly* so that atonement may be made through it. *Absolute* suffering is taken over, not just death in general, but all suffering to which ethical consent can be given, that is, intensely infinite temporal suffering: fear, pain, shame, death, even being forsaken by God in the highest degree, and without hardening against it, in the fullest feeling of it. There is no conceivable suffering above eternal godforsakenness. A human being is neither permitted to consent to this, nor can he be the object of the suffering of atonement, the concept of which is precisely to avert eternal punishment by means of a *temporal* one. In the end, atonement was made by Him who is *one* with the human race not merely in this or that respect but *absolutely*, of whom it is said that we are created in Him and through Him and in His image. That is the perfect and clear concept of atonement, which touches us there only in dispersed individual rays, by way of presentiment.

Justice is no less satisfied by such atonement than by punishment. Because, like punishment, it is the positive opposite of the transgression. The latter consists in the fulfillment of pleasure (the pursuit of satisfaction) against the supremacy of the commandment, the former in accepting pain (denial of the striving for satisfaction) to glorify the commandment and its author. The same rapport between mores and satisfaction, which are united (identical) in personality as their essence, explains punishment (§. 54) and atonement. In atonement, as in punishment, it is the real manifestation of the higher exclusive validity of ethical power, but in an even higher way. For in punishment this manifestation is only negative, passive, in the annihilation of the will which has rebelled; it is the act of ethical power and the suffering of man through which it shows its supremacy. In atonement, on the other hand, this manifestation is positive and active; it is human will itself which, by accepting suffering, thus through will and act, shows the supremacy of ethical power, the sanctity and inviolability of ethical commandment. In the former, what is contrary to the sacred is destroyed, in the latter it is transformed into the sacred itself. In the former, it is stated that God's will (objectively) alone applies, even with the annihilation of the evildoer; in the latter it is stated that the human will itself (subjectively) desires the sole validity of the divine will even with its own annihilation. It is the way of the final, supreme fulfillment in the *personal* kingdom. That is obviously something quite different from mere right action from now on; it does not redeem past guilt, nor cancel it, nor is such accomplished through mere repentance for itself alone which does not resolve the discord in the ethical order; redemption of transgression, fulfillment of justice is only the positive and contrary contradiction, *suffering* in relation to impermissible *pleasure* [Lust], be it the passive suffering of punishment or the active suffering of atonement.

Although atonement fulfills justice in the same way as punishment, it is by no means the same thing or of the same sort as punishment, for example only with a change in the subject, a punishment that is performed on the innocent instead of on the guilty, "substitute punishment." Rather, it is something very specific, as such opposed to punishment rather than identical to it. It is true that the suffering that the atoner assumes is undoubtedly a suffering for the guilt and for the guilty, a punitive suffering (Isaiah 53:5: "But he was wounded for our transgressions, he was bruised for our iniquities: the chastisement of our peace was upon him; and with his stripes we are healed") and he is *treated* as a sinner ("For he hath made him to be sin for us, who knew no sin; that we might be made the righteousness of God in him," 2 Cor. 5:21). But not only does atonement contain essential and inseparable features that are alien to punishment, even opposed to it, such as activity, the self-acceptance of suffering, but the power of atonement to satisfy justice – and this is the decisive point – lies not, as in punishment, in suffering as such, but in the act, in *obedience,* in *sacrifice.* It is not the *death* of Christ on the cross *per se,* but *obedience until death on the cross* that exercises atoning power. It is not the higher divine glory *being manifested in Him,* but *His own manifestation* thereof that is the satisfaction of justice. The justice of God is fulfilled, not because a bloody judgment was carried out on Christ – as it were on humanity – but because the Son of man, through this supreme human suffering, manifested the inviolability of the divine law itself and thereby annulled the discord in the ethical kingdom caused by sin, returning it to a higher harmony. Christ took our sins upon Himself, but that is why He did not become sinful Himself but remained sinless. In like manner, Christ took our punishment upon Himself, but did not for that reason become the object of an execution of punishment; rather, He remained the subject of an execution of atonement; while sin and punishment are laid upon Him ("the chastisement of our peace was upon him" [Isaiah 53:5]), they are only externally attached to him; they do not become His, but the sins laid upon Him become forgiven sins, and the punishment placed upon Him becomes an act of love. The execution of punishment, the death of the wrongdoer, is only the external quality of the process. Its inner eternal meaning in the ethical world is not *execution of punishment but sacrifice of atonement.* God's holiness does not become manifested *in* His passive suffering but *through* His active suffering, and we are justified not by the *execution* of Christ, but by the *death* and *merit* of Christ.

Just as this satisfaction regarding the holiness and righteousness of God consists not in punishment but in atonement, so is it not already accomplished with the death of Christ but only through the *acceptance of God,* i.e., through the resurrection of Christ. Namely, by the path of punishment, the work is accomplished with the execution etc. of the transgressor; this is precisely the act of ethical power, which maintains justice and therefore fulfills justice through it; but by the path of atonement the sacrifice is an act of the atonement, and it still needs that ethical power to accept this act and let itself be reconciled through it.

§. 58. If one grasps the atonement in its specific meaning in this way, instead of considering it as a punishment with a mere change of the subject (as a "substitute punishment") and the transfer of all aspects of the punishment to it, one overcomes a series of difficulties and objections that confront the doctrine of satisfaction usually presented by church dogmaticians. The entire inquiry as to whether and why the temporal death of a person can be an equivalent punishment for the eternal damnation of the whole human race, or whether first the voluntary acceptance of God (acceptation) is required in order to make an equivalent for them, can be put to one side because the sacrificial death of Christ and the deserved punishment of the human race do not need to coincide, because they are not equivalent satisfactions (both punishments) at all. The death of Christ need not be an equivalent of the punishment and therefore stand only in an indirect relation to sin, but is supposed to be an immediate equivalent of sin. Christ did satisfaction not for our punishment but for our sin. Obedience to the point of death on the cross is the opposite of disobedience out of pleasure; in relation to this violation of divine holiness, it is an overly sufficient, infinite equivalent unto the validation of divine holiness. Accordingly, however, it is also an equivalent (more correctly a parallel) of the punishment, but it must not be measured arithmetically with it according to the sum of the suffering, but only dynamically according to the sin-eliminating power, and the voluntary suffering of the Son of God, as we have seen, is of infinitely more powerful and infinitely higher satisfaction than the eternal damnation of sinners.

This also disposes of the question as to whether Christ did enough through His *active* or *passive* obedience, and whether the former was also *substitutionary*. Schleiermacher already emphasized the unity of suffering and acting in the work of the Redeemer, and indeed, as he understands it, because His suffering was an act, and all of His action by way of entering into the community of sinners was suffering. But this unity consists in something quite different from the fact that in every moment both doing and suffering are present, in this constant competition between the two; rather, it consists in the concept of atonement containing doing and suffering organically as being related to one another in a definite proportion. Doing, as the fulfillment of the law, as the life of love and holiness, is the precondition, the first link in the work of atonement, because only the pure can atone; doing as surrender to death is precisely the atoning act itself, and suffering is the object of doing, it is that in which lies the atonement. The atoning power lies in suffering, but only insofar as it is act, sacrifice, and insofar as it is the act of the pure one who has actively fulfilled the law everywhere. The fulfillment of the law does not in itself have sufficient power; suffering in itself (as execution, implementation of punishment) does not have sufficient power; but atonement alone has sufficient power, this specific articulated connection between doing and suffering. It is therefore an inadmissible scholastic division of indivisible units when it is said that through the punishment suffered for us, Christ acquired for us the forgiveness of sins, and through the fulfillment of the law (active obedience) acquired for us positive righteousness, so that in this manner His active and passive obedience is substitutionary each in itself and in terms of a different aspect. Active and passive obedience are *one* indivisible act and cause, as atonement, as has been shown, and this as *one* indivisible is substitutionary in terms of its nature; it is not so in its supposed aspects taken separately. Likewise, the forgiveness of sins and the imputation of positive righteousness, acceptance as a saint, are *one* indivisible effect; for as a person, man is everywhere active and of positive quality, never a mere blank slate, therefore necessarily either a sinner or a saint, and if he is not one, he must be the other; he cannot be considered as without act and without any quality. This entirety of effect is brought about by that entirety of cause, and it is inadmissible to separate such individual components and to set them in relation to one another. Dynamic effects cannot be disintegrated and dismembered into addition and subtraction. Who would say that children get their bones from the bones of their parents, their blood from the blood of their parents, and their soul from the soul of their parents? This also eliminates the question as to whether Christ as the Son of God was subject to the law (of love and holiness), or rather fulfilled it for us as a work which He did not have to perform (an *opus supererogationis*). That does not matter if it is not His holy walk taken on its own that was substitutionary, but His entire atonement, of which that was a part.

The doctrine of satisfaction, as founded here on the concept of atonement as something very specific, differs essentially from the scientific theories as they have been formed since Anselm and especially as they have developed among orthodox Lutheran theologians. But it is in no way in contradiction with the Augsburg Confession and the statements of the Reformers themselves, since these leave room for one or another; and it preserves all the moments that fill the Christian consciousness, and especially the evangelical-ecclesiastical consciousness: the justice and holiness of God which demand eternal damnation for human sin, the redemption of this sin through the vicarious satisfaction of Christ, imputed (not infused) righteousness. The primordial flaw of human, especially philosophical, thought is that it strives to eliminate specific concepts in order to re-deduce them from what is already given, in so doing impoverishing the infinite richness of creation and God's ethical economy. Such an impoverishment lies in the explanation of atonement by the determinations of the concept of punishment.

§. 59. As specific as the work of atonement is in itself, as the divine act of redemption, just as specific is the human act of appropriating it, through which it becomes atonement for the particular person – *faith*. Faith is an entirely specific virtue. In its most general concept, it means a sure confidence in the divine statements and promises. Now it seems downright absurd to the natural understanding to ascribe any ethical significance to the assumption or denial of facts (e.g., miracles, the resurrection), and especially to declare the former, faith, to be the highest duty and virtue, and the latter, unbelief, to be morally obdurate. Nevertheless, on closer examination, this is also rationally entirely well-grounded. All certainty is based on the presence and effect of an object. Even the lauded geometric certainty is not based on logical necessity but on the sensorial perception of space, the spatial world being present to us, working upon our senses. To have shown this is, in my opinion, one of Kant's greatest achievements. The defense against religious belief, the denial of a world of miracles (resurrection, signs) in opposition to the existing laws of nature is therefore based not, as one pretends, on the power of reason, but only on the power of the *sensorial present*. In the way that man stands higher than the beast because he looks to the future rather than having present sensation seem eternal to him, so it is again a higher state for him not to be overcome by the impression of eternity given by earthly visible conditions of the world. But the positive certainty of belief is necessarily also based on a presence of the object, i.e., God and the eternal world in our spirit and mind, only with the difference that the natural perception of this world is present in its entire development, whereas to faith the other world is merely veiled in its germ, i.e., in the power (in God) that will freely evoke and develop it. Faith therefore requires a presence of God in us and a power of our will to esteem the eternal, which is merely present in the germ, to be higher and truer than the temporal present in its entire development, and this includes a surrender of the human will to the divine and the ethical before the sensorial and natural.

On this rests the ethical value of faith and the equation of unbelief with carnal disposition. This is why Christ rebukes the Jews for demanding signs and wonders: Since the Son of God appeared in His divine love, truthfulness, unselfishness, the human mind should be so filled with this divine presence that it values His statements more highly than all sensorially present laws of nature; faith should be determined by the ethical power of the appearance of Christ and not the sensorial example of a breach of natural laws.[138] In the same way He rebukes His disciple Thomas for not wanting to believe the reported miracle of the resurrection: Thomas should be so filled with the divine impression of the Redeemer that this breach of nature should not alienate him. The present church is not in the position of the Jews, but in the position of this disciple. Therefore, if we emphasize miracles in relation to rationalism, it is something completely different than the demand of the Jews for miracles. The latter is based on wanting to have the divine breakthrough of nature as something present to the senses, while the former is based on believing it to be true even without a sensorial presence.

Now where faith does not refer to past facts (the assertoric), but to future fulfillments (the promissory), where it is a certain confidence in the divine promises, it contains at the same time another ethical and indeed a purely religious element: trust in the *divine will,* in the truthfulness and love of God. This trust is a virtue because God is a person, and relates purely to man's attitude towards God as a person. In relation to the world substance or the rational law of rationalism with its inner necessity, trust is inconceivable and impossible, and, if it were possible, it could not count as a duty or a virtue. But for the human bond to the person of God (instead of to the ethical law) there is no higher quality than this personal trust. This is why the entirety of philosophical learning and theology could only come up with *conscientiousness* [Gewissenhaftigkeit] but not *faith* as a religious trait (unless by ascribing thereto a completely different, foreign concept): because it either denies or ignores the personality of God and the purely personal behavior of man towards God. Everywhere,

---

[138] This also is the difference between belief and superstition. The latter renounces the laws of sensorially present nature only because it does not recognize them in all their strength, not by virtue of the presence of an ethical power, and devotion to that power; it therefore believes supernatural manifestations even if they lack any ethical significance.

therefore, faith is no mere act of judgment (considering something to be true historically, according to rational grounds), but an ethical act, an act of man according to his inmost personality. That is the general meaning of faith as it is praised in Scripture (e.g. Romans 4:17–22, Hebrews 11) as pleasing to God and almighty among Jews and even among Gentiles. In the economy of the New Covenant, however, it has an even more special meaning than the certain confidence in reconciliation in Christ. For here faith is at the same time a real confession of one's own guilt and the impossibility of one's own atonement, and it is man's complete coming out of himself in order to achieve reconciliation with God only through Christ and in Christ. It is the expression of the absolute need for redemption and the confident acceptance of the redemption commanded in Christ. As such, it is the means by which man becomes one with Christ, i.e., through which unity with Christ, which exists in and of itself as essential, since we are created through and in Christ, also becomes at the same time active (actual) for a particular person. But our unity with Christ, and only this, is what determines His atoning work for us.[139]

A coherent presentation of the dogma of the path to salvation and the confessional and theological divergences about the same, as goes without saying, is not the task here. It was only a matter of demonstrating and defining *atonement* and *faith* in a philosophical way, as basic ethical concepts.

[139] See my *Der Protestantismus als politisches Princip* [Protestantism as Political Principle], p. 9.

APPENDIX: THE RELATIONSHIP OF THEOLOGY TO PHILOSOPHY[140]

§. 61. *Theology* as the elaboration [Ausbildung] of revelation-knowledge for science, and *philosophy* as the culmination of secular science, are both *absolute sciences,* i.e., they each bring everything back to the supreme cause of being – the absolute, God – they view their objects in absolute terms. Now then, since there is only one absolute, it being impossible for God to be dual, so can there only be one real knowledge and science of the absolute, or God and things as they are in God. But this one science of the absolute divides itself in terms of both of those supreme relations of divine activity (§. 24) and this explains a dualism thereof as philosophy and theology, similar to a dualism of the ethic into morality and religion.

Philosophy, namely, is the knowledge of God as the world-creating and completing One, *theology* is the knowledge of God as the One who joins people to Himself; the former has for its goal human knowledge in itself, the completion of the creature, which lies precisely in that it itself comprehend the wisdom and glory of the Creator and His world plan, the latter by contrast the union of people with God, blessedness, the way of salvation. Accordingly, philosophy and theology *firstly* have a *different object* [Gegenstand]. Downward from that absolute point of unity, God, they part ways. Philosophy has a wide scope which remains outside of theology because it does not concern the union of people with God. Logic, ontology (the meaning of the categories), nature, speech, political science, all of this in its absolute relation is the object of philosophy, for all of this is the divine manifestation in the creation; but it is not the object of theology because it is not the means of union with God. But even to the degree that they have the same object, they still have it from a different angle. In this manner, the attributes of God are the object of theology to the degree that they stand in relation to the goal of union, e.g., the personality of God, the Trinity, creation by absolute power, justice, mercy, omniscience. By contrast, it is the

---

[140] This chapter is taken from the special edition of this book, *Fundamente einer christlichen Philosophie* (1846).

business of philosophy to investigate the manner of creation, whether it proceed from freedom or necessity, to investigate intellectual, moral, or artistic laws, why is there this particular class, this particular kingdom of nature? In the same manner, world history is the object of philosophy as the unfolding of human predispositions and conditions, as a work of art complete in itself, while it is the object of theology as the course of returning the human race to God and the means of expanding His kingdom. The former seeks in it the artistic, lawful, free manner (the appropriate or unsuccessful attempts by speculative construction), the latter the manner of God in favor of that union, the way in which He leads His own (answer to prayer, testing) and how He fulfills His salvation economy for the whole (bringing about the greatest things from the hidden, the inconspicuous). The former is inappropriate for theologians, the latter for philosophers. Likewise, the philosophy of religion treats religion not in its actual intention as religion, i.e., to unite people with God, but in its world-historical development in accordance with the lawful course in which ideas move forward, human consciousness undergoes a necessary process, etc.

Secondly, philosophy and theology accordingly have *differing interests.* The interest of philosophy is *purely theoretical,* since its goal is only human knowledge in itself. By contrast, the interest of theology in its innermost ground is *practical,* it being based on the longing to be united in reality (in terms of being and will) with God, apart from which there can be no real theology.[141] Schleiermacher expressed the truth for all times that the extent of dogmatics is restricted to the "interest of piety" in distinction to the "interest of philosophy." Similarly, no theology is possible without faith, without the already fulfilled restoration of the bond with God, which conversely is not necessary for philosophy.

§. 62. Accordingly, the distinction between philosophy and theology is founded in eternal relations, for which reason they remain for eternity in distinguishable

[141] In this sense, the expression "pectus facit theologum" [the heart makes the theologian] is entirely true. Namely, not subjective feeling by contrast with the objective, revealed Word and the clear content of its doctrine, but practical religious desire makes the true theologian rather than mere theoretical interest, the mere desire to comprehend, of speculative theologians.

spheres (orientations) of knowledge, of which the one will never merge into the other. This is the distinction between absolute *knowledge of the world* and absolute *knowledge of religion.* But for this reason, philosophy and theology are by no means sciences that are *separated* from each other. In terms of their eternal truthful character, they permeate each other everywhere, are inseparable at every point as the different relations of one and the same knowledge, and even in terms of their temporal character they have a shared center in God and a coherence and reciprocal effect through contact in the same objects.

In accordance with their necessary unity as mere aspects of absolute knowledge [Wissenschaft], they then must above all *agree* in their *results.* The world-view of philosophy and theology ought not contain any contradiction, not even any divergence. Here, nevertheless, is the moment at which, in opposition to the original idea of both of these sciences, an essential difference emerges between them in the empirical condition. The true knowledge of the absolute is only possible through real being in the absolute. Because man actually finds himself apart from God in the empirical condition, he is therefore incapable of any true absolute knowledge. For with regard to the one goal, union of people with God, God is active immediately already in temporality and establishes the real bond with people. In this manner an essential distinction arises between theology and philosophy which is decisive to their results.

In terms of the aspect of absolute knowledge, which theology represents, man is *supported by a divine revelation* which is lacking to him in terms of the other aspect thereof, represented by philosophy. For example, we have a revelation regarding the divine *redemption plan* but not one of the divine *world plan.* Likewise secular knowledge [Welterkenntniß] here below consists in *discursive thinking,* analogous to the externality of the state, while religious knowledge consists in *intuition,* at least to a certain degree, through that real union with God. In this manner, theology according to its inner ground is already in its true character, while philosophy is outside its true character, entirely analogously to the relation of church and state.

This gives theology an immeasurable advantage over philosophy. But not for this advantage can philosophy be given up in favor of theology, for it has an independent sphere that the latter cannot cultivate, as little as can the state, because it lacks inspiration, be given up in order for the church to take its place.

Accordingly, in the empirical condition philosophy and theology not only have differing objects and differing interests but a different *character* (another means and manner of knowledge); in this they are not only distinguishable but *heterogenous.*

§. 63. Even in this condition of heterogeneity, both sciences cannot give up their coherence and mutual reinforcement, and they have an impulse toward agreement within themselves in conformity with their original unity.

Theology cannot do without philosophy. As it puts the content of faith into the shape of science, it enters into the realm of discursive thinking, requires the forms, concepts, categories (substance and accidents, "ὁμουσια," "transubstantiation," with/in/under, "ubiquity"), the disclosure of which religion and revelation does not go into at all, as they are not concerned with the way of salvation – which in this manner withdraws them from secular science. In this manner theology is influenced in its scientific shape-taking by learning [Bildung] and hence in particular the philosophy of its time, even though it has the most decisive obligation to keep its content and results free from their effect.

Similar to the way in which the church comes under empirical conditions and the sphere of the state when she emerges from the supreme inwardness of faith community and furnishes herself with indispensable external organization, is theology in the sphere of philosophy. The great support theology can and should derive from philosophy through purification and elevation of natural knowledge therefore should not be denied.

On the other hand, true philosophy cannot do without the knowledge of religion. When it is being candid, it cannot hide the fact that this other need of the human spirit and this other aspect of knowledge exists, with which it must establish a relationship and fashion a unity if it is to be certain of itself. The manner of that unity – this constitutes the final decisive moment.

§. 64. *The true unity* between philosophy and theology by which the necessary independence and coordination of both is preserved can only consist in philosophy trying the worldview of the doctrine of revelation as *solution key* in its sphere and putting such to the test *according to its own laws.*

The course of all scientific investigation in fact is not, as one commonly assumes, to proceed from given data with logical consistency to conclusions with regard to the uncertain, but instead to ascribe something as-yet unknown, a hypothesis, to known phenomena in order to see if it explains them.[142] In the former manner, one makes calculations; in the latter, one arrives at scientific discoveries. For this reason, with all scientific advancement no less than with art, it mainly comes down to an inspiration. Scientific rigor does not consist in not making no inferences that have not been found by conclusions from an immediate knowledge [Gewissen] (pure unabstractable being etc.) but in not maintaining any hypothesis or allowing any hypothesis to stand which has not been tested against the object [dem Objekte] and its laws in terms of scientific rules.

According to philosophy's own law – not to ignore anything that exists – it is requisite to make such a use, as hypothesis, of revelation, which makes the claim itself to be the supreme knowledge. If the latter shows its mettle as the basis of the philosophical worldview, then the unity of the two sciences is achieved, namely the same foundation of supreme truth upon which they both rest, similar to the manner in which the state together with the church has religion as its ultimate foundation. Furthermore, the meaning which revelation attributes to itself is preserved, while without it the true worldview would not be capable of discovery. But this does not eliminate the independence of philosophy, for it takes on that foundation *not in faith, but only as, and to the degree that, it is tested.* Only then would philosophy step down from the claims that it hitherto has made for itself, for it would find its ultimate presupposition not of itself (the determinations of human reason) but by reception. In opposition to the foundational error of rationalism, this is the truth: philosophy receives all its

---

[142] It is well known that all great discoveries in the field of natural sciences have been made in this way. But this is no less the case in all other sciences, and especially in philosophy. All philosophical systems came into being by trying a hypothesis, even if they are not always conscious of it themselves. So even Hegel, who most resolutely disputes this course (see *History of Philosophy* on Leibniz), nevertheless did not proceed in any other way. When he discovered his system, he certainly did not proceed as follows: "I have being as immediate certainty, without any presupposition; in being there is nothing; and so on" as now appears in his system; but he had all things before him (and what is to be said here only parenthetically, already the pantheistic presupposition), and was looking for a solution. Then the thought presented itself to him that the unity of opposites would be the solution; he assumed it as a hypothesis, and by implementing it believed that he had found what really was explanatory. So did his system come about.

objects rather than finds them from out of itself, therefore can only receive what conditions and explains all other things even if this entails that the coherence of things is real and not merely logical.

The appropriateness of the relation between theology and philosophy here presented can only be assessed by *experiment.* Whether the content of revelation will prove itself to be the key to things can *a priori* only be believed, not known, and thus not accepted scientifically. In specific areas of knowledge, this experiment has already been made with success. Thus in particular in the area of morality. For the Christian revelation entirely explains the given condition of human knowledge, while no other assumption has been able to do so.[143] Nevertheless, on the whole the experiment still has to be made. May this little book as well as my collective legal philosophy serve as a contribution to this end, while I have made the Christian worldview the presupposition for the explanation of the world, and especially social conditions, not considering the authority of revelation to be the proof and guarantee thereof but simply the inward agreement in the presentation of the object.

But with this it must never be lost sight of that complete unity between philosophy and theology as well as the complete solution of philosophical problems is simply not attainable. Revelation is too restricted in its extent and philosophy too restricted in its power of implementation to achieve this; but philosophy can derive and establish its supreme foundation from the worldview of revelation and thereby gain an established position in harmony with theology, in that they, as the two sides of absolute knowledge, do not contradict each other even if they do not permeate each other across the board. But even this incompleteness of solution is explained in turn by the same hypothesis of the Christian worldview, according to which our understanding is clouded; it therefore is much rather a confirmation than an objection.

§. 65. The dualism of philosophy and theology, in that there can only be one absolute and one true science comprising them, has ever been an impetus to establish the difference between them. The most common and age-old form has been *auxiliary sources of knowledge.* Philosophy should be the *natural* know-

[143] In this regard, [Blaise] Pascal in particular may be regarded as a Christian philosopher.

ledge of God, theology the *revealed.* In consequence, only one can exist. Either revelation is deception, in which case theology manifests itself as the *bound* (and so untrue), philosophy as the *free* science of the absolute, the only one capable of truth. Or revelation is truth, in which case the converse, philosophy must fall as the insufficient and false knowledge vis-à-vis the true one, and at most can retain the significance that the external scientific form and method for theology is taken from it. This conception is indisputably correct that philosophy is based on natural knowledge while theology is based on revealed (§. 62); but it is erroneous to suppose that this constitutes the difference in concept and essence between them.

Deviating from this, Hegel puts the difference between the two sciences in their *organ* and *form*. Theology grasps the absolute through the *organ of feeling*, a knowledge that is still "interwoven with matter," or at best through the *organ of the abstract understanding*, therefore always only in the "*form of imagination* [Vorstellung]," while philosophy grasps it through speculative reason, hence in the *form of thought*. The difference is sometimes expressed as the difference in the object; religion has as its object the *undeveloped God* or the world in its reference back to the undeveloped God (that is something other than the person of God), philosophy the *developed God*, developed in the world and the (human) spirit.[144] In terms of thought, however, this is exactly the same as that first expression. Hegel's way of looking at things is precisely this: when viewed in their innermost, religion and philosophy are not at all two human modes of knowledge or knowledge of two sides or activities of God, but rather two *modes of existence of God Himself* (as cannot be otherwise in the pantheistic system). God, the unconscious demiurgic power (the "spirit in itself of nature and spirit") comes to its consciousness in man (becomes "for itself").[145] This is also the concept of revelation, not that the fully conscious God makes Himself known to man, but that He comes to His own consciousness in man, is revealed to himself, and therefore revelation is not an *act* of God, but rather God "*comprehends* the

---

[144] Hegel's *Propädeutik*; furthermore, Haman's review (*Vermischte Schriften,* vol. II, p. 88); cf. also §. 24 above, regarding the Hegelian school's conception of morality and religion. What is stated there applies here as well.

[145] "God is God only insofar as He knows Himself; His self-knowledge of Himself is furthermore His self-consciousness in man" (*Enzyklopädie,* §. 564).

manifestation of Himself," it is the concept of God, as unconscious power – of nature, etc., likewise directly having His consciousness as human being. Now this God becoming conscious in human beings is first of all a dark, real emotional state of consciousness – religion, and then a consciousness existing in concepts and thoughts – philosophy. Therefore religion (viewed from the side of man) is the general, real feeling of the world power in man, whose true relationship in itself as well as to the world he either does not even grasp in thought (this is devotion, cult, faith) or, however, compelled to do so, only grasped in the untrue, "reflective determinations" or the "imagination." That is to say, religion (in so far as it is knowledge and not merely devotion) makes the logical moments which are in truth world power and in truth only stand in logical relation to one another and to the world posited with them (in relation to being only moments of the concept), "into opposing presuppositions and into phenomena which follow upon each other and into a *coherence of happenings*." Thus the element of "universality" or of "universal being," which contains particularity as something different from it (universal being) and yet eternally identical with it, is what religion makes, according to the "reflection-determination of causality" (that is, the "coherence of happenings," an act) into the "Creator of heaven and earth" and to the "Progenitor of the Son," etc.; while philosophy recognizes the untruth of such ideas, presents world power, which is a logical relation, only as a logical relation (so that the truth is in the "form of truth").

Religion or theology and philosophy thus have the same object ("the spirit in itself of nature and spirit"), but the way in which this object is brought into consciousness (or becomes conscious itself, becomes "for itself") is in the former case untrue, the latter true. It is therefore obviously a delusion to pretend to have saved the independent significance of the two sciences or their unity. For it cannot be denied that, depending on the two organs and forms or modes of knowledge, the result is also different – with the former, the personal God, the historical act of the fall of man, the bodily future resurrection, the latter the idea, substance, the eternally uninterrupted fall into sin, the resurrection only through devotion to substance (see above §. 13), and then it is evident that the two sciences do not agree, and that only one of them can be the sole, true, the absolute. For all knowledge is concerned with its object. If this exists differently from what that envisions, it is not a harvest but an error. The consequence of this view, regardless of its packaging, is none other than that of the most common denial of revelation, that this religion and theology is only a temporary surrogate of philosophy, mainly a delusion, and therefore must cease with the times or the people in possession of philosophy. In this regard, Hegel in fact takes no other position than Strauss, Bruno Bauer, and so on.[146] From the standpoint of Hegel there is no theology, i.e., no dogmatics possible at all. What is called "speculative dogmatics" by this school is no dogmatics, "doctrine of faith," for, according to its own intention, it is not a representation of real *truths of faith*, but only a representation of the necessity of historical *imaginings*. Just as a Christian philosopher or theologian might explain the development of mythology, showing everywhere that its substance is nothing other than Christian doctrine in its clouded, displaced and fragmented conception, Christian theology is presented here as if its substance were only Hegel's logic in a clouded imagining, still interwoven with the material, and this clouding in its specific manner itself were a logical necessity. From this point of view, religion and theology are only the mythologies of philosophy.

The truth of the matter is, however, that religion does not have the undeveloped God as opposed to the developed God as its object; for the characteristics of God as a person and His actions to unite mankind with Himself are just as developed as is His act of creation of nature and man; the truth of the matter is, religion is not a knowledge of a different and lesser kind and form than philosophy, in the form of the imagination versus the form of the thought. For what Hegel calls the form of truth, i.e., the annihilation of the living connection of personality and act and cause and effect in mere logically (dialectically) immanent conceptual coherence – in terms of form and content that is absolute untruth, the untruth κατ' ἐξοχήν [par excellence].

§. 66. Schleiermacher's doctrine of the relation between theology and philosophy is infinitely closer to the truth than Hegel's. According to Schleiermacher, religion is a real human condition: feeling, immediate impression of consciousness (feeling of dependence, need for redemption, specific Christian experience of redemption). This feeling, or this state of mind, through logical reflection

---

[146] Already in the first volume of my *Philosophy of Law* (1830), I presented this entire way of thinking as the concealed albeit indubitable sense of Hegel's theory, as later so openly and surely confirmed by Strauss and his successors.

brought into developed consciousness and into scientific (dialectical) form, is theology (dogmatics, doctrine of faith). Theology has its object, its content and its measure only in this real state in which man finds himself. On the other hand, philosophy proceeds purely from intellectual contemplation in objective forms of thought and in this way finds the Absolute and the absolute coherence of the world. Accordingly, philosophy has the All of things (envisioned in the absolute) for its object, and the determinations of reason for content and measure. Thus there are two completely different principles and functions of the human spirit, one "subjective" and one "objective," which, however, because of the unity of human being, cannot contradict each other in their results.[147] Hereby is the independent truth of religion and theology recognized, that it is not a lower level of knowledge that manifests itself in philosophy as a higher instance, and that it must not be measured against that. There are two poles, two completely coordinated relationships between man and his knowledge.

But the conception of religion and theology, which is the starting point here, contains a shift in the true relationship. Because religion primarily is not a condition of man (feeling of dependency) but rather an activity of God, it is the quintessence of His enterprises and deeds for the unification (or reconciliation) of man with Himself. This, and then human piety as its product, are the object, content and measure of religion and thus of theology. But according to Schleiermacher, the object of theology is initially a merely subjective one (pious self-consciousness or pious states of mind) instead of the objective one (of the real God and His acts),[148] as well as the medium of knowledge, the source of reli-

---

[147] "Just as this (speculative consciousness) is the highest objective function of the human spirit, and pious self-consciousness is the highest subjective, a contradiction between the two would affect the essence of man, and such a contradiction can only be a misunderstanding" (*Der christliche Glaube nach den Grundsätzen der evangelischen Kirche im Zusammenhange dargestellt* [The Christian Faith Presented in Coordinated Fashion according to the Basic Principles of the Protestant Church], vol. I, p. 171).

[148] "Christian beliefs are conceptions of Christian pious states of mind" (p. 108). "We must therefore declare the description of *human conditions* to be the dogmatic basic form, but theses of the second and third form (about God and about the world) are only admissible insofar as they can be developed from theses of the first form; for only under

gious truth, being only the subjective, the "facts of pious self-consciousness" instead of the objective one: the Word of God. Rather than deriving dogmatics from the latter and showing its confirmation by the pious consciousness, he goes the opposite way; he derives dogmatics from pious self-consciousness and only then allows it to be confirmed by God's Word, indeed, he allows, where both of them in his opinion diverge, e.g., regarding the supernatural creation, the latter to be assessed and measured against the former and not the other way around.

This subjectivism is already expressed in the thread of its presentation. It does not follow the great objective existences, God, His properties, His deeds, His economy of salvation, but only the inner perceptions of the pious man and what attaches itself to them as a postulate, so that it even rends the doctrine of God. Omnipotence, omniscience, then justice and holiness, and finally love, are referred to their systematically necessary place in three different places of dogmatics, depending on whether they correspond to the different religious states of mind of man, the experience of dependence, sin, and redemption, similar to when a geographer does not follow a country by the thread of the rivers and mountain ranges but describes it according to the thread of the post road on which the traveler traverses it and puts that forward as the only systematic geography. By virtue of this subjectivism, doctrine and dogma have no other meaning for Schleiermacher that is different in nature (not merely in degree) from pious gestures (such as folding hands, kneeling); for it is only an expression of inner pious states of mind, which the gesture is as well, not at the same time the communication of objective existences and facts, which the gesture never is (pp. 110, 123).

But subjectivism necessarily includes *apriorism*. The Schleiermacher doctrine of the faith is therefore *logically apriorist* in terms of its scientific structure. Its course is by no means, as might seem, a continuous pursuit and observation of concrete full inner experiences, but only a logical unfolding of the two concepts which he has derived from two basic facts of the pious or Christian

---

this condition can they apply with certainty to *expressions of pious emotions*" (p. 177). For Schleiermacher, religion and piety are completely synonymous; even religion in the "objective sense" is for him only a common subjective piety and its product (p. 40). That, by the way, the essence of (subjective) piety is likewise incorrectly specified by Schleiermacher, it is not the place here to elucidate.

consciousness, i.e., the absolute feeling of dependence as the general substance of all religion and the feeling of redemption or the experience of redemption as the substance of the Christian religion. Indeed, nowhere does Schleiermacher derive his individual beliefs empirically (by means of inner experience), e.g., by examining whether the Christian consciousness does not demand the deity of Christ and find itself weakened everywhere when such is withdrawn from it, whether the fear of real eternal damnation, not the idea that death is brought about by the fall, be a fact and indeed an inalienable fact of that Christian pious consciousness – that alone would be a dogmatics based on inner experience – instead he merely examines whether or not such follows from the two basic facts, the feeling of dependence and redemption. He does not support individual beliefs, even the most important ones, directly from the Christian inner experience, but only supports them indirectly through a logical conclusion from one of these general basic assumptions about inner experience. But he does not take even these two basic facts in their full, rich, concrete content, as the real Christian inner experience everywhere indicates; rather, only in an abstraction which he has drawn from them in such a way as by virtue of simplicity they are suitable for an *a priori* system developing from a single thread. If he took the need for redemption as a fact of the Christian consciousness as it really is, he would not describe it merely as "inhibition of the easiness and steadiness of pious emotions," which is only one side of it, but at the same time as a feeling of the pressure of God as a hostile power outside of us, and if he would not describe the experience of redemption merely as "the restored easiness of those emotions" but at the same time as the certainty of reconciliation, by virtue of which God Himself, the objective personality outside of us, would unite with us again, and the like. But if, therefore, he accepted the part of those basic facts of Christian consciousness which necessarily lead to God and His acts outside of us and did not leave them outside his abstract concept, then it would no longer be possible for him to deduce a system of doctrine of faith that is "scientific," i.e., merely spun out of man. So it is only the two basic facts of the Christian inner experience, not the full complete Christian inner experience, and furthermore these two basic facts not in their full content but only in their concept, abstracted in a certain aspect, from which all beliefs (the properties of God, nature of the Redeemer, etc.) are derived. The investigation is conducted as to whether one has to posit God as Almighty, Omniscient, and in what sense, in order to maintain the absolute feeling of dependence, likewise which nature one has to ascribe to the Redeemer, whether immorality, perfection, whether just a full consciousness of God or real Godhead, etc., thus all that, but also nothing more than that, which is entailed by the concept of redemption (in the sense of a liberation from the bondage of the feeling of dependency). This entire dogmatics, expressed in scientific terms, is nothing other than the analysis of the concept of absolute dependence and redemption, as in what conditions man and, specifically, the Christian actually find himself. Schleiermacher's dogmatic method and Zinzendorf's "it is this to me" are very wrongly ranged together over against "it is written." However, both have in common a trait of subjectivism in opposition to objective words of Scripture. Only Zinzendorf draws his results from the Christian inner experience, from it and directly from it; Schleiermacher derives his own from the two terms to which he traces the Christian states of mind. His dogmatics is not built on the Christian subjective inner experience as opposed to objective research of Scripture, but on the logical analysis of two concepts extracted from Christian inner experience. According to its entire procedure (I am by no means saying according to its entire content) it is an *a priori dogmatics*, and in this it is a unicum in the history of philosophy and theology.

Namely, the speculative theology of the Hegelian school is also *a priori*, but it is precisely erected from *philosophical apriorism* (only an implementation of the philosophical system through this stage of the world, which is called religion) and therefore also is aprioristic according to its entire content. Schleiermacher's dogmatics, on the other hand, is a *specifically religious apriorism*. In his view, philosophy deduces *a priori* from reason (the determinations of thought) and dogmatics deduces *a priori* from the basic facts of pious or Christian self-consciousness, and the latter therefore also has a concrete albeit parched [verdürstigte] basis. In this respect, his dogmatic method is most similar to Fichte's philosophical method. Just as Fichte believes that he is systematically developing the world from the fact of consciousness, so Schleiermacher believes that he is developing religion from the fact of pious, especially Christian, self-consciousness. The fact that Fichte also accepts the world thus discovered as something merely present in consciousness while Schleiermacher accepts it as objective, is of course a very essential difference in the matter, but not in the method.

Now Schleiermacher demonstrated the truth for which theology must ever thank him, that the scope of dogmatics extends only to the "interest of piety" as opposed to mere "philosophy" [Wißbegierde]. It is only when Schleiermacher grasps this truth in a merely subjective way (making the subjective primary) that he comes to restrict the interest of piety in an inadmissible way. In fact, he declares everything to be outside the interest of piety that does not follow *a priori* from the absolute feeling of dependence or from the concept of redemption in terms of the content described by him. All of this is to him without "*dogmatic content*." This is the *key to his dogmatics*. In this way Schleiermacher banishes all "divine counsels" (that is, all positive, free acts of God which cannot be found *a priori* in the human feeling of dependence or the experience of redemption) from dogmatics, and limits them to "the properties of God" (*Glaubenslehre*, II, p. 24), he declares the "miracles and the prophecies to be foreign to them" (I, p. 100; II, p. 12.), and accordingly also the Old Testament document to lack the dignity and worthiness of the New Testament (II, p. 378), having superfluous authority (I, p. 160), Judaism being just as alien to Christianity, just as out of touch with it as paganism (I, p. 86). The supernatural begetting of Christ and, to a certain extent, His resurrection and ascension to heaven are dogmatically irrelevant to him (II, p. 70, 74, 92). The whole *objective guidance* of God's Old and New Testaments, since it is something so thoroughly positive, artistically applied, has no place in this doctrine of faith which only describes *subjective* pious states of mind. The Mosaic history of creation is dismissed from the doctrine of faith and relegated to natural science, not merely in its details, but in its general sense that creation is an act of God, a change in the previous state. In the doctrine of the properties of God, the positive divine omnipotence or the almighty act of creation is exchanged for the negative, the guard against "something being excluded from originating from God, or that God himself be placed under the determinations and oppositions which arose in the world and through the world"(I, p. 21). All this: positive omnipotence, creation through act, divine guidance, promise, prophecy and attestation of fulfillment is the highest interest of that piety, which is the mere effect and companion of objective divine deeds and events; but it certainly does not lie *a priori* in the postulates of the absolute feeling of dependence and the concept of salvation.

This is by no means to deny that Schleiermacher makes Christianity as "*positive* religion" the object of his dogmatics and the *historical Christ* (truly, not just as a symbol, as an expression of an idea) as its center. From the feeling of dependence, then, the main moments contained in it, and among these also that of redemption, are shown *a priori*, and so the position of Christianity is "constructed" (p. 83), but the fact that Christ is the Redeemer is recognized as something which cannot be demonstrated and constructed *a priori* but is only experienced through the real influence of Christ Himself, that is, of His Spirit, which He bequeathed to His community. This is also the moment at which Schleiermacher's doctrine of faith possesses the inalienable criterion of a Christian doctrine of faith, of a real theology, not just philosophy. But this historical Christ (although He is truly meant as such) *has no influence on the derivation of its statements of faith*. It is not as if all earlier deductions were only the way to Him, but now, after having reached Him, immediately only He Himself, this person outside of us, becomes the absolute source and measure of it. Schleiermacher does not arrive at the point at which, finally going out from himself and from his pious experience and the development of its basic concepts, he devotes himself to this historical person in His history and in His revelation (in His Word); rather, he always remains in himself and his inner experience, or rather his logical conclusion from those general facts established once and for all; these are not measured against Christ but, conversely, are measures of what Christ may and may not be. That Christ puts Himself forward as the one promised in the Old Covenant, that He puts forward His redemption as connected with the economy of the Old Covenant but not connected with paganism, is not determinative, for in terms of the apriorist construction of religions from the feeling of dependency into monotheistic and polytheistic, into aesthetic and teleological, it follows that Christ is alien to both Judaism and paganism in the same way. That is why Schleiermacher does not refer to *faith* in a biblical way as the certainty of what a free (objective) personality, God or Christ, will do in the future outside of us according to their promise (see above, §. 60), but as the certainty of what we perceive in ourselves as our own inner affection (feeling of bondage and the incipient liberation from the feeling of dependence) in the present. Faith is only a condition of higher "certainty accompanying self-consciousness" (p. 96). Christianity is therefore "positive religion" not in the sense that the objective deed and institution of God, through which it and only it is founded, by him is emphasized, but in the sense that, like Mohammedanism and paganism, it is a particular individual religion which has arisen through a historical (not necessarily divine) act, as distinct from the feeling of dependency, which merely forms the general basis of religions (p. 69).

In this, of course, there is an inner contradiction, that Schleiermacher does not make that which he establishes as co-cause of pious consciousness (God in general in the feeling of dependence, Christ in the particular experience of redemption of Christians) to be an independent primary principle of the doctrine of the faith; that he does not allow this cause of our pious emotion to have made anything else (e.g., a course of world history and the economy of salvation pertaining to it, a promise and fulfillment) than this, that he does not allow it to be something else than what can be found by analyzing our pious emotions. It is a contradiction that he recognizes the *that* of Christian salvation as a positive indemonstrable fact and yet demonstrates the *how* entirely from concepts. This contradiction is resolved to some extent by the fact that, according to Schleiermacher, Christ is "not supernatural" and "not superrational," i.e. precisely not superhuman, divine, but only "an effect of the developmental force inherent in our nature as a species" (p. 89), that "that which is produced by the divine spirit is in a certain way posited in human reason itself," therefore the "divine spirit itself can only be thought of as the highest exaltation of human reason" (p. 92). For if Christ and His work are only the highest potentiation of human nature without the addition of a purely and specifically divine quality and much less a free personal act of God or of Himself, then it is quite logical that non-potentiated (merely natural) man knows nothing of divine things, but whoever participates in this potentiation, who has once been fertilized by Christ, must also be able to find the nature of the Redeemer and the work of redemption merely by observing himself (the life and spirit in him). Apart from the fact that this directly contradicts biblical Christianity, this consequence would have to lead even further than Schleiermacher goes. Christ should then not be represented as the power that works in redemption, but only as the product of the spirit of the human species, which in truth would be this redeeming power, and Christianity should no longer be allowed (not even in its first fact of the perception of redemption through Christ) to be represented as something based on experience at all, in that it cannot be demonstrated (p. 98), but all reason would have to be expected to inevitably participate in the process of increase after we show it that this, apart from divine assistance, is its own law and nature. In short, one then necessarily arrives at Hegel's standpoint. But just as Schleiermacher is prevented from following the full content of his Christian inner experience by the requirement of the *a priori* method (which at that time was held to be the scientific be-all and end-all) and the same inseparable rationalistic-pantheistic basic views, so is he here discouraged by his Christian inner experience from following the full scientific consistency of that method and the standpoint contained in it. On this point the knot of contradiction, from which this man of mighty spiritual struggle could not free himself, is tied neither to one side nor to the other.

Schleiermacher's religious apriorism necessarily has the general flaws of all apriorism, as I have set out in great detail in the first volume of my *Philosophy of Law*. This method is scientifically untenable, in that Schleiermacher only apparently deduces a great deal from the feeling of dependency which he actually takes from objective religion (the Word of God and ecclesiastical teaching and tradition). As a result of this – which practically is the most important thing – essential components of true (positive) faith have been lost, above all the divinity of Christ (*divina natura*), which is made subject to the bare perfect consciousness of God, since in terms of the *a priori* deduction, the dignity of Christ ought not be higher than absolutely necessary for its function (as is postulated by the concept of redemption according to the abstract version thereof); likewise that the analysis of our feeling of dependence and the concept of redemption based on it should plumb the full depth and scope of the divine economy of creation and redemption, and so draw a line for God as to what grade of Christ He should send us; just so the immaculate conception and the like. Finally, the conserved doctrines of faith are not by any means, as one might think, the better guaranteed by their *a priori* proof, but on the contrary have confidence in them undermined. So for example the resurrection of Christ and the promise of our resurrection, as the Holy Scriptures proclaim them as positive facts and the simple Christian accepts them as positive facts, certainly enjoy a much greater confidence than Schleiermacher's artificial deduction as to whether the interest of piety really requires the "immortality of the soul," which after much deliberation is finally affirmed.

In addition to these general shortcomings of apriorism, Schleiermacher's specifically religious apriorism also has the specific shortcoming that it cannot be kept separate from philosophical apriorism, which is Schleiermacher's honest intention, but that both flow into one another. The objective standard of what aims at man's union with God and, correspondingly, what is revealed in the

Word of God, provide a safe, if only approximate, distinction between philosophy and theology. By contrast, in the mere investigation of what lies in the human being, the postulates of pious consciousness and those of philosophical consciousness, the endeavor to clarify the feeling of dependence and the endeavor to understand the coherence of the world, usually can hardly be distinguished. In this way a whole series of dogmatic determinations about God, which Schleiermacher puts forward as postulates of the absolute feeling of dependency, are by no means this but rather only postulates of the speculative consciousness of God as the Absolute. Among these I count above all the teaching that God absolutely must stand outside of all opposites, cannot restrict Himself,[149] that is, must after all be the All-Being, and in connection with this, the fact that omniscience is not knowledge of the doing and thinking of human beings as other than God who limits their existence, but is only knowledge of His own being or doing, for which reason divine omniscience and omnipotence are "*one*," likewise omniscience and wisdom (p. 322), and there is no difference with God between possibility and reality, but everything that is thought of by Him, and everything that God thinks, is real (I, pp. 319–324). In this spirit Schleiermacher rejects the "expression of redemption in relation to the divine council" (II, p. 18) because for God there is no sin (that would be the act of an existence that restricts God) "because the Almighty cannot rearrange anything for someone else's sake which He has not ordained." For the divine counsel the work of redemption is therefore not real redemption (i.e., the abolition of a free discretionary act of man) but "second creation." But all of that is by no means a postulate of pious self-consciousness, since on the contrary this, as all experience shows, everywhere clings to the self-restricting God, to the possibility that man may commit an act not decreed by God (sin in the real sense), etc.; it is rather the interest of speculation, "philosophy" [der Wißbegierte], the endeavor to make the relation of absolute to derivative existence conceptually imaginable, to save the logical consequence of the world-conjuncture. All these propositions are therefore exactly the same as those set out by Spinoza, who is determined not by religious but by speculative interests: that God can have no limit and no contradiction, that God's thoughts are always real things at the same time, that with God nothing could be *potentia* which is not also *actu*, that there is no good

[149] [cannot be] "of a limited being understood in [terms of] contrast" (II, p. 55).

and bad for God because nothing can be that God Himself has not ordained or accomplished. The proof that these propositions are incompatible with Schleiermacher's decidedly anti-Spinozist belief in the living God, in His free and conscious causality, His dealing in purpose and intent for the eternal continuation of human personality, etc., likewise the proof that these propositions need not necessarily be accepted in this way from a speculative standpoint (cf. Part I above) would here be out of place. Nor do I deny either the partial truth or the infinite difficulty of these things. The purpose here was only to show that in the implementation, Schleiermacher completely confuses the interest of piety and the interest of speculation, the strict separation of which is precisely his principal standpoint.

Schleiermacher did not just tread the path of return in a time of general alienation from Christianity, he also achieved lasting gains in theology; he is filled with a deep, living awareness of the need for redemption as well as the glory of the Redeemer and salvation solely in the personal bond with Christ. In addition to his critical activity, which cannot produce any advancement either in its results or in its impetus, he also showed positive relations in the Christian doctrine of salvation in a new or at least more lively and scientifically coherent conception. But none of this must determine whether we should recognize or even want to hold onto his subjectivism and apriorism, the shortcomings of his time, and the inevitable consequences of these, even in the case of personal, intimate religious needs. Schleiermacher's teaching is very different regarding Christianity than Hegel's: the latter, according to its basic disposition, is in marked opposition to the same, albeit expressing itself in an apparently even-handed manner, the former with a decided appropriation of the same but with a shift in its basic relationships according to the point of view of subjectivity. That is why they each left so different an effect, comparable to the waxing and waning moons. Schleiermacher's school gained far greater entry into positive Christianity than did the master (the greatest praise that can be given to a master); Hegel's school – accounting for a few honorable exceptions – developed further into a decidedly pronounced contrast and in several not insignificant individuals even frivolity against Christianity. [150] Nevertheless, it is not individual heterodoxies in

---

[150] With this, however, I am far from wanting to place Schleiermacher above Hegel in

Schleiermacher's teaching that the Christian church has to reject, but rather his theology taken as a whole.

§. 67. With such a view of the relation between philosophy and religion, the *content of philosophy* has remained completely unaffected by revelation. The philosophers from Descartes to Fichte completely ignored revelation, which of course came back to haunt them. The expressions of appreciation, for example, by Descartes or Wolff, in some cases only in tribute to outward circumstances, are of no importance where the thing itself, the system, certifies the opposite. Leibniz constitutes a major exception with regard to his personal position on revelation. But he proceeds as if philosophy were to come *a priori* to the same result that revelation contains as given, *a posteriori*, which is contradictory, for if such a thing is possible, revelation would be superfluous and convicted of untruth since it presents itself as indispensable and in terms of its content as undiscoverable by any human wisdom. The demand for demonstration in the sense in which Leibniz puts it is in itself incompatible with the acceptance of revelation. And so everywhere up until Fichte, philosophy proceeds without even a sideways glance at the revelation which it should have to take into account. Only with Schelling did philosophy come to the realization that it could not leave this great phenomenon, the center of the destinies of the human race, outside its realm; and since then speculative philosophy has made the demand upon itself and the claim to create the unity of faith and knowledge, of philosophy and revelation in each of its philosophical systems. But the standpoint of speculative philosophy is always that it recognizes revelation as a great *object of its explanation* (as with nature, mythology, the French Revolution, etc.), not as what revelation itself wishes to be, the *source of the explanation*, and it brings revelation into harmony with itself only in that it subjects the content thereof to a different, indeed opposite, sense than that by which revelation understands itself.[151]

---

terms of philosophical depth and significance. It is precisely through his deep philosophical view of the objective coherence of the world order that Hegel opened up access to true Christian knowledge for those who carried with them a religious need from elsewhere, but who were closed to Schleiermacher's view.

[151] This ingenious but deeply untrue conception of the Christian religion was first and

Such an agreement is only an alleged one; in fact it contains an even more radical abrogation of revelation than ever before, as has been shown above. The previous one was ignorance and thus indirect exclusion, the present one is direct denial of it. This is also the inevitable result as long as philosophy makes the claim to begin "without presuppositions" from the *a priori* conscience and "to complete itself in a pure process that does not accept anything from the outside." For this claim is from the start in and of itself an absolute contradiction to revelation that can never be reconciled. But it no less runs counter to all experience. Even a philosophy which would accept the facts of revelation but would undertake to bring a deeper key to its understanding than the latter itself contains, which sought a foundation behind that which is laid there, never would count as a Christian philosophy, nor would it ever accomplish such an undertaking. Revelation can offer a key to a deeper understanding of the world, but the wisdom of the world cannot offer a key to a deeper understanding of revelation. The church has never needed philosophy for enlightenment or to support her faith; if that were so, it would rest on weak supports.

Schleiermacher, too, who maintains the complete independence of dogmatics from philosophy, instead puts philosophy out of all contact with revelation, in that he likewise expects apriorism, namely purely intellectual apriorism, of it. If religion really were only, as Schleiermacher puts it, the "highest *subjective function*" of man like philosophy is the "*objective*," then that would be correct. But if there is a revelation as an objective act of God, then it is inconceivable that philosophy completely ignore it. In vain does Schleiermacher postulate that these two functions, despite their complete independence, cannot contradict each other in their results, "because the contradiction between the two affects the essence of man."

This new conception of the relation is now opposed to the other extreme that prevailed in medieval philosophy and is later only found sporadically; it is to make revelation the *norm* of philosophy and to subordinate the latter to

---

in essence also immediately fully presented by Schelling in his eighth lecture on academic studies. What has since manifested itself as the so-called philosophy of religion vouchsafes nothing more than a broader elaboration of the compact thoughts there presented. As is well known, Schelling himself has since progressed to a different point of view.

theology as its servant (*serva theologiae*). In the great advantage of theology, its support from revelation, there is indeed the temptation to impose such submission on philosophy. Similar assumptions can even be found with regard to the empirical sciences, namely that natural investigation should recognize the biblical narrative as the norm and should avoid contradictions with it. But this runs against the essence of philosophy, in terms of which it represents an independent side of absolute knowledge, and generally against the essence of all science. Philosophy can be subjected to absolutely no norm outside of itself, that is, no norm other than the laws and conditions of knowledge, just as little as natural investigation may recognize any other measure than the observation of nature and the laws derived from it. Accordingly, the true relation between philosophy and revelation is that the latter is accepted and so tested by philosophy neither as a *norm* nor as a mere *object to be explained*, but rather as philosophy's *explanatory hypothesis*.

WORKS CITED

Berner, Albert Friedrich. *Grundlinien der criminalistischen Imputationslehre.* Berlin: Dümmler, 1843.

Bernoulli, Nikolaus. *Göttliches Recht und der Menschen Satzung: Durch einen Freund des Vaterländischen Rechts.* Basel: C. F. Spittler u. Comp., 1839.

Feuerbach, Ludwig. *Das Wesen des Christenthums.* Leipzig: Otto Wiegand, 1841.

Fichte, Johann Gottlieb. *J. G. Fichte's ... Appellation an das Publikum über die durch ein Kurf. Sächs. Confiscationsrescript ihm beigemessenen atheistischen Aeusserungen.* Jena und Leipzig; Tübingen: Christian Ernst Gabler; J. G. Cottaischen Buchhandlung, 1799.

Geulincs, Arnoldi. *Ethica.* Leyden: Adrianum Serverini, 1675.

Groen van Prinsterer, Guillaume. *Ter Nagedachtenis van Stahl.* Amsterdam: H. Höveker, 1862.

Harleß, Dr. Gottlieb Christoph Adolph. *Christliche Ethik.* 5th. Stuttgart: Verlag von Samuel Gottlieb Liesching, 1853.

Hegel, Georg Wilhelm Friedrich. *Encyclopädie der philosophischen Wissenschaften im Grundrisse.* 2nd ed. Heidelberg: August Oswald, 1827.

—. *Encyclopädie der philosophischen Wissenschaften im Grundrisse: Tl. 1: Die Logik.* Ed. Leopold von Henning. Vol. VI. Berlin: Duncker und Humblot, 1840.

—. *Enzyklopädie der philosophischen Wissenschaften im Grundrisse.* III vols. Heidelberg: Oßwald, 1830 [1817].

—. *Grundlinien der Philosophie des Rechts, oder Naturrecht und Staatswissenschaft im Grundrisse.* Ed. Eduard Gans. Berlin: Duncker und Humblodt, 1833.

—. *Philosophische Propädeutik (Werke, Achzehnter Band).* Berlin: Verlag von Duncker und Humblot, 1840.

—. *Vorlesungen über die Geschichte der Philosophie.* Berlin: Duncker und Humblot, 1836.

—. *Vorlesungen über die Philosophie der Religion.* II vols. Berlin: Duncker und Humblot, 1840.

Jacobi, Friedrich Heinrich. *Werke.* Vol. VI. Leipzig: Gerhard Fleischer, 1825.

Jarcke, Karl Ernst. *Die Lehre von der Aufhebung der Zurechnung durch unfreie Gemüthszustände.* Berlin: Dümmler, 1829.

Kant, Immanuel. *Critik der praktischen Vernunft.* Riga: Johann Friedrich Hartknoch, 1788.

—. *Grundlegung zur Metaphysik der Sitten.* Riga: Johann Friedrich Hartknoch, 1785.

—. *The Metaphysics of Morals.* Trans. Mary Gregor. Cambridge: Cambridge University Press, 1996.

Locke, John. *Two Treatises of Government.* Ed. Peter Laslett. New York: New American Library, 1965 [1960]. First edition 1689.

Machiavelli, Niccolò. *Il Principe.* Rome: Antonio Blado d'Asola, 1532.

Melanchthon, Philip. *Philosophiae Moralis Epitomes Libri duo...* Mylius, 1546.

Montesquieu, Charles de Secondat, Baron de. *L'Ésprit de Loix.* Geneva: Barrillot & Fils, 1748.

Naugle, David K. *Worldview: The History of a Concept.* Grand Rapids, MI: Wm. B. Eerdmans Publishing Co., 2002.

Richter, Heinrich. *Das philosophische Strafrecht begründet auf die Idee der Gerechtigkeit.* Leipzig: Verlag der Hartmannschen Buchhandlung, 1829.

Rothe, Richard. *Die Anfänge der christlichen Kirche und ihrer Verfassung.* Wittenberg: In der Zimmermann'schen Buchhandlung, 1837.

Savigny, Friedrich Carl von. *Vom Beruf unsrer Zeit für Gesetzgebung und Rechtswissenschaft.* Heidelberg: bey Mohr und Zimmer, 1814.

Schelling, Friedrich Wilhelm Joseph. *Philosophische Untersuchungen ueber das Wesen der menschlichen Freiheit und die damit zusammenhaengende Gegenstaende.* Reutlingen: Ensslinsche Buchhandlung, 1834.

—. *System des transcendentalen Idealismus.* Tübingen: J.G. Cotta'schen Buchhandlung, 1800.

—. *Vorlesungen über die Methode des akademischen Studiums.* Tübingen: J. C. Cotta'schen Buchhandlung, 1803.

Schleiermacher, Friedrich. *Der christliche Glaube nach den Grundsätzen der evangelischen Kirche im Zusammenhange dargestellt.* 2nd. Berlin: G. Reimer, 1830–1831.

—. *Die Lehre vom Staat.* Ed. Chr. A. Brandis. Berlin: G. Reimer, 1845.

—. *Grundriß der philosophischen Ethik.* Ed. August Twesten. Berlin: G. Reimer, 1841.

—. "Über die Begriffe der verschiedenen Staatsformen." *Abhandlungen der Königlichen Akademie der Wissenschaften in Berlin* (1814–1815).

Spinoza, Benedict de. *The Ethics of Benedict de Spinoza.* Trans. "D. D. S." New York & London: D. Van Nostrand, G. P. Putnam's Sons, 1888 [1677].

Stahl, Friedrich Julius. *Der Protestantismus als politisches Princip.* Berlin: Verlag von Wilhelm Schultze, 1853.

—. *Die Kirchenverfassung nach Lehre und Recht der Protestanten.* Erlangen: Theodor Bläsing, 1840.

—. *Principles of Law.* Aalten: WordBridge Publishing, 2007.

—. *Private Law.* Aalten: WordBridge Publishing, 2007.

—. *Siebzehn parlamentarische Reden und drei Vorträge ... Nach letzwilliger Bestimmung geordnet und herausgegeben.* Berlin: Verlag von Wilhelm Hertz, 1862.

—. *The Doctrine of State and the Principles of State Law.* Aalten: WordBridge Publishing, 2009.

—. *The Recovery of Historical Law: Volume 1B of the Philosophy of Law: The History of Legal Philosophy.* Aalten: WordBridge Publishing, 2021.

—. *The Rise and Fall of Natural Law: Volume 1A of the Philosophy of Law: The History of Legal Philosophy.* Aalten: WordBridge Publishing, 2020.

Strauss, David Friedrich. *Die christliche Glaubenslehre in ihrer geschichtlichen Entwicklung und im Kampfe mit der modernen Wissenschaft.* II vols. Tübingen: C. F. Oslander, 1840.

Trendelenburg, Friedrich Adolf. *Logische Untersuchungen.* Berlin: G. Bethge, 1840.

Vatke, Wilhelm. *Die menschliche Freiheit in ihrem Verhältnisz zur Sünde und zur göttlichen Gnade wissenschaftlich dargestellt.* Berlin: Verlag von G. Bethke, 1841.

Wolff, Christian Freiherr von. *Vernünfftige gedancken von der menschen thun und lassen: zu Beförderung ihrer Glückseeligkeit, den Liebhabern der Wahrheit mitgetheilet von Christian freyherrn von Wolff*... 3rd. Halle im Magdeburgischen: Rengerischen Buchhandlung, 1752.

SCRIPTURE INDEX

GENERAL INDEX

Principles of Law

TABLE OF CONTENTS

NOTES ON THIS EDITION

The edition used for this translation is the 3rd edition of the *Philosophy of Law*, published by Mohr of Tübingen in 1854. I have endeavored to adhere as closely to the literal text as possible while maintaining readability. Words in German which are susceptible to multiple meanings or the meaning of which was ambiguous have been left in the text in square brackets. Square brackets are also used to insert interpolations for understanding or to provide supplementary material. Section headings do not appear in the original: they are of my own device.

Numbers which appear in bold between two angular brackets (like this: **<1>**) are page numbers of the original edition. Apart from the Table of Contents, references in the text and in the Index to page numbers in this book therefore refer to that page numbering.

Roman-and canon-legal terms in Latin are set off in the text with a boldface Roman font, e.g., **facultas**. Many of these terms may be referenced in William Smith, *A Dictionary of Greek and Roman Antiquities* (URL: https://books.google.com/books?id=HqUKAAAAIAAJ).

Weltanschauung, vision of the world, is translated in the accepted manner as worldview. Stahl was one of the original proponents of the worldview approach. The notion of worldview took wing when, in the face of the rationalism which was predominant in the 18th century, speculative philosophy began to postulate the primacy of prerational vision, the presuppositional framework on the basis of which reason operates. This had the effect of making explicit the subjectivism which was already rampant but lay hidden behind the guise of rational objectivity. Worldview-ism certainly is a product of that turn; worldview could be and has been abused in terms of subjectivism, but the abuse does not negate the use. Stahl demonstrates as much as he outlines here the Christian worldview in its philosophical and scientific application.

A note about the notoriously difficult words "Recht" and "Gesetz": as is well known, English has no direct counterpart to them; they both refer to "law." Often they are used synonymously, but just as often they are not. It is similar to the Latin words "jus" and "lex," which confront the translator with the same ambiguity. Be that as it may, "Recht" more often refers to law in the more elevated, transcendent sense, while "Gesetz" refers to law in the positive, man-made sense. For this reason, I often have translated "Gesetz" as "statute." And while "Recht" in the singular refers to law, in the plural ("Rechten") it refers to rights.

GENERAL PREFACE TO "THE DOCTRINE OF LAW AND STATE ON THE BASIS OF THE CHRISTIAN WORLDVIEW"

<ix> Together with the *History of Legal Philosophy*, *The Doctrine of Law and State on the Basis of the Christian Worldview* comprises Friedrich Julius Stahl's magnum opus, *The Philosophy of Law*. This multivolume production provides us with the philosophical foundations upon which Stahl's career as a professor of constitutional law, as a parliamentarian, and as a statesman in 19th century Bavaria and Prussia was based.[1] It is also unique: it is the only comprehensive work of legal philosophy produced by a modern, post-French-Revolution conservative, to wit, a follower of the pioneer in this regard, Edmund Burke.

Conservatism has always been in need of such a comprehensive philosophical system. For opposition to the Revolution did not necessarily lead to unity of worldview. Many conservatives were Roman Catholic and hence argued for a return to (idealized) pre-revolutionary conditions in church and state, thus for the primacy of the monarchy and the papacy – these generally bore the name Counter-Revolutionary. Others were Protestant, and thus perceived a need to move beyond pre-revolutionary conditions, albeit in a manner which maintained continuity with the political, legal, and cultural inheritance of Europe. Among the latter group Stahl was pre-eminent; he was the first of the so-called Anti-Revolutionaries, who in the Netherlands even formed a political party under the leadership of Guillaume Groen van Prinsterer and Abraham Kuyper.

<x> Stahl was a protege of Friedrich Carl von Savigny, himself the pioneer of the "Burkean" worldview in Germany. Savigny is best known for his argument against codification and in favor of legal continuity, including the primacy of customary law, as contained in his *On the Vocation of Our Age for Legislation and Legal Science*. Such arguments were com-

---

[1] For more on Stahl's life see Ruben Alvarado, *Authority Not Majority* (Aalten: WordBridge, 2007).

pletely in line with what Edmund Burke had argued in his *Reflections on the Revolution in France* and elsewhere. Savigny founded what came to be known as the Historical School of Jurisprudence, perhaps the most influential school of legal science Germany ever produced.

The problem with this school was that it lacked a solid grounding in legal philosophy. Writing in 1901, James Viscount Bryce, the noted legal historian and diplomat of late 19th-early 20th century Britain, claimed that in view of its methodology it is "more applicable to the law of any particular country than to the theory of law in general, for the details of legal history vary so much in different countries that immense knowledge and unusual architectonic power are needed to combine their general results for the purposes of a comprehensive theory" (*Studies in History and Jurisprudence*, II, p. 186). Indeed, Bryce considered the task so monumental that he doubted it had ever been done, though it "may be done, and so will doubtless be done some day. Everything happens at last."

As a matter of fact, the task had long since been accomplished, even by someone "of the requisite capacity" as stipulated by Bryce.[2] In fact, Stahl had already published the first edition of his *The Doctrine of Law and State on the Basis of the Christian Worldview*, presenting a legal philosophy sprung from the loins of the Savignian historical method, back in the 1830s when he was a young law professor in Bavaria. Savigny recognized it as providing the essential underpinnings in eternal veri- **<xi>** ties that he himself had failed to produce.[3] And in providing this service,

---

[2] For more on the curious ignorance of Stahl on the part of future generations, see the preface to G. Groen van Prinsterer, *In Memory of Stahl* (Aalten: Pantocrator Press, 2022).

[3] For an alternative interpretation of this development, see John E. Toews, "The Immanent Genesis and Transcendent Goal of Law: Savigny, Stahl, and the Ideology of the Christian German State," *The American Journal of Comparative Law*, 37, no. 2 (Winter, 1989), 139–169; idem, *Becoming Historical: Cultural Reformation and Public Memory in Early Nineteenth-Century Berlin* (New York: Cambridge University Press, 2004), ch. 5: "The Tension Between Immanent and Transcendent Subjectivity in the Historical School of Law: From Savigny to Stahl."

Stahl not only gave the Historical School a philosophical basis, he gave the Burkean common law school of thought a basis as well, although the Anglo-Saxon world of jurisprudence was unaware of it, then as now.

The English common law has never enjoyed the philosophical attention that has been lavished on Continental legal systems. The reason is of course its being a product of court practice without being made the continuous subject of scholarly analysis, as was done on the Continent. Even so, this did not preclude the development of a unique legal philosophy which, although it did not attain to the sophistication of Continental efforts, nevertheless developed into a full-fledged philosophical jurisprudence in its own right, inoculating the legal system from the challenge of natural-rights jurisprudence and enlightened-despot codification efforts the likes of which took over on the Continent during the 18th century Enlightenment. The common-law approach pioneered by Edward Coke, John Selden, and Matthew Hale (Coke and Hale were chief justices) provided the basis for Burke's political philosophy. And from this root came the Continental resurgence of conservatism, which had been driven out of business by Enlightenment rationalism.[4] **<xii>**

Regardless of the success this approach had both in preserving English common-law traditions and in reinvigorating Continental common-law traditions, in terms of legal philosophy it remained rudimentary. William Blackstone's *Commentaries on the Laws of England* (1769), which served as target practice for Jeremy Bentham and his utilitarianism, is paradigmatic in this regard. Indeed, from Bentham onward it might be stated that utilitarianism and pragmatism have been the leading philosophical approaches for dealing with the common law (e.g., Oliver Wendell Holmes, Roscoe Pound). And that legacy lives on into the present day (as witness its latest iteration, "Law and Economics," as exemplified in the work of Richard Posner and Richard Epstein). The alternative is a natural- rights school of thought based essentially on John Locke and the *Declaration of Independence*, and which in consequence is constantly fighting

---

[4] On this most interesting history, see Harold J. Berman, "The Origins of Historical Jurisprudence: Coke, Selden, Hale," *Yale Law Journal* 103, no. 7 (1994).

a rear-guard action against French Revolutionary principles.[5]

It might seem anachronistic that help on this front would come, of all places, from pre-Bismarckian Germany. But the sense of anachronism fades when one realizes the affinity between the pre-Revolutionary Continental and English legal systems. It is the divergence between these two which is constantly emphasized; but how is it, then, that Burke could postulate a fundamental legal continuity across Western Europe which was only ruptured by the French Revolution?[6] Indeed, Savigny and his followers recognized in English common law a cognate legal system to the German pre-codification legal system. Which is what makes Stahl's legal philosophy so interesting to common-law legal science. Stahl provides principles applicable to the English common law as well as Continental law, for he draws upon the common inheritance of Western legal science such as described in part by Harold Berman in his *Law* **<xiii>** *and Revolution*,[7] a legal science sharing essential characteristics, maintaining similar institutions, pursuing similar goals.

What Stahl does is provide an understanding of the solid, unchanging foundations to the evolving, adapting thing which is the common law. Considerations of utility and pragmatism are made subordinate to principles of justice and what he calls providential purposes, within the context of historical development. Burke's partnership "between those who are living, those who are dead, and those who are to be born"[8] finds a

---

[5] For details on this see my *Trojan Horse: Natural Rights and America's Founding* (Aalten: WordBridge, 2022).

[6] "If diffident of yourselves, and not clearly discerning the almost obliterated constitution of your ancestors, you had looked to your neighbours in this land, who had kept alive the ancient principles and models of the old common law of Europe meliorated and adapted to its present state – by following wise examples you would have given new examples of wisdom to the world." Edmund Burke, *Reflections on the Revolution in France,* vol. 2 of *Select Works of Edmund Burke* (Indianapolis: Liberty Fund, 1999), p. 125.

[7] Harold J. Berman, *Law and Revolution: The Formation of the Western Legal Tradition* (Cambridge, ma: Harvard University Press, 1983).

[8] Burke, *Reflections,* p. 193.

distinct echo here, as does his conceptualization of rights as inheritance rather than *a priori,* a-historical givens. Likewise, rights are made subordinate to law rather than being the source of law as conceived by the natural-rights school. What's more, Stahl provides subjective right with a clear position and demarcation within the legal system, which is a feat in itself and, perhaps more than anything else, is needed in today's confused, rights-bloated jurisprudence.

The concept he uses to establish these foundations is that of a *doctrine* of law and state. In the introduction he provided to Volume II as a whole (see *Philosophical Foundations*, p. 1), Stahl explains this notion of doctrine: it is something other than jurisprudence on the one hand and legal philosophy on the other. Jurisprudence is the science of a particular legal system as it exists in a particular country at a particular time; legal philosophy is its opposite, bringing "law and state into connection with the highest cause and the final goal of all existence" (*Philosophical Foundations,* p. 2). The doctrine of law and state occupies an intermediate position. It generalizes from jurisprudence while it particularizes from legal **<xiv>** philosophy. It operates in terms of universals but fleshes out those universals in terms of the particulars provided by jurisprudence. In so doing it provides universal criteria out of which particular legal systems can be generated and by which they can be judged.

Stahl bases this doctrine of law and state on the Christian worldview: because historically the nations of Western civilization likewise were based on that worldview, and because every such universal doctrine must base itself on one worldview or another. "Every philosophical system of whatever name in the final analysis rests on a foundational presupposition that is nothing more than faith, no matter what claim it may make to so-called scientific certainty" (*Philosophical Foundations,* p. 3). So, ultimately Stahl provides us with a Christian common-law legal philosophy, in doing so epitomizing the Western legal tradition in its conservative variant.

PREFACE TO THE "PRINCIPLES OF LAW"

<xv>This book is a translation of Book II of *The Doctrine of Law and State,* originally entitled "The Law" [Das Recht]. The title I have given it better reflects its contents: it contains the principles, the nuts and bolts, of Stahl's doctrine of law and state which then find specific application in Books III and IV, on private law and state law, respectively. It is, as it were, the wheelhouse: here in concentrated form are the elements which distinguish Stahl's common-law, Historical School approach, cast in terms of his Christian faith.

The Christian difference to the legal order is not to be found in any religious test or requirement of conformity but in the Christian character of legal institutions. Stahl accomplishes this by making institutions rather than actions the cornerstone of law (§. 3). Law is a general rule, not a specific command; and institutions, not persons, are its primary object. Persons operate within the framework established by law, but that law is an external, objective framework, not an internal, subjective one. The right of the person and the rights of persons are established and defended precisely by this objectively Christian order. Therefore, what is Christian about this legal order is the principles, the law-ideas, upon which it is based, not the level of faith of those living within it. Stahl assumes a Christian society but not individual Christians. In this his approach is similar to that of T.S. Eliot.[9]

This Christian orientation also demands a respect for the inheritance of the nation, conservation of its received institutions and laws – in Stahl's words, "piety" (p. 73 below). It calls <xvi> for obedience to the laws even where they might conflict with justice and the law-ideas, precisely because it recognizes the God-sanctioned authority of law and state as established by the people as something inviolable and as something to which God Himself has commanded obedience. Such an approach rules out a Lockean "right of resistance," but so does it likewise rule out a judicial activism which would overthrow laws on the basis of higher princi-

[9] *The Idea of a Christian Society* (London: Faber and Faber, 1939).

ples of justice. Law is rooted in custom and tradition, supplemented through legislation; only then do the courts have a voice, and it is a derivative, not an original one. The courts are bound to the law as the expression of the historical people, not ephemeral public opinion.

Key elements of the principles of law:

- law and state are dimensions of God's world order, but are entrusted to the people
- law therefore is a product of a specific people, of a nation
- law is historically conditioned: it is therefore not a mere product of the legislative power
- law is positive, which means:
  - natural law is not enforceable law
  - the law which is enforceable is that which has been previously established as law
  - enforceable law is established through custom and legislation, not by judges: judges are bound to the positive law and may not legislate from the bench
- principles of justice and ethics find their incorporation in the law through the medium of the people (custom) or the ruling authorities (legislation)
- the right of personality is natural, concrete rights are acquired

<xvii>

A Synopsis of the "Principles of Law": Law and Morality

Law is an outward, external order, and it is an order to be established by the human community as its own order. It is an order entrusted to the people, and although the people have this trust in subservience to God, they are independently empowered to generate and enforce it. Morality, by contrast, is an affair of individuals, of inward fulfillment, of positive virtues. Law is the order of the general rule and the common condition, morality is the order of the particular act.

Law concerns institutions. These institutions – personality and property, marriage and the family, local community, station, the state, the church – are the objects which law aims to maintain and promote.

The purpose of law is both to maintain God's order and to establish individual rights: God not only requires obedience, He provides individuals with the room to develop and establish themselves in the world. "These are the two factors of the ethical world: ethical power with its commands, and man in his free personality, which through law receive their determinate, precisely circumscribed validity in common life" (p. 16).

Law is grounded in the purposes established by God in the natural creation. These natural, factual functions (i.e., possession, procreation, community) form the kernels of legal institutions such as property, marriage, and the state. This is Aristotle's principle of entelechy properly understood. Law is thus rooted in material life and must accord with it.

Law does not command specific acts; it is a general rule. It therefore establishes negative boundaries rather than positive performances. "Law is not to realize the ethical idea of every institution *in its positive content*, but is only to preserve **<xviii>** its *outermost boundaries*, only enough to preserve the concept, to keep its opposite from manifesting itself" (p. 20). For law to command positive ethical fulfillment would be for it to become totalitarian; it would destroy individual freedom "and with it true ethics" (p. 21).

Justice, for its part, is not the formative principle of law – that is the inherent principles of natural life. But justice ensures that the principle of personality is preserved within those legal arrangements. Together with life purposes, justice determines law, ensuring that it responds to personhood.

The relationship of law to the state is twofold: the law requires the state for it to maintain itself in human life, while the state requires the law as the source of its very existence. Together they form the civil order. No "state of nature" preceded the establishment of the state per se – in this sense, the state is natural, not the product of human choice.

The major error of modern legal philosophy is its natural-rights orientation, which makes law and the state into creatures of individual choice, in which individuals through a social contract choose to leave the "state of nature" and form a government and a set of laws under which to be ruled. Furthermore, the principle upon which social life is supposed to have been established has been steadily watered down from Grotius's "desire for community" to Thomasius's "pursuit of happiness," finally leaving us with Kant's "live and let live" principle of coexistence as the only bond of the social order. This whole approach is oblivious to the fact that human social order, being an inheritance, is a higher order transcending individual choice: "In truth, the life of human commonality (the people) is not mere coexistence... rather, it is the common unified fulfillment of a higher order, the ethical world plan; the freedom of individual men is not the sphere of law, but only a part of it" (p. 27). He- **<xix>** gelian and other forms of "organic" philosophy, despite their shortcomings, have this merit, that they restored the recognition of this supra-individual concept of legal order.

Positive Law and Natural Law

Modern legal philosophy compounds its error by either making natural law into a directly applicable legal standard or abandoning law to the play of interests, cutting off any influence from higher principles. Neither is appropriate. There are two principles to be affirmed in this regard: 1) positive law is law in the strict sense: there is no other law, and it is owed obedience as such; 2) positive law is to be subordinated to "law-ideas" (the principles of law as described in ch. 1), but only during the phase of legal formation by authorized organs, not by individual citizens – the sources of law are to be subordinated to the principles of law. God's divine order is the archetype of law, but it is not directly applicable as law. In fact, God commands that the law as it stands is to be obeyed, regardless of its correspondence to the principles of law. Human freedom under God is the freedom to crystallize and make concrete those principles of law as a positive legal order. Natural law lacks objectivity, universal recognition, publicity in the sense that it can be known by everyone ahead of time; it therefore cannot be enforced by the state. In fact, to do so is to establish opinion and thus injustice as law. "The rule of natural law is therefore in truth only the establishment of the arbitrariness of any opinion over the common public order; it is the establishment of the war of all against all" (p. 38). This was the principle underlying the French Revolution.

Besides the principle of subjection to the law-ideas, positive law is generated in terms of historical continuity. Continuity is crucial to the regard for law, for if law is created in a haphazard, arbitrary fashion by lawmakers from above, it loses its **<xx>** sanctity as the expression of the "wisdom of the ages." The primitive condition in which law, justice, morality, and the like exist commingled, without distinction one from the other, is left behind; but in this process of differentiation, if continuity is maintained, then the original correlation of law and justice is never lost sight of.

The law as revealed in the Old and New Testaments serves two purposes: as a source of law-ideas, along with reason and conscience; and as the source of specifically revealed law unique to it, such as Sabbath regulation, marriage among close relations, divorce, and church law. Hence, "the commands of the Christian revelation, like those of reason and justice, form a binding standard for the establishment of law, a claim on the legislator. But they are this in far higher degree and in an entirely different form than the latter, because they enjoy the special sanction of God, and because He Himself indicated their particular form, which otherwise is left to human freedom" (p. 43). In particular, the Christian nations of Europe are bound to this law, Christianity having been formative to their development.

Modern natural law theory has gotten to the point that it accepts natural law as a subsidiary standard in addition to positive law. By contrast, the Historical School of Law made the advance of recognizing in positivity the true nature of law, rejecting the direct enforcement of natural law by the state. On the other hand, it must guard against the opposite error of rejecting subordination to the principles of law altogether.

The Romans were the first to realize the principle of the positivity of law in its purity; it is a misreading of the sources to attribute to them notions of natural law. **<xxi>**

The Origin and Sources of Law

Because law arises through the human community, it takes two basic forms, in accordance with the two main forms human community exhibits: statute, via the ruling authorities who represent the people, and custom, or observance by the people themselves.

Custom is the original form of legal generation. It is produced when the people observe certain norms in a certain way over a period of time such that those norms-in-practice come to be considered a part of the social fabric enforceable by the state. Statute or legislation arises on the foundation of custom; it is generated through deliberation on the part of the ruling authorities and is thus the product of reflection rather than spontaneous generation. Even so, it presupposes custom for its very existence, and must never presume to replace custom.

Neither custom nor legislation must answer to the popular viewpoint regarding law at any given time. Both custom and legislation may at a specific point in history diverge from public opinion. Their validity is inherent in themselves; the law has validity above and beyond what public opinion may think of it. The law is conditioned both by its history and by the principles embodied in it; neither can be discarded should the popular viewpoint change. Public opinion must first be applied through the medium of the sources of law (custom and legislation); therefore, its application must answer to the received body of law; there can be no question of willy-nilly lawmaking on the basis of swings in the popular conviction. And if one divorces the law from God and His order as its ultimate ground, one delivers it over to the exclusive dominion of this popular conviction, with all the consequences thereof.

Therefore, codification is a bad idea, for it wishes to remake the law in a single act of rational creative power, disavowing the wisdom and the lessons embodied in the received **<xxii>** legal order. It is legislation gone haywire, have lost all connection with that order.

Legal science, while not a source of law, is a crucial discipline to the development of the legal order, for it helps to discover custom, to interpret existing law, and consequently to discern the underlying principles of the law, making them available for the future generation of law. In so doing, "it ... brings the latent content of the law to full and harmonious development" (p. 64). For example, legal science played a crucial role in the development of Roman law, apart from any form of legislation. It finds direct application in court practice, through "the evenhanded application of a norm," by which "the courts become the actual organ, i.e., means of determination, for legal science, in the way custom is for the popular consciousness and statutes are for the will of the ruling authorities" (p. 66). Court practice thus takes its place alongside custom and legislation as a third source of law, albeit a derivative and not a primary source.

The legal order as so construed is one in which the law places great stock on historical continuity, in fact as inheritance. It was the Historical School of Law, especially Savigny, who brought this truth to light "in the teeth of the leading orientation of the times" (p. 73). The natural-law school of thought had even gone so far as to consider language to be the product of convention, of mutual agreement.

The Popular Character of Law

Although not the expression of public opinion, law is an expression of popular character. This is the consequence of law being the vocation of a people, of a nation. Every people and nation has a specific character. This character as expressed in the law is the popular character of law. Thus peoples and nations are the proper subjects of law. This does not absolve **<xxiii>** peoples and nations from the obligation to submit to God's order and commandments; rather, it locates the appropriate basis for realizing that order in free expression. The principle of popular character embodies the idea of the nationality of law, that law is in principle indigenous rather than being imposed from the outside, and that of the popularity of the law, meaning that law is to be generally comprehensible and accessible.

Roman law occupies a peculiar position here in that it has had such an impact historically especially on German law. The popular character of the law does not entail the rejection of this influence, not even of the Reception of Roman law in Germany. The Reception is a fact of life that cannot be undone; furthermore, it mainly affected areas of private law in which indigenous German law was undeveloped.

The popular character of the law has been subverted into the principle of popular sovereignty over the law. In this approach, the popular conviction and public opinion are made into direct sources of law, rather than being mediated through custom and legislation. It leads to the condition wherein the law can be changed from day to day, wherein there is no continuity, no predictability, hence no chance to anticipate future conditions. Such a notion of popular character runs directly contrary to that of the Historical School, which views the people in terms of the historical continuum, not the isolated present.

Legal Obligation

Legal obligation is twofold: the requirement of the ruling authorities to uphold the law, and that of the people to obey it. It is a restricted obligation, in that it, in line with the distinction between law and morality, does not mandate specific perfor- **<xxiv>** mances but rather prohibits infringements of the general rule which is the law.

Rights: Law in the Subjective Sense

Rights form an essential component of the legal order. They are the expression of subjective personality within the objective common order. They are the expression of a person's inherent ethical power vis-à-vis others, leading to duties on the part of others. But rights are not the be all and end all of law; rather, they form a secondary principle of the legal order. The primary principle is the life purposes ingrained in the natural order, which provide the basis for rights and brings them into coherence.

Rights are not derived from duties; instead, rights create duties. But rights and duties find a higher coherence in the concept of vocation. Vocation determines both rights and duties and serves as their standard of judgment. "It is the *ethical, specifically Christian conception to consider rights only in the light of vocation*" (p. 100).

Rights are of two forms: innate and acquired. Innate rights are: "life, liberty, honor, afterwards the general capacity for property, family, political and ecclesiastical rights" (p. 103), while acquired rights are all those rights actually formed through that general capacity. Therefore, many so-called natural rights are actually acquired rights and so cannot be considered to be the portion a person has by nature, such that the lack thereof (e.g., property) can be considered a violation of such rights. It was the error of the French Revolution to confuse acquired rights with rights such as they would exist in an ideal situation. But, as Stahl points out, "There exists just as little an opposition and a dividing line between primeval [i.e., natural] right and the rights of positive law as between the law of reason and positive law. In terms of his idea (thus by na- **<xxv>** ture), man of necessity has rights just as the community has a legal order, but which rights he has is everywhere first more specifically determined by positive law" (p. 104). The Revolutionary doctrine is to consider property, participatory government, and the like to be the natural birthright of all people the absence of which indicates an unwarranted deprivation, while in reality these are institutions subject to development through positive law, without a priori specification. They are the product of the advance of civilization, not the properties of an original state of nature.

The System of Law

Legal institutions are the formative components of the legal order. Such institutions are "complexes" of factual relations based on life purposes, put into a legal form. These legal institutions stand in reciprocal relation to the factual relations upon which they are based, both influencing them and being influenced by them. The sum total of these legal relations integrated into a coherent whole is the legal system.

Every people forms its own legal system, each however merely adapting those general legal institutions in terms of specific conditions.

Rights are always a subordinate component of the legal system; they are determined by legal institutions and therefore are creatures of those institutions. Therefore, law is not primarily freedom and entitlement, but order, and the legal system is not a coherency of rights but of orders (legal institutions). **<xxvi>**

Private Law and Public Law

The legal system has two main areas, private law and public law, corresponding to the dual relation of common life, which is individuals in themselves and individuals as members of the whole. Private law serves the purposes of the individual, public law those of the whole. Private law involves integrity and freedom of the person, property, family; public law, state and church. The principle behind public law is not common utility but a common rule, thus a higher order above utility.

Civil Justice and Equity

Civil justice is justice as applied in the civil order. It has two main forms, protective and retributive. Protective justice serves to restore infringements of rights, where such infringements do not likewise involve an attack on the legal order itself, or on the authority of the state to maintain that order. It is satisfied when the wrong is righted by way of compensation. Retributive justice, on the other hand, is meted out by the state as a violation of its own right, as it were; the state punishes those deeds done with an eye to the active frustration of the maintenance of legal order. "This is the concept of *crime,* and its consequence in terms of justice is punishment as restoration of the regard for the violated legal order" (p. 126).

For its part, equity stands in opposition to the law, restoring an original equality of advantages and disadvantages where the law does not obtain, as for instance in a situation of confused boundaries. Where entitlement does exist, equity cannot be called upon to overrule that entitlement. The Romans had a system of equity (**bonum et aequum**) which they set up to make up for shortcomings in positive law (**strictum jus**). Where equity is applied, it does not express an objective norm nor the national conviction, but rather, since it attaches only to the particular case, it is solely personal judgment without fur- **<xxvii>** ther effect. In that sense it is thus a subjective rather than objective principle.

PRINCIPLES OF LAW

CHAPTER 1: THE CONCEPT OF LAW AND ITS RELATIONSHIP TO MORALITY

§. 1. Law as the Outward Order of Human Community

The place which law assumes within the entirety of the ethical field has already been shown [in *Philosophical Foundations*].

The ethical field has two relations: the *image of God* in *persons* and God's *world order* in the *human race.* The former is the likeness to God, holiness, to which each person is called, each for himself. The latter is the form and order that God ordains for the entire human race in its common life, its common uniform existence, the edifice of social relations He established for mankind's natural preservation and ethical fulfillment, the plan of the ethical world. The former is concerned with the *virtues* (truthfulness, courage, love, compassion, continence, ascesis), the latter with *institutions* (protection of life, property, marriage, respect for elders, ruling authority [Obrigkeit]); each in mutual permeation and unity (*Philosophical Foundations,* §§. 25, 26, 30).

While the preservation of the image of God in man is God's business, through His commands and His inner power in the conscience, along with free fulfillment by men, the human community itself is to uphold God's world order in the human race through a *human order,* an order which it is to establish, and under which it is to subordinate all individuals through outward power. This order is *law.*

God Himself indeed maintains His world order in the human race, and He does so directly, through His commands and His power in conscience by means of the free fulfillment **<8>** of individuals. Lacking this, the edifice of the ethical world would collapse, security of life, property, and ordered family could not exist; indeed, these realize their fulfilled existence in accordance with their full requirement purely and simply through conscience in free fulfillment. However, in order for God's world order not to be dependent on the conscience of individual persons but to exist regardless, uninterrupted, at least at a bare minimum, at the outermost boundaries of His commands: for this reason human community shall establish the order of law over all individuals.

There is a dual ground for this: firstly, given the fortuitousness of human fulfillment – in fact, the dominant tendency to disobey God's commands – God's world order would not be maintained without such an order of law, and while there would be individuals acting ethically, the collective existence of the human race would not exhibit an ethical form and could not maintain itself against the destructive power of evildoers. Secondly, the maintenance of God's world order by the human race is itself a fulfillment of human existence and therefore itself an essential part of this world order. For this expresses the ethical will of the human community as such, as a unity, to fulfill God's commands. Even if men truly for conscience's sake refrained from murder and theft, lived in monogamy and raised their children, honored their parents – all that would only be the ethical deed of individuals, each for himself; God's world order as a whole should also be the ethical act of the human race as a whole.

Now then, in accordance with the self-reliance and unique originality [Ureigenheit] that runs through the entire realm of personal being, the human community is to establish this order, through which it maintains God's world order, *on its own as its own order*. In return, it is to give shape to the ideas of the world-plan, which in themselves are a creative conception <9> of God, with creative spirit, each community according to its own understanding and natural disposition in terms of time and lineage [Stamm] and in accordance with its wisdom regarding the prevailing situation; it shall even combine and permeate these with its own humanly proposed goals, and establish and maintain the thus-formed order under God's authorization by virtue of its own regard [Ansehens]. That is the high position and worth to which the human race is called. It is not simply to fulfill God's commands but also to establish and maintain this order as an instrument and vessel of world rule under God's influence. Man thereby assumes the godlike position of ethical steward, of lawgiver and judge.

For this reason, this order is entrusted to the *people,* whether naturally or politically formed, because only a people has the unity of worldview and the seeds of creative formation – it being in fact a form of higher personality – and for this reason such an order is not charged to the people as a mass of individuals but in their unity, that is, in their organization as a state, in their obedience to ruling authority. In fact, the ruling authority is itself the highest element of that order.

This is the sphere of the civil order – the sphere of law and state – opposite the spheres of religion and morality, an external kingdom, founded on authority and the arrangement of human ruling authority opposite the kingdom founded on God's immediate command and immediate power in conscience. This is the origin of that *dualism of commands,* moral and legal. For God Himself there is no dualism. His image in man and His world order in the human race are determined in complete unity and agreement through His own thought, and effectuated through His own command, being made known in conscience. However, with that world order also being entrusted to human ruling authority, independently, and thus in certain situations outside <10> of God – for this reason a second ethical order arises, law, separated from the original divine order, deviating from it, in fact often opposed to it.

Law therefore is the life-order of the people and of the community of nations for the preservation of God's world order. Although it is a human order, it serves the divine order, is determined by God's commands, is founded on God's authorization.[10]

The relationship of law to morality (including religion) is this: morality contains God's immediate commands, law the commands of human

---

[10] The conceptual delineation of law in the second edition of this book was yet insufficient on this point, in that it only brought forth one characteristic, common existence in distinction to individual existence, while leaving aside the second distinction, law's being ordered through human community itself, and thus human ruling authority as distinguished from an immediate divine command. However, it would be just as insufficient if one were only to bring this second characteristic to the fore, whereby law is the embodiment of the commands of human ruling authority, for then it would be a matter of indifference if the ruling authority were to prescribe ascesis and complete holiness in its commands, while furthermore all arrangements of common welfare [polizeilich Verfügungen] would fall within the sphere of law.

ruling authority. Morality is an obligation on men, each for himself; law is an obligation on the nation in its unity. Morality includes the entire ethical sphere; law excludes sanctification, the virtues of men, and only includes the ethical construction of human common existence, and even this only in accordance with its barest existence [nothdürftigsten Bestande]. Morality inspires the activity of will of individuals, law an objective external order; the former, ethical action, the latter, an ethical form of public condition; the former, the particular act, the latter, the general uniformly observed rule. All of this will be explained in more detail in the following exposition. <11>

§. 2. The Subject of Law: The People

The *subject* of law is the people in *its unity*, thus the *state,* not the individual as such. This means that law is the vocation of the people. It is a command, initially extended to the peoples and their ruling authorities, which they are to realize in their common life. It is required of the people and its ruling authority that public security, property, marriage exist in their true shape; when the people and its ruling authority tolerate robbery, incest, anarchy, they are answerable to God. It is similar to what the Apostle Paul wrote to the church in Corinth that "your glory is not His" while one in their midst had taken his father's wife.[11] The individual, on the other hand, stands under the commands of the law only in and by means of the people, as a member of the whole, not immediately for himself, as individual; as *civis,* not as *homo;* he only observes it with an eye to and under the assumption that all others will likewise so observe it. For this reason, the standards of law are established through peoples and states, not left to the judgment of individuals, and are maintained by peoples and states, not left to the will of individuals. For this reason as well, however, only what truly is an obligation of the people, only such actions of individuals the allowance of which holds as an act of the people, as an expression of the ethical judgment and will of the people, belong to the sphere of law. Law is the *common ethos*, the *national ethos.*

Law is nevertheless the vocation of the people only in relation to the

[11] [1 Corinthians 5:6, Luther's translation.]

enduring shape of life which is established to preserve God's world order in the human race. Ethical obligations on the people and its ruling authority when they do not con- **<12>** cern this life arrangement, for example to come to the aid of an oppressed people, to reward a deserving man, are therefore only moral obligations on the nation, not elements of law. Law is the *objective ethos,* the *outward shape of life.*

For this reason, law everywhere only comprehends the *ethical rule,* not the ethical obligation of the *concrete case,* and its most prominent characteristic is *continuous realization,* that is, unfailing fulfillment by individuals, uninterrupted continuity as a whole. Law is not a bare norm but an *order:* precisely an implemented, continuously observed norm. The necessity of unfailing fulfillment, which accordingly pertains to the essence of law, is expressed as *physical coercion* undertaken against the resistance of individuals. Coercion therefore from ancient times has appeared the primary, that is, the most evident distinction between law and morality. Hence the ethical power of law is not based directly on ethical ideas, as is morality, but in this external, pre-existing order, and the law precedes the acts of individuals and even the acts of the people, as something already implemented, although it in turn is only implemented in and through this action. Law in this manner is on the one hand an obligation on the will – an *ethical command* – and on the other hand an *institution mechanically preserving itself.* This dual nature is the peculiarity of the law.

§. 3. The Object of Law: Institutions

The *object* [Gegenstand] of law is the arrangements, institutions of God's world order, thus the relations and bonds among men which make up common existence, which comprise the existence of the human race as a whole. These institutions are the following: **<13>**

1. The *preservation of individual existence:* integrity and freedom of the *person,* protection in the acquisition and use of means of subsistence (*property*).
2. The *expansion of the race:* the organic bond of procreation, which in the ethical sphere becomes a bond of will, thus elevated to

enduring individual shared identity – the *family*.

3. *Common existence as race:* the mutual complementarity of the species [Gattung] in its activity – *local community, estate* and *corporation*, and their common higher rule in accordance with ideas and purposes as an ethical intellectual kingdom – the *state* and the *community of states*.
4. The *common bond with God:* the institution to reconcile mankind with God and to glorify God through mankind – the *church*.

All these relations, even those initially existing only among individuals, such as for example property and marriage, have the character of *impinging upon the whole;* they are the general bearers of human existence. They stand together in a (not merely logical, but real) unity, while they generate and condition each other. Together they are the natural furnishing for the preservation of the human race and the ethical shape of its common life. They are the plan of the ethical world. For this reason, their order is the task of the community, and thus the law.

Excluded however from the sphere of law, and belonging to morality alone, is the entire *conduct of individuals* which either merely concerns oneself, such as truthfulness, moderation, frugality, or, although it involves other individuals, its effect ends with those individuals, such as friendship, gratitude, hospitality. For example, if one were to consider marriage only to be a bond among the two spouses, without its connection <14> to other married couples [den übrigen Ehen] and the remaining human relations which make it a general necessary institution, it would be as little a legal relation as friendship is. Likewise excluded among these relations of common existence are all those relations which turn on total fulfillment by individuals, and not merely the preservation of relations in general in accordance with their ethical continued existence. In the family, for example, the never-ending manifold expressions of love and piety, which must ever be individual, the value of which lies in inventive feeling ever creating afresh, are simply of a moral nature. It is not through them that the individual family takes its place in the enduring edifice of the general condition. On the other hand, community of station [die Gemeinschaft des Standes], the duty to provide sustenance, the bounds of mutual esteem must exist in every family in the same manner and with the same effect. This is the necessary foundation of human common existence, such that the possibility of dissolving into individuals must destroy the condition of the whole. Therefore, through these unshakable foundations operating in the whole, the family enters the objective life-order, the law.

This partition runs through all relations. Accordingly, individual devoutness or orthodoxy does not form part of the law and its coercion, while the preservation of the church as a public institution upon its true foundations, with its pure doctrine,[12] does; not individual chastity in accordance with the standard of the Sermon on the Mount, but rather the preservation of marriage as a general institution in its purity (legal prohibition on divorce, polygamy, etc.); not individual probity <15> in wealth transactions [Vermögens-Geschäften], but rather the establishment of general property exchange on the basis of fidelity [Treu] and trust (**bona fides**). This is the boundary of the sphere of law over against the sphere of morality, the compelling ordinances of the government as against free fulfillment of conscience. Self-evidently this borderline is a fluid one.

§. 4. The Twofold Purpose of Law: God's Order, Man's Rights

The *purpose* of law is the preservation of God's world order, albeit in independent and free human implementation. Its first priority is therefore *God's commands;* its other is *rights*. This is because God's world order is not only concerned with the ethical well-being of men but also the natural preservation and the guarantee of their personality, their worth, their vocations; it not only obliges men but secures and shields them as well. And in accordance with the nature of personality, ethical commands to the degree that their content consists in the protection and benefit of men likewise become an ethical power over against others, intrinsic to these men and inhering in them – this is the concept of *entitlement*

---

[12] The fundamental error in the system put forward by Thomasius lies in this, that because devoutness and orthodoxy are not an object of external power, church government does not have the task of preserving pure doctrine.

[Berechtigung] or *law in the subjective sense*. The efficacy of law therefore consists in this, that it establish and secure on the one hand a definite range of inviolable validity for *divine commandments* in human common life, on the other a definite sphere of existence and power for men, that is, *rights*. So on the one hand it sanctions the divine command of pure marriage (monogamy, prohibition on divorce and incest), the divine command of submission to authority (from which also conscription, the duty to pay taxes), the divine command of punishment for murder, theft, incest, blasphemy; on the other hand it preserves for men the right of <16> life, property, privileges of marriage, the authority of parents and civil government. These are the two factors of the ethical world: ethical power with its commands, and man in his free personality, which through law receive their determinate, precisely circumscribed validity in common life.

For this reason, the arrangements made by the ruling authority for common life, even for those institutions of the common condition, are an element of law only when they have as their object either the commandments of God or the rights of men. If they on the other hand merely contain technical means on behalf of such commandments or human praiseworthy goals and human utility, they fall under the area of administration and the common welfare [Polizei]. Everything that above was urged as a component of the legal order – property, government, punishment for murder, incest, blasphemy – is the assertion or more precise specification of immediate divine commands: thou shalt not steal, thou shalt not kill, honor thy father and mother (thus all ruling authorities), thou shalt not commit adultery, thou shalt not take the name of the Lord thy God in vain. On the other hand, such things as military, passport, or post regulations, instructions for the administration of demesnes or a decree to lock houses at night, to quarantine contagious disease, all of these are mere technical means to safeguard the power of ruling authorities, life, and property, or for human comfort and mores [Sitte], rather than being immediate results of a divine ordinance. While these certainly may be categorized as law in a broader, merely formal sense, because they are issued by the ruling authorities and therefore are legally binding, they are not so in the actual and material sense; although they are the commandments of legal authority, they are not themselves components of the legal order.[13] **<17>**

This is the delimitation of the sphere of law over against the sphere of administration and the common welfare. As with its delimitation over against the moral sphere, this stems from its concept, which is that it is the human order for preserving the divine world order. Accordingly, everything is excluded that is merely the affair of individuals (*morality*); but no less so is everything, even that which is common and public, which is merely technical and pedagogical [Paideutik] rather than a necessary ethical ordinance in itself (*common welfare* [Polizei]).[14] **<18>**

---

[13] When with us public indecency is punished only in terms of public welfare measures, then that is a symptom of a lax condition of public mores, not a basis for erecting a concept of law and its delimitation over against public welfare. In accordance with the true requirement and the nature of the case, such indecency, to the degree that it falls under the purview of the state, is to be treated as a violation of the public ethical family order in the sphere of law, and thus falls under penal law (albeit in the lowest degree, although classified under the law); the sphere of public welfare in this case only pertains to prevention of indecency (e.g., against offensive dress, movement at night, mixed bathing, etc.), thus only such as the violation of which does not in itself constitute an offence against the divine order.

[14] This yields that which Grotius sought, a concept of "natural law" (the sphere of law) delimited both over against morality and against politics. Usually, one sets the criterion of law as opposed to social welfare or other activities of the state in the fact that it determines *rights*. But, as is shown elsewhere, the law does not restrict itself to this, and furthermore this would make social welfare appear only as a higher (objective) goal, law on the other hand as an aggregate of (subjective) entitlements. On the contrary, the law makes the opposite impression, that precisely it is the higher sanctified order, prior to all other spheres of the state. Its field is formed by the institutions of God's world plan and unconditional divine commands, albeit in the freest human implementation, over against other objects of common interests and humanly-proposed goals. Rights are only a part of that sanctified order.

§. 5. The Principle of Law: The Purposes Inhering in Life Relations

The *principle* and *standard* of law, that which provides its commandments with their content, are the concepts and commands of God's world order, thus not, as with morality, the idea of fulfilled personality, but rather the idea of complete common existence, the complete edifice of social relations; this is indeed the divine plan for the ethical world, the *ideas of Providence* (*Philosophical Foundations*, §. 30). On such Providence is based in equal manner both the factual existence of those relations as natural institutions, and their ethical shape as the ethical world, which is in fact law. The activity of law is therefore the *force of formation and determination;* by it the separated existences of men and institutions, and their fixed boundaries, arise in the ethical sphere, all the while being related to each other as a coherent whole. It is the development of a world with its determinate constructions, similar to the natural creation.[15] A providential idea inheres in every individual life relation (property, marriage, the parental relation, estate activity [Standesthätigkeit] and the like), which strives to be fulfilled in it, and the fulfillment of which is the task and criterion of the law. As law is an ethical order founded on natural institution, every legal institution has a natural basis: property for example is based on possession, marriage on procreation, the state on the union of the forces of the people, etc. The providential idea of that legal relation is already present within this factual basis and is active as a disordered inclination which, when elevated to permanence and clear shape, controls that factual **<19>** basis through an ethical, or better legal, norm. So for example in possession, the idea of individual gratification through things; in procreation, the idea of the union of the sexes, etc. The idea of each life relation having a self-propelling action beginning in natural inclinations and progressing to ethical order fulfills Aristotle's view, which he characterized as the τὸ οὗ ἕνεκα [the cause for the sake of which], or as the τέλος [goal], that is, an *inclination and purpose of nature* characterizing relations

---

[15] It is therefore an error to assume that, assuming the perfection of man, love would replace law. Love can only replace coercion, not law, because love is not form-giving.

themselves and being realized in them. In accordance with the Christian understanding, however, this likewise appears as a *divinely established purpose* for life relations and as a *vocation* for that purpose established for men. *This purpose* (τέλος) *characterizing life relations is the objective and real principle of legal philosophy* as opposed to all merely subjective or merely logical principles. It is the leading principle in the entire exposition which follows.[16]

§. 6. The Boundaries of Law

The law does not have to take up the ethical ideas inhering in life relations *to their full extent*, but only to the degree that they, in accordance with the above (§. 3), form the permanent, **<20>** uninterrupted shape of common existence and are to exist as the work of the community (the nation) in its unity as manifestation of the ethical spirit of the ruling authorities. Their complete and higher fulfillment, by contrast, pertains only to God's immediate commands and immediate operation in the soul, not to the human order, which is only to support that, and therefore is much more the work of public mores [Sitte], which in turn themselves have their source in the conscience of individuals rather than in governmental coercion. Certainly in the given condition of human nature – the separation

---

[16] This is however an *absolutely positive* principle, because the purpose of each life relation (family, state) must specifically be recognized as given, which can only be found by observation of itself and not through statutes or concepts outside of and prior to it. Contrary to this, Hegel for example does not make the particular inner significance of property, the family, the state to be the foundation of his assessment; on the contrary, this is to issue from the concept of will, in accordance with the substantial and subjective moment and, even farther back, the law of dialectic. For this reason it can and doubtless will happen that we hit the truth in some matters and miss it in others, in accordance with whether we have rightly discovered the particular purpose of the one institution and not with another. A legal philosophy with the claim, such as is being made up to the present time, that it is either entirely true or entirely false according to whether its principle (supreme axiom or method) is true or false, is totally foreign to our standpoint.

of the common will from the individual will, and the impurity of each – the sphere of the common condition and therefore of law must be restricted to the *negative* (*Philosophical Foundations*, §. 45); that is, law is not to realize the ethical idea of every institution *in its positive content*, but is only to preserve its *outermost boundaries*, only enough to preserve the concept, to keep its opposite from manifesting itself. So for example the legal protection of personality does not contain the positive recognition of individuality but only the negative, that the concept of the person not be abolished, thus that one not be bodily violated by another, be injured by another; the law of marriage does not include the positive union and devotion of spouses, which public ethical opinion demands as generally necessary apart from all particularization, but only sees to it that polygamy, divorce, arbitrary change of marriage, abandonment, not providing for one's wife, do not take place, thus only that the concept of marriage exist. Therefore the law of the state does not require the permeation of the general and the individual, as Plato and Schelling (unjustly) require of the state institution, but only obedience, fulfillment of performances, etc.

Law and morality, the two sides of the human collective ethos, accordingly stand together in a bond of unity. The same ethical (providential) ideas provide the content of law and the **<21>** content of morality, to the degree that morality is concerned with the relations of common existence: for example, faithfulness and fairness in property transactions, chastity, piety, care, obedience in the family, etc. One may express it virtually definitively like this: the law, like morality, rests on the Ten Commandments and solely on them. Therefore, all deeper minds sense that a separation of law from morality in terms of content – such as is done in abstract natural law – must of necessity be untrue. Regardless of this, however, the commingling of these two areas is strictly out of the question, because morality realizes these ideas in their full extent and from their positive side while law realizes them only from their negative side, only at their outermost boundaries.[8] Both positions, that the law retain

[8] This is true even in the sphere of property [Sphäre des Vermögens], although

ethical content and be determined by ethical ideas, and that it not incorporate any more of these ideas than belong to its sphere, are likewise necessary for its true operation. Complete or at any rate positive incorporation of the contents of ethics into law and its coercion (§. 2) destroys individual freedom and with it true ethics. On the other hand, leaving this entirely up to individual freedom, e.g., the allowance of concubinage and the like, is in itself unethical simply as lack of **<22>** acknowledgment of the ethical common will, and has the consequence of eliminating the solemnity of the ethical command from the objective shape of life and from constant view, as well as from the public mind, and thereby in the end from ethics itself. So for example the true attitude regarding the ethical essence of marriage will not be maintained when divorce is arbitrary or is viewed as being a matter of entire indifference in public institutions. When however public life in its constant appearance displays the purity of marriage, the ethical view of individual persons regarding marriage also receives confirmation. The burial of suicides with all otherwise customary ceremonies must end in smothering the notion of the sinfulness of suicide. The public observance of Sunday, that is, the prevention of workaday labor making its appearance in public, will actively maintain in the general consciousness the necessity of dedicating this day to religious gathering; and the reverse is also true: it must be left up to individuals to

---

that sphere is usually considered to belong simply to rights. Here as well we do not have mere moral demands of neighborly love, beneficence, etc., regarding use, which however belong to an entirely different sphere, but a *moral probity* of a wider extent than the fulfilment of the law and even lawful **bona fides**; e.g., overcharging in the case of a sale, while irreproachable before the law, is not so before morality, and the moral law against which it offends is by no means the law of love but the law of moral probity as distinguished from juridical, precisely positive probity as opposed to negative, whereby one does not deceive or cheat. Another example in which the law is fully satisfied but where on the contrary moral probity (to be distinguished from love) feels outright offended is this: suppose a banker detaches an officer to the army; after a victorious battle, this officer immediately informs him thereof, which information the banker uses to immediately embark on a buying spree on the exchange.

decide whether to observe Sunday or not, etc. This is the general guideline for the level of moral and religious requirement. There is however no clear dividing line, the less so because the given makeup of the human condition – the contradiction between the true ethical shape of life and the human will – should never have even existed, but rather a broad amount of leeway for adjustment according to time and condition, and particularly in terms of the capacity to bear on the part of the persons for whom the laws are to be given.

§. 7. The Place of Justice in Law

These things, the purpose inhering in life relations and the ethical characteristics contained in that purpose, differ for each: freedom and the free expansion of personality, the bond of the sexes, sanctity of mores, honor and piety, etc. But one <23> characteristic runs equally through them all – and that is *justice*. Justice, its essence being to uphold regard both for the ethical power and its laws and the right of men in equal inviolability, is the inseparable attribute of all ethical order of law, both divine and human. Every individual relation as well as the entirety of the legal order must be determined in accordance with this, so that both the command of God's providential order and the rights of men owed them as a person and for each and every relation be manifested and attested in inviolable sanctity. The providential ideas on the one hand and justice on the other are together the poles of the ethical world order. The former determine (objectively [sächlich]) the structure of this order, while justice determines (subjectively [persönlich]) the relation of ethical power established and sanctified by that order to men vested with rights derived from it. The former are the organic constructive power of the world order, the latter its self-confirmation and self-empowerment as a kingdom of living wills under a supreme immutable will. Both of these mutually condition and permeate each other.

Justice therefore is not the sole nor even the original and form-giving principle of law. Instead, it already presupposes a content of commandments and rights which through it are to attain the guarantee of inviolability, and this content stems from the purpose inhering in life relations, in accordance with the plan of the ethical world (§. 5).

The original order of legal institutions (property, marriage, paternal power, state, church) therefore in no way rests on the idea of justice, but rather on other ideas peculiar to each institution in its own right. It is only in accordance with these, not justice, that the commandments which hold for property, for marriage, are determined, as are the rights which are to be ascribed to spouses, fathers, heirs, property owners. However, justice is nevertheless a determining factor in all these institu- **<24>** tions to the degree that the right of personality which is bestowed on men from the beginning is to be preserved inviolable in all of them and in each according to its peculiar nature.

Furthermore, justice also has a sphere over which it exclusively and originally rules, appropriate for the preservation of the entire legal order which is its essence. The administration of criminal law in its entirety, the inviolability of positive law, the preservation of acquired rights, the general regard for the merit and guilt of men in all civil and criminal, private and public relations, rests on the concept of justice alone.

Justice is not the original and form-giving principle of the legal order; but it is its preserving and confirming principle, its final seal.

§. 8. The State as the Necessary Upholder of Law

The law *realizes* its existence only through the *state*. Just as the law is the human *order* of common life for the sake of the maintenance of God's world order, so is the state the institution of human *rule* of common life in proxy of God and for purposes set by God. The first of these purposes is however precisely such order.[17] Law and state have an all-encompassing purpose, which is to form the human race into an ethical world. They condition each other mutually in this, but without coinciding with each other. The state derives the norm for its order, and in fact derives its entire

[17] Law therefore comprises all the actions of men, including those done for their individual purposes, and gives them a common rule only for the sake of their common relation; the state, on the other hand, to the extent of its operation, everywhere unifies the actions of men only for common purposes. The former is a norm for life relations, the latter is itself a life relation, and a real power.

existence, through the law,[18] <25> while the law gains its realization only through the state. However, the law orders other relations besides the state, while the state pursues other purposes besides the law. Both together form the concept of the *civil order* (**status civilis**) and exhaust the ethical world in terms of its objective existence.

A so-called "*state of nature*" neither factually preceded the civil order nor is it scientifically to be presupposed, such that one has first to discover it in order to start out from it as terminus a quo. One only arrives at such starting points when one goes awry and obliterates the entire connection with objectivity, putting himself first (rationalistic standpoint). On the other hand, one may posit the civil order as a given situation over against the state of nature as a conceivable situation in order by these contrasts to illuminate it and confirm it.

§. 9. Misrepresentation of Law in Legal Philosophy

Philosophy, both ancient-pagan and modern-rationalistic, does not see in law what it really is, the order of the living personal God, since it everywhere leaves Him out of consideration. It treats the law just as it does morality, as a command of *reason* (laws of thought, human nature striving after harmony). Because God's influence in the earthly condition is not visible, outward observance also perceives the law as a mere self-contained order, the regard for which is by no means conditioned by faith in God. Such mere outward observance likewise takes morality to be independent of faith in God, and nature as existing in itself without a Creator and Lord who grounds and maintains it. This viewpoint, restricted to what is observable on Earth, is considered by that philosophy to be the only scientifically secure one. Yet the dualism of the ethical field is inexplicable from this standpoint, it being based precisely upon the dualism of world-ordering authorities, upon <26> the free world plan of God, whereby the human race, in the law, itself is called to a godlike world-ordering position. Both spheres furthermore are presented in an inex-

---

[18] The other relations have a factual or ethical existence apart from all rights (property, family), while according to its very concept the state is a legal institution.

plicable inadequacy. Morality, the true ethical action of man, appears fully isolated, arbitrary, detached from a grand plan in which it intervenes, and the law, the ethical shape of the common condition, appears in the unsatisfactory manner of mere human order. It does not yield a world order maintained by God Himself and fulfilled through the inward ethical action of man. Finally, there are the inexplicable contradictions in which the law empowers what morality prohibits and reason requires obedience even to irrational law.

Philosophy did not in the same manner close itself off to that other truth, that the requirement of common life, the common order of the human race, termed in an inappropriate expression "sociability" [Socialität] form the ground of the law. This truth is accessible even in abstraction from God. It was recognized by Aristotle, following him the entire Middle Ages,[19] in the same way by Melanchthon,[20] then finally by the founders of the just-mentioned "sociabilistic" systems (Grotius, Pufendorf). However, apart from Aristotle the basis was conceived to be the mere empirical datum of the need for society, rather than ethical common requirements, and likewise mutual necessity rather than original unity; this ten-

---

[19] E.g. Thomas Aquinas, *De regim. Princ.* [Of the rule of princes], l. IV, c. 3: "Appetitus videlicet humanus, ad communicandum opera sua multitudini, ut molestum sit eidem aliquid virtutis agere absque hominum societate....– Patet igitur hominum sive ex parte corporis, sive partis sensitivae, sive considerata sua rationali natura necesse habere vivere in multitudine. Ex qua parte necessaria est secundum naturam constructio civitatis" [There is the human appetite to share one's works with the multitude, which makes it difficult for him to do something virtuous in the absence of human society.... It is therefore clear that men, either because of their bodies, or their sensitive part, or their rational nature, must live in multitudes. For this reason the construction of the state is necessary by nature]. – Nearly all writers of the Middle Ages put the Aristotelian πολιτικόν ζῶον ("sociale animal") at the basis of politics.

[20] Melanchthon, *Phil. Moral* (edit. Basil. Tom. IV.) p. 214: "Homo conditus est ad societatem" [Man was created for society] – which is however followed by: "doceantur homines et praecipue de deo" [let men be taught, and especially of God].

dency was **<27>** realized fully by Grotius, who conceived of sociability simply as the instinct of the individual. When, however, Thomasius replaced the drive toward sociability with the *drive toward happiness*, by which the individual of necessity becomes isolated, the last remnant of an objective legal principle was eliminated. For this reason, from the outset it was impossible for natural law, in its entire development up until Schelling, to discover the proper relation between law and morality in that it derived everything from the nature of the individual, while the law has its derivation only from the equally original existence and task of the community.

So the ultimate consequence was the arrival at the strong expressed fallacy by which the legal sphere is restricted to the *external freedom of individual men* and the *coexistence of this freedom* (Kant, Fichte). Accordingly, the prohibition on polygamy and incest, in fact even the duty to provide for and care for children, was excluded from the legal order, and law generally and everywhere lacked higher sanctification because it existed only for the benefit of man and not for the order of God.

In truth, the life of human commonality (the people) is not mere coexistence; it is not a mere existence of men alongside each other, in which they pursue their purposes as individuals, protect themselves from each other, and at most promote each other; rather, it is the common unified fulfillment of a higher order, the ethical world plan; the freedom of individual men is not the sphere of law, but only a part of it.[21] **<28>**

---

[21] Now that the nullity of this standpoint and doctrine has been irrefutably demonstrated, the attempt is being made, despite this, by those who cannot separate themselves from it, to introduce it in another, less clear and determinate form. Law is certainly not restricted to the mere freedom of men; nevertheless, its distinction from morality, they say, is that it only establishes *rights of men* (claims), and duties merely as the consequence of the claims of others, while by contrast morality merely burdens with duties and does not confer rights; or, expressed in another form, law contains the rules which stem from justice, i.e., the suum cuique [to each his own], while morality contains the rules stemming from charity. (For example, Warnkönig's legal philosophy, among others;

The Greeks, on the other hand, even though they apparently were not yet aware of the distinction between law and morality, nevertheless possessed the elements of a more just distinction, in that Plato distinguished between the justice of man and of the state, and Aristotle distinguished between ἁπλως δίκαιον [absolute justice] and πολιτιχον δίκαιον [political justice]. Now then, when these distinctions were carried through willy nilly, law seemed merely to be an attribute and tool of the state, and thus both concepts coincided falsely with each other (see above, §. 8).

Lately, *speculative philosophy*[22] emphatically has presented the law as an objective ethos, albeit muddled by the pantheistic dislocation of all viewpoints. This holds mainly for the basic principle of its legal teaching, that of the "*general will*" in the sense in which first Schelling[23] and then Hegel

---

regarding this, see my countercriticism in the appendix to *Philosophical Foundations;* apart from this, such a viewpoint in a less extensive form is extremely widespread as a relic of the older form of natural law.) However, religion and morality confer rights (claims) just as well as law does, e.g., spouses and fathers have rights derived just as well from the Gospel as from the civil code, and vice versa, the law itself just as well establishes original duties and requirements which are not the consequence of the entitlement of others as does morality, e.g., the prohibition on incest, prohibition of divorce by mutual agreement, likewise the duty of subordination which inheres in state power and which by no means is the mere consequence (effluence) of the entitlement of men, as well as the entire administration of penal law. In the same manner, many commandments and demands follow from justice which nevertheless belong not to the sphere of law but to the sphere of morality, such as the justice of a father with his children, the justice of a critic, and vice versa, the legal order contains demands and commands that are derived not from justice but from purity of mores and piety; and regarding all of these justice itself is not merely the suum cuique (give to every man his right), but at the same time the soundness of an ethical order (§. 7).

[22] Schelling, *Acad. Stud.* Hegel's *Philosophy of Law,* also Schleiermacher's *Ethics;* cf. Book I of this volume [*Philosophical Foundations*], §. 30 (paragraph 4).

[23] See Fichte's and Niethammer's *Philosophisches Journal einer Gesellschaft*

in his own way furnished a system of legal philosophy. This concept, distinguished absolutely from the volonté générale of Rousseau and <29> Sieyès, signifies a power over individual men which is neither the will of the people (be it as collection of individuals or as a unity) nor the will of God, but rather the power and necessity of the *impersonal* (logical) *world law* (in this stage of the development of the *concept* of will) which in a pantheistic manner of speaking is ascribed the attribute of will. Apart from the fact that this conception necessarily denies the existence of a personal will over men – thus God – this "general will" entails that, because in truth it cannot will anything, legal content not be derived from its will (the world plan contained in its creative intelligence) but simply from its concepts and abstract aspects (positing a general possibility, a specific content, and the union of both, etc.).

In this manner Hegel arrives at his bizarre notion that the ethical world can be dissected into three spheres: 1. Private law ("abstract law"), 2. Morality, and 3. Family and public law ("ethics"), with morality as the connecting link between private and public law, similar to the way one wishes to conceive of the human soul as a connecting link between the members of the human body.[24] The central meaning of this conception is that it is not the eternal content of the will, love, etc. that is to be realized in human community, but the abstraction of a will-function, of aspects of that which is general, etc.; and the ethical world consists in their realization. If we however prescind from this central meaning and consider the matter simply in terms of its results, there is in these three spheres nothing else presented than three basic forms: human *entitlement* ("abstract law," law of the individual will), human *obligation* ("morality"), and *objective organic connections*. Entitlement, or the law of individual will, consists in property and obligation (contract), in mine and thine; <30> duty ("shall"), in the pursuit of the good; the objective organic communities (ethics), in family, corporation and state. Hereby Hegel falsely states these

---

teutscher Gelehrten [Philosophical journal of a society of German scholars], vols. 4 and 5.

[24] Compare my *Philosophy of Law* (2nd ed.), vol. I, p. 428 [*The Recovery of Historical Law*, pp. 83ff.].

three basic forms as being in a dialectic development, the one following after the other, thus successively and side-by-side, as three different spheres of life, while in reality all three are equally original, mutually permeating the spheres of life. Entitlement does not stop with property and obligation ("abstract law"), it runs through all spheres (e.g. rights of marriage, royal rights); morality is not restricted to the pursuit of the good but likewise permeates all spheres, even those of so-called abstract law; and objective ethical institutions ("ethics") are not simply the family and the state but also property, etc.; for though the latter is no organic connection, like them it is a part of the construction of human common existence. Morality therefore likewise is no connecting link between property on the one hand and family and the state on the other, but, to the degree that these are legal institutions, their common opposite. In this manner entitlement and morality, which run through all life spheres, are inappropriately set over against other spheres (family, state) as separate spheres of life, classified along with them. There are in truth two totally different foundations for the distinction: 1. Men have entitlements and duties; 2. Men have both an individual existence and an existence as a member of the objective ethical world structure and of specific organic connections (in both of which they have entitlements and duties). Hegel however unnaturally makes three members out of one distinction, which then is the structure of his legal philosophy. Despite this, the distinction between "morality" and "ethics" does prepare the way, even though in extremely confused fashion, for the proper realization: that *morality is the ethical completion of the individual, while law is the ethical order of the common life of the human race assigned to it* (the people) *as a whole.*

CHAPTER 2: POSITIVE LAW, NATURAL LAW, REVEALED LAW

§. 10. Law is Positive

As has been explained, law [das Recht] is human order, albeit for the sake of maintaining God's world order (§. 1). It therefore exists as men in a particular time, in a particular country, have established it, and it exists because they *have* so established it, whether good or bad, and not because they in that manner *had* so to establish it, in accordance with a necessity in God's command. This means that law [Recht] is *positive*, but that in the concepts and commandments of the world order of God it has a higher law [Gesetz] to which it *ought* to answer, according to which men *ought* to establish it.[25] Therefore *positive law* [Recht] has over against it a *God-commanded, just, rational* law. Even so, this rational law, the concepts and commandments of God's world order, are not themselves a law – a so-called *natural law* or *law of reason* – since the essence of law is precisely to be an independent human life order, therefore positive law. Even so, they are the determining power in positive law, its original ground and archetype, the standard by which it is measured and judged. <34>

§. 11. Positive Law is Authoritative by Divine Right

God's world order is the archetype of all positive legal construction, but it is not itself a legal construction. Its concepts and commandments, the purpose inhering in life relations, are the principles and the guideline for the laws, but not themselves laws, such that human relationships could be put in order and controversial cases could be decided in accordance with

[25] Regarding morality, no such distinction exists between positive and rational since nowhere does it rest on *human* ordinance, but only on God's command. Even mores that are traditional to a certain people, which one might call positive morality, do not bind the individual person in the way positive law does; he is only to follow God's command.

them.

For this they firstly are lacking in a determinate shape, the provision of which is the vocation and the freedom of the people. The people themselves, in accordance with the particularity of their spirit and their conditions and with their own creative power, are to give definitive shape to them, to particularize them and thus also to individualize them; and only then do they become applicable norms, or law. The process is similar to the way in which the archetype of the beauty of the human body functions as the guideline which determines the sculptor and by which his sculptures are judged, although itself this archetype is neither a body nor a sculpture, with determinate forms and lines which may be cast or sketched. The foundational concepts and relations of the law are in similar manner grounded in God's world order, are divinely necessary, but the specific way in which they are implemented is humanly free – it may be done this way or that way, and therefore it is the way it is, positive. Human freedom is not left simply to sharpen those eternal ideas to a point, so that e.g. positive law need only supply the time interval of prescription or the forms of testament, but it is entrusted with the plan of its realization in general. Thus e.g. property is a concept and commandment in God's world order. Whether however a longer period of possession can establish objection [Einrede] or acquisition, or **<35>** whether transfer can occur by contract or only by cession, or whether the honest buyer must return stolen merchandise without compensation, even whether the entire institution of property is to be regulated in accordance with the Roman law or with Germanic law, etc., all of this is a free human conception which, although moved and determined by divine commandments, nevertheless has its coherence and coordination only in itself. All legal construction therefore has a dual aspect, a divine necessary (natural-law-oriented) and a human free (positive), both permeating each other without dividing line, existing in indissoluble unity.[26]

---

[26] Already Aristotle (*Ethics*, Book V, ch. 7) divides the content of law (πολιτικόν δίκαιον) into a natural (φυσιαόν) law, which everywhere must be equally in force, and a positive (νομικόν) law that can only be law when it is so established, e.g.,

In the same manner, God's world order is the ground of the regard for law. This human order has a binding power and sanctity only because it serves to uphold that divine order, and because there is truly no law, not even the worst, that does not in some way uphold that order, that is bereft of all reasonableness and justice. Nevertheless, the concepts and commandments of the divine world order have no legal (externally binding) regard in human common life, as long and as far as the human community has not made them into commandments of its order. Only thereby do they become *norms in effect* – laws. This is because the human community is to establish the law as its own life order (§. 1), and it is the human order itself, not the claims on it such as they correspond to the divine order, which has God's sanction externally and commonly to bind men. <36>

§. 12. Law is Positive Law, not Natural Law

In this manner the human order, which is law, is rooted in the divine; but it is independent in itself, and in this independence consists the *positivity of law.*

The law is *positive in terms of its content.* Although its principles and ideas lie in God's world order, its specific laws are humanly constituted, positive. It is *positive in terms of its validity.* The final ground of its binding regard is God's world order, but the locus of that regard is nevertheless the humanly established order, the existing law. In terms of this independence, the law can even come into conflict with God's world order, which it is to serve; human community, which is called to give the concepts of

---

the custom of sacrifices in a specific city. However, he sets them up more as externally separated spheres beside each other. By contrast, Melanchthon (*Loci Communes*, p. 229) recognizes the proper relation in saying: "Verum quia jus positivum determinatio est juris naturalis, facile intelligi potest, jus positivum tamen habere aliquam regulam, videlicet ne pugnet cum jure naturali" [Verily since positive law is a determination of natural law, it can easily be understood that positive law has validity to the degree that it does not conflict with natural law]. More extensively in Hegel, *Philosophy of Law*, §. 3.

law a specific shape in accordance with freedom, might turn it into its opposite, ordering the unjust and irrational, and even in this God-opposed makeup the law retains its binding regard. In this the character of *positivity*, which is accorded the law, has its most extreme demonstration.

Law and *positive law* therefore are synonymous terms. There is no other law than positive law. Underlying the idea of a "natural law" are in fact those concepts and commandments of God's world order, the law-ideas; the latter, however, have neither the required specificity nor the binding power of the law. They are grounds for determination of the further development of the common condition, not norms already in force for the common condition. There are therefore *rational demands* on the law, but there is no *law of reason*. Subjects may not oppose positive law, either as individuals or in the mass, by leaning on natural law; this is the iniquity of the Revolution. The ruling authorities are to uphold the positive law, not the natural law. In particular, the judge is not to pass judgment in accordance with natural law, be it against the positive law, be it only in addition to positive law (subsidiary). <37>

The application of natural law in decisions cannot be realized even factually. It fails in the lack of *objectivity* – common equal recognition – and in the lack of *precision*. The judge would be referred thereby only to his judgment as to what he regards to be natural law, at best he would speak therefore only as an individual (as a mere arbitrator) rather than as a real judge, i.e., as an organ and a representative of national legal judgment, and even with respect to his own judgment he would only find a general legal maxim and not a specific manner of restoring the wrong, which insofar would be arbitrary or based in vague equity.[27]

---

[27] The same is true of the general motives or tendencies of legislation, even where, inappropriately enough, one has included them in constitutional documents and codes and not merely in their prefaces and declarations of promulgation. For example, "equality before the law," "equality of burdens," "the duty of reimbursement on the part of the state, when by necessity required to sacrifice the rights and advantages of subjects in favor of the common good." Immediate applications of these declarations, in the manner that everywhere is attempted

The application of natural law in the courtroom is however also impermissible legally; it is contrary to justice. Every man has the right not to be subjected to any other norm than those which are established as the objective order of the common life, which are sanctioned by the ruling authorities, as the norms of positive law. It does not come into the head of any judge learned in the law to decide in accordance with natural law, be it against, be it outside positive law. Would there have been, prior to recent times when positive law contained laws against unauthorized reprinting, a judge who would find in favor of a lawsuit against reprinting because of natural law? Would there have been a judge in a slave-owning state of North America who recognized a natural right of freedom for <38> slaves against owners? The rule of natural law instead of or in opposition to positive law has the appearance of establishing the order of God over the order of men: but it is precisely the human order, the law, which is consecrated by God; it is the only common public order that He has ordained over men on earth. The rule of natural law is therefore in truth only the establishment of the arbitrariness of any opinion over the common public order; it is the establishment of the war of all against all.

§. 13. The Nature of the Case

Something else altogether than so-called natural law (law-ideas) is the *nature of the case* [Natur der Sache]. This designates, not *ethical* (legal) *principles* outside the principles of positive law, but *factual relations* previously unforeseen but now emphasized as providing indications for decisions according to the *principles of positive law.* So for example our decisions regarding eviction were inferred by Roman jurists from the nature of the case: namely, that because positive law recognizes the binding nature of

---

by the participants or by the political parties, must lead to a frightful confusion of the legal condition. The confusions precipitated by the judicial application of that stipulation of the Prussian Civil Code had to be countered with a special law of 1851. (This passage, which appears on p. 183 of the 2nd ed., I have retained at least as a note, to confirm that I had already then expressed the principles which I later asserted).

contracts, liability to vacate an object ensues because of then non-existing right, not because of subsequent events, etc. In the same way, whether newspaper advertisements or lithographed orders by trading houses are to be treated as written documents, whether promises made in a constitutional document have legal consequences, whether in a German state the powers of ancient national representative bodies [Landstände] devolve as a matter of course to a contemporary chamber of deputies, all of this can and must be decided in terms of the nature of the case in accordance with positive law, not natural law, with principles of justice outside and alongside positive law. **<39>**

Something other than so-called natural law are likewise the supreme principles regarding the binding nature of positive law itself, such as that one must obey the ruling authorities, whether there is a limit to such obedience and what that limit is, whether active resistance is permissible. All of this is of course not a matter of positive law but exceeds positive law. Neither is it a matter of natural law, but of *morality*, and therefore each man must judge for himself according to his own conscience before God, not in reference to the stance of others, not according to a common public lawful norm (§. 2).

§. 14. Positive Law the Most Immediate Ethical Standard

Accordingly, with regard to the law-ideas – the realization of which is its task – positive law is subject to the standards of *justice, morality, efficiency,* and the like; but it itself, as positive law, is the primary, most immediate ethical measure for the actions of men, and that measure is the standard of *lawfulness* [Rechtmäßigkeit] as opposed to justice and the like. What agrees with positive law is lawful, and vice versa.

§. 15. The Supreme Rule of Legal Development: Continuity

The original condition of the peoples contains the various ethical spheres yet in the compactness of a bud. Law and morality, positive law and the claims of justice on law (natural law) are as yet undistinguished. There exists the simplicity of awareness in which that which is existing law is viewed as just, and that which is just is viewed as existing law. There exists also, however, the fortuitousness, arbitrariness, injustice, whereby ruling authorities, judges and the people apply in individual cases that which they hold to be just law, even that <40> which they hold to be moral, without such being established and sanctioned as a general enduring legal order. Therefore, it is a desirable advance when the ethical spheres unfold, when law and morality, positive law and the claims of reason on law, are set apart in their uniqueness, when positive law, this human order, maintains its full independence, only judged and applied in terms of itself. With the Romans and the Germans – the law peoples par excellence – this development was completed already at the start of their appearance on the stage of world history. Nevertheless, despite this independence, positive law is not to withdraw from the unity of the entire ethical sphere, and the awareness of this unity is not to be eliminated. Even here it is not to be separated from the higher order which it serves. Even in this developed condition, it should not pass in the nation as something merely human, but as the necessary, albeit freely formed, fulfillment of reason and justice, as the maintenance of God's commandments.[28]

In particular, the *continuity* of law serves this purpose, which is why it is the supreme rule of legal development. Continuity does not rule out change and further advance in terms of changed conditions and advancing knowledge; it is not *stagnation* (stability). On the contrary, it is precisely such advance that is required in order for positive law to gain the recognition of being just and rational. But it demands that all that is new and improved be derived from that which exists, and with all changes in particulars the existing law as a whole never be abolished and another put in its place. Its opposite is the *inco-* <41> *herence* of legal development, the termination of existing legal conditions and erection of new ones,

---

[28] So for example, according to firsthand reports in England the judge in pronouncing sentence on the criminal customarily charges him with meriting such a heavy punishment because he violated God's command. In Germany the judge as a rule will only explain that such and such a section in the civil code prescribes the punishment. In the former case, the human order appears in its unity with God's command; in the latter it is totally separate, as something purely human.

whereby one switches legislation and chooses among various options thereof as if that which now exists does not matter to us, in the way one picks and chooses clothing. The former is a development from inside out and therefore gradual, the latter is a change from the outside, therefore abrupt. In the former case, the legal condition certainly becomes essentially different during the course of time, perhaps centuries, and there is no moment in which change can be shown to have taken place; it always maintains its roots in all ages of the history of the people taken together. In the latter case, a specific occurrence causes a line to be drawn at one fell swoop through the history of the people; what lies beyond that line no longer holds for what lies before it. The former is the manner of development of all living things; the latter is the manner of treatment of things mechanical. In the former, the plant and the human body grow; in the latter, man changes and exchanges a machine.

Through such continuity of law, the original simplicity of the popular mind, in which that which is existing law is seen as just and that which is just is seen as existing law, is preserved. This is because it effects a situation in which the law in itself is known as none other than the law of the fatherland, by which the existing law in general is considered to be necessary and cannot be otherwise, in spite of many faults in particulars. Against this, the abolition of what is received by picking and choosing among bodies of legislation produces in the public consciousness a complete divorce between what is just and what is positive law. What is just loses its objective existence and exists only in the mind of men, is different for each person; and positive law loses faith in its necessity and justice. Should the necessity and justice of the existing law be brought into ques- <42> tion at a fundamental level, in its entirety, then the question would arise in everyone's mind as to what should be put in the place of this now abolished legal condition, and, since everything human is questionable, the solution would always be subject to a facile rejection.

§. 16. Revealed Law

God's commandments for the institutions of His world order (property, family, state) are, as are all of His commandments, partly given in human *conscience*, partly through *God's revelation* in the Old and New Testaments. That is why, in the elements of law which we set over against positive law, we must consider the revealed commandments to be a special component of the God-given, the reasonable for the human common condition. The ancients accordingly distinguished between a positive law, a natural law, and a divine (revealed) law. Even if we cannot accede to the concept of a revealed law, as little as to a natural law, there nevertheless exist revealed commandments for the law.

All commands of conscience are likewise corroborated by revelation, and therefore all legal institutions in their basic concepts likewise are based on revelation, in fact on the Ten Commandments: "Thou shalt not kill, not steal, not commit adultery." Therefore, only those commands are to be considered by the law purely to be revealed which are known to men solely through revelation, or which include a certain predetermined shape and institution based on a revealed divine ordinance, such as Sabbath observance, the commandment regarding divorce, marriage among close relations, institutions of the church. Accordingly, there is no sharp line drawn between mere commands of conscience (reason) and those given by revelation. **<43>**

Even when composed clearly and precisely, the commandments of *Christian* revelation have no immediate validity as law, as little as do the commandments of reason and justice, which likewise are none other than God's commandments. This is based on that one decisive principle: law is the order *established by men*, not the one *enjoined by God.* One cannot call upon the Holy Scriptures as a legal norm in a court of law; even in the church, one may only refer to the church's understanding of the Holy Scriptures.[29] This is the ground as to why no revealed law exists, as little as does natural law, but only revealed requirements for the law.

By contrast, the commands of the Christian revelation, like those of reason and justice, form a binding standard for the establishment of law, a claim on the legislator. But they are this in far higher degree and in an

---

[29] When e.g. a Catholic clergyman invokes Holy Scripture to bestow the blessing on the remarriage of innocently divorced spouses, or vice versa when a Protestant clergyman refuses to do so, the courts and officials of the concerned church will not go along with it.

entirely different form than the latter, because they enjoy the special sanction of God, and because He Himself indicated their particular form, which otherwise is left to human freedom. This is where the claims grounded in revelation (**divinum jus**) are to be distinguished from those general commandments of justice and reason. This special regard is owed the commandments of the Christian revelation above all because the Christian revelation is the eternal truth, the actual will of God, but furthermore because it is the public faith of the nations of Europe. Christianity cannot refuse obedience to the commandments and declarations of God in the Old and New Testament even in its public institutions, without fearfully sinning and contradicting itself.

Certainly, those commandments of revelation are not <44> valid for the *law of Christendom* the purpose of which is only the sanctification of individuals, such as "he who looks upon a woman to lust after her commits adultery," "should someone take your belt, give him your cloak also," and no less those the purpose of which was for the Jewish nation, such as the Levirate marriage, the Jewish priesthood. Nevertheless, the revelation in the Old and New Testaments does also contain commandments for Christendom, which therefore has the duty to maintain them in its common public condition, and thus as law. So for example regarding divorce or marriage among close relatives. Which commandments are of this character, which of that, can only be decided on the merits of each.

§. 17. The Error of Modern Natural Law

The quarrel among the ancients concerning the existence of a **jus naturale** as precipitated by Carneades' denial, and which was again taken up by Grotius in Cicero's train, has to do with ethics in general and therefore mainly as to whether all mores were introduced merely because of prudence, for the sake of utility. Only since most recent times, however, does the struggle date as to whether natural law in our special meaning, a law derived immediately from reason, exists in distinction to positive law. Although the objectors in this struggle do recognize subjective ethics (morality), they state that objective ethics (law) measure up only to the standard of utility. This contradicts natural law as developed since Grotius. The fact that no specific decision and no institution stems directly from the law-ideas as necessarily and precisely so arranged, leads them to deny the independence of the law-ideas themselves.

Grotius's entire enterprise however was based on the error of attempting to discover from the law-ideas that which is *lawful* rather than that which is appropriate or just (see above, <45> §. 14). In this process he did perform a signal service for the law of nations, by bringing to clear awareness norms which were already in observance and removing doubts as to their obligation. However, in natural law, of which he justifiably is viewed as the creator, he produced a worthless science. For legal philosophy already existed prior to him, but his science postulated legal philosophy serving also as jurisprudence. Even here, Grotius did the great service of making the task of legal philosophy the ideas of *constitutional* law (legal relations between ruling authorities and subjects, etc.); these hitherto had been saddled with *political* ideas (the ideal shape [plastische Vollendung] of the state, power, welfare [Wohlstand], mores, etc.). But he presented these *ideas* behind constitutional law as if they comprised constitutional *law* in general.

Following Grotius, the teachers of natural law posited a concept of natural law as a legal order existing prior to and outside of the state (in the state of nature), continuing in the state alongside positive law, even, as the most consistent among them viewed the matter (Rousseau above all), as an inalienable right of men valid against the state order, so that this latter, when not in agreement with natural law, is null and non-binding. But even among the teachers of positive law, the manner of conceiving the matter became general in the 18th century in which two norms exist for deciding cases, the natural, derived from the natural law (law-ideas), and the positive. The positive law takes precedence where there is a conflict; but in cases where positive law cannot decide, natural law holds as a subsidiary source. One hereby of necessity considered natural law as a self-contained complete body of legislation, on the one hand certainly enriched by positive law but on the other hand richer than positive law. Such a manner of conceptualizing was implemented especially in Weber's then celebrated book[30] <46> regarding natural obligation. But it is also contained in all the textbooks, such as Thibaut's *Pandects;* it has even crossed over into legislation, as for example in the Austrian Law Code, which declares natural law to be a subsidiary source of law in place of the common law, which hitherto has served that function.

The *Historical School of Jurisprudence* dropped the entire theory, and it did so implicitly, that is, without taking precise account of the ground as to why one may deny the validity of the law of reason, without asking whether positive law is entirely arbitrary, whether in so doing one denies all absolute ethical standard for the law, leaving only the relative standard of suitability to people, time and conditions. Considerations of the latter sort are supposed of the Historical School, and they might be harbored by many of its supporters wishing to put right their relationship to the earlier viewpoint. Nevertheless, these supporters are entirely oblivious to the true spirit of this school, which consists instead in a *direct pervasion of the recognition of the positiveness of law*, as it has here been attempted to deduce from philosophical principles.

In life itself, the concept of *positive law* – that is, the sole validity of norms established in the common life of the nation, to the exclusion of those derived from ethical motives or mere law-ideas – was first realized in the Roman era, just as the Romans were the first to realize the concept of *acquired rights* and their inviolability. The law, both in its objective and subjective signification, consequently appears there for the first time in world history in its pure form as an independent sphere of life. This is why the Romans justifiably are considered to be the classic people in the cause of civil order.

Any validity for "natural law" is therefore least of all to be sought among the Romans. Even so, their terminology can easily lead to misunderstanding. For them, "**jus naturale**" <47> signified the component of law necessary by nature, not an embodiment of legal principles; **jus gentium**, that portion of positive law which contained generally observed legal determinations, not those peculiar to Rome, which therefore were

---

[30] [*Systematic Development of the Doctrine of Natural Obligation and its Historical Effect.*]

accustomed to be seen to have come from general law-ideas (**naturalis ratio**), not however a law separate from positive law, which might be derived immediately from the law-ideas.

CHAPTER 3: THE ORIGIN AND SOURCES OF LAW

§. 18. Human Community as the Source of Law

The way in which law arises is commensurate with its essence, to wit, the human order of the common condition for the maintenance of God's world order. Law arises through the human community, through the people and ruling authorities, but with the consciousness of a necessity and an authorization in God's order – either through establishment by the ruling authorities, since they have the vocation from God to maintain order – *through statute* [Gesetz] or through *observance among the people* with the consciousness that a norm is part of the legal order to which one is subject from God – through *custom* [Gewohnheit] and *tradition* [Herkommen].

The law thus proceeds from the people as an originally given unity, either through uniform regard for the ruling authorities or through the uniform consciousness of the people, which fills them all and determines their actions; not from the individual people who first come together in order to establish the law in mutual agreement.

The law arises from the awareness to fulfill a commandment of God to which man is bound (or, where faith in God is lacking, to fulfill an ethical necessity), and not in the manner of an arbitrary institution or for mere human protection and utility. For this reason the people's ethical valuation of life determines the law's content, and it therefore arises originally, apart from choice or intention, out of a direct impression of necessity, which preponderantly determines even the regulations of the ruling authorities *(principle of the Historical* <50> *School).* Now free reflection as to what is just or unjust, and the consideration of utility and wholesomeness, immediately manifests itself, and this free activity expands with advancing culture. Nevertheless, it remains reflection on the basis of the immediate ethical and legal judgment of the nation, the consideration of utility remaining ever rooted in the ground of the commandments of justice; and the entire law-developing action, even in free reflection and consideration of utility, is permeated with the sentiment of duty and the principles and commandments given beyond human choice.

The law arises first through establishment as external order in the life of the community. The mere consciousness of law among the people does not yet have the binding power of law until it is transferred to external life, there coming to expression and form. The will of the ruling authorities must be proclaimed in a determinate form; the legal conception of the people must be activated in custom in order to become law. Legal consciousness is only the power and action of God's requirements in the soul, and, like these requirements themselves (the law-ideas), it does not yet ground any law. First this establishment in external life, which is the act of men, grounds the human order, which is the concept of law. First this establishment produces the common external shape of life (objective ethos); this objective ethos is the concept of law. The law thus established as external objective order then separates itself from the grounds of its origin into an independent existence. It is not valid *as* the will of the ruling authorities or *as* the popular consciousness, but only *as* law. God's order inheres in the external objective order as such, which is to support it. For this reason the law remains no less in force even when the legal consciousness of the people and the ruling authorities has long become something else, when everyone considers the law to be irrational and unjust, and, <51> with regard to valid legal norms, when one no longer even considers their origin; in fact, they gain in sanctity to the degree that such awareness sinks into oblivion.

Such a transition from inward valuation to external *establishment* and validity is the concept of the *sources of law,* and accordingly in general there are only two sources: *custom* and *legislation*, i.e., observance as law, and establishment by authority.

§. 19. The Two Sources of Law: Custom and Legislation

Custom is determination for the *popular* consciousness, i.e., the consciousness of the people who abide by the law, and insofar as they do so – be it only the high nobility; custom therefore concerns the necessity of *observance* of a legal rule (**opinio necessitatis**).

Legislation is determination for the *ruling-authority* consciousness, i.e., the consciousness of those whose vocation it is to establish the law – be it only the democratic assembly; hence legislation concerns the necessity of the *introduction* of a legal rule in accordance with justice or utility.

Custom thus rests on an immediate legal judgment, legislation on a reflected-upon (legal-philosophical or political) judgment. The content of custom is therefore derived from that legal consciousness that fills the community as ethical substance, as a determining inclination; the content of legislation comes from deliberation and the will of certain persons, based on the foundation of that consciousness. With the former, establishment in external life follows from the gradual ongoing subjection of conduct; with the latter, it comes through a sort of command. The former is the organic manner of gradual unobservable emergence, analogous to mores and language, while the latter is the manner of the mind, of personality, emergence from intention through action in a specific **<52>** moment. For that reason, the subjects of customary law are *natural* communities: region, station [Stand], people; the subjects of legislation are *legally constituted* (i.e., fashioned into an acting personality) communities: municipality, corporation, state.

In consequence, law exercises its power over men immediately in custom; in legislation it does so by means of the human authorities sanctioned by the law itself, and therefore through free human establishment. This corresponds to man's twofold position as *creature* and as *personality:* human community first has law as a given reality over itself, and then, on the basis of this given reality, establishes law over itself through its own action. The former given reality is customary law. Its legal rules have established themselves through their own inherent power over consciousness; they were not decided upon by any man and are not supported by any regard for those rules, but are valid in themselves. The legal rules of legislation, however, are introduced by men and are valid because of regard for their originator. This removes the objection made against customary law as to how subjects can bind others through their previous actions. It is not regard for *them* which binds later generations, but regard for the power which continually determines men in their actions independently of each other, and for the rule and order which they hereby establish in their inner valuation and external life. The persons through whose observance custom develops are not the originators but only the medium of customary law.

Customary law accordingly by no means rests on a concession of the legislator; it is an independent, in fact the original source of law. For legislation itself presupposes customary law, since an immediately given law must already exist for there to be legal authorities, by means of which it from that point arises. Every constitution, thus the legislative power itself, is originally customary law. But legislation <53> certainly enjoys a higher regard, in that it includes in its concept free rule over the encountered legal order. The legislator therefore has the power to abolish custom or to cut it off in advance to the degree that he factually can intervene.[31] At any rate, to the degree that he can prohibit and does not do so, he is the cause of customary law, albeit a negative, not a positive one.

§. 20. The Binding Force of Customary Law

In accordance with its origin and seat, the binding force of customary law lies in both aspects: legal consciousness (**opinio necessitatis**) and observance in consequence thereof. The latter apart from the former is meaningless; but likewise the former without the latter has no validity, is not yet law (see §. 11). Custom as such is therefore by no means a mere characteristic, or the "irrefutable witness of a law which arose prior to it and from elsewhere," "so that the origin of law is independent of custom," but an aspect of the origin and binding power of the law that is just as necessary as legal consciousness itself. This is analogous to how the criminal will and the criminal act are both equally essential aspects of crime. Both, inner consciousness and outer realization, must be in evidence in the entire legal sphere, in accordance with its character as external ethos.[32]

---

[31] For example, the Austrian Code, §. 10.

[32] For this reason, repeated use and a certain duration are essential requirements to establish a legal custom. For it is precisely in this that establishment consists as an independent moment. The consequence of this spiritualistic description

The binding power of legislation however has its seat in the lawful regard for the legislator and the proclamation of his will (promulgation – Royal Assent).

The ground of this binding power is however the same for both: and that is the *regard for the law* itself, i.e., the given external order over men. Legal norms arise through custom, in that through it they become elements of this existing order <54> (and indeed it is not the origin of custom but its continuance that is the basis of its validity) and through legislation, in that they proceed from the authority which the existing order designates. It is therefore not the national conviction or the national will which is the ground of the binding power of the law; it is instead the law which is the ground by which the national will binds individuals, and the manner in which it does so. To ground the regard for law on the national conviction is analogous to grounding moral laws on conscience. Law, like morality, has the ground of its binding power absolutely in itself, but in accordance with its peculiar character it has this power not merely in its idea but likewise in its external continuance. In terms of its provenance,

---

of customary law would be that one would have to identify the law that "arose elsewhere," i.e., the national legal conviction, the bare characteristic of which is custom, by other characteristics if necessary, and then grant it legal validity even without custom and observation, but in particular abandon the requirement of duration. Neither Puchta, who put it forward (and indeed without needing it for his salutary reform of the theory of customary law), nor Savigny, who accepted it in part, derived this consequence from it. Lately, however, this has been done by Beseler. He really does posit a folk consciousness valid as law without custom at all – "popular law" – as opposed to customary law, and therefore also designates the sources of knowledge of the latter. Incidentally, such a view is by no means confirmed by the Roman assertions that custom cannot defeat **ratio** [reason] or that it cannot arise against **ratio** through error. For even if we concede the full applicability of these sayings, which are more philosophical than juridical (who is to decide on the **ratio**?), on the one hand the **ratio** is something other than the view of law arising in the consciousness of the people, and on the other hand it still does not follow that a popular view of law can become lawful without custom.

it is a potential in the nation, while in terms of its continuance and its validity a power over it. The national conviction therefore is certainly the source of the determinate content of the law, and the necessary means by which it comes to its external, objective existence. But the ground of the regard for law does not lie in that national conviction but in law's own ethical power, which in fact effected that national conviction, and in its existence, mediated through this and no less through outward establishment, although now having become independent. In this independent existence it passes through the generations, without any of them being able to lay claim to it as its work, as the order over the nation which connects the nation and the ages.

The regard for the legislator therefore is not based on the fact that he is the organ and representative of the national conviction but that he is the organ of the law and its power over the nation. The consequence of the opposing viewpoint would be for customary law and legislation continuously having to measure up to the national conviction, with their validity dependent upon the verdict regarding their correspondence. The teaching of the Historical School in its innermost motive **<55>** does not consist in deriving the *validity* of the law from the popular *will*, but in deriving the *content* of the law from the popular *consciousness.*[33] Its intention is not to set persons, the people, over the law, but on the contrary to put persons and therefore also the legislator under the law, that is, its development in national history. The subjectivity principle, to which such an error belongs, has however ensconced itself so deeply in the intellectual culture [Bildung] of the times that its expressions perhaps every so often brush on the same thing.

In the final analysis it is the power of God's world order which produces the law and lends it its regard. It moves the peoples and their ruling authorities to establish norms which in greater or lesser degree answer to it and which for that reason they recognize to be that which is just, rational, imperative. It is the ground of the regard for ruling authorities and therefore for the binding power of the laws. It is also the true and

[33] This is a frequent misunderstanding. In such confusion, Gönner attributes to Savigny a democratic tendency.

reasonable ground of the binding power of custom; because it is that which, as an awareness of constraint (**opinio necessitatis**), determines the actions of men. Regard for *it*, not regard for observing men nor for the popular intent, consecrates custom, which has arisen out of the awareness to obey it. This has nothing to do with an "immediate connection of law with the divine will." The law derives its content immediately from the national consciousness and its regard immediately from itself. But its final ground lies in a higher order of the ethical world, which is nothing other than the commandment of the living personal God. Thusly does law lend itself to religious faith, which does not deceive. Thus also must true science understand it. Since no ethical power is possible apart from a living subject, if one sep- <56> arates the law from God, one gives it the people for its subject, no longer treating it as law but as national conviction, and the eternal divine content of the law comes to be considered mutable according to people, time and conditions, and to be at man's disposal.

§. 21. The Wrongheadedness of Codification

In accordance with the dual position from which they arise (see §. 19), both manners of law's origin, custom and legislation, are always necessary, each with its own particular value and own sphere of application.

Custom has the merit of greater venerability,[34] the undoubted merit of legal consciousness entirely undisturbed by the possibility of something else, and, in the initial shape it gives to the legal condition, also of greater harmony. This is because nature always works more harmoniously than reflection. Legislation for its part is a higher attestation of the human spirit and has the merit of freedom and reflection, and thus the greater power of correction, direction toward purposes, and greater precision and forcefulness.

Custom thus develops the legal condition *originally* and in its *totality.*

---

[34] Thus Aristotle (*Politics* III. 16): "῎Ετι κυριώτεροι καὶ περὶ κυριωτέρων των κατὰ γράμματα νόμων οἱ κατὰ τὰ ἔθη εἰσίν" [customary laws have more authority and they have it on more important matters than written laws]. In the same manner Lycurgus prohibited the writing of the laws.

It arises together with life relations themselves and provides them with the norm; it makes them into legal relations. Legislation then enters the picture. When a situation presents itself to legislation's scrutiny, as a rule it has already for some time been taken hold of by that invisible constructing power of law and brought to a certain level of development. Scrutiny is precipitated partly by contradiction between law <57> which arose in past times and the conditions or the values of the present, partly through immediate present need (because for a newly arisen relation often no corresponding observance has been developed, especially with regard to those relations resting more on utility than justice), and partly, finally, by purposes for the future. For the purpose [Sinn] of the ruling authorities, the outflow of which is legislation, is a purpose of intention, of guidance and direction for an end; legislation therefore does not restrict itself to providing the seal of approval to already developed life relations but also has the vocation to call forth future life relations primarily by means of institutions in a creative and intuitive [divinirend] manner (Beseler).

Certainly, custom remains at all times a fertile source both for the new production of law and for the further advance of the written law; in the period of higher consciousness and freer reflection, however, legislation must engross a greater sphere over against it, and the higher the degree of systematic character the law gains, the more it must itself increase in consciousness. Therefore when one demands that law's conditions grow in a gradual unconscious manner, in the manner of the middle ages, one opposes the principle of our time. Despite this, the legislator in no way takes the place originally occupied by custom: he may not undertake to create the legal condition *starting anew and in its entirety*. For human freedom is not absolutely creative.[35]

This yields the assessment regarding *codification*. By codification one

---

[35] Man of course possesses an unlimited power to destroy in accordance with free reflection, but only a limited power so to build. For instance, how difficult would it be for us to produce a constitution according to the Greek manner or on the basis of medieval feudal principles! Even the French Revolution, with its apparent absolute free reflection, was locked into an extremely small circle of specific concepts.

understands the composition of law *codes* <58> which are intended to contain the *total law*, be it for a specific area of life (civil constitution [Civil-Verfassung]), be it even for the entire public condition (e.g., the Prussian Civil Code). It is the extreme form of legislation. It provides the legal condition with an entirely different character. Originally and up to that point, the legal condition of all peoples rests in its entirety on custom, which supports and encompasses it. A few more or less comprehensive laws are added to this, which in their place intervene in that entirety, which date from various times and collectively [sämmtlich], the earlier and the later, are independent of each other. With codification, however, the legal condition is based in its entirety on the code, which supports and encompasses it. Custom is only a mere exception within the code, but individual laws are likewise mere exceptions. Laws dating back to before the code are no longer valid; laws dating from afterward appear as appendices ["Novellen"], and when they begin to mount, one treats it as an invitation to a new codification.

Thus by means of codification the legal condition in its entirety is based on statute instead of custom, on the work of human reflection rather than on the drive to develop given by nature. This of necessity entails the disadvantage on the one hand that given the restriction of human reflection and perspective, even the most successful implementation leaves a significant incongruity with real life and its requirements, and on the other hand that continuity, the historical unity of the legal condition, is broken, divided into a before and after the Codex, by which the awareness of necessity, which to that point was on the side of the existing law, gives way to the notion of arbitrary selecting and changing (§. 15). For this reason, codification is an unnatural, a bad form of legal condition.

This does not mean that all codes under all circum- <59> stances are to be rejected. They might be justified by way of exception following profound shocks and uprootings, upon wholesale changes in life relations or mores which perhaps over longer periods of time had remained unaccounted for, upon actual and not merely presumed confusion in existing legal material, a confusion which in fact arises most easily through legislation itself.[36] They are also less questionable in spheres which merely regulate the actions of state power than in those which regulate the life relations of the people, e.g., less so for procedural or criminal law than for civil law or above all for constitutional law, and are most appropriate for certain relations involving a less deep ethical relation and with those concerning which agreement across the entire nation is desirable, such as the law relating to bills of exchange. Beyond that, its profitableness depends on the historical and systematic insight of the age and on the possession of persons sufficiently gifted for the work, who, like geniuses in art, are not born every day. Under all conditions, the first step from the historical form of legal condition to that of the code remains extremely hazardous and should not be taken except in extreme necessity.

However, even where codes seem appropriate and even indispensable, they should, to the degree possible within this form, maintain the *continuity of the legal condition*. Accordingly, the legislator firstly should not change the received *structure* of the law, that is, the legal concepts, without need and clear awareness, even when he must change legal provisions. This holds <60> equally for individual statutes and for entire codes. A new structure which does away with the past voids, in terms of result, the entire received legal condition, because although it appears to have stayed the same, in fact it has changed into something else, since in the new relation it realizes a new effect. This total change in legal content does not lie within the purpose of legislation; even with codification, such a purpose instead extends only to secure command of that content and to sifting and improvement in details. It is entirely ungrounded, for real life has no need for it. It leads to confusion, because the relation of the new to the old cannot be overlooked; and finally, it makes it impossible to utilize

[36] "But if laws heaped upon laws shall swell to such a vast bulk, and labor under such confusion as renders it expedient to treat them anew, and reduce them into one sound and serviceable corps, it becomes a work of the utmost importance, deserving to be deemed heroical, and let the authors of it be ranked among legislators, and the restorers of states and empires." Sir Francis Bacon, *The Advancement of Learning,* edited by Joseph Devey (New York: P.F. Collier and Son, 1901 [1605]), book VIII, ch.3, aphor. 59.

earlier experiences because it has changed precisely the conditions which they had undergone. Rather than truly sifting in order to eliminate the faulty and discordant, every legislation in this manner becomes an entirely new experiment.[37] And another thing: the legislator is not to *annul in principle* previous law, even where he formulates the legal condition newly in systematic form, but, to the degree that it is not either directly or indirectly definitively abolished, to allow it to con- **<61>** tinue in force. This is not a mere *subsidiary* validity, the kind which one can likewise attribute to a foreign received law, but *immanent* validity, as existing in the continuity of the legal condition; accordingly, former law does not find its application merely in the areas in which the new law is silent but also in those in which new law speaks, as the explanation and root of that law, along with it and in it. The principled abolition of existing law in order to put into force only that which is contained in the new code leads at once to material shortcoming, since no human legislator is capable of exhausting life.[38] Hence, it destroys the unity of the national law and legal

---

[37] So for example Justinian in the *Const. De transform. usucap.* and in the *Nov.* 115 entirely wisely and appropriately changed the legal provisions but, without knowing or wanting to, also changed or, as the case may be, confounded the legal concepts (of **usucapio**, **praescriptio**, nullity, inofficiousness, etc.), thus producing highly disadvantageous confusion. How totally must this be the case when entire codes take that course! In the transition from old to new legal conditions, knots should be untied rather than cut through, which is why the vocation for new codes requires historical and systematic insight in the existing law. For this reason Savigny's book *On the Vocation of Our Age for Legislation and Legal Science* mainly assumes the lack of insight into the structure of existing law and by extension the danger of producing a new edition. By no means does it oppose material reform. That such a lack of insight truly existed at that time, and not merely in terms of degree, and thus susceptible of infinite improvement, but in its very nature, has adequately been demonstrated through the insight attained since then.

[38] So for example the Bavarian constitution arranged nothing for the *apanage* [provision for the subsistence of royal descendants] in the case of a prince of the

consciousness. Instead of the further development from its original national foundation being continuously preserved, as in the case of that immanent validity of previous law, here all future effect is founded simply on the coincidental viewpoint of a specific point in time and a specific individual who happens to be the legislator. Finally, it cuts off from the legal system [Rechtswesen] the fruit of the scientific might and achievements which were attached to the preceding; this is especially grievous with regard to the new civil legislation, because it is precisely in the area of civil law that its most illustrious achievements are rooted in the classical common law. The more the codes in this manner fundamentally and in point of fact grant validity to the pre-existing, naturally grown and historical law, the less they fall under the strict definition of codification, and the more they retain the charac- **<62>** ter of simply more extensive statutes. The degree to which this is possible and profitable depends on the circumstances which brought on the necessity of the code in the first place.

This then is the criticism of the newer codification, that the procedure associated with it is the opposite of all of that. Codification per se is considered the normal, the higher sort of arrangement of the law, and one therefore needlessly resorts to it, merely for the sake of the excellence of this form, in order for the entire law to be a consciously thought-out work of men, in order for the present purely to stand on its own, divorced from the past. One furthermore approaches the matter by treating existing law not as binding and determinative – questioning, without having a practical need to, whether better material determinations exist than those which it contains, giving it a new structure, taking away its entire validity, annulling everything not contained in the code. Instead of bringing the received legal condition to clear awareness, reforming where needed, one

---

blood ascending to a foreign throne. When this case came up, there were no grounds for decision in accordance with the codification principle. In terms of the principle of ongoing validity of past [vergangenen] law, however, grounds were available in the *nature of the apanage*, as contained not in the constitution but in never-destroyed German constitutional law [deutsche Staatsrecht] and in historical precedents.

destroys it in order to put an entirely new one in its place. Here the purpose is not to create the *content* of the law a priori by reason – one has for the most part come back on this error – but to ground the *validity* of all law a priori on the new code, referring the people and the jurists simply to the code, so that in a manner of speaking the existence of the law first dates from the code. Apart from all these negative consequences, this in itself is a diminution the *sanctity of the law*, since law is no longer treated as a power existing from nature which merely undergoes the legislative act, but rather in its entirety is treated as a product of the human action of legislation.[39] **<63>**

A form of code that does not interfere quite as much as this is the *corpus* [Sammlung], examples of which are Justinian's Codex and the Decretals of Gregory XI. Here previous laws are listed in their own original

---

[39] A good deal of new legislation has furthermore gone astray by construing legal principles themselves a priori as a philosophical system, or by defining them as in a textbook. The definitions then become for it not only a negative, the border guard, which keeps out certain things it wishes to exclude, and of which it therefore is conscious; but it aims thereby to exhaust the matter itself, and everything it does not include in the definition – those things of which it is not aware, as well as those things it excludes consciously – is stripped of juridical consequences. Instead of e.g. pointing out the concepts of robbery, of theft, burglary as the nation and the jurists have done so in accordance with practice up until now, and only to guard against what it recognizes as a specific shortcoming, either of an overly narrow or an overly broad formulation, or where it fears confusion with a related concept, it instead constructs these living facts from categories and characteristics and only accepts that which it fortuitously has comprehended thereby as theft, as robbery, as burglary. There will then certainly be cases which do not fit these characteristics and nevertheless truly constitute such crimes. And when legislation considers it necessary to teach e.g. what burglary is, let's say forcible breaking into a repository, it will, if it is consistent, not be able to leave it to human consciousness to decide what is forcible, what is breaking into, what is a repository; it will have to keep on going with its determinations of concepts until, as in Hegel's philosophy, it arrives at the definition of pure empty being.

form and on the strength of their own original authority. Hence it is not based on the principle that the entire law is first sanctioned *today*, and the requirement exists neither systematically to fill out the entire sphere of law nor theoretically to examine every rule now for the first time. Nevertheless, the corpus lacks any principled inner motive; it is virtually solely oriented toward the external goal of facilitating usage, and therefore in no way can serve as an example for us.

Another form of code to be distinguished from codification is the *register* [Aufzeichnung] of previous law, either combined with significant reform qua content or not. It indeed proclaims all its laws as new and sanctioned for the first time by itself – this in contradistinction to the corpus – but it is not conceived as a conclusive and therefore exhaustive <64> system. Hence it is the form in which historical continuity as stipulated above is maintained. An example of this is given in the Twelve Tables legislation. Although extending across the entire area of law, it laid no claim to cover it and, to the degree that it did not, it left room for the old norms. Just so the Law of Moses, to the degree that it concerned secular relations; no less so the most ancient codes of the Germanic peoples. This manner of composition is just as applicable at our level of scientific advance and is truly the appropriate one.

§. 22. The Role of Legal Science and Court Practice

Legal science has the task of bringing the law to complete and systematic awareness in order to apply it either to future rules (*theory*) or to obtain judgment regarding an existing case (*praxis*). Its activity is to discover customs and to delimit them in sharp outline, as well as to interpret the laws, and regarding both, to discover the underlying principles from which to gain new legal rules, to grasp the system of the law as a whole, i.e., its mutual integration to form a total effect, and to arrange its application in terms of that spirit. It thereby brings the latent content of the law to full and harmonious development.[40] In this manner it is truly productive; it is an element of legal development, no less fertile than custom

---

[40] Puchta has exceptionally concisely formulated the meaning of legal science in his *Pandects*, 2nd ed., §. 16.

and statute, but in no way original and independent the way they are, rather ever dependent upon a given reality before it, so that its results are continually to be measured in terms of agreement with that reality. The class [Stand] which in more mature times has the special vocation of performing this function in no way does so as representative of the popular conviction, as little as does the legislator (see §. 20), but as representative of the law, this higher power over the people. Hence it is due to the necessity of the law and not to the representation of popular opinion that because this or that principle is valid for the legal condition, the appropriate development of it must be valid, and that that which has been determined in consequence of legal application is valid as a component of the existing legal order.[41]

The harmonious development of legal content and its principles to their full extent, covering all of life, is accordingly a scientific and not a governmental vocation, and it is a mistake to desire to use the legislative power to take care of this. Where the necessary norms can be derived from existing principles, one should not pass a law but rather refer jurists to their own scientific activity. It is a mechanical conception of this day and age that a law must always be thought up in this manner, and it was not the least of the accomplishments of the Historical School to combat this mechanical conception. How excellent are the principles in Roman law regarding eviction, accident, negligence, compensation for damages, etc., which were gained purely through scientific activity without any help from legislation! But then legal science cannot replace legislation. Only legislation may make independent isolated decrees or wholly new principles and life arrange- **<66>** ments, or do away with valid ordinances.

Giving legal science full play therefore does not conflict with legis-

---

[41] Puchta's designation of the legal profession [Juristenstandes] as "representative of the people," and similarly Savigny's, does not have the significance of its being the representative of the laity and its convictions, but of its being the bearer of a national vocation and therefore the bearer and true representative of the national consciousness (see above, §. 18). This rebuts the objection that in consequence of this designation the learned law [Juristenrecht] must first be measured against the popular (read: lay) conviction.

lation according to its true vocation. It is just as little in conflict with the influence which is continually exercised by the popular consciousness, and therefore custom, on legal formation. For the latter is able originally to produce norms, while legal science can only systematically assimilate existing ones. That legal science, like every specialized activity and no less legislation, might detach itself from the collective spirit of the nation and become one-sided does not abrogate its natural [naturgemäss] significance, but it may render institutions desirable which reduce this danger, as long as such are otherwise capable of being implemented and profitable.

Legal science finds its transition into life *indirectly* in many ways, through custom and legislation, in that it determines the viewpoint of the people and the ruling authorities; it does so *directly* however through *court practice* [Gerichtsgebrauch], that is, the evenhanded application of a norm by the courts. In this manner the courts become the actual organ, i.e., means of determination, for legal science, in the way custom is for the popular consciousness and statutes are for the will of the ruling authorities.[42] As ongoing observance of a norm in the awareness of already existing obligation (**opinio necessitatis**), it is a species [Gattung] of customary law in the broader sense. Nevertheless, it has its own unique character, in that the legal valuation from which it springs is a *legal-scientific* judgment in the broadest sense, or a *juridical* judgment, that is, a judgment **<67>** regarding the validity of a norm *on the basis of principle* and in coherence with the *whole law*, be it a legally expert judgment [rechtskundiges Urtheil], that is, a judgment as to whether a legal norm (namely custom) already exists, as occurred with the ancient lay assessors [Schöffen], or a *true legal-scientific* judgment, that is, one in which the legal norm is to be derived from the existing law. A legal-scientific function nonetheless underlies the former, be it ever so imperceptibly, namely in the substantiation of the norm, particularly e.g. custom, through conscious conclusions

---

[42] A legal perspective of the people can certainly be established by court practice, it being likewise the organ for this, but always mediately, through the activity of jurists (administering justice [Rechtssprechenden]), which, as is shown below, absolutely has a legal-scientific character in the broadest sense.

gained from observances, and the specification of the norm with regard to the remainder of the law. This decisively characterizes the standpoint of the judiciary as opposed to the standpoint of the people, out of which custom arises. Custom is the consciousness of subjection under a norm, immediate and isolated. The binding power of court practice therefore is based on the general ground of customary law, viz. gradual establishment in the external order, but it has a special character in accordance with its peculiar nature.

Since in fact court practice is the product of a legal-scientific judgment, which for its part, in accordance with the above, has a given reality ever before it against which it always is tested, the validity of court practice is also dependent upon this test to the degree that such legal-scientific judgments exist in ongoing application, e.g., court practice regarding the three degrees of **culpa.**[43] Should however **<68>** court practice be detached from the juristic operation that evoked it, and should this be lost to consciousness so that the practice in the end manifests itself as something independent, it then acquires unconditional binding force (**legis vicem**); for example, the court practice that *pacta* are actionable or that a compensation payment can be claimed from a marriage engagement. This occurs of necessity and in short order[44] where jurists follow a custom or

---

[43] ["culpa: Fault, neglect, negligence. A term in civil law, meaning fault, neglect, or negligence. There are three degrees of *culpa: lata culpa*, gross fault or neglect; *levis culpa*, ordinary fault or neglect; *levissima culpa*, slight fault or neglect, and the definitions of these degrees are precisely the same as those in our law. This term is to be distinguished from *dolus*, which means fraud, guile, or deceit." From *Robertson's Words for a Modern Age: A Dictionary of Latin and Greek Words used in Modern English Vocabulary.* URL: http://www.wordinfo.info.]

[44] Precisely this result is based by Savigny in the presumption of a twofold sort of court practice, one being the same thing as actual custom, and by Puchta in distinguishing two sorts of juristic activity, with jurists in their immediate judgment, as the representatives of the popular conviction, being unconditional sources of law, while in their legal-scientific judgment always being subject to scrutiny. In accordance with my entire conception of law, I cannot evade also attributing a significance to established court practice as such.

are determined by an immediate requirement of life; but it can also occur where they attain that result through mediated scientific activity, even perhaps through historical misunderstanding, as for example in our summary procedure regarding possessory interdicts. Here then court practice differs fundamentally from custom, which has unconditional validity since popular consciousness, the organ of which it is, is an immediate element of legal generation which undergoes no further examination.

On the other hand, however, there is a special consideration attending to court practice: for the sake of both legal certainty and seemliness, every court must be in agreement with itself. For this reason court practice, already in the stage in which it began to develop, enjoyed a certain degree of regard while custom did not, as long as it was not fully developed and settled. To wit, *precedents* [Präjudicien] and *praxis* are to be distinguished, **<69>** i.e., individual observable occurrences [Vorgänge] as opposed to lengthy continuous application, usually no longer capable of being accounted for. The former is incipient, the latter settled, established court practice.[45] Mere praxis is capable of attaining to unconditional validity (**legis vicem**) in accordance with the above-mentioned preconditions. But a court shall not deviate from its precedents even in cases of doubt. Beyond this, the regard for precedents can be intensified through positive

[45] Thus for example our bankruptcy procedure rests on praxis, not precedents. Furthermore, cf. Bacon, *op. cit.*, aphor. 95 and 96 [95. If judgment be given upon a case in any principal court, and a like case come into another court, proceed not to judgment before a consultation be held in some considerable assembly of the judges. For if decrees are of necessity to be cut off, at least let them be honorably interred. 96. For courts to quarrel and contend about jurisdiction is a piece of human frailty, and the more, because of a childish opinion, that it is the duty of a good and able judge to enlarge the jurisdiction of his court; whence this disorder is increased, and the spur made use of instead of the bridle. But that courts, through this heat of contention should on all sides uncontrollably reverse each other's decrees which belong not to jurisdiction, is an intolerable evil, and by all means to be suppressed by kings, the senate, or the government. For it is a most pernicious example that courts, which make peace among the subjects, should quarrel among themselves.]

law and in consequence of national organization (high-court rules of procedure [gemeine Bescheide] – Prussian and Bavarian law regarding precedents).

§. 23. The Role of Court Practice in the Generation of Law

And so the elements of legal generation are popular consciousness, the purpose of the ruling authority, and legal science. The *sources of law* in the technical sense however are custom, legislation, court practice. It is imprecise to count legal science as a source of law. For the concept of the sources of law designates the bases or organs through which legal rules <70> obtain validity, not those through which they arise in consciousness. A source of law is only the statute [das Gesetz] and that which has the force of law ("**legis vicem obtinet**"). This cannot however be said of legal science. The doctrine of legal science as such (**communis opinio**) is simply incapable of obtaining binding regard from the judge since it lacks that establishment in the external order, just as little as does the popular consciousness. Only court practice, which does embody such establishment, is capable of this under the above-mentioned conditions.[46] It is entirely appropriate to construe those elements of legal generation and the sources of law corresponding to them (their manner of establishment) in their unity and accordingly to designate them as elements of the total legal condition: popular law [Volksrecht], learned law [Juristenrecht], and legislation. But one must guard himself from the error of considering the aspects of popular consciousness and of legal science to be detached from custom and independently established court practice.

---

[46] When positive laws grant force of law to legal science, in so doing they make certain jurists into judges, similar to the councils of law professors [Spruchkollegien (bodies of university law professors who provided courts with legal opinions)] (**responsa prudentum**) or certain writings on codes (Citiredikt) – but they do not make legal science as such into a source of law. Maurenbrecher (*De auct. jurisprud.*) reckons the **opinio jurisc.** to be a source of law in that he puts legal scholars on a level with judges, through the erroneous presupposition that the regard for court practice rests on judges being legal scholars.

The external determination of the law, which resulted from its nature as common external life arrangement (objective ethos), therefore is everywhere just as essential an element as is the national consciousness from which it springs. It is that which is the seat of law's independent power, detached from the national consciousness and its vagaries. Therefore, among all true law-peoples prior practice is held in high esteem already as such, apart from its inner reasons. Among the Romans, this <71> was true of everything which had become **tralatitium**; among the English, the precedents.[47] In its independent existence, <72> existing law deter-

[47] Bacon, *op. cit.*, aphor. 21ff. ["Precedents and the Use of Forms": 21. We come next to precedents; from which justice may be derived where the law is deficient, but reserving custom, which is a kind of law, and the precedents which, through frequent use, are passed into custom, as into a tacit law; we shall at present only speak of such precedents as happen but rarely, and have not acquired the force of a law, with a view to show how and with what caution a rule of justice may be derived from them when the law is defective. 22. Precedents are to be derived from good and moderate times, and not from such as are tyrannical, factious, or dissolute; for this latter kind are a spurious birth of time, and prove more prejudicial than instructive. 23. Modern examples are to be held the safest. For why may not what was lately done, without any inconvenience be safely done again? Yet recent examples have the less authority; and, where things require a restoration, participate more of their own times than of right reason. 24. Ancient precedents are to be received with caution and choice; for the course of time alters many things; so that what seems ancient, in time may, for disturbance and unsuitableness, be new at the present; and therefore the precedents of intermediate times are the best, or those of such times as have most agreement with the present, which ancient times may happen to have more than later. 25. Let the limits of a precedent be observed, and rather kept within than exceeded; for where there is no rule of law, everything should be suspected: and therefore, as this is a dark road, we should not be hasty to follow. 26. Beware of fragments and epitomes of examples, and rather consider the whole of the precedent with all its process; for if it be absurd to judge upon part of a law without understanding the whole, this should be much rather observed of precedents, the use whereof

mines the legal consciousness of the nation in no less degree than it originally was determined by it. Law therefore is also in terms of its content not merely the expression of general law-ideas and the national consciousness, but likewise the consequence of certain events of its establishment, and thus partly free personal act (by the legislator, leading jurists, merchants influential in legal affairs, landholders, etc.), partly accidental, often merely external influences and motives (ruling authorities, parties etc.). For this reason, law can become alienated from the national consciousness in high degree, even to the point of contradicting it. But as long as it is not altered (in the manner set out by itself), the law asserts its full power and sanctity, this contradiction notwithstanding, for the sake of that independent existence.

---

is precarious, without an evident correspondence. 27. It is of great consequence through what hands the precedents pass, and by whom they have been allowed. For if they have obtained only among clerks and secretaries, by the course of the court, without any manifest knowledge of their superiors; or have prevailed among that source of errors, the populace, they are to be rejected or lightly esteemed. But if they come before senators, judges, or principal courts, so that of necessity they must have been strengthened, at least by the tacit approval of proper persons, their dignity is the greater. 28. More authority is to be allowed to those examples which, though less used, have been published and thoroughly canvassed; but less to those that have lain buried and forgotten in the closet or archives: for examples, like waters, are wholesomest in the running stream. 29. Precedents in law should not be derived from history, but from public acts and accurate traditions; for it is a certain infelicity, even among the best historians, that they dwell not sufficiently upon laws and judicial proceedings; or if they happen to have some regard thereto, yet their accounts are far from being authentic. 30. An example rejected in the same, or next succeeding age, should not easily be received again when the same case recurs; for it makes not so much in its favor that men sometimes used it, as in its disfavor that they dropped it upon experience. 31. Examples are things of direction and advice, not rules or orders, and therefore should be so managed as to bend the authority of former times to the service of the present.]

§. 24. Law as Inheritance

Due to its subjective standpoint, the period of legal science and legal philosophy prior to the Historical School had no inkling that law arises in any other manner than through conscious human action, first through contractual, later through legislative establishment. People even thought that speech itself often came about through agreement! Custom, which despite all of this was encountered in life and in positive law, therefore was derived from the sanction of the legislator, even made into mediate legislation (Thibaut). Hugo was the first to emphasize the fact that custom is an independent source of law of no less importance than legislation. Savigny invested this fact, that law <73> springs from the popular consciousness through custom and later through scientific activity and thus develops in an organic manner, with its intellectual significance. This insight into the origin of law gained its juristic implementation through Puchta, to which Savigny added the finishing touches. In this manner a juristic science of the sources of law was gained which in its essential results appears to be assured for all future time. Moreover, Niebuhr and Savigny brought to awareness, in the teeth of the leading orientation of the times, the ethical principle of the venerableness of tradition and human circumspection, not to create an entirely new legal condition on his own strength. It is therefore a feature of piety, reverence for the higher constructive power over men, which characterizes the Historical School.

Certainly with this manner of doing things the danger arose of making the organic origin of law, which by all means recedes in later periods and only serves as a foundation, into the dominating and even the sole principle. This is the objection of "*naturalness*" [Naturwüchsigkeit]. In terms of principle this objection misses the mark, although in its initial assertion the application of the new principle may have gone overboard. This has been moderated for quite some time now. Adjustment in this sense has always been praiseworthy and still is. Instead of this, however, opposition has arisen from the Hegelian school, which completely ignores this great and valuable significance of the Historical School and for its part puts forward an entirely opposed principle: the *absolutely free generation of the legal condition through the human spirit*. This principle, even though it is foreign to Hegel's own doctrine and in fact stands in opposition to it, is nevertheless the consistent result of a philosophy which elevates reason, coming to consciousness in men, into God. It is the principle of arrogance over against that of piety. The same spirit of allowing nothing validity but that which is <74> produced by man freely by his cognition likewise once filled Fichte. However, that which once was an innocent error acquires a different character when the truth has been brought to clear awareness. For the rest, this philosophical intention is not in any sense new. It is entirely the same conviction, in a somewhat more convoluted speculative form and in a more lackluster edition, as that which was attested to by the Revolution of 1789 in simplicity and powerful action.[48]

---

[48] The latest polemic against the Historical School, from Beseler in his book *Popular Law and Learned Law,* is of an entirely different sort. The writer professes the viewpoint of the Historical School but characterizes its implementation until now to be defective. The new doctrine of the sources of law which he opposes to it consists primarily in the assumption of a *popular law* distinguished in the same way from *customary* as from *learned law* and to be asserted over against both. This rests however on the same unacceptable presupposition as the previously commonplace concept of natural law, to wit, that a law exists which has not externally been fixed and implemented. Certainly, a *popular consciousness* exists which is to be distinguished from custom, and which possibly no longer corresponds with custom, just as there exist law-ideas which are distinguished from positive laws. No one denies this. Then as to whether in Germany the existing law truly contradicts the popular consciousness and to what degree, and furthermore whether the reception of Roman law in its entirety and in specific areas took place through jurisprudence against the popular consciousness and popular need, are not principial but historical-factual questions regarding which therefore only individual opinions obtain, not the profession of a school of thought. However, a popular *law* alongside customary law can as little obtain as a law of reason alongside positive law. Popular consciousness which has not been fixed in custom – and it is the duration of observance which embodies the fixing – has no justification, no binding power, no capacity to be observed by the judge; and were the latter to attach such status to it, it would lead to the

inexpressible confusion and uncertainty of law. For the inner requirement (τέλος) of legal transactions and the intention of concerned parties (merchants, landowners) in such transactions are certainly norms for the judge, but that is not, and is not valid as, popular consciousness or popular law, as little as natural law, but as the nature of the case (§. 10), which is not disputed from any standpoint.

CHAPTER 4: THE POPULAR CHARACTER OF LAW

§. 25. Law is the Product of Human Community, not Public Opinion

The law is to be the free human manifestation of God's order, thus at the same time the manifestation of the human community's own ethically reasonable spirit and the subordination of its entire external condition to that order (§. 1). Accordingly, law arises from the consciousness of the people (§. 18), from its valuation of life, its innermost individuality (Savigny), and it arises in consonance with the entire condition of the people, the makeup of the land, climate, extent, means of subsistence, mores (Montesquieu); and precisely because of this, law arises in a living manner in the consciousness of the people, more or less generally known and understandable, or even, where such is not the case, at least generally recognized as that which is peculiar to it and indigenous. All of this taken together can be termed the *popular character* [Volksthümlichkeit] *of the law*. It is the condition in accordance with nature, it exists everywhere at the dawn of history, and there is great value in its being maintained.

By no means does it follow, however, that law must be in agreement with the prevailing opinion and legal point of view of the people. This firstly because the law above all must be in agreement with God's order, with reason and justice, to which even past customs and popular characteristics must be subordinated. For example, in the case of the Romans and the Germans the pagan laws, even though <78> popular, had to give way to Christian ones. Popular character has its worth as the special peculiar implementation of that which is just and reasonable, not in what it is in itself, and especially not in opposition to the just and the reasonable. Furthermore, popular character is something entirely different from the prevailing opinion of the people; it is the peculiarity implanted in the people, growing during its entire history, the effluence of its divine vocation, and the embodiment of the actual, natural and spiritual requirements of its particular condition. Prevailing opinion, on the other hand, is the judgment adopted by the people possibly on the basis of passion and error, which might even be an apostasy from its own popular character, as in the case of the Jewish people considering Baal and Moloch worship to be necessary and advisable, or the same with the French people in 1789 regarding the republican form of government; there could be nothing further from the popular character, in that Jewish popular customs and traditions were based on Jehovah-worship, French customs and traditions on the monarchy.

However, it most certainly follows that the maintenance and restoration of indigenous laws as opposed to a law received from outside – the *nationality of the law* – and the general comprehensibility and accessibility of the law – the *popularity of the law* – are an advantage and a goal. Still, the historical leading of the peoples does not always allow of the attainment of this goal everywhere and in full measure. Individual legal institutions of previously developed peoples, sometimes even their entire legal edifice, press upon and to that extent suppress original legal generation, leading in the developed situation of later times to a technical development of the law which no longer allows for the easy comprehension and general understanding of the law. The law itself, however, ever stands over the <79> popular character of law. This means that the justice and appropriateness of norms, even continuity, as that which in fact maintains the awareness of this justice and necessity in the people (§. 15), form an even higher consideration than whether the law originated in this nation and whether it now is generally understandable to, and known among, this nation.

§. 26. The Gradual Detachment of Law from Popular Consciousness

Initially, national legal consciousness is itself naive and, since custom and tradition predominate, it builds law in an immediate manner. There therefore exists a complete and immediate unity between it and the existing laws as its expression. After reflection awakens, after legislation and science extend their activity and external events step in with their effects, this immediate unity must cease. The spiritual permeation of the law in the national consciousness must then become historical and systematic rather than naive, that is, the legal norms are to be retained as to their causes, fates, past applications, and explanations, and in the coherence of their effect. Such a permeation in its heightened degree is ever a matter of special vital activity, and therefore of a special class [Stand]. Not to allow the gap which then arises between the general popular consciousness and the legal condition, or the scientific knowledge thereof, to become excessive, and to try to reduce it, is a worthy goal; the attempt to eliminate it, a vain one. Codification in the misconceived version described above is an example of the latter. Its intent is for the popular consciousness mechanically to reappropriate the <80> legal condition (that is, through external indoctrination or reference works from codes) which once was its own organically, i.e., as its own construction. In so doing it provides no true appropriation, while it endangers that historical and systematic permeation. One cannot give up scientific, historically developed theology in order to return to the simple undeveloped consciousness of God of the first Christian congregations, or wholly to replace it with the conceptless, bare theology of emotion of the current school. One cannot abandon scientific medicine based on anatomy, physiology, chemistry, in order to heal merely in accordance with mere doctor's discretion or even with simple natural means. One cannot give up the technically developed art of war and allow the peoples to pound each other *en masse*. One cannot give up the comfort and mores of contemporary society in order to return to a simple state of nature. Just as well may one give up our legal science and legislation, which has gone far beyond the popular consciousness, in favor of a popular law. Simplicity, upon which general wisdom is founded, is always to be pursued, but never at the cost of truly appropriate, fruitful development.[49]

§. 27. Roman Law as Germany's Received Law

In the same manner every people initially had its self-constructed, purely

---

[49] The now so widespread viewpoint that non-jurists could pass better judgment than jurists precisely because of their lack of knowledge which makes them impartial, is thereby similar to allowing laymen unprejudiced by medicinal systems to treat the sick, or civilians to command armies.

national law. Events can occur, however, through which such a law is irretrievably lost. Our German people was forced to accept the entire body of Roman law as formally valid for private law, as they have <81> in recent times had to accept English-French concepts, at least de facto, with regard to public law. Regarding the former, the matter certainly cannot be undone, regarding the latter virtually not. With respect to private law in particular, the complaint might be lodged that the reception of Roman law suppressed legal formation stemming from the peculiar spirit of the German nation in broader extension. What an advantage England had in this matter, where although it certainly underwent the influence of the learned Roman law, it gave that law no formal validity, and the generation of law was effectuated entirely out of the peculiar national conviction. Even so, it cannot be denied that a higher leading was behind this. The Roman people had a mission from God to develop this aspect of human existence, the law, in an excellent manner and with an enduring truth, similar to the Greeks regarding art and the Jews regarding religion; and the appropriation of its handiwork therefore cannot simply be termed an evil. Indeed, the Roman law is not owed an unconditional decisive regard, as little as is Greek art, but in the same way that the ancient world provides an indispensable foundation for the self-reliant creative artist, so is the Roman law in certain degree the indispensable foundation of private law, not simply through its exemplary method but also through a range of apt decisions, through the disclosure of the nature of the case in relations of property law [Vermögensrechts].[50] Furthermore, a large portion of legal relations for which to us the Roman law is valid <82> had little connection with the national character, as for example purchase, exchange, tenancy, eviction, etc., and the reverse is also true, Germanic law

[50] See the appendix to *Private Law*. In this appendix (first in 1845) the question was examined in general terms which came up at the Germanist assembly of 1846. There on the one hand Roman law was recognized simply as an example of juristic method, on the other as a mixture of natural law and the nature of the case as written reason, from which the untenable result was derived that Roman law only "then is valid to the degree that it is justified by reason or has come into force in German form." Even so, voices testifying to the truth were not lacking.

maintained and independently developed in broad degree those legal relations inseparably connected with the national valuation of life, as for example the entire law of persons, law of the family, rights of property within marriage, relations based in landed property. All of this must therefore significantly moderate the complaint about the invasion of Roman law.

Be that as it may, the Roman law has become the law of Germany and has the power and regard derived from historical, centuries-long existence. Therefore it is never advisable to throw the Roman law overboard as a matter of principle, like something extraneous, in order thereby to restore the old Germanic law or entirely to make a newly to be created Germanic law tabula rasa. This would be a violation of the sanctity of law in itself; in fact it is a violation of nationality itself, in that the reverence for this law, with which the German imperial crown was bound up, is itself a deep-seated trait of German conviction and German history. As little as it is advisable, so little is it possible. The original generation of law by the German people cannot be set into motion again at the drop of a hat following three centuries of suppression. As something peculiarly Germanic and youthfully productive, this has not existed for a long while; there is therefore now neither a power of German legal generation available, nor can that now be retrieved which in the meantime would have proceeded from it had one preserved it from the Roman law. On the other hand, the historical rootedness of the Roman law is no hindrance to the truly advisable task of revitalizing German law, to the degree that vital power still resides in it; even to interpret it according to its own spirit and principle through science, praxis, legisla- **<83>** tion, rather than according to analogy of the Roman law; to bring Roman law closer to German law by following its history and correctly understanding its modifications in German practice, and in so doing – regardless of whether codes exist or not – to make ready a uniform legal consciousness through science.

§. 28. The False Understanding of the Popular Character of Law

The movement in favor of the popular character of law which manifested itself shortly before the catastrophe of 1848, and prior to that as symptom and precursor of that event, is based on entirely different principles from the ones laid down here in connection with Savigny and Montesquieu. Here for the first time the popular character of law – nationality and popularity – is considered to be the supreme, in fact the only viewpoint, against which the continuity of legal development, in fact justice itself, scarcely comes into view. Furthermore, the popular character of law is increasingly being invested with the meaning that law must answer to the current judgment and will of the people, and thus from now on must be determined by the people. In this manner indeed it is not so much the nationality and popularity of the law but instead *popular sovereignty for the law.*

As means for this popular character, one therefore demands firstly the most extended codification *carried out by the popular assembly,* in order for the currently existing people to refound the entire legal condition. Accordingly, one demands *judges from the people* in twofold opposition, against the jurists [Rechtsgelehrten] and against the officials [Beamten], thus laymen elected by the people for a determinate periods of office: jurors [Geschworne] in criminal cases, lay assessors [Schöffen] **<84>** in civil cases. These popular judges are not to be bound to the existing law but are themselves to make law, to be legislators in the individual case. In this manner lynch justice in particular is given a hitherto unheard-of significance. While jury members in terms of the English institution are bound in every respect by law, and in the French institution, while free from legal rules regarding evidence, are not free from legal characteristics regarding crime, and thus are only left to their personal (moral) conviction with regard to judgment of facts – in terms of this requirement of popular character jury members without exception will also pass judgment regarding the law in accordance with their personal conviction, thus e.g. not merely regarding whether the accused is guilty of high treason but whether high treason is punishable. The same thing will of necessity occur with the popular judge in the administration of civil justice. Actually, proponents have gone even further: the popular judge is not only not to be bound to existing law but not even to scientific rules, legal concepts and their consequences and coherence, but is to judge only according to his natural common sense (bon sens – cf. Kirchmann). Thus, legislation will continuously flow from the current sovereign people via their representative (to whom the king will not dare oppose a veto) and the administration of justice will yet be emancipated from this legislation under popular judges with sovereign power over the individual case. This will have the effect of the law complying with the contemporary opinion of the people, the latter finding no resistance in established laws and ordinances; but rather every one of its pulses immediately determining judicial decisions, as when e.g. the people, public opinion, no longer view high treason, lèse-majesté, adultery as crimes and therefore no longer punishable (even though still on the books as crimes), or when the people deems rental payments from peasants to be unjustified, and no judge recognizes them. **<85>**

Beseler provided the initial impetus for this conception of the popular character of law, in that he was the first to depart from the proper conception of the Historical School.[51] For this runs in greater or lesser degree through the Germanist gatherings as a common characteristic.[52] In the

---

[51] Beseler, *loc. cit.* Beseler's viewpoint, unlike that of the subsequent movement, is not to furnish the objective structure of the law with its order, which although established and structured through history, practice, and science, is neither the product of the people, nor fully understandable by the people, nor any longer in correspondence with its will; but only to foster the newly generating powers of the present, scientifically to investigate the continually new forms of national commerce (e.g., among landowners, merchants); in this, his national tendency is justified. However, he first posits the principle of the legal validity of the popular consciousness, and substitutes a law of determinative popular consciousness, the principle of this movement, for the popular consciousness bound to the law, which is the principle of the Historical School, and he proposes to some extent the means which the subsequent movement is pushing to the limit.

[52] At the Germanists' assemblies at Frankfurt and Lübeck in 1846 and 1847, the well-grounded and timely pursuit of German nationality and thus of the nurture of Germanic law was permeated and, I might add, thwarted by this false notion of popular character. Regardless of the moderations and protestations of

final analysis, it **<86>** is men of secondary importance who have fully developed it and carried it out to its most extreme expression.[53] But even now in popular opinion, in many cases there is a lack of clarity and the confusion of the popular character of law, which is natural and advantageous, with the popular sovereignty of the law, which is overthrow and destruction.

This movement in pursuit of popular character has advanced together with a polemic against Roman law, in a certain connection with Germanistic efforts. Although by many these efforts were meant seriously, the strength of the current at that time went against the Roman law not simply because it was Roman but because it was a historically developed

---

estimable voices, the leading element of these convocations nevertheless was the lack of recognition for the continuity of law and its many hundreds of years of existence – the desire for a radical elimination of Roman law, either immediate or gradual – the imperceptible substitution by which the concept of Germanic law passes over into the concept of today's popular opinion and the legal judgment of the intelligentsia, the capacities of which one became convinced in the chambers of Baden etc. – the demand for universal codification – the conception of the institution of the jury as the voice of the people, which with regard to the laws discovers the justice and actual guilt of individual cases, replaces the princes' right of pardon, purges unjust laws – the argument against Roman law, that the laity cannot become versed in it, that their right depends on whether the judge has studied in Berlin or Heidelberg, as if one might not, through a good handbook, become just as well versed in the common law as in a new code, which itself is not lacking in amendments and determinations from practice, and as if a modern constitutional or civil law code does not have its controversies just as well as Roman law does – an argument which besides is much more valid against German private law and therefore demonstrates that it is not so much the national as it is the modern form of legal condition (codification according to the current popular viewpoint) which this movement is aiming for.

[53] E.g., Kirchmann, *The Uselessness of Jurisprudence as a Science* (see in opposition to this my booklet, *Legal Science or Popular Consciousness?);* Eberti, *Journal;* Leue, *German Lay Tribunals* (a writing which received the approval of Mittermaier in Lübeck).

law binding the present and binding the current popular will. And it aimed for Germanic law as little as it did Roman; rather, it merely aimed for the will of the contemporary German people. The people, to whom one wishes to hand a codification, from whom one wishes a sovereign judge to arise, will never produce Germanic law but a law in accordance with contemporary political science, precisely as good as and in fact much closer to the doctrine of the Romance peoples. Experience has demonstrated this. At the German national assembly in Frankfurt in 1848, where the proponents – moreover, the moderate proponents – of this viewpoint exercised decisive influence, everything (after in 1846 having proclaimed that "in the great act of founding a German collective legislation only German law can be laid at the foundation") that remained of actual Germanic law was eliminated root and branch: family estates [Stammgüter], estates in fee [Lehngüter], rights of estate [Standesrechte], corporations founded in hierarchy [Abstufung] **<87>** and superiority; and in their place pure Romanistic institutions were proclaimed as German fundamental rights: Roman simple property, French-style corporations based simply upon the number of votes, etc. This undeniably testifies to a democratic rather than a Germanistic tendency.

This trend confronted the Historical School in pronounced animosity, even though the latter was the first to bring to awareness the coherence between the law and the consciousness and peculiarity of the people, and even though from it and only from it did the actual revival of Germanic elements of our legal condition stem, and only through its method can they actually be furthered. There is however this distinction: the Historical School bases the law on the people in its collective history, while the popular-character movement bases it on the contemporaneous people. In the former case, the law is based upon the people in terms of its full extent and articulated relations, in which the ruling authority and jurists are an essential and specially called part of it; in the latter, upon the people in the modern democratic sense, in opposition to ruling authority and jurists. In the former, the people are to generate law in order to obey specific norms as being bound to them – in custom and tradition; in the latter, in order to command the norms that it considers good.

In its complete development (and the more so, the more it approaches this) the popular character of law as hereby pursued is an emancipation from everything toward which a constraint should exist: emancipation of the present from the past, emancipation of subjects from the injunctions of the ruling authority, emancipation of the subjects from the legislative power, emancipation of human judgment from the laws of the matter [Gesetzen der Sache] as presented by science. It is a consolidation of the democratic principle, established in the area of the admin- **<88>** istration of justice as well as that of the constitution. Because when in this manner penal authority simply is opened up to the people as it sees fit, no ruling authority can stand against the will of the people. In the end, however, it is the *destruction of the administration of justice:* through it, that which it is the primary, in fact sole, business of the administration of justice, justice itself, is banished from it. Justice demands that the judicial verdict be declared simply according to immutable laws, in accordance with merit and guilt; a historically developed, evenhandedly administered law provides a guarantee of this, with its clearly determined norms and learned judiciary [gelehrter Richterstand], for whom at least, even though everywhere subject to that which is human, it is the spirit and honor of the profession [Standesgeist... Standesehre] to subordinate all personal inclinations and disinclinations to the laws. Against this, such popular judges render decisions, as the nature of the case and as experience everywhere confirms, in accordance with emotion and passion, be it according to hate and jealousy, estate partiality [Stände], or according to prevailing currents of political opinion or party, or according to sentimentality. And justice no less means that the verdicts in the entire country for all similar cases be in agreement with each other, the entire administration of justice be ordered by one and the same (ethical) order of life, all cases be determined as if by one act, all men weighed with an equal balance, and this safeguard is also achieved by a historically developed law and a learned judiciary. By contrast, popular judges are informed only by their own conviction, and under the same exact conditions render one decision in one case, a different decision in another; their decisions are unpredictable, for one and the same act here passing down a death sentence, there acquittal and praise; under equal conditions the contracting party, the pensioner, **<89>** hereditary tenant here triumph, there are defeated. The entire administration of justice thus becomes a chaos of individual, mutually conflicting decisions.

CHAPTER 5: LEGAL OBLIGATION

§. 29. The Twofold Nature of Legal Obligation

The obligation imposed by the existing (positive) law is *legal obligation.* Accordingly, it comprehends both the obligation of individuals to obey the law, and the obligation of the community, i.e. the ruling authority, to maintain the law. The obligation first to restore the law according to its true ideas is, by contrast, a moral duty of the community and its power-holders.

§. 30. Legal versus Moral Obligation

In line with the nature of law, the character of legal obligation is that of *external duty*, i.e., that it proceed to men from external (objective) existence; and it has this external existence as its aim. From this are derived the individual characteristics which distinguish legal from moral obligation:[54]

1. Legal obligation is concerned *merely with the action*, not, as is the case with moral obligation, with the *motive*. This is because the latter is not necessary to maintain the external order – Kant's distinction between *legality* and *morality*. **<92>**

2. Legal obligation is only *negative*,[55] for its goal is already fulfilled: it is the already realized external order of common life. The requirement of legal obligation is simply not to interrupt that order in its regular operation. When for example a debt is paid or a police order is carried out, it is

---

[54] The earlier natural law made its primary task the elucidation of this distinction. Since the advent of speculative legal philosophy, one considers himself absolved of this task. But despite the intrinsic value or lack thereof of the former's general construction, the abandonment of the implementation of keen determinations of judgment is by no means justifiable.

[55] This is something other than the mere negative character of the *content* of law in our given condition, regarding which see above, ch. 1.

not that anything new occurs, but only that routine existence is not interrupted. By contrast, the aim of moral obligation, the inward completion of men and their devotion to persons and ideas is a matter of a continuously creative positive act. The fulfillment of ethical obligation therefore is capable of infinite elevation; legal obligation, on the other hand, is either fulfilled or it is not. From this as well comes the characterization: "right" [recht – lit. "straight"] the negative, that which cannot be omitted, in opposition to "good," the positive good.

3. Precisely for this reason, ethical obligation in each specific case first obtains its individualization through the individual and his freedom, and therefore *is not recognizable* ahead of time with regard to that case ("in concreto"). Legal obligation, on the other hand, has already gained its individualization through the common will (this is precisely positive law) and therefore is exactly and completely predetermined and recognizable for each specific case ("in concreto"). So for example it is determinable in concreto that the debtor must pay, and how much; but as to sharing from a motivation of love, the form, the measure, the person of the **<93>** recipient are all indeterminate.

4. Finally, legal obligation must be *unfailingly fulfilled*. As objective order, it cannot depend on either the judgment of the individual regarding his duty in a specific case (consideration of conscience) or from his considerations to obey. It is therefore *coercible*, which is to say, coercible *via legal action* [von Rechtswegen], so that the one coerced is aware of yielding not to a physical power but physically to an ethical power. The inward perfection of men excludes coercion; the uninterrupted continuance of external order requires it.[56] Even with legal obligation, however, coercion remains in the background. Law is not a natural order, from the outset realizing itself through physical force; it ever remains an ethical order, an order for human action, and since, in terms of the true structure of the human race, that order is always freely fulfilled, so it is also in our given condition meant freely to be fulfilled, and coercion only arises when men

---

[56] Accordingly, coercion is not derived from the requirement of individual freedom (Kant, Fichte) but from the requirement of the uninterrupted order of common life.

resist. Because law is an ethical order, it is *freely to be* fulfilled; but because it is an *objective* order, it *must* be fulfilled. In normal circumstances this coercion is exercised by the *ruling authority*. However, where such does not exist, prior to or outside of the state relation, the requirement of uninterrupted continuance expresses itself in the authorization of *self-help* and the obligation upon all *others to provide aid.* **<94>**

§. 31. Legal Obligation versus Coercibility

In line with this, however, coercibility is only the consequence, not the primary characteristic of legal obligation. The latter instead consists in the commonality (objectivity) of the norm and thus in the requirement of unfailing fulfillment independent of all subjective considerations of conscience. For this reason coercibility and especially ordered, fully guaranteed coercibility is by no means a decisive criterion for legal obligation. On the contrary, there are exceptions in which legal obligation cannot be coerced – when either the real power punishing those who are refractory or the higher authority representing the legal order fails to exercise coercion – without it thereby ceasing to be legal obligation and coming to coincide with moral obligation. These exceptions are primarily two:

1. *The duties of the law of nations*, for example to keep treaties, to respect the extraterritoriality of ambassadors, which obviously have an entirely different character than the duties of the *morals of nations* [Völkermoral], for instance to come to the aid of an oppressed people, not to interrupt the trade of another nation; they are the common norms, recognized as inviolable and unfailingly to be fulfilled; for this reason the law of nations is unjustifiably denied a juridical character.

2. *The duties of princes to the laws of the state,* namely *the national constitution.* These are essentially different from the *ethical* duties of regents. The latter depend on their moral judgment in each individual case, in which they are to decide merely in accordance **<95>** with their conscience; the former, by contrast, are an unconditional requirement, independent of examination by conscience, which are simply to be fulfilled if princes are not to act in a manner contrary to law, and thus unconditional-

ally unethically.[57] It is therefore erroneous to consider these duties to be coercible in the way that the French Revolution declared them,[58] but just because they are not coercible it is no less erroneous to consider them to be mere moral duties in the manner in which the Hallerian school, at least in part, considers them. The former abolishes all authority and thus the legal order itself; the latter places the entire legal existence of common life in the conscience of the prince, so that he vouchsafes it in the same way as almsgiving, and therefore is the true absolutism.

The distinction between uncoercible legal obligations and moral obligations is by no means hairsplitting. Legal obligation always has external effect even when not the final one of coercibility and its guaranteed result. The violation of the duties of the law of nations grounds *lawful war* (**casus belli**), and thus coercion by legal action, albeit accompanied by factual uncertainty; and the violation of the nation's constitution and the laws of the land by the prince entitles subjects to *protestation* and *passive resistance*, while nonfulfillment of moral duties of regents only lead to remon- **<96>** strations. [59]

---

[57] So for example a prince, even though he have the strongest conviction of conscience that the new constitutions are no good, may not abolish such a constitution existing in his country.

[58] 1793. *Declaration of Rights* Art. 35: "Should the government infringe the rights of the people, the insurrection of the people and every individual part of the people is the holiest of its rights and highest of its duties." Lafayette has lately spoken publicly along these lines.

[59] Accordingly, the duty of Protestant territorial princes only to exercise their ecclesiastical power according to the **consilio** of the clergy [des Lehrstandes] belongs to the legal (constitutional) duties, even if not enforceable. Omission justifies not merely remonstration but protestation. Richter's statement (*Textbook of Ecclesiastical Law*, §. 50) that the prince has "the *ethical* obligation to be advised by theologians" rests on an improper concept of legal and ethical duty. Even so, in that he includes this apparently only moral duty in his book on ecclesiastical law, Richter gives unwitting testimony that it must after all have a juridical character.

CHAPTER 6: LAW IN THE SUBJECTIVE SENSE OR RIGHTS

§. 32. Subjective Right as the Power of the Individual

<97>The law as the objective-ethical form of life gives specific form to human life relations, while also allotting and ethically protecting the spheres of the existence and action of men, and their satisfaction in those spheres (§.1., §. 4.). But by virtue of the personality of men, the essence of which is self-causation and concentration (relation back) upon himself, the sphere which is allotted to him through the ethical power of law is of necessity *his own ethical power inhering in himself over against others,* who then are ethically bound *to him* – not merely to God or their conscience or the legal order with respect to him – he is not merely an *object* of their duty but the *cause* of it. This is law *in the subjective sense* or *rights.*[60]

Accordingly, law in the subjective sense is the *ethical power* which a man has over against others in the sphere allotted to him by the legal order, by virtue of that order. Its essence is not merely the negative of allowance or the intransitive [lacking a direct object] of freedom, but the positive and transitive [having a direct object] of ethical power against others. Although allowance and freedom are frequently the same with regard to content, they are not always so. In particular, freedom does not coincide with law in the subjective sense. It is partly more extended, man having natural freedom from God which as such is not yet entitlement,[61] and

---

[60] Rights thus construct the existence of people in the ethical world, which is their own ethical power, in the same way that their existence in the physical world is their own physical power.

[61] Here belong the use of our corporeal organs, e.g., "the nose to smell," the freedom to sleep or to awake and the like. To conceptualize as a right anything which does not refer to other people, thus to the ethical world, leads to the absurdity which confronts us in the question regarding the "right to smell." Cf. Book III [*Private Law*], §. 2.

partly more re- **<98>** stricted, there being rights which freedom does not underlie, as for example life. Neither does law in the subjective sense come to the same thing as will, but instead to the power a will (better, a personality) has over other wills.

By its concept, law in the subjective sense can only be attributed to a personality, and only by virtue of a higher order. We therefore do not attribute rights to legal institutions as such (e.g., marriage), since they are not personalities, although they are treated in that manner through artificial transference; and we attribute no rights to God, because He does not have ethical power over us by virtue of a higher order – He Himself is that ethical power.[62]

Law in the subjective sense, e.g., the right of man due him in all his life positions, forms, it being his own power inhering in him, a true center about which the entire external world (things, actions of others, etc.) is related as controlled object, and in accordance with which the content of legal norms is often determined. It is therefore a *secondary principle of the legal order* alongside the primary and absolute principle: the *purpose* (τέλος) of *life relations.* As secondary principle, however, it is always based upon this latter. Its own content and **<99>** range is originally and essentially derived from, and the coherence of all the rights of all men lies in, this objective higher principle.

---

[62] To speak of a right of the world-spirit, as Hegel does, is therefore from his own standpoint entirely inappropriate. Likewise one cannot really speak of a right (e.g., entitlement) of marriage, of the family, to wit, in a manner similar to Schelling when he says: "all desire is will, will is that which puts up resistance in matter": in this manner one might say that all existence in the ethical world is law (in the subjective sense), this is what offers resistance to the one who is transgressing. Even so, it would be improper. As little as we may ascribe will in the actual sense to matter, as little may we ascribe rights to institutions as such. In matter it is a higher will that has placed the physical power of resistance in matter; in the ethical world it is the same higher will that has placed its ethical power in this institution. It is not its own power, as in the case of the personality of human beings.

§. 33. Rights are Independent of Duties

Rights arise from God's world order and belong to it in the same way that the ethical form of life relations does, hence no less than does the existence and power of personalities. Therefore our rights are not the consequence of the duty of others; instead, that duty is the consequence of our rights in the specific case. They are not the consequence of our own duty but the original immediate content of the legal order. Certainly, rights are preconditions of dutiful action; devotion is not possible apart from existence and power. But they are in no way mere means to that end[63]; rather they are due to one simply because of his personality. They are an original independent purpose, no less than is fulfillment of duty. For God desires the existence of personalities – and the rights attendant to them – as an end in itself, to the same degree that He desires their duty-inspired decision as an end in itself. Rights therefore are *imparted to man with the first breath through which the divine essence is imparted to him.* Even so, our rights stand in coherence with <100> our duties. For it is one and the same world plan from which both spring and in which they are related to each other in unity. The higher uniting factor which embraces duties and rights is *vocation* (§. 5). Duties arise from vocation, as do rights, and vocation is the standard against which both are measured. It is the *ethical, specifically Christian conception to consider rights only in the light of voca-*

---

[63] According to Kant, man only has external freedom (entitlement) with a view to morality, that is, he has it in order that reason (the logical law of universality together with the law of non-contradiction) has absolute causality in the world; he does not vindicate this causality for human personality *as such*. It is therefore according to his own standpoint consistent but improper when Kant deduces the right of personality in terms of duty (*Rechtslehre* [Doctrine of Law], XLIII): "do not allow yourself to be used as a means." This duty to safeguard my independence is something entirely other than the right of personality, i.e., the ethical power over others, in order that they *may* not use me as a means. With regard to the insoluble difficulties encountered by the old natural law in deducing the concept of right in the subjective sense, see Vol. 1, Book III, Part II, Ch. II [*The Rise and Fall of Natural Law*, p. 108].

tion. Certainly, in the condition of perfection men's rights and their ethical will are always somewhat different, each being arch-independent, albeit without contradicting each other: the entitled will seeks nothing other than that which is ethical. But although man no longer answers to his true ethical nature, nevertheless his personality and therefore also his entitlement are for that reason by no means extinguished, precisely because this is an independent goal that does not coincide with morality. The human will yet exercises power over others even where it itself has ceased to will that which is ethical. Rights therefore are to be considered holy by men even where they are abused for goals counter to morality (egotistical). This therefore answers to that divine purpose wherein that which is innermost in men, whether good or evil, is to manifest itself decisively here below (Matthew 13: 29).

§. 34. The Relationship between Rights and Duties

And so rights are not derived first from duty but from the immediate original content of law. Nevertheless, they do not form *the* content of law pure and simple, that is, its sole and "actual" content, in which case legal duties are not original but derived from rights; rather, they belong together with them to the content of law. For the law does not merely impart to men their determinate existence and position in the ethical world; it above all gives shape to the ethical world itself, and therefore consists just as much in commands for the maintenance of the <101> proper form of institutions as in commands for the security of human positions. The content of the former commandments therefore is mere duties or necessities but not rights, e.g., the prohibition on incest, polygamy, divorce by mutual agreement, the command to punish crime, and the like.[64]

---

[64] Therefore when Puchta bases his system on the contention that "the *actual* content of law is rights" (preface to *Pandects*, I, 6th edition), for this reason alone (apart from the untenability of making the category of the object the basis for division) it must be rejected by us. It cannot be along the lines of rights of the community that one maintains the prohibition on incest, the punishment of crime, etc. The community does not maintain this as its right but as an order

Therefore, although a duty must correspond to each right as its effect, in no way must the reverse be true, that every right (or every necessity) must correspond to a duty as its cause.

In a higher sense, certainly that which is an ethical law of life relations, which is God's order over men, at the same time is also a right of man itself by virtue of the unity of its innermost essence with this order. So for example spouses who divorce by mutual agreement or who live in incestuous marriage not only violate God's order but at the same time also the right of others and themselves; blasphemy is not merely sacrilege against God but at the same time also an affront to the one who confesses God, to the believing congregation. It is even the right of the murderer to be put to death. Nevertheless, it is not the bare entitlement of the human will, by which <102> it seems to manifest itself as determinative principle, as prime cause and final goal; it is entitlement by virtue of the fulfillment of the ethical world order; and therefore, that order is perceived as their right only by the ethically deepest and purest men, while by the general and initial view it seems simply to be a limitation of their right.

Those duties which correspond to the rights of others are therefore something entirely specific, something other than legal obligation in general as distinct from moral duty (§. 29). Legal obligation in general is that which is laid upon us by the legal order as distinguished from morality, even when it does not stem from the entitlement of another; for example, the prohibition on incest, the duty on the part of subjects to serve in the

---

over it, which is transferred to it for safekeeping. I have not denied that law includes rights in its essential content; therefore, the citation from Genesis 1: 26 was unnecessary in this context. On the contrary, I asserted, in opposition to my previous conception, that rights form an immediate content and independent purpose of law by virtue of the personality of men, and not in consequence of duties or as means for duties, that they "are imparted to men with the first breath imparted to him by the divine Being" (p. 130 of the 1st edition). On the other hand, I am unable to recognize that "rights form the *actual* content of law" and thus that those higher ordinances and requirements are only an *improper* content of law. Aside from this, Puchta (*Institutes*, 1841) described the significance of right in the subjective sense in its full intensity.

armed forces. With this specific class of duties, however, there is the peculiarity of having the right of another as ground and center. One must consider all duties which lack their origin in such an entitlement to be the logical opposite of this class. In particular, though, the *duties of love* form an opposite to these duties, because while these are the consequence of the ethical existence and power of others and consist in their not being violated, duties of love are the preservation, usually through self-sacrifice, of that which does not yet belong to the ethical existence and power of others, to the disadvantage to one's own existence. Not to murder one's neighbor, not to poach his wildlife, is a duty arising from his existing right. By contrast, to come to the aid of one's neighbor against rapacious animals, to protect him from them or to help him put them down, is not the consequence of existence in the ethical world as guaranteed him by God, but an expansion and enrichment of his existence through his own devotion. The duties of love do not however exhaust all moral duties and do not exhaust all original duties not derived from any entitlement, but simply form the material opposite to that other rela- <103> tion in which allocated, secured existence is not violated.

§. 35. Public Rights

The primary sphere of rights, since it has the individual person as its goal, is private law. Nevertheless, the position or power assumed by a person in his relation to public law becomes his right by virtue of his personality and in accordance with his nature. There are therefore public entitlements as well, that is, those which exist in public relations and for public goals (§. 48.). But entitlement as such is always a person's. In terms of competence, of the relation to the subject, it is private, since a right or entitlement is in fact an attribute of the individual. Only the relation in which, and the final goal for which, the entitlement exists makes it into a public one, for the content and manner of use are determined by this.[65]

---

[65] This applies in particular to the question as to whether the royal power is a public or private right.

§. 36. Innate versus Acquired Rights

Rights are due a person either simply for and with his existence as personality, or for specific conditions and therefore in consequence of specific characteristics, actions and circumstances. The former are termed "*innate*," the latter "*acquired*" rights; perhaps more appropriately, *general* and *specific* rights. To the former belong life, liberty, honor, then the general capacity for property, family, political and ecclesiastical rights; to the latter belongs every actually existing right issuing from that general capacity.[66] <104>

An entirely different opposition as this is that of the *primeval right* [Urrecht] of men versus *actual rights*, that is, the rights (and in fact both sorts, the general as well as the particular) as they *ought* to be due to men in line with the idea of man, versus rights as they actually *are* due him in the given situation. German natural law theory intermingled both oppositions, putting primeval right and innate rights on a line, and setting particular rights, instead of the existing inadequate legal condition, in opposition to the primeval right. For its part, the French Revolution's theory of the rights of men holds fast to the latter opposition with clear awareness, but it conceives it falsely. That is to say, it understands by "the rights of men" those which are to be derived from the concept of man as *valid a priori* and which therefore supposedly have no need of positive law, which cannot *lawfully* and in a *legally* binding manner be deprived or restricted. Their opposite thus becomes the positive-legal rights, which then however have no validity in conflict with these and which in fact, as is desired, are to be eliminated altogether.

However, *in the first place* this concept of the primeval right, or the rights of men so conceived, that is, which have the effect it ascribes to them, is worthless. There exists just as little an opposition and a dividing line between primeval right and the rights of positive law as between the

---

[66] The literal concept of innate and acquired does not adequately describe the distinction here intended; for e.g. the nobility or sonship in a family do not form part of innate rights in this sense. I summarize so-called innate rights as the right of personality and therefore treat them as such in *Private Law*.

law of reason and positive law. In terms of his idea (thus by nature), man of necessity has rights just as the community has a legal order, but which rights he has is everywhere first more specifically determined by positive law.[67] The latter can be unjust in this, but <105> lawfulness can be decided only on its terms. The claims of serfs and peasants [Grundholden] deduced therefrom for the emancipation of their persons and possessions, or those of burghers to equal political position to the nobility, or those of the people to participate in sovereignty, were, leaving aside the question of truth or untruth, in none of those cases *actual rights*, i.e., already valid, made effective by coercion, over against which existing rights could be considered unlawful.

In the second place, that concept of primeval right or the rights of men is not the true primeval right in terms of content. On the one hand, the rights which it is to include, such as e.g. equal participation in state power and the like, are in terms of the law-idea themselves not claims that can be realized everywhere and unconditionally, in the way that for instance the abolition of serfdom in truth is such a claim. On the other hand, they are insufficient to exhaust the right which is due men by virtue of his idea. For in the case of political rights which make up the content of the "rights of men," which moreover only concern formal equality, the individual citizen might die of hunger, as chides the Communist doctrine, or stultify in barbarism.[68] The *true primeval right* due to men as personality is not simply the fullest freedom and political entitlement but also the fullest *satisfaction* and *highest spiritual perfection*. The primeval right therefore

---

[67] For this reason the concept of "*natural* coercive law" put forward by most natural-law proponents is as untenable as is the concept of "*natural law*."

[68] The German natural-law theory, certainly of the primeval right of men, is of course even more threadbare than the French rights of man; because in consequence of that confusion it only includes the rights described above as "innate," these mere possibilities, as its content, and in fact arrives at the conclusion that the primeval right only consists in negatives, in being "non-means," "non-things" (see Vol. I, 2nd edition, pp. 138–139 [*The Rise and Fall of Natural Law*, p. 120]), or in the abstract capacity to be able contractually to obligate anyone else to the same thing to which anyone may obligate him (Kant).

cannot be realized but is only amenable to steady approximation. While civil society is to strive to realize the idea of primeval right, it cannot "reclaim <106> it" since it never was in its possession.

On this depends the erstwhile oft-discussed question regarding the *inalienability of rights*. Properly understood, the inalienability of rights, just as the disposability of rights in general, focuses on whether rights are due a person for a position ethically necessary to him, or merely for his satisfaction or his freedom. Accordingly, not only innate rights (life, freedom etc.) but also many acquired (particular) rights, e.g. the right of marriage, paternal power, are not disposable and not alienable. Such rights ever remain just as much duties as well. To use the ancient expression, they may be a **potentia activa** since in accordance with the above every right is a power inhering in man himself, prohibiting violation by another, but they are not, at least not in every respect, a **facultas**. This is the true and simple principle regarding the alienability of rights. But in that discussion one understands by alienability and inalienability the question as to whether men (i.e., the great majority) may in terms of legal obligation lack certain rights (to wit, the right to govern, to make laws), which one views, under the false supposition that the civil order rests on contract, as an alienation of that condition,[69] and consequently one wishes to decide whether they belong to the primeval right of men in that sense. The untenableness of the question itself as well as that of the standard of judgment is clear from the above. The question, thus corrected, as to the degree of restricted legal capacity allowable in terms of the law-ideas, will be dealt with in the section below[70] concerning the right of personality.

§. 37. The Origin and Cessation of Rights

<107> The grounds of the origin and cessation of rights are infinitely

---

[69] Thus Fichte in his anonymous writing: *Beitrag zur Berichtigung der Urtheile des Publikums über die französiche Revolution: zur Beurtheilung ihrer Rechtsmässigkeit* [Contribution to the Rectification of the Public's Verdict Regarding the French Revolution: An Assessment of its Legality] (1793).

[70] Book III [*Private Law*], §§. 2ff.

manifold, each in accordance with the content and sphere of life in which they intervene.[71] Nevertheless, in general they may be classified under two main headings in accordance with the two principles of the legal order: the purpose of life relations, and human entitlement and freedom. Accordingly, rights arise either:

1. through *will* and *act*, be it one's own, be it another's, be it both at the same time (e.g. occupation, testament, contract, tort, royal grant, popular election and the like); or,

2. *of their own accord, through given processes and relations* (accession, **versio in rem**, lineage, kinship, and the like), in particular as the consequence and result of a more comprehensive – originating either voluntarily or involuntarily – legal relation (e.g., the right to alimony by filiation and the like). In the first case, rights arise by means of human freedom; in the second, "directly through the law" (**lege**).[72]

§. 38. The Doctrine of Prescription

Finally, another general ground of the origin and cessation of rights is *prescription* [Verjährung]. This is deeply rooted in the essence of the law; for law has the twofold root of its existence in the general consciousness and in establishment in outward life. Time, and time in its further exercise (positive or negative), exerts a power on both, on the consciousness and habituation of men as well as on establishment in outward conditions, the latter through entanglement with infinitely many lawful relations and infinitely many reasonable transactions already erected upon this practice. The prescriptive condition is in this manner transformed into a legally consecrated one, entirely analogously to the manner in which cus-

---

[71] It is self-evident that property, obligation, inheritance, trade privilege, nobility, royal power, civil office, ecclesiastical office, easements, etc., do not originate and are not extinguished through the same or similar grounds.

[72] Only in this sense is it proper when partly the Romans and partly the moderns talk of *legal* [gesetzlichem] rights of pledge, *legal* inheritance, *legal* claims as a separate class; for in the final analysis the other class must also be grounded in the law. The more appropriate distinction is: the action of the participants, and the relation inherent in the thing.

tomary law develops.[73] Now then, an expression of this inward necessary power of time and practice is the confusion which arises in case one does not recognize it. This principle of prescription therefore has its effect in many areas of law, for example the adverse possession of property, real rights, regalia, the statute of limitations regarding accusation, the (German-legal) acquisition of a higher station through exercise into the third generation, the (factually valid) eventual legitimation of a usurped throne, and even the statute of limitations on punishment.

The duration of prescription must of necessity vary according to the nature of the right in question. Regarding rights of a public character, it is usually, in accordance with nature, the time of general human memory (**quod memoriam excedit**) or more precisely stated, the length of three generations.[74] **<109>**

In terms of the standpoint of the older school of natural law, no origin of rights can be conceived apart from the free will of the acquirer and of the one obligating himself. Prescription is therefore viewed as a means of acquisition not by natural law but only by positive law. Indeed, however, from that viewpoint neither can the **in rem versio**, the obligation from the **negotiorum gestio**, the **condictio sine causa**, in fact even intestate succession and the like be recognized as truly lawful. The objection to the "natural law" validity of prescription, that reason cannot give the measure thereof, rests on the false assumption that the other legal institutions have a precise and determinate form already by virtue of their law-ideas. The other objection, that one's right cannot expire apart from his will, would, if it were correct, affix the label of injustice on the positive institution of prescription; but it is incorrect, because rights resting on the will of the

---

[73] It is self-evident that this parallel is not meant to contradict the distinction made by Puchta between customary law and prescription, with its practical consequences for the demonstration of the former. Prescription has a ground and significance for law in the subjective sense similar to what custom has for law in the objective sense. To the degree that law in the subjective and in the objective sense are to be kept apart, to no less degree are prescription and custom to be so.

[74] See Savigny, *System*, IV. 481ff., and Homeyer, *Saxon Mirror*, II. 2., pp. 305 and 643.

entitled require, in accordance with their nature, continuous actualization of that will. Now then, even though – in line with the limitations of human nature – an uninterrupted awareness and assertion of rights cannot be required, still the complete absence of actualization has a limit beyond which the loss thereof must follow.

CHAPTER 7: THE SYSTEM OF LAW

§. 39. Legal Relations and Institutions

If law is the order of human common life, then the system of law is the coherency of *life relations in their legal order,* i.e., a coherency of *legal relations* and *legal institutions.*

These are complexes of facts and factual relations and their legal norms, which together, through the unity of the *purpose* (τέλος) *inhering in them*, form an indissoluble whole.[75] To wit, I understand by legal relation the life relations which have the purpose of being a part of the legal order (e.g. property, marriage, inheritance)[76]; by legal institution, the same relations to the degree that they already have attained their legal ordering. Each legal institution is accordingly in turn itself an order, and the law, it being the total order of human common life, thus in turn unfolds itself in orders, i.e., in just those legal institutions.

§. 40. Factual and Legal Relations

The coherence of law as ethical power with life relations is however a coherence in which law takes hold of these <112> relations as its factual material and sets them into an ethical form. The law as ethical constructive power thus advances in life relations as factual material; this, then, is the course the system takes. But the same purpose (τέλος) which is effec-

---

[75] For example, the pledge relation *and the law of pledge* arises from the purpose of vouchsafing security to the creditor by means of objects of property. From this spring the law of pledge's manifold concepts in their entirety – the dependent nature, the restriction of the right to mere alienation, the real action [dingliche Klage (i.e., **actio in rem**)], the distinction between movable and immovable collateral, the consideration of priority, etc.

[76] Therefore I cannot for my part accept the example used by Savigny of **lex frater a fratre**. This **lex** contains a legal *case*, not a legal *relation* in this technical sense.

tuated by the legal arrangement is also already active in the bare factual relations (§. 5) and vice versa, the legal order for its part creates a multitude of factual relations. For this reason, the factual and the legal (life relations and legal institutions) are distinguishable but not separable, and the system, conceived as total effect, advances in legal institutions, although these institutions have natural life relations as their presupposition, as their a priori. This is the succession of legal institutions, or of life relations to the degree that they maintain their legal content.

§. 41. The Ongoing Development of Legal Institutions

The sequence of legal institutions, first the life relations and then the already legally active institutions, therefore rests upon their actually (**realiter**) preceding and following each other as conditioning and conditioned. Whether in terms of logic they are simple or complex is not decisive. So for example, private law naturally precedes public law, personality precedes property, marriage precedes paternal power, family law precedes the law of inheritance. But with everything organic a member is not a mere precondition of the other; it is ever and again is conditioned by the other, at least if it is to fulfill its purpose. So, for example, the state already manifests itself as determinative and form-giving for private law as well. Furthermore, legal relations are always jointly generating new such relations: for example, the law of inheritance springs from the purpose of property and the family together, the law of pledge from the law of <113> things and of obligations together. Such institutions therefore depend on a double root.

§. 42. The Enduring Character of the Legal System

Just as the content of law changes, so of necessity does its coherency. The legal construction of each people, and of each epoch of its existence, therefore has its own system. But the character of the legal system, which is that of a coherency of legal institutions, remains always. In the same way, it is also these same fundamental relations that equally make up the legal condition of all, or at least all civilized, peoples, albeit developed and modified by each of them in a particular manner.

§. 43. The Subordinate Character of Rights

Law in the subjective sense is a central point on the basis of the objective coherence of legal institutions (see above, §. 32 at the end). That is, by virtue of the recognition of personality, it is an independent principle which reacts back onto the order of the legal institution in which it arises. But the content of the entitlement is everywhere first determined by the nature of the legal institution, for which reason the totality of the legal order can never find its supreme principle and coherence in subjective entitlement. This even holds true for Roman law, where it is an independent principle more than in any other legal construction, in many cases entirely detached from higher considerations. <114>

§. 44. Freedom is Not the Supreme Criterion of a Legal System

According to the subjective-rationalistic conception of the legal system, private law is a *division of rights*, public law a *division of powers*. Here everything is related to the entitled person as center. With the former, the distinguishing category is then the *object* [Gegenstand] *of rights* (rights to things, actions, persons), with the latter the *form* of *activity of power* (legislative; judicial, i.e., subsuming[77]; executive, superintending power).

This system above all lacks *logical agreement*. Public and private law are erected upon different concepts, and in private law not even the category of object can be implemented. So for example, property and servitudes have the same object, the thing, and are distinguished only by their *content,* i.e., the acts allowable upon the object; the right of pledge through its conditionality, its dependent nature, etc.[78] Furthermore, this

---

[77] [Subsumption is the use of the syllogism in legal science. In *The Rise and Fall of Natural Law,* Stahl describes it like this: "It is based on there being, apart from the rational rule, which is the major premise, also matter separate from it, as the minor premise. Scientific activity brings both together and draws a conclusion."]

[78] When it is said that with property the object of the right is the thing, while with easement it is the usage, this is unacceptable; one should much rather say:

system does not answer to the requirements of a *juridical* system, because its principle of distinguishing – law in the subjective sense, or even the object according to its variation – is not the <115> principle which *brings about* juristic determinations. For example, it is certainly not because of any distinction of objects that the fourth part of the inheritance must be deducted in favor of the legatee[79] or that children cannot be disinherited; rather, it is the nature of inheritance as a legal institution. Finally, this system only includes a *separation, classification;* it does not, as the term suggests, show the interrelation. How thereby "the organic relation of rights to one another and to the whole, the members of which they are"[80] is to be shown is simply impossible to foresee. This whole is in fact nothing other than the legal order. Starting from the legal order and thus legal institutions, one arrives entirely naturally, in fact of necessity, at rights; but starting from rights one will never arrive at legal institutions; the matter remains a plethora of rights. On the contrary, here the natural coherence is disrupted; so for example one must, to be consistent, classify the right of succession in a different category than the right of inheritance, and legacy must appear in both real rights and personal rights (**vindicationis** and **damnationis**).

---

the object with property is complete usage and complete disposition, while with easement it is only particular usage. This is however not an object in the sense that things and actions initially were declared to be objects of rights, but rather *content.* In the same way, the innermost essence of the law of pledge is not expressed when one describes it as the right to the *value* of a thing, it is much rather the dependent nature, the purpose to serve as guarantee for another right, which constitutes its peculiarity, and not the distinction of objects.

[79] ["According to the Roman law, one who became heir or **legates** with the condition of a **fideicommissum** (i.e., of transmitting his inheritance or legacy to another after his death) had the right of deducting the fourth part from the inheritance or legacy, which was not transmitted; this fourth part being known as the Trebellian quarter." From Francis Schaefer, "Influence of the Church on Civil Law," *The Catholic Encyclopedia* Vol. 9 (New York: Robert Appleton Company, 1910). URL: http://www.newadvent.org/cathen/09066a.htm.]

[80] Puchta, *Pandects,* 1st ed., VI.

Despite all objections, this system in recent times has found in Puchta an advocate as consistent as he is persistent. It is based on Puchta's *conception of law itself*, as lately has found especially clear expression. For him, the essence of law is not *order* but *freedom*, and the entire content and purpose of law even in the objective sense is *simply the recognition of personality and its will*, its freedom. "The fundamental concept of law is freedom."[81] "Law accordingly is the recognition of legal *freedom*, which expresses itself in the person and his will, and its effect on objects. It is itself a will, firstly God's, and then of the total- **<116>** ity of men, who are joined through it, a will *aimed at the recognition of the person and his will*."[82] But is not law, precisely in accordance with this pronouncement, itself much rather order than freedom, since "a will of God" cannot be understood as the freedom and entitlement of God? And with regard to rights does the divine will (or the collective will) truly concern only the recognition of personality and its will and not also the maintenance of certain bonds and rules in human community over men as sacred orders in themselves, which are His will and not the will of human personality? In any case, according to this the question of system shows itself to be a mere corollary and leads back to a quite simple viewpoint: if law is *primarily freedom* and entitlement (so that law in the objective sense is none other than the recognition of this freedom or rights), then, I concede, the system of law is a coherency of *rights*. If, however, law is *primarily order* (and freedom is only one side, one part of the content of this order), then indisputably the system of law is a coherency of orders, that is, of legal institutions (see above, §. 34).[83]

---

[81] Puchta, *Lectures on the Institutes*, 1841, p. 4.

[82] *ibid.*, p. 11, 12.

[83] Puchta's reply to me (*Textbook of the Pandects*, 1st edition, 1838, p. VI) is based on a complete confusion of the point at issue. In no way did I oppose the *factual* (relations) to the *juridical* (legal institutions), as is here understood, but the *objective* (law and its institutions) to the subjective (entitlement and its objects). I have nowhere otherwise expressed myself than in joining both together: "a coherence of legal relations *and legal institutions*," and then "complexes of facts *and*

their legal norms." Where I asserted the *factual* (complexes of factual relations), this was not done in opposition to the juridical but in opposition to the merely *logical*, in opposition to the *abstract category* of object (e.g., in the case of the law of pledge etc.; see above). The conception that the *purpose of life-relations* (which I express alternatively as "τέλος," "inward striving," "drive" of life-relations) is the principle from which juridical statements [Sätze] proceed, and that the ethical power of law draws on the (factual) life-relations in order to subject them to itself, and therefore likewise that the sequentiality within the system depends upon the factual sequentiality and real reciprocal action of life-relations or legal institutions, as the case may be – this conception certainly is not the *subordination* of the legal to the factual, is it? It is not otherwise in Puchta's system, so that here as well the ethical, the will of the person, draws on the *factual of objects*, and has this factual as its basis, its first. In this respect as well, Puchta's system makes *factual* relations its foundation, for the variation in object (thing, action, etc.) is undeniably factual. The divergence in our conceptions therefore certainly is not located here. That entire argumentation that it is not the "factual substrate" but the juridical that must be the main issue for a juridical system therefore is not appropriate to the question being dealt with here. Furthermore, it would be well to keep in mind that the system does not have its locus in its results but in its ruling principles. Rights, i.e., that which is owed to you and me, are of course *juridically relevant results*, but the system rests on the principles of the legal institutions by which it comes about that we have such and such rights, and according to which it is decided whether we have them, and that is of no less juridical interest.

Puchta has now, despite these decisive objections to the system of *relations*, nevertheless lately expressed himself in this manner: "The personality of man and thus his *legal relations* differ according to how they are conceived in the following characteristics: 1) as individual, 2) as a member of an organic connection: a) the family, b) the people, c) the church. *Legal relations* are distinguished in accordance with this distinction into property, family, public and ecclesiastical legal relations, and the law itself into private law (property and family law), public law, ecclesiastical law" (*Institutes*, p. 54). This cannot possibly mean, as the words seem to indicate, that legal relations follow after the characteristics of men as members of a family or the state. For this would be a reversal of things. Consequently it can obviously mean nothing else than that personality and the rights of man are determined in accordance with the legal relations of property, family, state and church. Legal relations are therefore that which primarily determine, while the rights of man are that which are determined. After all, the system is located in that which determines and not in that which is determined!

Therefore, in the most recent edition of the *Pandects* Puchta has dropped his previous system of obligation according to object and, as in my case (1st edition, p. 152), accepted the foundational division in "obligations of transaction and tort" as well as a broader implementation according to the content of the obligations. Accordingly, our controversy regarding system should be brought to a close. At this point in time (1854) I do not believe that I need to argue with my colleague and friend as to whether the plethora of damning epithets contained in his preface, triggered by zeal against my entire legal philosophy, was justly poured out.

CHAPTER 8: PRIVATE LAW AND PUBLIC LAW

§. 45. The Legal System Reflects the Dual Relation of Common Life

The entire legal system is divided into two main areas. To wit, in accordance with the dual relation of human common life, legal relations are of two sorts. The one serves to satisfy the *individual person*, to complete his existence (of course, only to the degree that it forms an element of the common condition); the other serves to rule men collectively, to join them into a common existence and to complete it as such. The former make up *private law*, the latter *public law.*

Accordingly, the relations of private law are the integrity and freedom of the person, property [Vermögen], family; the relations of public law are church and state.[84] That which is a function or part of the state naturally belongs for this reason to the category of public law – thus municipal law, welfare and criminal law, civil procedure, the law of nations. Even so, a relation can belong to both areas depending on its various as- <120> pects.[85]

---

[84] "Publicum jus in sacris, in sacerdotibus, in magistratibus consistit" [Public law consists in the sacred, in the priests, and in the magistrates] (I. I. §. 2 *de just. et jure*). One may view the church since it has been separated from the state by Christianity and especially the Reformation as a third entity alongside private and public law to the degree that it is conditioned by subjective faith, by which both the participation of individuals and the recognition of the state is arbitrary and fortuitous. In that case, the church appears *relatively*, namely to the people who do not believe it and to the state which does not recognize it, as a mere *private affair*. But in itself and for those who share its faith, it is always and of necessity a *public* institution no less than is the state, i.e., just such an institution which binds them into one subject and rules them by necessity.

[85] Thus, e.g., the relation of estates [Stände], i.e., their delineation, their place in the state (requirements on and privileges of nobility, guild ordinance, freedom of trade and the like) are part of public law, while the modifications which act

The essence of public law is customarily sought in the *common utility*. But its essence is not the common utility as goal, but the *common rule* (union into one common condition) as object and content of relations. What is public is not simply that which serves the utility of all but that which serves a *higher order* over all utility. The other viewpoint leads to consequences such as public punishment having to target the common utility (protection) – the relative theory – or public power only having as goal the utility of men and therefore put at the disposal of those for whom it is of use, etc.[86]

§. 46. Private Law for Individuals, Public Law for the Community

In the relations of private law, man stands in his own right [für sich], and as a complete whole, by virtue of his independence and personality; in the relations of public law, as part of the human community, he stands subjected to a higher power which in its unity has commandments and goals over itself. The former therefore are realized by individuals, the latter through the act of the community. Hence, in private law the individual is always the goal of the arrangement, even when the manner of arrangement conforms to public goals; in public law, it is the whole. In the former, men always appear as individuals <121> – apart or joined with individuals – in the latter, only in the greater community. This or that concrete private relation therefore is a relation among *specific persons*, while this or that public relation is one of *objective* institution; the former therefore ceases to exist with a change of personnel, the latter does not. An obligation, a state of marriage, a guardianship is no longer the same obligation, marriage, guardianship, when it no longer embraces the same

upon estates in their other private relations (family trust – inheritance of farmers – commercial and exchange law) fall under private law. Civil procedure (the order of the administration of civil law) is a part of public law, albeit, in terms of the points of dispute here treated, with a private-legal side.

[86] The Romans expressed themselves indeterminately: "quod ad statum rei publicae spectat – ad singulorum utilitatem" [that which concerns the condition of the public affair – that which concerns the utility of the individual]; even so, this refers to the public *condition* rather than the common *utility*.

persons. By contrast, the state is and remains this particular state through all changes of generations. In the same manner, the civil and criminal procedural law of a state remain the same regardless of changes in individual legal transactions and transgressions.

§. 47. The Effect of Public on Private Law and Vice Versa

Public law encompasses private law to the degree that the latter is conditioned by position (membership) in the commonality and attains the security of its execution through public institutions (legal prosecution).[87] On the other hand, the right and freedom of the person have no less significance for public as for private law. Man is the center for both.

§. 48. The Proper Delineation of the Spheres of Private and Public Law

<122> In earlier times confusion was brought into the distinction between private and public law, as for example in putting the church and welfare [Polizei] arrangements under private law, the family under public law, primarily on the grounds that one comprehended these concepts as a division of *legal norms* (laws). To wit, just as the entire legal system is a system neither of statutes nor authorizations but of legal relations and legal institutions, so also this indispensable fundamental division. *Legal norms* in analogous manner may also be divided into public and private, that is, those which are given in the *public interest* and those which are given only for the *advantage of the individual.* The latter can be *altered* by

---

[87] Bacon, *op. cit.,* aphor. 3 and 4. [3. But private right lies under the protection of public laws; for law guards the people, and magistrates guard the laws. But the authority of the magistrate is derived from the majesty of the government, the form of the constitution, and its fundamental laws; whence, if the political constitution be just and right, the laws will be of excellent use; but if otherwise, of little security. 4. Public law is not only the preserver of private right, so as to keep it unviolated and prevent injuries, but extends also to religion, arms, discipline, ornaments, wealth, and all things that regard the good of a state.]

the entitled in his case, the former cannot.[88] But this latter division, although of great practical relevance, nevertheless cannot form the foundation of the legal system. Nor does it in any way coincide with the first. Private law is full of determinations having public interest (are **publici juris**) and public law often contains determinations to the advantage and at the disposal of the entitled (e.g., civil servants). Should one ask whether the family, welfare administration, the church belong to public or private law, one of necessity intends the division of legal institutions, since family, church are institutions and not norms; upon answering the question, however, one substitutes unawares the division of legal norms, since one has not based the question at all on the concept of relations and institutions, and consequently one reckons the family to public law because many of its determinations are in the public interest and therefore are immutable, and vice versa. In this manner, one asks with one concept and answers from another. The Romans used the same expression **<123>** for both divisions, without however mingling the matter. In the first edition of this work, I used for the latter division the designation "prohibitive and dispositive norms." More appropriate perhaps is the designation now proposed by Savigny: "absolute and mediating law."[89]

In the same manner one may divide *law in the subjective sense* into public and private (§. 35). Private rights are those which have the satisfaction and advantage of the entitled as content and goal, even though in relations of public law; public rights are those which have as content their influence on the whole, and thus as their final goal a consequence for the whole. Accordingly, not simply property, paternal power etc. but also the right of domicile, right of emigration, tax exemption, etc. are private

---

[88] "Jus publicum pactis privatorum mutari non potest" [public law cannot be changed by private agreements], [Digest 2.4] l. 38, de pactis. Just the same is intended where it says "reipublicae interest, dotes salva este" [it is in the interest of the state that dowries are preserved] or "testamenti factio non privati sed publici juris est" [the act of testating is an act of public not private law]; **dos** and testament do not for all that form part of public law.

[89] See my first edition, II. I. p. 125, and Savigny, *System of the Modern Roman Law,* I. p. 58 [English translation pp. 45f.].

rights, while royal warrant, mediatized status of erstwhile imperial nobility, estate suffrage, freedom of the press and the like are public rights. Nor does this division coincide in extent with that of public and private law. An application of it will be made when discussing the doctrine of the limits of legal procedure [Rechtsweges].

CHAPTER 9: CIVIL JUSTICE AND EQUITY

§. 49. The Forms of Civil Justice

<125> Civil justice is only the expression in the area of civil order of the eternal essence of justice as already set forth (I. [*Philosophical Foundations*], §. 55). It is ever a determining power for the original construction of law; in particular, it is the power for its maintenance through protection and retribution.

Protective justice is instigated by the *disturbance of another's rights.* This can be either of a negative sort, *nonfulfillment* (e.g., nondelivery of a legal object, nonperformance of an owed service), or of a positive sort, *infraction* (e.g., damage to things, overcharging). The expression of justice in the former case is the command of fulfillment, in the latter compensation, in both cases in the final analysis coercion. With infraction, the act of the infringer is the decisive consideration, with nonfulfillment it is simply the entitlement of the infringed, which is why in the former case accountability (**dolus**, **culpa**) is presumed while in the latter it is not; meanwhile nonfulfillment, continued with awareness, in fact becomes infraction. However, neither manifests itself as an instigation of retributive justice, as being punishable. Certainly, every knowing and willed disturbance of the rights of another, and especially by infraction, infringes the commandment, and infringement of the commandment, in accordance with ethical principle, is generally an offence to higher regard, which calls for punishment. Nevertheless, because the civil order as mere external order does not lay any requirement upon the attitude of men, it is therefore no infringement of its regard that the subject not voluntarily perform <126> what is owed (be it either the initial fulfillment or the commanded indemnification), instead allowing it to come to coercion.

Against this, *retributive* justice is instigated by the *infringement of the civil order as such.* This is the case when the violation either affects an unrecoverable object of the legal order (e.g., life, state constitution) or a recoverable object in such a manner that the perpetrator's aim is precisely to evade the redressing public power (theft, criminal deception). For that is *active* frustration and thus destruction of the legal order, not the mere *passive* awaiting of punishment. This is the concept of *crime*, and its consequence in terms of justice is punishment as restoration of the regard for the violated legal order.

Protective justice only issues a command to the infringer (conviction, determination regarding compensation); when he fulfills this, the public power does not intervene (execution), in that all that matters here is satisfaction of the one infringed upon. Against this, retributive justice requires that the redress simply be carried out by the public power, since only in that manner does the majesty of the civil order preserve itself over the criminal; punishment is therefore only punishment if carried out by the ruling authority.

§. 50. Equity as Opposed to Justice

Equity forms an opposite to justice. The essence of justice is to maintain a given order, law and right inviolably intact, while the essence of equity is simply to restore the *equality of advantages and disadvantages* (**aequum**) among those concerned, precisely while *leaving aside* all previously given order, all previously granted law and right. So for example the Law of Moses provides that when one's ox gores another to death, the living and the dead are to be common to both. The right of the former, which ac- **<127>** cording to justice must be accorded if he does not forfeit it, is thus left out of consideration. This might be an unconditional quantitative equality or even a proportional one in accordance with the measure of the needs of those involved, or their having (through no fault of their own) caused damages, etc. One often however reckons considerations to equity which are grounded in justice and are not considered in positive law only due to its shortcoming. Considerations of this sort are especially contained in the equity system of the Romans (**bonum et aequum**) which they oppose to their system of strict justice (**strictum jus**), such as, e.g., compensation, defense against fraud [Einrede der Arglist].[90]

[90] [The Roman **exceptio doli**, in which a person who is sued may plead fraud on the part of the plaintiff.]

In terms of its deeper root, equity rests partly on the original equal entitlement of men and partly on the equal love for all, which yields an equal standard everywhere that no special law, right, or right-founding act effects a preference. In this root, equity is reunited with justice, it consisting merely in disregarding those intervening grounds. A decision in accordance with equity is therefore in order where such facts grounding a specific inviolable right are truly lacking, e.g., in the settlement of confused boundaries,[91] while in the contrary case it is a censurable violation of justice. Only the entitled himself may forfeit his right and exercise equity. Equity is only to fill in the gaps left where justice does not extend. We therefore do not attribute equity to God, since his justice fills all things.

Legislation may follow the principle of justice or the principle of equity, and the function of the judiciary can then be referred to the one or the other. The principle of justice expresses itself differently with regard to legislation than with regard to the function of the judiciary, in that with the former **<128>** it consists in the consistent implementation of law-ideas in each and every institution, with the latter in the consistent implementation of specific (derived from the law-ideas) *statutes* and *positive-legal* principles. The consistent upholding of granted entitlement is the same in both respects. To the degree that the function of the judiciary depends on equity, any objective norm of decision-making expressing the national conviction is lacking, in that the equality of advantages and disadvantages merely attaches to the particularity of the case; the judge therefore is simply referred to his own personal judgment. Hence, he is not actually a judge (**judex**) but only a *referee* (**arbiter**).

---

[91] To this category belong, e.g., cases in which the Romans were wont to appoint a majority of judges (**arbitri, superatores**).

WORKS CITED BY STAHL

Aquinas, St. Thomas. *On the Government of Rulers* [De regimine Principum: various editions]. Cited on p. 26.

Aristotle. *Ethics* [Presumably the Nichomachean Ethics; various editions]. Cited on p. 35.

Aristotle. *Politics* [various editions]. Cited on p. 56.

Bacon, Sir Francis. *The Advancement of Learning,* edited by Joseph Devey. New York: P.F. Collier and Son, 1901 [1605].Cited on p. 59, 69, 71.

Beseler, Georg. *Popular Law and Learned Law* [Volksrecht und Juristenrecht]. Leipzig: Weidmann, 1843. Cited on pp. 74, 85.

Eberti, *Journal* [Zeitschrift; further information lacking]. Cited on p. 86.

Fichte, J.G. *Contribution to the Rectification of the Public's Verdict Regarding the French Revolution* [Beitrag zur Berichtigung der Urteile des Publikums über die Französische Revolution]. Berlin: 1793. Cited on p. 106.

Fichte, J.G., and F.I. Niethammer. *Philosophical Journal* [Philosophisches Journal einer Gesellschaft teutscher Gelehrten]. Jena; Leipzig: Gabler, 1795–1800. Cited on p. 29.

Hegel, G.W.F. *Philosophy of Law* [Grundlinien der Philosophie des Rechts], 5th expanded edition. Hamburg: Meiner, 1995. Cited on pp. 28, 35.

Homeyer, C.G. *The Saxon Mirror* [Der Sachsenspiegel]. Berlin: Dümmler. 1835–1844. Cited on p. 109.

Justinian, *Corpus Iuris Civilis.* Cited on p. 60, 119, 122.

Kant, Immanuel. *Doctrine of Law* [Rechtslehre; many editions]. Cited on p. 99.

Kirchmann, J.H. *The Uselessness of Jurisprudence as a Science* [Die Werthlosigkeit der Jurisprudenz als Wissenschaft: ein Vortrag]. Berlin. 1848. Cited on p. 86.

Leue, F.B. *German Lay Tribunals* [Das deutsche Schöffengericht] Leipzig : Kollmann, 1847. Cited on p. 86.

Maurenbrecher, R. [editor's surmise] *De auctoritate prudentum*. Bonnae: Weber, 1839. Cited on p. 70.
Melanchthon, Philip. *Philosophiae Moralis* [Moral Philosophy; further details lacking]. Cited on p. 26.
Melanchthon, Philip. *Loci Communes* [various editions]. Cited on p. 35.
Puchta, G.F. *Lectures on the Institutes* [Cursus der Institutionen; presumably vol. I: Introduction to Legal Science and the History of Law among the Roman People (Einleitung in die Rechtswissenschaft und Geschichte des Rechts bey dem römischen Volk)]. Leipzig: Breitkopf und Härtel, 1841. Cited on pp. 101, 115.
----------. *Pandects* [Lehrbuch der Pandekten], 1st edition. Leipzig, 1838. Cited on pp. 115, 116.
----------. *Pandects* [Pandekten], 2nd expanded edition. Leipzig: Barth, 1844. Cited on p. 64.
----------. *Pandects* [Pandekten], 6th expanded edition. Leipzig: Barth, 1852. Cited on p. 101.
Richter, A.L. *Textbook of Ecclesiastical Law* [Lehrbuch des katholischen und evangelischen Kirchenrechts: mit besonderer Rücksicht auf deutsche Zustände], 4th edition. Leipzig: Tauchnitz, 1853. Cited on p. 96.
Savigny, F.C. *System of the Modern Roman Law* [System des heutigen römischen Rechts], vol. I. Berlin: Veit, 1840. Cited on pp. 109, 123. English translation by Wm. Holloway, Madras: J. Higginbotham, 1867.
----------. *On the Vocation of Our Age for Legislation and Legal Science* [Vom Beruf unserer Zeit für Gesetzgebung und Rechtswissenschaft]. Hildesheim: Olms, 1967 [reprint 1840 ed.]. Cited on pp. 3, 60. English translation by Abraham Hayward, London: Littlewood & Co., 1831.
Schelling, F.W.J. *Lectures on the Method of Academic Study* [Vorlesungen über die Methode des academischen Studium]. Tübingen: Cotta, 1803. Cited on p. 28.
Schleiermacher, F.D.E. *Ethics* [Ethik: (1812/13): mit späteren Fassungen der Einleitung, Güterlehre und Pflichtenlehre]. Hamburg: Meiner, 1981. Cited on p. 29
Stahl, F. J. *Legal Science or Popular Consciousness? Casting a Light on the*

Lecture given by Mr. von Kirchmann, Public Prosecutor, entitled "The Worthlessness of Jurisprudence as a Science" [Rechtswissenschaft oder Volksbewußtsein? Eine Beleuchtung des von Herrn Staatsanwalt von Kirchmann gehaltenen Vortrags: Die Werthlosigkeit der Jurisprudenz als Wissenschaft]. Berlin: Verlag von Albert Förstner, 1848.

—. *The Rise and Fall of Natural Law: Volume 1A of the Philosophy of Law: The History of Legal Philosophy*. Aalten: WordBridge Publishing, 2020.

—. *The Recovery of Historical Law: Volume 1B of the Philosophy of Law: The History of Legal Philosophy*. Aalten: WordBridge Publishing, 2021.

—. *Philosophical Foundations*. Aalten: WordBridge Publishing, 2022.

—. *Principles of Law*. Aalten: WordBridge Publishing, 2007.

—. *Private Law*. Aalten: WordBridge Publishing, 2007.

Thibaut, A.F.J. *System of Pandect Law* [System des Pandekten-Rechts], 1st edition. Jena: Friedrich Mauke, 1803. Cited on p. 46.

Warnkönig, L.A. *Legal Philosophy as Natural Doctrine of Law* [Rechtsphilosophie als Naturlehre des Rechts]. Freiburg im Bresgau, 1839. Cited on p. 28.

Weber, Adolph Dieterich. *Systematic Development of the Doctrine of Natural Obligation and its Historical Effect* [Systematische Entwickelung der Lehre von der natürlichen Verbindlichkeit und deren gerichtlichen Wirkung]. Schwerin, Wismar und Bützow, in der Boednerschen Buchhandlung, 1784. Cited on p. 46.

INDEX

N.B.: The page numbers given in the Index refer to the page numbering of the original edition.

Private Law

TABLE OF CONTENTS

NOTES ON THIS EDITION

The edition used for this translation is the 3rd edition of the *Philosophy of Law*, published by Mohr of Tübingen in 1854. Words in German which are susceptible to multiple meanings or the meaning of which was not totally clear have been left in the text in square brackets. Square brackets are also used to insert interpolations for understanding or to provide supplementary material. Section headings do not appear in the original: they are of my own device.

Numbers which appear in bold between two angular brackets (like this: <**1**>) are page numbers of the original edition. References in the text and in the indices to page numbers in this book refer to that page numbering.

Roman- and canon-legal terms are set off in the text with a boldface Roman font, e.g., **successio universalis**. An index of such terms is provided at the end of the book, along with the page numbers of their appearance. Many of these terms may be referenced in William Smith, *A Dictionary of Greek and Roman Antiquities* (URL: https://tinyurl.com/ 48au6euy).

A word about the word *Vermögen*. As explained in the text, this refers to "property in the broad sense" as opposed to *Eigentum,* property in the strict sense. As such, *Vermögen* is an umbrella term covering both property and contract. The origin of this legal concept lies in Roman law. In the Roman legal tradition, property and contract together form the "law of things." This law was further developed in the German legal tradition, in which the Roman concept of things became the concept of *Vermögen*, which roughly corresponds to "assets." Therefore, in the German tradition both property and contract are forms of assets. To indicate this distinction, we translate the word *Vermögen* as property* (with an asterisk).

Sections (parts of §§. 69, 70, and 76, along with §§. 77–79) left out of the first edition have been included in this second edition of *Private Law*. The text has been corrected where necessary and improved where appropriate.

GENERAL PREFACE TO "THE DOCTRINE OF LAW AND STATE ON THE BASIS OF THE CHRISTIAN WORLDVIEW"

<xi> Together with the *History of Legal Philosophy*, *The Doctrine of Law and State on the Basis of the Christian Worldview* comprises Friedrich Julius Stahl's magnum opus, *The Philosophy of Law*. This multivolume production provides us with the philosophical foundations upon which Stahl's career as a professor of constitutional law, as a parliamentarian, and as a statesman in 19th century Bavaria and Prussia was based.[1] It is also unique: it is the only comprehensive work of legal philosophy produced by a modern, post-French-Revolution conservative, to wit, a follower of the pioneer in this regard, Edmund Burke.

Conservatism has always been in need of such a comprehensive philosophical system. For opposition to the Revolution did not necessarily lead to unity of worldview. Many conservatives were Roman Catholic and hence argued for a return to (idealized) pre-revolutionary conditions in church and state, thus for the primacy of the monarchy and the papacy – these generally bore the name Counter-Revolutionary. Others were Protestant, and thus perceived a need to move beyond pre-revolutionary conditions, albeit in a manner which maintained continuity with the political, legal, and cultural inheritance of Europe. Among the latter group Stahl was pre-eminent; he was the first of the so-called Anti-Revolutionaries, who in the **<xii>** Netherlands even formed a political party under the leadership of Guillaume Groen van Prinsterer and Abraham Kuyper.

Stahl was a protege of Friedrich Carl von Savigny, himself the pioneer of the "Burkean" worldview in Germany. Savigny is best known for his argument against codification and in favor of legal continuity, including the primacy of customary law, as contained in his *On the Vocation of Our Age for Legislation and Legal Science*. Such arguments were completely in line with what Edmund Burke had argued in his *Reflections on the Revolution in France* and elsewhere. Savigny founded what came to be known as the Historical School of Juris-

---

[1] For more on Stahl's life see my *Authority Not Majority* (Aalten: WordBridge, 2007).

prudence, perhaps the most influential school of legal science Germany ever produced.

The problem with this school was that it lacked a solid grounding in legal philosophy. Writing in 1901, James Viscount Bryce, the noted legal historian and diplomat of late 19th-early 20th century Britain, claimed that in view of its methodology it is "more applicable to the law of any particular country than to the theory of law in general, for the details of legal history vary so much in different countries that immense knowledge and unusual architectonic power are needed to combine their general results for the purposes of a comprehensive theory" (*Studies in History and Jurisprudence*, II, p. 186). Indeed, Bryce considered the task so monumental that he doubted it had ever been done, though it "may be done, and so will doubtless be done some day. Everything happens at last."

As a matter of fact, the task had long since been accomplished, even by someone "of the requisite capacity" as stipulated by Bryce.[2] In fact, Stahl had already published the first edition of his *The Doctrine of Law and State on the Basis of the Christian Worldview*, presenting a legal philosophy sprung from the loins of the Savignian historical method, back in the 1830s when he was a young law professor in Bavaria. Savigny recog- **<xiii>** nized it as providing the essential underpinnings in eternal verities that he himself had failed to produce.[3] And in providing this service, Stahl not only gave the Historical School a philosophical basis, he gave the Burkean common law school of thought a basis as well, although the Anglo-Saxon world of jurisprudence was unaware of it, then as now.

---

[2] For more on the curious ignorance of Stahl on the part of future generations, see the preface to G. Groen van Prinsterer, *In Memory of Stahl* (Aalten: Pantocrator Press, 2022).

[3] For an alternative interpretation of this development, see John E. Toews, "The Immanent Genesis and Transcendent Goal of Law: Savigny, Stahl, and the Ideology of the Christian German State," *The American Journal of Comparative Law*, 37, no. 2 (Winter, 1989), 139–169; idem, *Becoming Historical: Cultural Reformation and Public Memory in Early Nineteenth-Century Berlin* (New York: Cambridge University Press, 2004), ch. 5: "The Tension Between Immanent and Transcendent Subjectivity in the Historical School of Law: From Savigny to Stahl."

The English common law has never enjoyed the philosophical attention that has been lavished on Continental legal systems. The reason is of course its being a product of court practice without being made the continuous subject of scholarly analysis, as was done on the Continent. Even so, this did not preclude the development of a unique legal philosophy which, although it did not attain to the sophistication of Continental efforts, nevertheless developed into a full-fledged philosophical jurisprudence in its own right, inoculating the legal system from the challenge of natural-rights jurisprudence and enlightened-despot codification efforts the likes of which took over on the Continent during the 18th century Enlightenment. The common-law approach pioneered by Edward Coke, John Selden, and Matthew Hale (Coke and Hale were chief justices) provided the basis for Burke's political philosophy. And from this root came the Continental resurgence of conservatism, which had been driven out of business by Enlightenment rationalism.[4] **<xiv>**

Regardless of the success this approach had both in preserving English common-law traditions and in reinvigorating Continental common-law traditions, in terms of legal philosophy it remained rudimentary. William Blackstone's *Commentaries on the Laws of England* (1769), which served as target practice for Jeremy Bentham and his utilitarianism, is paradigmatic in this regard. Indeed, from Bentham onward it might be stated that utilitarianism and pragmatism have been the leading philosophical approaches for dealing with the common law (e.g., Oliver Wendell Holmes, Roscoe Pound). And that legacy lives on into the present day (as witness its latest iteration, "Law and Economics," as exemplified in the work of Richard Posner and Richard Epstein). The alternative is a natural- rights school of thought based essentially on John Locke and the *Declaration of Independence*, and which in consequence is constantly fighting a rear-guard action against French Revolutionary principles.[5]

It might seem anachronistic that help on this front would come, of all places, from pre-Bismarckian Germany. But the sense of anachronism fades when one realizes the affinity between the pre-Revolutionary Continental and English

---

[4] On this most interesting history, see Harold J. Berman, "The Origins of Historical Jurisprudence: Coke, Selden, Hale," *Yale Law Journal* 103, no. 7 (1994).

[5] For details on this see my *Trojan Horse: Natural Rights and America's Founding* (Aalten: WordBridge, 2022).

legal systems. It is the divergence between these two which is constantly emphasized; but how is it, then, that Burke could postulate a fundamental legal continuity across Western Europe which was only ruptured by the French Revolution?[6] Indeed, Savigny and his followers recognized in English common law a cognate legal system to the German pre-codification legal system. Which is what makes Stahl's legal philosophy so interesting to common-law legal science. Stahl provides principles applicable to the English common law as well as Continental law, for he draws upon the common inheritance of Western legal science such as described in part by Harold Berman in his *Law* **<xv>** *and Revolution,*[7] a legal science sharing essential characteristics, maintaining similar institutions, pursuing similar goals.

What Stahl does is provide an understanding of the solid, unchanging foundations to the evolving, adapting thing which is the common law. Considerations of utility and pragmatism are made subordinate to principles of justice and what he calls providential purposes, within the context of historical development. Burke's partnership "between those who are living, those who are dead, and those who are to be born"[8] finds a distinct echo here, as does his conceptualization of rights as inheritance rather than *a priori,* a-historical givens. Likewise, rights are made subordinate to law rather than being the source of law as conceived by the natural-rights school. What's more, Stahl provides subjective right with a clear position and demarcation within the legal system, which is a feat in itself and, perhaps more than anything else, is needed in today's confused, rights-bloated jurisprudence.

---

[6] "If diffident of yourselves, and not clearly discerning the almost obliterated constitution of your ancestors, you had looked to your neighbours in this land, who had kept alive the ancient principles and models of the old common law of Europe meliorated and adapted to its present state – by following wise examples you would have given new examples of wisdom to the world." Edmund Burke, *Reflections on the Revolution in France,* vol. 2 of *Select Works of Edmund Burke* (Indianapolis: Liberty Fund, 1999), p. 125.

[7] Harold J. Berman, *Law and Revolution: The Formation of the Western Legal Tradition* (Cambridge, ma: Harvard University Press, 1983).

[8] Burke, *Reflections,* p. 193.

The concept he uses to establish these foundations is that of a *doctrine* of law and state. In the introduction he provided to Volume II as a whole (see *Philosophical Foundations*, p. 1), Stahl explains this notion of doctrine: it is something other than jurisprudence on the one hand and legal philosophy on the other. Jurisprudence is the science of a particular legal system as it exists in a particular country at a particular time; legal philosophy is its opposite, bringing "law and state into connection with the highest cause and the final goal of all existence" (*Philosophical Foundations,* p. 2). The doctrine of law and state occupies an intermediate position. It generalizes from jurisprudence while it particularizes **<xvi>** from legal philosophy. It operates in terms of universals but fleshes out those universals in terms of the particulars provided by jurisprudence. In so doing it provides universal criteria out of which particular legal systems can be generated and by which they can be judged.

Stahl bases this doctrine of law and state on the Christian worldview: because historically the nations of Western civilization likewise were based on that worldview, and because every such universal doctrine must base itself on one worldview or another. "Every philosophical system of whatever name in the final analysis rests on a foundational presupposition that is nothing more than faith, no matter what claim it may make to so-called scientific certainty" (*Philosophical Foundations,* p. 3). So, ultimately Stahl provides us with a Christian common-law legal philosophy, in doing so epitomizing the Western legal tradition in its conservative variant.

PREFACE TO "PRIVATE LAW"

<xvii> This book is a translation of Book III of *The Doctrine of Law and State.* It provides Stahl's detailed outworking in private law of the principles of law developed in Book II, *Principles of Law*. "In accordance with the dual relation of human common life," it says there (§. 45, p. 119 in the original pagination), "legal relations are of two sorts. The one serves to satisfy the *individual person*, to complete his existence... the other serves to rule men collectively, to join them into a common existence and to complete it as such. The former make up *private law*, the latter *public law*." Here follows, then, an elucidation of private law, the law as it relates to persons in their individual relations.

Permeating the work is the understanding of private law having a twofold basis, a rootedness in the natural creation – a givenness of nature determining all legal institutions – and the principle of personality acting within those creation givens, resulting in the institutions of private law. "Private law therefore springs from a dual principle: *the objective purpose* (τέλος) *of life relations* as grounded in the arrangement of nature... ; and the eternal *idea of personality* which, on the basis of the former, in the final analysis gives legal institutions their shape" (p. 2). This is the twofold basis of law developed by Stahl in *Principles of Law* (§§. 5, 7, 39, 40).

The starting point is the right of the person. This right of the person is the primeval, inalienable right, the basis of all further rights in civil society. It entails integrity, freedom, honor, legal capacity, and protection of acquired rights. This basic setup is inherent in each individual person; upon it is erected the positive rights which go into every separate civil constitution.

So then, "personality is the substrate of free action," the basis for the range of civil rights; but it does not itself contain that range of civil rights. The latter are positive, acquired through one's effort or that of one's forefathers, or are entered into as part of a greater institution, as for example entering into marriage puts one into the position of husband or wife, father **<xviii>** or mother, head of household, testator. In particular, far from establishing an equality of rank or property, it establishes the preconditions precisely for inequality in rank or property. For "*equality* is a primeval right of man, albeit in precise measure, according to a determinate relation. It does not rule out distinctions and rank, the inequality of actual rights, the inequality even of the capacity for rights. Abstract and unconditional equality ('égalité') is by no means a primeval right of man" (p. 22).

Freedom is likewise subject to misunderstanding. The modern concept of freedom is choice between good and evil, and the greater the range of choices available, the better. But this is not freedom at all. True freedom consists in the ability to choose the good and the right. Such a capacity is not just *there*, it must be fostered and conserved, and a just and free legal order recognizes that. "The first condition of legal freedom is thus the reasonableness of laws. The unreasonableness and thus immorality of laws is the first suppression of freedom. By contrast, the maintenance of a public life-order in the people and this order's restriction of our actions is not in itself a reduction of our freedom but rather a postulate of it. When this order truly is morally reasonable, it sets us not against our actual self but in accordance with it" (p. 16).

The modern viewpoint also has it that full humanity is the principle of all civil society, and that human rights are the fulfillment thereof. But it forgets that there is another principle of society, the fear of God, and that it is that principle, in its Christian form, which preceded the appearance of the principle of full humanity *and in fact engendered it.* Both principles are necessary to a healthy and just social order.

Following upon these basic considerations, the "meat" of the law is addressed, beginning with the institution of property. **<xix>**

In line with Stahl's understanding of legal institutions as combining creation imperatives with the higher calling of personality, he understands property as the means through which man expresses his personality. Things are the medium through which he does this, through which he gives shape to his life; and freedom is the necessary prerequisite for him to be able to accomplish that. Property then also serves an ethical purpose, in that through property man can fulfill ethical duties which otherwise he could not. "Therefore property is not simply the satisfaction of human self-interest or the necessary means of maintenance, nor is it merely the purposeless rule over things; it is the material and means for a vocation, and therefore is itself a vocation" (p. 44).

The community of goods short-circuits this vocation and therefore cannot be what it claims, a higher sort of ethical condition; the inequality of property is in fact the just outworking of a social order in which personality and freedom of expression are given free rein, and where God's providential ordering is respected.

In its origin, property is collective and it is landed. Nations, not individuals, take possession of the land, from whence it is parceled out. This forms the basis of all further forms of property. Although its origin lies in grant, such a grant is irrevocable; the further course of property-holding and exchange lies beyond the distributing hand of government. "In its initial origin, [property] is not grounded in one's own power but on authority, it is not something attained but something received. On the other hand, its independence begins immediately; the initial distribution is irrevocable, and upon this basis property is further acquired through the particular act and destiny of each individual" (p. 52). Furthermore, property in its origin is as original as is contract and the state. Therefore, to found property on contract, as the natural-rights theorists such **<xx>** as Grotius would have it, is as foolish as to found the state on contract.

Property involves two elements: satisfaction and control. Satisfaction is the purpose for which property exists: to provide for human needs and wants. Control is the indispensable means through which it attains to this purpose. Control is the means by which personality is injected into the workings of attainment of satisfaction.

Property can be construed broadly and narrowly. Property narrowly speaking is the absolute right to a certain material thing. But there is also property broadly speaking, which embraces all forms of entitlement. In German the term for this is *Vermögen;* as there is no English translation for this word, "property*" (with an asterisk) will have to suffice. For all forms of entitlement, including both partial rights to things, such as usufruct, and rights to the performances of persons – obligations – are likewise means of establishing control over media of satisfaction, thereby making one's world more secure, one's future more certain.

The Communist-Socialist repudiation of property, for its part, obliterates this plan of free personality working through things and performances; but most of all, it denies the reality of God's dispensation. "As is the case with all efforts at all times to achieve a community of goods, the error of Communism therefore consists in general in the denial of the ethical meaning of property and the illusion regarding the ethical value of the community of goods; but in particular it consists – and this is its innermost distinguishing characteristic – in the non-recognition of the leading of God in the distribution of goods" (p. 64).

In line with the two main forms of property* (i.e., in the broad sense) described above, the law of property* is divided into two main forms of rights: real and personal. Real rights **<xxi>** are rights to things; personal rights are rights to performances by others. (Personal rights are not to be confused with the right of the person as discussed above.)

Real rights are those which establish control over a thing, where "the thing must serve one person fully and completely as the object of his will, so that he freely disposes over it" (p. 71). The most complete control is property in the strict sense; but particular powers can be fragmented and made into partial rights, such as easements, servitudes, usufructs, liens, leases, and the like. Joint ownership is also possible, with Germanic law providing better forms than Roman. Acquisition of property occurs in two main ways: original and derivative. Original acquisition is gained where ownership did not previously obtain; derivative acquisition occurs where ownership is assumed from a previous owner. A form of real right which does not attain to the status of property is possession: this is merely protection in a factual state of affairs, in which one has physical possession of a certain thing; the law requires that this factual condition be preserved even where title is lacking.

Personal rights establish, in line with their character as property*, control over the performance of another. "Performances [Leistungen] by other people serve the needs of our existence just as much as does the possession of things, and the activity of personality in freely giving shape to the way of life, which requires property in things, therefore also requires the same power of free disposal and the same enduring secure right over that other means of existence" (p. 95). These personal rights are called obligations. Their significance lies "not so much [in making] possible services or the communication of things – this can be achieved by mere factual performance – but much rather that security of the future exist, partly by making possible a present performance or communication... without damage and hazard, and partly through which the future **<xxii>** possession of an object is secured in a manner often not afforded even by continuous possession" (p. 95).

In accordance with the nature of property* as being an affair of freedom, two basic forms of personal right exist, categorized in terms of the role of the will in them: contract, engaged voluntarily, and tort, engaged involuntarily. Contract is "a mutual stated agreement among specific persons regarding a legal relationship to be founded amongst themselves" (p. 100). It has two forms. The one establishes relations the continued existence of which is independent of this contract, as for example marriage; the other contains within itself both the foundation and continued content of the relation, "so that complete fulfillment continuously proceeds only in pursuance of the agreement and according to the standard it sets.... The former are contractual *acts*, the latter contractual *relations*, that is to say, the former arise through contract (agreement) without themselves being contracts" (p. 101). This underscores the importance but also the subordinate character of contract. Just because a relationship is established by contract does not mean that its content is freely to be determined: this is especially important in the understanding of marriage. And vice versa, contract can serve as a true source of law where its contents are legally valid; by it, the agreeing parties may set up for themselves various legally binding arrangements which serve as a law for them.

The law of the family follows the law of property*. Here as well, the key factors are the forces of the natural creation being harnessed to the exigencies of personality and freedom.

> Solely by virtue of the personality of man, these relationships, which in the lower reaches of creation only form momentary passing acts, with him becoming enduring bonds permeating all of existence. The complement of the sexes becomes a bond of imperishable full personal devotion, be- **<xxiii>** comes *marriage;* procreation becomes an enduring bond between parents and children, namely *upbringing,* this being the free communication of one's own human essence in accordance with its ethical spiritual side, just as procreation is the natural communication of the same in accordance with the mere natural side. As such, in this spiritual ethical character, they are the *institution of the family* (p. 111).

The family is the central institution of society, "the center of human existence, the bond of individual life and common life, as it constitutes the complete satisfaction of the individual while also being the means by which the race, and thus the community, civil and religious, arises, both corporeally and ethically-spiritually (through upbringing)" (p. 114). Although a legal institution, it is (uniquely among legal institutions) primarily of a moral character, "in that according to its entire being it is the inner union and devotion of specific persons" (p. 113).

The cornerstone of the family is, of course, marriage. Here the complementarity of sexes comes to the foreground, in which this natural phenomenon becomes elevated into the realm of the personal: "from the mere union of sexual functions it is elevated into the union of persons for which the former only serves as substrate, thus into a bond not of mere momentary complementarity but of the persons concerned immutably becoming as one in feeling, knowledge, and will, into a *living union*" (p. 118). Its indispensable prerequisite is consent, but its form and structure are entirely independent thereof. And although it is primarily an ethical and secular relation, serving earthly society, its essence as pure devotion lends it a religious dimension which cannot be ignored. It therefore requires the blessing of God as bestowed by the church.

Restrictions on marriage involve near relation. The primary reason for this lies in the fundamental difference between the marriage bond and the bond between relations, especially **<xxiv>** between parents and children and between siblings. The marriage bond is a bond of mutual need, "a bond of necessitous, fulfillment-seeking, yearning love" (p. 135). The bond between parents and children, by contrast, is a bond of selfless love downward and reverence upward, while that between siblings is one without need, with "the organic purpose of *being* the family, of realizing its goal, not of *generating* the family, of being a means for it" (p. 135). These bonds cannot be confused or mingled. Furthermore, it serves the greater purpose of the human race for families not to close off to each other but rather to intermarry and so, in Augustine's words, to expand the bond of love.

Marriage is in principle indissoluble. There is only one true ground for dissolving a marriage, and that is adultery. In this day and age, civil government may extend the grounds of adultery by analogy to this ground, thus granting divorce on the basis of serious fault; but the church must remain faithful to Jesus' statement as recorded in Matthew ch. 5. Modernism has invented an alternative ground for divorce, which it even has the temerity to regard as the ethically superior ground – the spouse's happiness in life. To elevate such a principle to the grounds for divorce is to elevate personal satisfaction above the higher ethical order. It spells the destruction of ethical order.

Regarding religiously mixed marriages, marriages between persons of different religions are, for Christians, sinful unless concluded prior to conversion; but for persons of different Christian confessions, they are not per se sinful although in most cases they are to be discouraged. This can cause problems especially regarding the upbringing of children.

Paternal power is the power of parents over their children, not as an end in itself but with the goal of bringing them up to a state of civil and financial independence. (Stahl speaks **<xxv>** of paternal power, but he does so representationally; the discussion makes clear that both parents participate in this power.) It includes protection and representation vis-à-vis the outside world, and the power of upbringing, to determine what kind of education the children receive. Following independence, paternal power per se disappears, but the bonds of paternal love and filial piety remain.

The power of upbringing means that parents have the right and duty to determine the education of their children. But the state likewise has a "vocation and right" in this area. Broadly speaking, the paternal power extends to individual upbringing, state power to that which is involved in "national education," involving mores and culture, in particular with regard to training for public office. Furthermore, the state has the duty to ensure that schools meet minimum standards of quality. For its part, the church has the right to insist that nothing in the schools is taught contrary to the Christian faith.

Inheritance is the means by which personality extends itself through the generations. It therefore is not a mere transfer of property but a transfer of the entire sphere of rights and obligations from one generation to another. By means of inheritance, the human race maintains its coherence, by maintaining the separate legal spheres of its members integrally through the generations. The original form of succession is intestate, and it remains the model, even where testate succession is implemented. For intestate succession assumes that surviving spouses and children have the most right to the inheritance. Originally the male line was preferred in succession; but with the rise of Christianity the equality of the sexes has been increasingly realized in this regard as well, although with certain necessary exceptions (e.g., where landed property is connected with political position). **<xxvi>**

Stahl includes in an appendix a brief discussion of the value of Roman law. This discussion concisely reveals both the greatness and the shortcoming of that law. Firstly, Roman law was the first to realize the idea of law, without admixture either of morality or politics; secondly, it realized the principle of individual entitlement in a thorough, uncompromising fashion. But it failed to recognize other important principles, such as the connection between rights and duties, which led it to lopsided oddities, as Stahl details. But besides this, Roman law was able to implement a systematization of the law which remains exemplary for all time: that which Stahl characterizes as a codex of the nature of the case. For Roman law was more than a mere example of logical consistency; in terms of content as well, its system provides universally valid material, not certainly in terms of the law-ideas themselves, which is where the Romans fell short, but in terms of the nature of the case. "Should one consider that value [of Roman law] to lie in logical consistency, systematic completion, antique simplicity, that which is commonly understood as the scientific exemplariness of Roman law, thus only the *formal* aspect of the method of treatment, one thereby fails to appreciate that Roman law also contains a plethora of outstanding *material* decisions just as true for our conditions as for Roman" (p. 197).

PRIVATE LAW

INTRODUCTION

§. 1. The Principle of Personality in Law

<1> Private law comprises the relations in which the life of individual persons is fulfilled: *protection of the person* and his free action; *property**; *family*.

The principle through which the series of these relations appears as a unity, as a system, therefore is *the concept of man itself:* as ***personality,*** *built up from the* ***natural*** *creation and based on the natural creation.*

Accordingly, relations on the one hand develop subject to the conditions of natural, more specifically material, existence in accordance with their inherent *providentially administered goal* (τέλος): integrity of existence – maintenance and satisfaction through things – connection of generations and procreation.

On the other hand, however, these relations are elevated into the *essence of personality:* natural (material) existence is transformed into existence as a person, from which *freedom, honor, legal capacity,* etc.; natural satisfaction through things becomes material for the free manifestation of personality through the ordering of his lifestyle – from which *property;* and to this end persons may freely, by the power of immutable personal will, choose mutually to obligate themselves in an enduring fashion – through *contract.* The natural union of the sexes is elevated into that which is personal – into *marriage;* procreation, into upbringing *(paternal power)* and enduring bonds of piety, and <2> finally, through the extension of property beyond the grave to descendants, into *inheritance.*

Private law therefore springs from a dual principle: *the objective purpose* (τέλος) *of life relations* as grounded in the arrangement of nature (deeper: in the free divine providential administration); and the eternal *idea of personality* which, on the basis of the former, in the final analysis gives legal institutions their shape; both principles however in indissoluble permeation and unity.

The Kantian concept of "sensate, reasonable existence" would thus actually be the principle of private law if it were properly conceived. To wit, the "*sensate*" is not simply (subjectively) to be related to the nature of men but (objectively) to the economy of nature. Thus, legal relations (things, acts of others) are not as with Kant dead matter, idea-less objects, simply to be subsumed under an otherworldly abstract legal concept; on the contrary, precisely the aspect of legal formation lies within them, and not merely in the rationality of the person. Instead, then, of "the rational essence" we would more properly say "person," from which not only freedom would follow, as Kant and even more so Fichte one-sidedly and arbitrarily assume, but all those qualities belonging to the broad compass of the concept of personality as well, such as for example customary behavior [Sitte], steadfastness and so forth. These principles are just as much original elements of legal formation as is freedom.

PART ONE: THE RIGHT OF THE PERSON

Chapter 1: The Right of the Person in General

§. 2. The Rights of Personality

<3> Being a person, man is an original, independent and thus absolute end of creation and the world-plan (Book I [*Philosophical Foundations*], §. 6): not mankind as a genus, not the concept of man, but the individual, each individual person. The law must also conceive him as such. The individual person is consequently an absolute end in the legal order – this is the *right of the person* or the "*innate right*," the "*primeval right*." The content of this right therefore comprises the things belonging to the *existence of the person: integrity, freedom, honor, legal capacity, protection in acquired rights*. Individually these rights are viewed as "innate," though more properly they are viewed as rights inhering in the essence of personality.

The final ground of the right of the person is his being the *image of God*. This is also the case in his fallen condition, albeit in muddled, disturbed fashion. It is simply his essence, his concept. Therefore, his life must be held to be holy, room for his freedom and activity preserved, his value recognized.

Personality is the substrate of free action, not its allotted object, for which reason these fundamental rights are neither alienable nor disposable. From this follows the criminality of murder by another at one's own behest, the impermissibility of <4> Germanic feud law and dueling, contractual slavery, alienation of general legal capacity.

The *maxim of coexistence* is valid for these rights, and only for these rights, because they belong to each person independently in himself, and are not derived from a common higher organic relation, although even here this maxim is insufficient to ground a decision in the case of conflict; such can only be found in the specific nature of the rights concerned, as shown below (§§. 3 and 5).

It is as impossible as it is senseless individually to add up the objects and actions included in these rights of personality (such as for example the right to "speech instruments," to the use of members, such as "of the nose to smell," the right to make bodily movements, to dance, to wash oneself), should one desire to make an exhaustive list. Integrity and freedom include them all. Law, however, the concept of which after all is ethical power over others, only concerns the hindrance of others; my own use is not grounded in my right, but in my natural freedom, because God has given me a body (Book II [*Principles of Law*], §. 32). The exclusion of public restrictions, as for example that the state can make no laws regarding free passage or freedom of the press because such would infringe my right to free movement or the use of my speech instruments, therefore cannot be derived from the right of the person: natural freedom of the person must subordinate itself to the higher claims of common existence.

Because the right of the person is due men prior to any civil order as a primeval divine conferment, the atrophy of it in the civil order takes on the appearance of injustice (Book II [*Principles of Law*], §. 7), whereas the malign arrangement <5> of most of the other spheres largely seems only to be transgression of mores or inappropriateness.[9]

§. 3. The Right of the Person: Integrity

Integrity consists in the protection of life and limb, corporal inviolability, "peace" in the Germanic manner of speaking. It is the initial claim on the legal condition, thus preceding all others; in particular, it is the initial restriction on freedom. One's freedom should not infringe another's integrity.

§. 4. The Right of the Person: Freedom

Freedom is the power to act, that is, to be a cause in the external world according to one's own will and choice, to affect a *factual* situation (both to change one's spatial relation to actual situations, what the English call "vis loco motiva," and

[9] Hegel leaves no specific place at all for the rights of the person but rather confuses them with real rights [Sachenrechte] and considers them, to the degree that he gives them any attention at all, under the category of property. "As a person I have both my life and body, *like other things*, only to the degree that it is my will" (*Philosophy of Law*, §. 47). Therefore, I can *sell* my life, my members, my spatial freedom as well? The total divergence in meaning in which in the former case personality purely as such is the goal while in the latter case it is material satisfaction, as well as in the consequences, that in the latter case full disposability and alienability holds while in the former case it is ruled out, offers him no obstacle. The abstraction: "a thing is that which is entirely external to freedom, to which my life and body also belong," seems to him a sufficient ground for this confusion.

to act upon corporeal things and persons), and thus especially to affect *legal* situations.

It is part of the essence of personality that action is inseparable from its cause and becomes a component of the actor's existence. Therefore man expands his legal situation <6> through an act, his act (just as his personal existence itself) becoming binding on others; and he restricts it through an act, his act becoming binding on himself (for example occupation, dereliction, entering into inheritance, damage and so forth). What sort of act it must be, and what sort of legal consequences it has, are of course determined by the legal institutions in which it intervenes.

Because freedom arises from the law as an ethical order, it is not unrestricted but from the start has a specific content, standard and boundaries.

Legal freedom is bounded *first* by *higher duties* to which persons must subordinate themselves; not, of course, by claims of (subjective) morality, but indeed by ethical ideas of life relations maintained in common life (objective) – namely the ethical form of marriage, the state, the church and so forth; these are the one principle of the legal order, human freedom is the other. The kind and degree of this restriction can therefore only be determined by the nature of the legal institution concerned.

Freedom *furthermore* is restricted by the *equal freedom of others* (the maxim of coexistence). All legal objects are open to all. The conflicts that follow from this are not decided according to the consideration that these objects are to be distributed equally among all (the principle of equity: Book II [*Principles of Law*], §. 50), but, as is made clear above, simply according to the right of the person, his essence being *causality*. Therefore, the *act* is decisive. This is the preference of *priority* [Prävention], which comes into play whenever considerations grounded higher in the purpose of legal institutions are lacking. Others must take a back seat to those first making actual use of their freedom, who in taking possession of objects have put themselves in a favorable position. This priority is expressed differently according to the nature of relations, whether priority in a factual situation (place- <7> ment of nets in a stream, taking one's place in the theater), in the acquisition of a right (occupation), or in the grounding of a legal function (competence of the court).

§. 5. The Right of the Person: Honor

Honor is the consciousness people have of their *absolute value as a person*. Initially it is something internal. Others can do nothing to give or take away one's true honor. It is however a person's right to see this, his absolute value recognized by everyone in *common* life – this is *legal honor.*

The *basis* of honor, however, is above all *ethical integrity* as the true essence of a person, and therefore, especially with regard to the common life and thus legal honor, it is the public conviction of this integrity – *blamelessness* (**existimatio**). Honor therefore entails a double right, the right to it directly and the right to its basis. The former is *honor in the strict sense*, the latter is a *good reputation*.

There are therefore two forms of insulting a person's honor, underlain by various considerations. The former is infringed by acts directly demonstrating another's *contempt* (refusal to recognize honor) – *slander* (**injuria**); the latter through expressions that undeservedly deny one public recognition of blamelessness – *libel* and *calumny* (**diffamatio** and **calumnia**). Slander is unthinkable without *premeditation* to show contempt (**animus injuriandi**); this is not the case with the injury to the good name of another; on the other hand, libel is not unlawful if it is *true* (**exceptio veritatis**), while slander as such is by no means justified by the truth of the accusation. Slander and defamation [Diffamation] therefore are entirely different things, although they may vie in one and the same act. This essentially likewise <8> gives the sense of Roman law.[10] Against this, newer legislation often runs slander and calumny into each other.[11]

§. 6. The Right of the Person: Legal Capacity, Protection of Acquired Rights

Legal capacity in general is the characteristic of being the subject of rights – including the three mentioned general ones – and in this sense is the same thing as legal personality. In particular, however, it is the possibility of having specific rights (Book II [*Principles of Law*], §. 36), that is, the right to a certain object or a certain status as provided in the legal order in terms of its various subject areas.

Protection of acquired rights is maintenance in just these objects and statuses, the holding of which as a right is the concept of legal capacity, in particular in

---

[10] Walter in *Archiv für das Kriminalrecht* Vol. IV, p. 278.

[11] e.g., *Cod. Max. Bavar.* P. 4 cap. 17.

objects and statuses that can be gained or lost as an external possession, such as for example property or aristocratic privileges, rather than the ones that, once established, are immediately inseparable from the particular person to which they adhere (such as paternal authority and the marriage bond).

§. 7. Slavery

The complete lack of recognition of these rights located in the essence of the person is *slavery*, as it was found in ancient states, as it also still exists among contemporary Asian peoples, but also as it is found even in the southern states of the Union of North America. **<9>**

Slavery consists in the treatment of men not as a person, not as an end in himself, but as a thing, as a mere means for others. It is therefore to be rejected out of hand. It is no justification that some men are incapable by nature of caring for themselves (Aristotle), for this leads only to the conclusion that they need to be put under the guidance and power of another, not however that they be made into mere means for that other. There is no justification for it in the rationale that otherwise prisoners of war will be killed (Hugo), for it is precisely this killing that is to be rejected. Even if there are laws that effectively protect slaves from murder, mutilation, destruction by punishment, exhaustion through labor, the separation of families (spouses from each other, children from parents) through sale or disposal by the owners, the sale of a man as such, the position as a whole of being a mere implement of labor and object of use for another and to be entirely at another's disposal, one's own lack of legal capacity, which furthermore renders inoperative those protective laws – these things taken individually and as a whole unconditionally constitute the destruction of the right of the person, a disparagement of the image of God, a violation of the commandments of God in the hindering of slaves in their observance of those commandments.

Now then, where slavery exists and as long as it exists it is, as is all positive law, lawful and binding. It could certainly have the appearance that the slave, for whom the social order preserves no right but confronts him merely as something oppressive, would also have no duty of obedience against it, and that resistance, insurgence, any form of self-defense, would be allowed to him. Nevertheless, ethics preserves, even in ever so slight degree, that which the law denies, and the order which curtails him is still always an order and therefore also an order <10> for him. Therefore, the Christian commandment says: you slaves, obey your masters in the flesh!

Transition phases, similar for example to German serfdom, to maintain order, the protection of the ruling class or for the entire economic condition of the total population may be necessary and therefore justified. But there is no justification for maintaining the condition of slavery itself, even if only for a period of time.

Germanic *serfdom* is not an annihilation of personality in the way slavery is. The serf is the subject of laws, is not a thing, is only subject to conscription in his person, is not an object of property. But the serf nevertheless lacks essential rights of the person, such as the free choice of occupation, the freedom of domicile. Serfdom had therefore also to give way, as is recognized, and that the serf often had it better than the contemporary free proletarian could and should not have halted a development based in an ethical postulate, the fundamental recognition of the right of the person.

§. 8. The Right of the Person: Inalienable Freedom

The thought of the absolute claim that the person qua person has rights and is to be protected in those rights was lacking in the earlier epoch of natural law; hence, even the condition of slavery (for example von Oldendorp, Grotius, Thomasius, Wolff, Höpfner)[12] was considered permissible. First Rousseau and then Kant made inalienable freedom an absolute right of the person – as Kant put it: "a man must not be made into a bare means!" However aside from the fact that Rousseau et al. conceived this right only negatively and therefore without <11> content,[13] while ruling out protection in acquired rights, they founded the entire objective legal structure one-sidedly on the rights of man. Against this, Hegel, as already mentioned, restored the legal status of ethical institutions, the family and the state; but to do this he in fact gave away the *right of the person* through his pantheistic standpoint, substituting for it simply the bare concept (aspect) of personality or subjectivity. According to him, the *individual* person is simply "an accident of general being"[14]; this aspect of subjectivity rather than the individual particular person is for him the goal of creation and therefore also of law.

---

[12]See Vol. I (2nd ed.), p. 155 [*The Rise and Fall of Natural Law,* pp. 133–134].

[13]*Ibid.*, p. 150 [*The Rise and Fall of Natural Law,* pp. 128ff.].

[14]Hegel, *Philosophy of Law*, p. 145.

Chapter 2: Freedom and Equality

§. 9. Moral Freedom

<13> *Freedom,* being an inseparable attribute of personality, is a primeval right of man. Its circumference is discerned from its proper understanding:

The essence of freedom is *to be determined only by one's own self.* Inner, moral freedom, therefore, is to be determined only by one's own self in one's own resolutions, while outward, legal freedom is to be determined only by one's own self in one's actions in human community. The former is freedom of the will in the strict sense, the latter freedom of action.

The innermost self of man is however a *determinate ethical essence;* it is *consciousness* of the same and the decisive exclusion of what is opposed to it; it is *individuality,* and so unending creative choice as the manifestation of individuality (Book I [*Philosophical Foundations*], §. 39). Inner, moral freedom thus does not exist where man cannot act according to his ethical essence and in consciousness of that essence, and according to his individuality. Man, determined by sin and the passions, submitting to the flesh rather than to the spirit, is not free, but unfree; because sin and the passions are not the self of man, but a power standing in opposition to his essence. A child who obeys before having full cognizance of commands is at the least less free. But man is still not free when in religion he stands under the law, in morality under the maxim, in art under a style, instead of under grace, love, creative conviction; for although law, maxims, <14> rules do not stand in opposition to his ethical essence, they do restrict his individuality.

Therefore *choice* certainly forms part of moral freedom. Moral freedom means not being bound to an exhaustive blueprint that in itself and thus completely, positively determines our actions, that subordinates man only to that which all men have as a common equal essence, which leaves no room to individuality which is ours and which is originally productive. Man is not free when, in fulfilling his duties as son, father, relative, citizen, he does so not by being original and special but rather by thoughtless imitation. Even so, the release from strictures, this choice, must always be based on necessity and constraint. Choice in terms of the good, not the choice between good and evil, pertains to ethical freedom. The choice between good and evil which actually confronts man is a consequence of a division of his being, the consequence of being ruled, tempted, by a power alien to his essence – evil – and is not freedom but disturbance; it is an attack on his freedom. The more perfect the character, the higher the level of freedom; the less of a choice between good and evil, the less possibility of evil, ignoble, dishonorable decisions. Will the man who considers whether or not to steal, to lie, who being a soldier at his post, considers whether to abandon it, be considered freer, or the one for whom there is no possibility of stealing, of lying, of fleeing his duty, who can act only according to conscience and honor? It is not the vacillating character, still in a position to choose between good and evil, which is free, but the steadfast character that has become a law of unavoidable nature and necessity (Book I [*Philosophical Foundations*], §. 40).

In God, the highest personality, the aspects of freedom are present absolutely: an absolute immutable essence, which is God's holiness and wisdom – the absolute conscious exclusion of everything ungodly, unholy – absolute boundless, immea- **<15>** surable individuality and creative power, all in complete harmony. Human freedom on the other hand needs to advance and is called to advance in all its aspects, and considering that the essence of man is permeated with sin, it is divided and in contradiction in all its aspects. Man is to advance by gaining in consciousness and in decisiveness in excluding that which is contrary to his essence, which is evil. Therefore, the one who through reflection has succeeded in gaining this advancement occupies a higher level and is freer than the naive and childlike man; the attainment of this decidedness is the reason God allowed and allows temptation. At the same time man is to advance to a greater expression and freer revelation of individuality; he is called to greater creativity. But while the essence of man is not divine and holy but is capable of providing a basis for an existence separated from God, a basis for self-seeking – for this reason the consciousness of the contradictions in his ethical essence became a temptation to him and brought him to a fall; and after having fallen, the free revelation of his individuality also became a burgeoning revelation of this sin and the advance and confirmation of the same. Therefore, a conflict arises among the relations of human freedom, with the preservation of man's ethical essence threatened by the advance of consciousness and individuality. The advance of consciousness threatens innocence and purity, and the advance of individuality (in the particular sense of Christian freedom) threatens the strictness of laws and adherence to duty. The leading of the human race and the moral development of each individual moves through these hurdles.

§. 10. Legal Freedom and Freedom of Choice

Outward, legal freedom concerns external actions in social life, determined not by other persons, in particular the ar- <16> bitrary will of the ruling authority, but by one's self. It therefore is characterized by these elements: that this order to which we are subordinated be in accordance with our true inner self, which is the truly ethical, reasonable life-order; that insight into its laws and its foundations be accessible to us so that we consciously can obey it; that it provide our individuality with all the room it needs. We are not free in the legal sense when we are put under immoral [unsittlichen], unreasonable laws, or where law remains a secret of a certain class, or where otherwise reasonable laws through obsolescence cease to allow room for our individuality, either by suppressing our national individuality or by restricting our personal individuality. Finally, we are totally unfree in the legal sense where a tyrannical government simultaneously suppresses that order which accords with our ethical essence and our individuality as well.

The first condition of legal freedom is thus the reasonableness of laws. The unreasonableness and thus immorality of laws is the first suppression of freedom. By contrast, the maintenance of a public life-order in the people and this order's restriction of our actions is not in itself a reduction of our freedom but rather a postulate of it. When this order truly is ethically reasonable, it sets us not against our actual self but in accordance with it. When we are required by the legal order not to divorce arbitrarily, to obey our elders, to provide for and educate our children, etc., all of this is only the condition of our true inner self. And vice versa, if a legal order loses sight of all of this, we have not gained any greater freedom, because we dare not make any use of such latitude; we are left with only the support of our own ethical essence for our actions and have thus lost a support of our freedom. This leads to the collapse of mores among the great mass, uncertain of its own ethical essence, as well as in the upcoming generation; thus we have gained unfreedom. <17>

But there is more! The ethical life-order of the people is likewise the general validity of our own ethical essence in the external world, and therefore the highest guarantee of our freedom. This is because that which is in the highest degree my freedom is realized when my ethical essence and fiber, thus my inner self, my true will striving for realization and dominion, finds expression not simply in my own actions but also in the condition of the nation, and it is a violation of my freedom when contrary actions remove the prospect and impression of an ethically ordered common life – removes what we might call the ethical atmosphere – when I must tolerate what violates my ethical or religious sensibility – when public institutions neglect what this sensibility requires. Therefore the freedom of each entails the right to the existence of such a life-order in which the family is maintained in its ethical shape, the church in its purity of faith, the entirety of public life in discipline and honor and unto the glory of God. It is not a violation of freedom to forbid and punish public disrespect, blasphemy, convenience divorce, but rather its establishment; it is not the maintenance of church confessions, church discipline, Sunday observance but rather their abandonment, not church marriage but civil marriage which violates freedom.[15]

No less a demand of freedom, however, is the full expression of our individuality. The maintenance of this kind of ethically reasonable life-order among the people should not go so far as to cut this off. Partly it must not encroach upon the sphere to which our innermost personality or the creative use of our God-given gifts belongs; partly it must progressively leave more and more room to individual decision in such areas as choice of occupation, choice of spouse, choice of faith, free scientific research and dissemination, free political endeavor. <18>

Therefore choice is also an indispensable element of legal freedom, in fact it is the blossoming of freedom, because choice is the expression of individuality. Even so, in legal freedom as well this choice must have a basis in ethical necessity. Just as the ethical essence of man forms the basis for inner ethical freedom, the ethical life-order of a people forms the basis for external legal freedom.

The ethical life-order of the people and the free manifestation of individuality by individual persons permeate each other without a specific dividing line, with the result that with the latter a conflict arises for external freedom (as it does in the former case with internal freedom), that the strictness of the ethical life-order of the people – especially while it is in the hand of human and thus imperfect magistrates – might prejudice true ethical individuality, and vice versa: the full development of individuality might prejudice the ethical life-

[15]Stahl, *Seventeen Parliamentary Speeches*, p. 61.

order. Therefore, true legal freedom must rest on both bases, with the point being to bring them into harmony in the most appropriate way and in accordance with circumstances.

Calvin's order in Geneva preserved a high degree of freedom for the believing congregation, because it expressed and put into practice to a high degree its innermost self, a truly religious, and more to the point a specific religious conviction; tolerance of libertinism lost its freedom. Considered in itself, however, this order restricted the expression of individuality, the more so as it was not lacking in a heavy admixture of human one-sidedness and narrowness, and thus did not entirely answer to the general human essence. On the other hand, to drop ethics from legislation as occurred at the end of the 18th century is the other extreme; this is not freedom but the abolition of freedom. **<19>**

§. 11. Freedom versus License

These considerations lead to the following fundamental theses:

Legal freedom is bounded by the equal freedom of others: the maxim of coexistence.

Legal freedom is originally and in itself bounded, or better, determined by the ethical life-order of a people, and thus by the law of life-relations (family, community, station, church, etc.), differently according to each.

No right to unrestricted freedom can obtain in any area. Thus for example there is no right to unrestricted establishment of sects, no right to the unrestricted use of the labor forces in the society (Turgot). The public order of religion or of production for gain require limits and these themselves then form a postulate of true freedom.

There can be no right to that which is bad and repulsive in itself and unconditionally, for example to an atheistic religious confession and the education of children in the same, to an immoral lifestyle, total profligacy, and the like.

It is not society's responsibility to increase the choice between good and evil, so as to make men freer. Such a choice is not freedom, and its increase is not progress. To lead into temptation for the sake of resoluteness is a matter for God alone because He also provides the strength to triumph over the temptation; it is not a matter for human government and leading (Book I [*Philosophical Foundations*], §. 40).

By contrast, the task is to augment individuality and the possibilities for its manifestation. This is true freedom and thus true progress. By extension this requires the tempering or abolition of preventive measures such as censorship, denial of freedom of association, and enhancement of the freedom to choose a calling since no class is any longer restricted from any <20> vocation. But this augmentation of individuality and its free manifestation can in no way serve as the basis for a freedom that undermines ethical public order and the meaning behind that order. Thus for example when a people preserves its religious ethical substance, as did, it must be recognized, the English people in the 16th and 17th centuries despite the plethora of errors, it also had a right to freedom of the press, which was useful to it and constituted a true elevation of its freedom. When however a people has abandoned that religious ethical substance, like the French at the end of the 18th century, then there can be no right to freedom of the press; in fact the latter becomes an affront to justice and does not elevate its freedom but rather helps to destroy the people's ethical goods and thus also that portion of freedom which it still had.

§. 12. The Modern Concept of Freedom

The fundamental error in this age's claim to freedom lies in the fact that it sees freedom as an empty formal possibility without content or goal, without a determinate ethical essence. Accordingly, a person appears to be morally the freer the greater the choice he has between good and evil, the more his consciousness becomes a tabula rasa, until finally reaching the zero point, a person bound and determined by nothing decides whether to be the most repulsive cad or the most elevated wise man. Thus legally a person appears the freer the more the public order allows all thinkable, including the most repulsive, options to be displayed before him: God-denying confession, an unrestrained press, riotous unions, frivolous carousals, the pursuit of gain which destroys the common welfare.

Rousseau's train of thought rests on just this error. He also detaches the freedom of men fully from the ethical substance of men, which is their true concept. Rousseau was en- <21> tirely correct, that freedom is inalienable and hence could not be alienated by participating in the state, nor could it be alienated to the state, and he was entirely justified in thinking that for this reason the problem of the state relation is this, that every man, in that he obeys the state power, only obey himself and therefore remain as free as before ("chacun s'unissant à tous, n'obeisse pourtant qu'à lui-même et reste aussi libre qu'auparavant" [*Du Contrat Social,* I. 6]). But since he formally conceived of freedom as unrestrictedness, as arbitrariness, he arrives, as elaborated elsewhere (Book I [*Philosophical Foundations*], §. 50), at a solution to the problem in the *formal* criterion of how the laws come to exist, in the equal competition of all in the state power, by which indeed freedom does not remain unalienated, but becomes completely alienated to the majority. In truth, however, freedom is not separable from the ethical essence of men, and on this basis the solution to this problem lies only in the *material* aspect, in the content of the laws and the government, that they only command what my own ethical essence and my own rational life-purpose requires. For in this case and only in this case do I, in that I obey the ruling authority, obey only myself (that which is my true self) and hence remain as free as before. That this solution, given the shortcoming of the earthly condition, only imperfectly and approximately can be achieved, is self-evident. One must accept this just as one must accept mortality and imperfect health. The false conception likewise obstructs the solution as much as possible, however, leading to a situation where the formal participation of all is accompanied by content that is virtually contrary to the claims of ethics and human reason, for which reason everyone becomes oppressed as never before. **<22>**

§. 13. Equality

Equality is a primeval right of man, albeit in specific measure, according to a specific relation. It does not rule out distinctions and rank, the inequality of actual rights, the inequality even of the capacity for rights. Abstract and unconditional equality ("égalité") is by no means a primeval right of man.

In fact, the essence of man as person requires the equality of right: that to which one can lay claim because he is a person (image of God) must also be claimable by the other. But the plan of the ethical world requires inequality of rights. Because this plan gives people differing positions and tasks, they must also have different rights. As a person, man is an absolute totality for himself; this is the basis for equality of rights. However, man is also a part and member of organic connections and institutions, and no organism is composed of equal members; this is the basis for inequality of rights.

The considerations decisive to inequality are the diversity of natural characteristics, the diversity of vocation, the diversity of prior acts, and destiny.

Inequality of rights is grounded above all in the *natural diversity* of people: sex, age, health, even education. Inequality upon this basis is still seldom disputed even though examples are not lacking of philosophers, consistently carrying out the concept of equality, declaring the exclusion of women from public offices and legislative bodies to be a violation of human rights. Even rights that otherwise must be generally accorded can be denied due to natural hindrances such as insanity.

Inequality of rights is further grounded in the *diversity of vocations* and the characteristics, both natural and civil, which relate to those vocations. The law [Das Gesetz] of the relevant relations provides each the measure of his rights according to <23> his position in those relations. This is the case with the family; husband, wife, and children each with their own task and their own rights – this is disputed by no one. This is no less the case, however, with state and church. Inequality in the state is not simply connected to the diversity of intellectual gifts, something which even the French Revolution recognized, but to the difference of every other quality decisive to the proper ordering of the public condition. The essential character of the state, rather than the right of personality, is decisive to the question whether this inequality consists in a simple function or an enduring right, whether it is personal or hereditary. So for example it is part of the essential character of the state whether participation in its confession of faith is required for participation in its administration; whether a material interest in land, especially landholding, is required to take up a position in the representative body, princely birth to inherit the crown, etc. Just as people are not mere means for the state, the state is not a mere means for the people: participation in its administration must not be motivated by honor, income, enjoyment of ruling, etc., or by the sense of equality as such. Accordingly, inequality on this basis is then to be related to political rights per se, not to private law and not to class-based occupations and branches of industry, except where these are inseparably associated with political institutions. And they must not extend beyond the limits of the vocation. An inequality of rights, thus a privilege, which is not grounded in any vocation, is a **privilegium**; this is an unfair relation, or where it is grounded in historical occurrences and thus justified, nevertheless a relation to be restricted to the strictly necessary. So for example it is no **privilegium** that a large landholder has a dominant share in a country's representative body, but it is a **privilegium** when he is exempt from quartering soldiers or mortgage duties or when his sons have exclusive capacity for state offices. To eliminate privileges is <24> natural progress, to eliminate rights of station [Standesrechte] is a disturbance contrary to nature.

Finally, inequality of rights is grounded in the *dissimilarity of preceding acts and occurrences* and the rights acquired through them. When someone gets a wife and raises a son, he has a family-right over them that a bachelor does not have. It is the same when property is acquired or inherited. It is the same when a class, a city, a family has acquired political rights in the previous history of the country (more over this in the following chapter).

§. 14. Essential Equality, Accidental Inequality

All these inequalities must however preserve as their basis the essential equality of rights residing in the essence of the person. This is the truth in the error of the Revolution. There is a general civil right and honor which must be the substance of the legal condition. Inequalities must only be accidental to this, just as personality and its essence is the substance of man and the variety of vocations only the accident. So for example where in their previous position the Jews, and indeed often Christian confessions, were not allowed religious exercise, human existence atrophied. This essential equality was contradicted by gradations in penal law, where violations against nobles were punished more strictly than violations against civilians, or where one class was subject to corporal punishment and the other not. Thus it is a proper progression in equality that civilians can attain to manors and attendant positions in the representative body, that public offices in civil and military service be open to all. In the area of ethics such an essential equality should also exist; this is an advance of the times; nevertheless, differences ought not cease to exist: the elderly are entitled to a different sort of honor than the young; <25> the upper classes, the ruling authority are entitled to a different sort of honor. The task of this age does not lie in the elimination of distinctions, the leveling of political conditions, as the Revolution would have it, but in the *recovery of essential equality in the maintenance of grounded distinctions*. As in the Middle Ages knightly honor and law formed the common substance (albeit for a restricted circle) in the light of which distinctions were less significant, and regardless of superiority and inferiority, regardless of the deep subjection to the power of kingship, even the humblest knight was considered the equal of the king – this is Burke's impassioned description – so in our time (for society as a whole) function human right and human worth.

Equality before the law is a truth and an advance of the times when understood as this essential citizenship common to all; it is an error and worthless notion when it is made to mean the abolition of legal distinctions, especially distinctions of station.

The false concept of equality is the major force of destruction since the end of the last century. It entails unconditionally the impermissibility of kingship, of state religion, of political rights of landholders, and everything of this sort, it entails the abolition of the organic edifice of the state.[16] The most foolish effort along these lines had to be the enterprise of carrying through this equality not simply in the area of law but also in the area of mores, to achieve through laws or moral coercion the fully equal treatment of the "citizen general" and the "citizen barbarian."

---

[16]Kant, *Doctrine of Law* XLV, understands this equality only formally, not to obligate oneself to another in greater degree than one *can* bind another to oneself; this is of course theoretically erroneous, in that society does not rest on mutually engaged commitments, but is practically without consequence, in that it admits true inequality when only the mere possibility of the highest entitlement for everyone remains conceivable.

Chapter 3: Protection of Acquired Rights

§. 15. Acquired Rights as the Expression of Personality

<27> Protection of acquired rights is an original right of man.

Acquired rights, as the name itself suggests, are not coeval with the existence of the person but presuppose certain actions or certain occurrences and conditions, and thus do not form part of the rights of personality. What does form part of the rights of personality is the inviolable maintenance of acquired rights *after* they have been acquired. The rights acquired by individuals stand in opposition to innate rights, but the protection in acquired rights is itself a natural right. The complete worth of man as a person is found only in this stability of all legally acquired rights. This is because it is part of the essence of the person to be active for his condition and to be certain of his condition. The person is an *acting* subject; if therefore man is a person, his *act* must be recognized, and thus the *rights that arise from his act.* A person's legal condition should not simply be the result of his *concept as personality;* it must also, to some degree, be his *own work* as well, the result of his *actions* and the actions of other persons. And because in the existing order these are appropriately (legally) grounded or have been gained through achievement, so they must remain inviolable as an expansion of his self, as his world, over which his will is established for the present and future. Otherwise he is not truly treated as a person but simply as a concept or object to which certain effects are due of neces- <28> sity. Thus the most masculine, powerful peoples hold acquired rights in the highest honor: the Romans, the Germans, and – in particular up until the present age – the English; and where this high honor does not exist, as with the Orientals and the Greeks, there it is that this whole depth and strength of personality is lacking. It is therefore a great error of the Revolution – and more or less the natural law theory – that in protecting, even imposing, what it derives from the concept of man it believes that it is upholding man and his rights, but yet refuses to recognize the result of his actions, *acquired rights*. It thus removes from him his self-causality and refuses him the certainty of his legal sphere; it preserves for him only what at any given moment others regard as his right, not what is his right in an unambiguous objective order. This is not the restoration but the destruction of the rights of man.[17]

Herein lies a broader ground for legal inequality beyond that contained in the organic nature of legal institutions, especially the state, as was already indicated in previous sections. In the private sphere, distinctions in wealth arise hereby, and it would mean the dissolution of society should one, as the Communists aim to do, wish not to recognize acquired rights but rather the equality of possessions, presumably in accordance with the nature of man. But political positions are also ac- **<29>** quired as rights in this manner, partly as the individual historical formation of an organic position grounded in the essence of the state (e.g. rights of the English peerage), partly however as truly accidental rights without any inner ground in the essence of the state. It should be said however that the legal situation is not perfect, nor even appropriate, in which these accidental political rights and inequalities can arise; nevertheless, once having arisen in a legal manner they must be held in regard and protected by virtue of the right of the person. This is especially true for so-called feudal rights. Their appropriateness to times past or present is irrelevant. One may dispute about that and come to a differing judgment for differing rights. Their legality in former times is beyond doubt, and since then they are equal to all other acquired rights. No time is called to hold court over the past and rights arisen in the past, and to recognize or abolish them in accordance with its verdict regarding their appropriateness.

---

[17]This error is most closely connected with the rationalistic principle: recognition only of that which follows logically, exclusion of everything the cause of which is personality, freedom, act (cf. Vol. I, p. 142 [*The Rise and Fall of Natural Law,* p. 119]). Hence Hegel as well, although asserting the organic coherence of the state over against the aggregational conception of liberalism, nevertheless had no sense of *acquired rights.* This is shown in his treatments concerning the Württemberg territorial estates and the English Reform Bill, but most blatantly in his *Philosophy of History* (p. 263), where he pictures the Roman respect for existing laws and acquired rights, in consequence of which e.g. "It took Licinius ten years to carry laws favorable to the plebs" and the like, with the greatest revulsion, characterizing them as a "disposition and character" the "foundational aspect" of which lies in "that primal *robber-community.*"

§. 16. Limits on Acquired Rights

Like all human freedom and action, acquired rights are bounded in their validity by that which the idea of the common condition and the legal order, or the natural continuing development of the same, promotes or excludes with unavoidable necessity. From this follows:

1. Acquired rights cannot be considered inviolable to the degree that they eliminate another's right of personality, e.g., the slave trader appeals in vain to his **jus quaesitum**. It is similar to the way the freedom of the one cannot be allowed to violate the integrity of another.

2. In developed state constitutions, in which each member has an organic position designated for the sake of the <30> whole, *for the future* essentially no acquisition of new political rights, no inequality, can take place through mere incidental actions of individual members.

3. In the overarching world-historical development of the public condition in its entirety, acquired rights of individual persons or classes in the final analysis must give way, because they are in constant relation to the entirety and only derive their protection from that entirety; they can be changed, even absorbed. However, even then they must, where the public well-being no longer can support them, give place *as rights* and be *recognized as such*, and in the most considerate manner, if at all possible with compensation. The violent abolition of acquired rights out of political considerations is not a progressive and regular function of the state organism but the work of extraordinary times, and therefore is better viewed as a world-historical than a juridical phenomenon.

§. 17. Rights versus the Common Good

The newer school culminating in the French Revolution does not recognize the concept of acquired rights; for it, rights arise at any moment, like new from top to bottom, through reason and the popular will. This is the view not only regarding specifically political rights (rights to rulership) but also regarding all rights of acquisition and property* as far as they are, or appear to be, involved with a political institution – for example, so-called feudal rights, toll and trade rights, immunities and the like. This school only recognizes the concept of acquired rights as regarding pure private property, which is a right which completely isolates the one against the other; and it does so inconsistently, because if the present is at all called to judge the past and to investigate the title of rights derived from the past, then this calling holds for all rights without distinc- <31> tion, and this great investigation must concern itself not only with the rationality of feudal rights but also with the rationality of property.

Since it does not go this far, the newer school (liberalism) does recognize acquired rights, justifying their abolition by way of exception, in terms of the undeniable admissibility of what is required to maintain the public condition. Even here, however, it far exceeds the true principle in manner and measure. It considers abolition to be justified for the common good (**salus publica**, bien publique), by which it understands not *public necessity*, which is the irrefutable need for healthy, salutary continuity and organic development, but rather *bare utility* (**lucrum**), and often by this utility intending the utility of the *majority*, thus the people over against the upper classes, rather than the well-being of the whole. There are however no legal grounds for removing the rights or possessions of individuals or minorities because *advantageous* to someone else, or the majority, or even the state. And then it is often a simply imaginary utility, a mere doctrinaire ideal for which acquired rights are violated, as for example with the so-called liberation of landed property. Furthermore, these rights are not yielded up as rights, as in the case of conflict between the development of the public condition and individual rights, with the latter considered inferior; it does not even recognize these individual rights where they are, or appear to be, an affront to the common existence; it wipes them out at once as something unlawful.

This entire approach led to the more or less inconsiderate and unjustified abolition of acquired rights, eventually to the radical destruction of the legal situation and the refusal of compensation. Taking the lead in Europe in this regard was the notorious night of August 4th 1789 ("the St. Bartholomew's Day of property"). The recognition of this fact cannot be denied out of consideration of the motive of personal sacrifice <32> for the public welfare, nor from the fact that multiple legal institutions (serfdom, incidental tribute and the like) needed to be abolished or changed. Apart from the degree to which terrorism, false sentimentality, womanizing vanity determined actions, this abolition of existing rights in individual cases was often entirely unfounded and even partly chimerical – e.g., the abolition of guilds, hunting laws, the inequality of imposts (?), fees for ecclesiastical services – and as a whole was carried out in such excess and upheaval of social conditions and gave such a shock to legal principles that it could not have been guided by true political or economic utility. The *Declaration of the Rights of Man* in the same year constituted the fulfillment of the announcements made that night, and by way of completion the matter was closed through the law of July 17th 1793, which abolished all feudal rights without compensation.

In Germany, such a radical implementation of these false principles did not take place because the Revolution did not there become fully realized. On the other hand, such was at least contemplated and announced in 1848, in the "basic rights" of the German national assembly, and was realized in at least a few acts, such as the abolition of all rights of previously entitled orders, the knighthood, the Prussian hunting law. Even after 1848, the oft unfounded abolition of rights was proclaimed either with insufficient compensation or none at all. The worst example of this was the intervention in the property rights of the church; the grossest irony is that this was viewed as taking place out of a supreme consideration for the public welfare (**salus publica suprema lex esto**) when in fact the majesty and security of the church's property was offered up to benefit individuals.[18] While all this forms part and parcel of a volatile <33> period, it continues to be the widespread opinion that every forced renunciation of acquired rights for the true or alleged improvement of the public condition is justified, especially where money compensation is offered. The most extreme and factually unrealizable exaggeration from the opposite end of the spectrum is that of the Haller school, which considers rights once they have arisen to be absolutely inviolable for all eternity. This makes the rights of man just as much an exclusive principle as does the liberal theory. It is the consequence of the private-law absolute isolation of rights.

§. 18. Expropriation of Property

Differing from the *abolition of rights*, which removes the recognition and operation of an entire genus of rights in the state, is the *expropriation* of things, which extorts from individuals individual objects of continuously recognized rights, namely property rights. The former is a legislative act and is based on the continuous development of the legal condition, the latter is an administrative act

---

[18] Stahl, *Speeches*, pp. 63ff., "The Liquidation of Church Revenues" [Die Ablösung der Kircheneinkünfte], and 70ff., "The Forced Liquidation of Assets" [die Zwangsablösung unter dem Werthe].

based on the continuous movement of material (industrial, commercial and the like) conditions. Therefore expropriation is a continuously exercised function of state power, while the abolition of rights is not. However, the principle behind both is the same: the *public necessity* as distinguished from mere *common utility*. This is of fundamental importance. In accordance with this, expropriation is appropriate for fortifications, dikes, roadways, railways, to build churches, schools, hospitals where this otherwise would not be possible or at least not in any useful way, in particular for the expansion of previously existing buildings. On the con- <34> trary, it is not appropriate to expropriate the house of a private individual because it would provide the most advantageous solution for a public establishment [Etablissement], nor to expropriate private land because it would be the most efficient for new construction sites and the like, and especially not for state buildings, because even without expropriation these can always be built through additional spending. Most of all, expropriation cannot be justified for mere *beautification*. Expropriation for *any "public goal"* is therefore a despicable maxim. The presumed advantage that it brings does not in the least offset the damage done to the security of property, because the security and strength of property and the attitude it fosters are certainly no less significant components of the common welfare than are enterprises of common utility.

Grotius, the first person scientifically to put forward the foundational statement of expropriation (**dominium eminens civitatis**),[19] ascribes appropriateness simply to *public utility* in opposition to *extreme need* (**summa necessitatis**). The latter he understands only as the so-called *right of necessity*, that is immediate, extreme physical need (for example, fire), which even empowers private individuals to infringe alien property (**quae privatis quoque jus aliquod in aliena concedit**). But the concept of public utility lacks necessary, strict boundaries. In this unrestricted manner, a point of view has taken control leading in the end to the excessive extension of expropriation, as witness recent legislation.[20] By contrast, the *Berlin Political Weekly* does not wish to restrict expropriation to the case of physical need, danger of flooding and fire, if the development of general trade requiring e.g. railways is not likewise an undeniable need to the country. <35> However, the principle of expropriation is not the right of necessity as

---

[19]Grotius, *De Jure Belli et Pacis,* Book III, ch. 20 §.7, likewise Book II, ch. 14 §. 7.

[20]e.g., the Baden legislation of August 28th 1835.

proposed by the *Political Weekly*, which knows no commandment, and which, as Grotius already indicated, also accrues to any private individual, as little as it is the advantage of the majority or of the state; but rather, the necessary organic development of the common condition and the necessary participation and thus shared involvement by individuals in it.

Chapter 4: The Principle of Humanity

§. 19. Universal Human Value

<37> The image of God in man is the final ground of the right of the person (§. 2). In it lies the obligation on the civil order not only to preserve the rights necessary merely for the existence of the person, but also to elevate him to an ever higher level of entitlement, freedom and gratification, which we described above as the primeval right (Book II [*Principles of Law*], §. 36). It is this power which motivates our times at their deepest level.

Among the many partly true, partly misconceived efforts of these times, one appears in full clarity: the *recognition of the rights of man*. This does not belong simply to the area of law. More deeply comprehended, it is the *principle of humanity:* the idea that the well-being, the right, the honor of every individual, even the most humble, is the concern of the community, which views each person in accordance with his individuality, which protects, honors, looks after him without regard for descent, class, race, gift, as long as he has a human face. This is the characteristic principle of the times and what constitutes its true worth. From it stems the abolition of serfdom, torture, the toleration of deviant religious confessions, the elevation of lower classes to equal civil honor, the many philanthropic pursuits, the effort to provide a satisfactory existence for the starving masses. This principle was alien to previous times, even that of the Reformation. Certainly, where Christian faith exists, love of neighbor and thus humanity is of necessity the motiva- <38> tion of life. However, this neighborly love in the past only concerned corporeal and spiritual well-being, not entitlement, freedom, the honor of men, and only provided the motivation for personal action, not the civil order. The outlook of improving entire classes out of a motivation of humanity, of spiritual individuality, of recognizing the honor of each person, did not inspire any institution in those times. Only in the most recent period has humanity in its full concept become an energetic virtue, the principle determining the entire society.

§. 20. The Fear of God as Principle of Order

On the other hand, earlier periods of European Christianity had the *fear of God* as the motivation for the public order, the unconditional devotion to God's command and ordinances and the zeal to glorify God. Recent times prior to the revival of Christian faith (that is, the end of the 18th and beginning of the 19th century), had eliminated this motivation. Every trace of the recognition of an unconditional divine command, every obligation to fulfill the will of the living God disappeared from it. Only the recognition of men and their convictions and opinions, and the care for men, remained as guideline. Thus in the area of religion only tolerance remained a recognized and praised motivation, not however the zeal for God's Word and God's honor, that previously was the only such recognized motivation. Tolerance has no boundaries; all religious or much rather irreligious doctrines are to have equal rights and equal honor; and even deistic and pantheistic doctrine of every stripe is to be recognized as Christian and as a church as long as it considers itself to be so. On the other hand, fidelity to divine truth, to maintain the true revelation of God, finds no consideration when it maintains its true measure, much less so when it in any way oversteps its boundaries. It is the same in the po- <39> litical arena. The state is based solely on human rights, not on higher goals; this is the sympathy for all opposition against all authority; it lacks the recognition of unconditional commands for the legal order. From this springs opposition to the death penalty and in fact to any sort of punishment. In the absence of a higher command that the criminal must be punished, that where blood is shed, blood must be shed, this becomes an institution for improving the criminal or a means of providing for the security for others. From this springs the claim for unconditional divorce, making the happiness of the spouses, their sense of what is agreeable, the decisive concern and not the higher, unconditional command that what God has joined together, let no man tear asunder. From this everywhere stems the revolt against all discipline, against all restrictions established for the fulfillment of a higher order of life.

§. 21. The Two Poles of World Order: The Fear of God and Full Humanity

The fear of God and full humanity are the twin poles of the ethical world order. The fear of God puts the seal of elevation on the individual man and the public condition. This elevation consists in being fully subsumed in the will of God and therefore in the unconditional fulfillment of higher commands without regard either for one's own life and well-being or the life and well-being of others. It elevates man above himself and all the powers and frailties of the earthly world. A picture of such elevation and unconditional devotion to God and, at least in accordance with our knowledge and our standard, virtually without humanity-inspired motivation, is found in the colossal appearance of Samuel in the Old Testament. Similar character, perhaps tempered by the spirit of the New Covenant, runs through the great men of <40> the Puritan church.[21] Humanity however is what provides the stamp of beauty, love, and kindness, the final consummation. The fear of God everywhere in dignity is the highest, in time the first. It begets humanity from itself. This is the eternal law, the course of history. Upon reaching maturity, however, it dare not close itself off, for in that case it becomes rotten and kills, it becomes Pharisaism in its manner of thinking, in institutions becomes a despotic and grotesque oppression. On the other hand, humanity dare not free itself from this, its true root. Otherwise it softens into the weakness of live and let live, into mutual interests merely regarding corporeal, earthly existence, the short-term indulgence of others to their long-term damage, as well as to that of the whole. Thus, love becomes the practice of worldly well-being, freedom the acclaim of arbitrariness. Following Kant, it is false humanity to make the man of appearance (homo phenomenon) the linchpin rather than man as he truly is (homo noumenon). For the public order, however, humanity freed from the fear of God leads on the one hand to fanaticism, as in the Revolution when the rights of man were imposed through the guillotine, and on the other hand, because human society can only be held together through God's ordinances, first to the slackening and then the dissolution of society.

---

[21] A similar elevation shows itself in the engrossment of men in higher ideas apart from a final relation to God, e.g., Roman civic virtue which did not even spare its own sons. But this virtue does not, as does Christian fear of God, give birth to humanity from itself as its other principle.

This is therefore the shadowy side of recent times along with its higher worth: that it only seeks man while being detached from what stands above man. Of the two parts through which the law is fulfilled – you shall love the Lord your God above all things, and your neighbor as yourself – it has arbi-
<41> trarily picked out the second while ignoring the first, it has demolished the first of the two tables of the law while proposing to establish only the second. This is however contrary to the eternal ordinance. No building can stand when one removes the foundation, no tree can live when one lays the ax to the roots. The task of the times is therefore not the ongoing one-sided advance of humanity and the rights of man, but the restoration of the fear of God as the energetic principle in both hearts and public institutions, while in it and through it preserving humanity and the rights of man. This is the union of the truth of former times with contemporary times. It gives the testimonies of the one and the other principle their pure shape and their complete meaning and worth.

PART TWO: PROPERTY IN THE BROAD SENSE[22]

Chapter 1: Concerning Property* (Property in the Broad Sense) in General

§. 22. Property* as the Manifestation of Individuality

<43>Man is lifted out of the material base of his existence into the essence of the spirit. He is made from dust, but a divine breath has been breathed into him. For this reason he is on the one hand dependent on the material world outside of him, needing it for his maintenance and gratification; on the other hand he is elevated above it: it is for him a serviceable medium and material. In this manner, man is set in the creation as *lord*. The objects of the external world are allotted to him for the *satisfaction of his needs*, initially corporeal, and through them spiritual ones as well. However, in the *manner* of achieving satisfaction, that is, in the *arrangement of lifestyle and conduct*, the *personality* of man is to *actively involve itself*. For this reason man has, <44> from nature, power over things; for this reason in human common life there must also be *freedom* for each vis-à-vis everyone else *to do as one likes with those things;* things must be *enduringly and securely* subjected to one's will.

This is the basis for *property** in the broadest sense. Property is the material for the *manifestation of the individuality* of man. His innermost being reveals itself in the manner and measure in which he acquires and uses property. The manner of gaining a living, clothing, habitation, use for sensual enjoyment, for taste, art and science, for hospitality, liberality, goals of common utility,

---

[22] [This is Stahl's own definition of *Vermögen*, an umbrella term covering both property and contract. In the Roman legal tradition, property and contract together form the "law of things." In the German legal tradition, this concept of thing was developed into the concept of *Vermögen*, which roughly corresponds to "assets." Therefore, in the German tradition both property and contract are forms of assets. The implications of this understanding cannot be further explored here. In this translation the word *Vermögen* is translated as **property***, in order to distinguish it from property in the strict sense, which in German is *Eigentum*].

employment for acquisition and profit, for spiritual activity, for the contemplative life – this total way of life, resting on the foundation of property, is the image of man.

Property is however especially and primarily the material for the fulfillment of man's *ethical duties*. A man has particular *duties* that are *his alone*, which are not at the same time of others or of the community, duties stemming from his individual vocation and course of life, chiefly duties to his family. For this reason he must also have means which are *his alone*, in order that through their acquisition and use those duties can be fulfilled. In the manifestation of individuality and the fulfillment of special duties, for which property thus provides the necessary foundation, consists the activity of the personality of man.

Therefore property is not simply the satisfaction of human self-interest or the necessary means of maintenance, nor is it merely the purposeless rule over things; it is the material and means for a vocation, and therefore is itself a vocation.[23] Herein lies the ethical consecration of human relations to the goods <**45**>of the earth, that in their use the innermost character of men be made manifest, and that these goods be the means for them to uphold the family bond and family life. They are this however only by means of property.

§. 23. The Community of Goods

The community of goods, often contrasted with property as a higher, more ethical institution, does not answer to the purpose of property*. It does not even satisfy material needs, or if it does it does so insufficiently, and certainly not in a fair manner, because it neglects the incentive of production of goods, and values the lazy as highly as the productive. Above all, it eliminates the activity of personality, which is what truly consecrates property. With the distribution of goods by the community, the entire arrangement of life, it being built on goods, is likewise distributed by the community, and equally to each and every one. The human spirit hereby loses a portion of the material upon which it imprints its unique stamp, like taking from the artist the material he uses to express his thoughts. No less does it deny the fulfillment of ethical obligations to one's own.

---

[23]The expression lately arisen, that property is an *office* [Amt], is inappropriate. For office merely describes an activity for the entirety, for the public, while with the institution the first thing and basis is one's own satisfaction, by which free disposition is predominant; here the concept of office has no place.

Society, immediately or mediately, then provides for one's wife and children, comes to the aid of one's parents and relations. This in large part eliminates the ethical claims and activities of love from the holiest of bonds, and conversely eliminates ethical motivation from the relationship to goods. These goods then sink to the level of bare means for sensual maintenance and enjoyment.[24]

<46>The derivation of the community of goods from "Everything is common to those who love each other," as with Plato, rests on a misunderstanding. This is because the community of goods, being an expression of love, has to be a work of action (and thus of sharing), not a given condition. If the human will were immutable, which it should have been in accordance with its divinely created nature, then of course immutable love would have fomented the community of goods, albeit as a *perpetual act* (uninterrupted sharing). But because the human will is mutable, the community, that is the sharing of goods, can only be fleeting[25] and a community of goods as an institution, existing of itself apart from any action, would not make the human condition a whit more ethical.

The teaching of Christianity is based on this community by sharing, though by no means in opposition to the institution of property, and the first Christians did not at all live in a community of goods. "No one said of his own goods that they were his, but that they were everyone's in common" (Acts 4:32) refers to use, not to right. In order for Barnabas to lay the proceeds from his land at the Apostles' feet (Acts 4:37), he first had to own land and realize proceeds. Furthermore, such an act is praised as an exceptional example of love and not viewed as a Christian *duty*, as Peter expresses in his speech to Ananias (Acts 5:4): "you could have retained it (the land) in your possession, and when it was sold, it remained in your power." To the degree however that a propensity for community of goods is found in the early church, it differed fundamentally from the later political sects, namely the Communists. In the former case, the propensity was for those who <47> own goods to give; in the latter case there is the desire and the claim of the have-nots to take.

---

[24]Thus Aristotle (*Politics*, Book II, Ch. 3) rightly offers Plato the objection that he, in that he denies his "Guardians" separate property, also cuts them off from the virtue of generosity, communication to friends.

[25]In this sense the older writers are justified in viewing property as a consequence of the Fall.

A true community of goods is seen partially in the ancient world, and generally at the time of the initial development of peoples: for example, Oriental priests' landed property was considered common, and in Greek states a portion of the land often was allocated to all jointly. This community, which furthermore usually was restricted to certain objects, had, just as in the beginning, the lack of development of human individuality as its precondition – such a priest and even such a Greek citizen usually had their day-to-day activity in common with each other as well – and was based on the notion of common devotion to a higher calling (priestcraft, the state) in which the collective still formed an undivided unity – not on a bare equal claim to satisfaction on the part of separate individuals; and finally, its purpose was only bare maintenance, maintaining life in the highest degree of moderation, even to the point of an asceticism-oriented life, not to extend the luxurious pleasures of an overly cultured time to the poorer classes as well. This therefore can only be the calling of exceptional times and exceptional groups. Its significance is clearest in the monasteries. This same significance is also seen in the community of goods of the Pilgrim Fathers in New England. Earthly goods were far less important to them than the zeal to establish the kingdom of Christ. On the other hand, the movements for a community of goods in Europe after the Reformation – Thomas Munzer, the peasants' rebellion, the Levelers – were precursors of contemporary Communism, just as the political movements accompanying them were precursors of the Revolution. Then, it was the breaking of God's ordinances out of religious fanaticism; now, out of the lack of religion. **<48>**

§. 24. Inequality of Property*

The *inequality of property** is a necessary consequence of property. Whether it originally arose through occupation or distribution, equally or unequally, property must straightaway, in consequence of independence and thus independent destiny, lead to *inequality*. This is because property includes among its factors not simply nature and its available objects, which man to a certain degree can maintain in equal distribution; two other factors come into play, the *action and labor of man* and the *blessing of God*. These are however always and everywhere different. The one is industrious, the other is indolent, the one gathers, the other uses up. The one is a disciplined hunter, fisherman, shepherd, farmer, craftsman, the other performs these functions without talent. God also distributes his blessing differently. He determines that the one is born earlier than the other. He allows the one to succeed and the other to fail, He leads the one to the game and to the fish and not the other, He preserves for the one his fields and makes his herds fruitful while dispensing to the other hail and epidemics. Certainly such inequality of property*, which is to be attributed to the particular relations and gifts of each individual and the special leading of God, appertains to God's world order on earth and to the full development of the personality of men, similar to the way special gifts develop, and in like manner as all special destinies. In general therefore the legal basis of property as an institution is based in the vocation of men to actuate their personality; hence, presupposing this, the legal basis for specific property (of every person) lies in these three: the original inheritance through all generations reaching back to the initial distribution; the particular act of men (labor, saving or the lack thereof); and the dispensation of God. None of these three aspects should be **<49>** denied recognition and legal consequence.

In accordance with this, the *equality of goods* – while allowing separate property – is no command or goal of the legal order, as little as is the community of goods. It is contrary to justice that the industrious and the lounger, the thrifty and the profligate be put on the same line, and it is contrary to justice that the special gift of acquiring property* extended by God to a person and the special blessing extended by God to a person should bear no fruit to him. And in terms of outcome, it does not constitute a higher level of earthly condition that one person has just as much as another; but that, in the form and measure of property* there exist diversity and mutual supplementation as members of society.

The maintenance of the poor is by all means a command for the legal order as well (poor relief institutions, arrangement of contributions for the poor). The human community must in the extreme case provide for the life and existence of each and every individual. However, it does not do this by virtue of material solidarity in the goods of the earth, meaning that as soon as one has them in possession one must for that reason provide for another; but by virtue of the personal solidarity of the human race, in accordance with which, regardless of who possesses what, the race maintains its existence by personal performance and service. For this reason what is involved here is, firstly, not equality but only extreme need, and, secondly, even here not as property but as support, alms. This is not based on any entitlement on the part of the poor but on the ethical-legal duty of the community[26]; and he <50> who is unable to provide for oneself, be it his own fault or the special dispensation of God, is not owed full entitlement and full honor in the community.

§. 25. Equality of Distribution of Land

Somewhat different from the community or equality of goods is the concern to maintain each family in its landed property, and in the case of solely agrarian peoples, for each family to have landed property distributed to it. Although not a command, because of the impossibility of its unconditional implementation, it should nevertheless be a goal of the legal order. Here above all belongs the *Mosaic year of Jubilee*, the consequence of the idea that divine love extends to each family its own property, which human freedom cannot change without limit and contrary to this goal. Here belong the Germanic stipulations of inalienability, or difficulty of alienation, of landed property in the family. This is not in the least contrary to community or equality. Even with the institution of the Jubilee year, inequality remains in accordance with the increase of the family and the utilization of the land. These institutions are not an elimination but much rather the implementation of the idea of property, because they have in prospect nothing else than that property exist not merely in general (**in abstracto**) but with specific persons (**in concreto**).

Nor is the concern to combat excess inequality to be rejected. For example, Plato in his book *The Laws* and other writers listed by Aristotle taught that through the establishment of a maximum, or by some other means, a greater equality of property* should be promoted, and Greek institutions, especially in the Dorian states, were based on the same intention. Nevertheless, the goal here is more of a negative, compromising sort, that the one not receive too much at the start, rather <51> than being of a pure, exemplary character as with that other case, which is of an affirmative, independent provision, providing that each family for its own sake, apart from any comparison to others, have property to maintain or distribute.

Nowadays one unjustifiably seeks to abolish all institutions of this sort as being contrary to free private disposition. Although property itself is by nature a thing of free private disposition, the purpose for men to have property is still

---

[26]With regard to there being original legal duties and necessities which are not the consequence of the entitlement of another, see Book II [*Principles of Law*], §. 34.

a public one. Therefore, although no positive guidance of private disposition is admissible, the restriction of free private disposition, to wit, alienation, is so. None of these institutions are, like community of goods or equality of goods, contrary to the institution of property, but only modalities of the acquisition of and trade in property. Their further evaluation therefore forms part of the doctrine of national wealth (see Book IV).

§. 26. The Origin of Property

The vocation of man regarding property requires an initial distribution of the goods of the earth that are open to all. This was everywhere to take place in an orderly fashion. Thus, in the first human society this was to take place through allocation by forebears or through taking possession by reciprocal consent, as Abraham said to Lot: "if you decide to go to the left, I will go to the right; or if you decide to go to the right, I will go to the left." In this manner, the peoples were to divide the possession of the earth among themselves. However, in accordance with the character of the human race, from the beginning violence and struggle came in the place of amicable settlement.

The beginning of property among the peoples is therefore occupation of the land. This is based in the vocation of <52> peoples, which is to carry on an ordered ethical existence, the necessary condition of which is the exclusive possession of a certain land. The right of the people to its land is therefore based not on the mere act of taking possession, which is much rather only a precondition, but on the ordered ethical existence that it in fact establishes on that land, and on its power to maintain that existence. Therefore, the lack of an owner in the initial occupation is by no means the decisive factor.

The beginning of property among a people already in possession of its own order is not occupation through individuals but distribution through the ruling authority. For all property in the final analysis is derived from landed property. The material of enjoyment and labor are the product of the ground, and the pasturing of livestock and the hunting of game presupposes property in land. Among nearly all peoples landed property is originally divided out rather than left to arbitrary occupation. The Promised Land was conferred to the Jews by tribes and families, in Greek states the citizens kept the landless out of the state, and in Rome private ownership of land took place through assignation; the kings and princes of the Germanic peoples distributed conquered land as fiefs among their followers. This is in accordance with the essence of property. In its initial origin, it is not grounded in one's own power but on authority, it is not something attained but something received. On the other hand, its independence begins immediately; the initial distribution is irrevocable, and upon this basis property is further acquired through the particular act and destiny of each individual. <53>

§. 27. The Ultimate Justification of Property

The law-idea of property is as original as that of contract or the state itself; for this reason, the validity of property by no means presupposes either a contract to that effect or the state. Something different than contract or the state is however a *community of legal consciousness and observance*. This is by all means a precondition for the realization of property, because without it the law-idea of property would lack the specificity necessary to its realization, e.g., how is property acquired, through occupation or only first through usucapion? And how is it lost? etc. This is however no less true for every other legal institution, especially contract and the state itself. The controversy concerning whether property is binding in itself or only in consequence of agreement is hereby settled by reference to the fact that no law-idea (rational law) is in force in itself but must first be positivized (Book II, ch. 2).

§. 28. Property* Extends to Acts

The object of property* is first of all *material things* [Sachen], the right to which is *property* in the strict or technical sense. However, the acts and performances [Leistungen] of other persons are also the object of property* because they generate effects in the material world, and therefore – be it through the bestowal of things, be it even direct – they serve to provide satisfaction no less than do material things. In accordance with the general significance of property* – in which personality freely manifests itself in the manner of satisfaction, in the shape given to lifestyle – control and the power of disposition are required with regard to these performances as well, in like manner to material things; here in particular, this is the security by which they can be counted on, so as to be able to appoint <54> one's life. This guaranteed power of disposition over another's actions is the concept of *obligation* (**obligatio**) and is the other part of property* besides property, to be distinguished from bare factual performance (**datio**). In this manner, one person serves the other as material, as a thing, but only for individual outward actions. The person himself and the inner personal bonds or outward expressions of the same cannot be the object of property. The object of obligation is therefore neither the person of another nor the performance directly, considering that there can be no immediate disposal, even factually, over performance; rather, the object is the performance of another through the *instrumentality of his will*, thus this will itself as bound, in order by means thereof to be able to bring about performance according to place and time; this is the *legal bond* (**vinculum juris**). Therefore, the obligation always firstly has a *future* object in mind, and when this moves into the present, in fulfillment, it also spells the obligation's termination (**solutio**). In accordance with the solidarity of men, there exists (**potentia**) a general mutual capacity for performance and therefore also of obligation. On the other hand, in line with their freedom, in order for obligation to make a real appearance (**actu**) there must be a special occurrence (**causa**), as a rule voluntary acceptance; accordingly, the obligation is always a bond between specific persons (creditor and debtor).

As a result, the total idea of property* is this: the earth with its goods (including human performances) is the substrate of human satisfaction, realized however by means of guaranteed special entitlement of individuals, the goal being the free shaping of individual life. In this manner there arise just as many centers of property* spheres as there are people, the material of which is partly things, partly legal obligations to perform on the part of other men.

<55> Property* is however typified by property because material things are the sole indispensable and the most significant means of satisfaction, while obligations are dissolved in the bestowal of things or, in more developed social conditions, virtually always find a complete equivalent in things. Property is therefore the central point to which all other property* rights relate. All property* however has to do with goods of general and exchangeable value. This lies in the nature of the matter, it being corporeal means. The representative of general and exchangeable value is *money*. Only that which has money value can be an object of property.

§. 29. The Twofold Purpose of Property: Satisfaction and Control

The purpose (τέλος) of property* is dual: *satisfaction* through external objects and *control* over them in order *freely to give shape to one's way of life;* however, the two are inseparable and stand only in relation to the other.

Satisfaction of needs is the constructive impulse of the law of property*; through it the various institutions comprising that law take shape, e.g. that there be property, servitudes, lien, purchase, exchange, hire, etc. However, the general character displayed by all its institutions is *control*, the free, secure disposal by the individual, unconditional subjective entitlement. The former determines the shape of the institution, the latter the role of the person in it. Therefore *rights* are the *only* content of the law of property*, duties only as the consequence of those rights; external matter is merely passive, it imposes no commitment, and the rights here concerned are freely disposable. This is its peculiar character, which is found in no sphere of law outside it.

<56> The character of control in property* rights is the general requirement that cannot be lacking in a legal system; but the excellence of a legal system consists in satisfaction being made possible in the most various and complete manner, while leaving this character inviolate. The older legal structures were mainly determined by the consideration of satisfaction as the first and natural goal of property. The idea of free unconditional secure control first makes its decisive appearance in the Roman law, but in such a one-sided and rigid manner that the initial goal of satisfaction or utility (**utilitas**) often led, for example, to legal transactions being seen merely in terms of the bare will and its justification, not according to their inner purpose of gratification; for this reason, for example, no exception of deception or repayment could stand against a stipulation. This was offset in later development (**praetor, Caesar**). In German law, both principles permeate each other. Thus, in contrast to the former, property* in its full organic correlation is viewed as an institution [Anstalt] of human common satisfaction, and therefore the law of property* is not conceived apart from the relation to the creation of property*. While the Roman law conceived the world of goods simply as pre-existing, the objects of which are appropriated and mutually distributed by individuals through their will, Germanic law views goods likewise as being produced continually anew by the human community, according to which the consideration of this production and its stimulation has to be a decisive aspect likewise for the manner of appropriation and distribution. As a result, the vocation of estates, in accordance with their manner of earning a living and the political position based on this (the landowner in general and the nobility in particular, followed by the industrial and commercial classes, etc.), has its influence on the law of property*. This is an advantage of Germanic law over Roman law. The Romans brought the law of <57> property to fulfillment simply with reference to itself; but the relation of the law of property to the economy

and to political conditions must be granted essential influence, in the spirit of Germanic law, although in terms of its content this naturally must change with changes in the economy and political conditions themselves, and with the changed position of classes.

§. 30. False Justifications of Property: Kant, Hegel, Locke

The older school of natural law taught an original community of goods (**communio primaeva**); in this concept it usually confounded the legal establishment of common usage and the factual condition of general arbitrary seizure. Property however it conceived as the consequence of a mutual contractual establishment.[27] This continued up until Kant, who by contrast deduced property as an original right of the person, actually simply from the idea of freedom and the will, and thus also with the meaning of a *purposeless power* over the thing. The acquisition of property according to Kant is therefore the act by which a person subjects the thing to his will – *seizure*. Hegel follows him in this.[28] Both men merely consider the power of people over the thing, not their dependence on the thing. Not only is the first aspect of property, the satisfaction of needs, hereby nullified or contrary to nature made into something secondary, but even the other aspect, free disposal and control, is not conceived in its true signifi- <58> cance. The meaning of property does not lie in its being an expression of human freedom, that man has a passive object at his command and in so doing celebrates his triumph as a person (this is much more merely the factual power of mankind over nature, not the legal power of a person over against another) – but that by means of this command he freely gives shape to his way of life and in this way manifests his individuality.

Besides this theory of Kant's and Hegel's, there is the fundamentally divergent one of Locke's. Locke deduces property from *need and utility*, because man, as experience teaches, cannot exist without property, and the acquisition of property is therefore to him the act by which a person produces a thing useful

---

[27]For more on this see Vol. I, p. 145 [*The Rise and Fall of Natural Law*, pp. 126ff.].

[28]"The rational in property does *not* lie in *satisfaction of needs*, but in this, that the bare subjectivity of personality is subsumed" (*Natural Law* [Naturrecht – a.k.a. *Philosophy of Law*], §. 41). This selfsame property is further described as "the reality of my freedom in an external thing," which just for that reason "is a poor reality" [eine "schlechte Realität sey"]; see §. 39 as well.

to human need – *labor*. Here we have the reverse conception: the higher meaning of property, the activity of personality, is completely disregarded. The former theory of property is the consequence of the rationalistic viewpoint, the latter the empirical viewpoint.[29] Neither deduction provides an answer to the question as to what it is that gives a person the right over against others to take possession of a thing for himself or to process a thing for himself.

[29]See Vol. I, p. 317 [*The Rise and Fall of Natural Law,* pp. 259ff.].

Chapter 2: The Communist-Socialist Repudiation of Property

§. 31. The Rationale Behind the Repudiation of Property

<59> During the entire development of legal philosophy, agreement reigned concerning the necessity and justice of property, with opinions differing only about the manner of its foundation. In our day a doctrine has arisen and achieved power in the world putting this necessity and justice itself in question – *Communism* and *Socialism*.

In terms of their goals, Communism and Socialism indeed are a system of economics and not law, but nevertheless they are based on a certain overarching foundational principle of law, the *repudiation of property*. Apart from this it must a priori appear inadmissible to set the social condition on a foundation opposed to property.

Within this new doctrine, there exists, apart from the many subordinate deviations, a foundational difference in terms of economic viewpoint, finding expression in the dual appellation; namely, that Communism is a community of goods while Socialism is only a community of economic activity (as further explained in Book IV of this volume [*The Doctrine of State and the Principles of State Law,* §. 22]). Just so, there exists a fundamental divergence in legal perspective. To wit, the one denies property in the objects given by nature, the other by contrast denies all property plain and simple, thus also in those objects which one's own labor or special competence and ability in labor provides him; one may have a particular <60> right in virtually nothing. So Fourier aims for a distribution of the yield attained by society according to the standard of labor and talents which each has contributed in society, and therefore allows labor and talent and that which they effectuate as property for each individual, for the sake of which they have a claim to a higher share of consumption. By contrast, Proudhon rejects any preference for talents and quality of labor, determining the value of objects merely in terms of the *time* of labor; accordingly, men have no more property in their own abilities and skills, these are common property, only the time applied to labor is one's own. Finally, Louis Blanc goes beyond that, establishing that the yield of social labor be distributed merely in accordance with *need*, so that the laborer who is also the most gifted, competent, and assiduous, nevertheless receives the least if he needs the least, e.g., if he has no children, and vice versa. This is the culmination. According to this, one simply has *nothing left* which is his own.

Indeed, both of these divergent legal viewpoints correspond to both divergent economic viewpoints, albeit not in complete correspondence. Babeuf and the committed Communists, although they do not state the question clearly, in essence nevertheless go as far as the complete denial of property, in that they do not even allow for the development of special talent, while conversely the entire national-economic school called into being by Fourier goes only as far as mere partial repudiation of property.[30] The entire Communist-Socialist school then is united in this, that there can be no property in **<61>** things in the true sense, in objects which are the mere gifts and products of nature; the only difference in viewpoint consists in whether property can exist in the products of one's own labor, in the values created by man himself.

§. 32. Proudhon

The total repudiation of property is stated by Proudhon in his celebrated book: "What Is Property?" (qu'est ce que la proprieté?). The answer he gives is: property is theft (la proprieté c'est le vol). This rendition is however likewise the only attempt at all at a scientific justification of the unlawfulness of property, which is presupposed by the entire Socialist-Communist orientation.

Proudhon's method of proof is to demonstrate the unlawfulness of all titles of property:

One cannot derive property from *occupation,* for the arbitrariness of the seizure could not justify any right, and the possession itself could at most command respect only as long as the possessor is on it, and only as far as he exercises it personally and directly, just in the theater nobody can occupy more places than he occupies with his body; one cannot derive property from *labor,* because the authorization to labor already presupposes ownership of the thing, and the

---

[30] In the distribution of the social product Fourier does take into account capital brought in, but with regard to the future such is only to be the product of prior labor; for the initial beginning, Fourier only allows it by connivance, because to be consistent Fourier cannot recognize property as such, it deriving from the current unlawful condition of civilization. Nor does Fourier at any time allow for property as a separate object of labor.

labor only creates a higher value of the thing, not the thing itself; one cannot derive property from *positive law* (i.e., as the elders taught, from a contractual stipulation at the founding of the state society), for positive law may not order anything that is not justified in itself, i.e. contrary to reason and justice. Since property can in no way be justified according to this, it is illegal, and for this very reason it is a withholding of the equal share that belongs to the rest, i.e., theft.

His entire method of proof rests however on a flawed line of reasoning. He demonstrates the injustice of property by arguing that no title of acquiring property (occupation, labor, contractual establishment) can justify that property. But the title of acquisition is not the basis of property; property is the basis of its title of acquisition. It certainly is foolish to say that while men can take possession of things, can cultivate them, for this reason there must be property; this is what Proudhon refutes, and he doesn't have much trouble doing so. On the contrary: occupation, cultivation, prescription and the like, all are titles of acquisition under the presupposition and on the grounds that, apart from them, the necessity and justice of property is established in and of itself. If property in land, in game etc. does not exist on other grounds, occupation of the same does as little to ground property as does the occupation of a spot in the theater or on the lake shore. However, when property in land etc. is necessary and justified in itself in accordance with nature and the vocation of man, **<62>** there must then be actions to acquire it, from which follows acquisition through occupation, cultivation and the like, from the lawfulness of property and not the reverse. The final and decisive question is therefore whether property in itself is a postulate of human nature, the ethical condition of the human race, and this question, upon which everything else turns, is left untouched by Proudhon. Therefore, while he is able to refute the usual method of justifying property (from the will and the act of volition of man) – something which had already been done before him, in this book – he did not refute property itself, and in fact did not even bring up the question of property.

§. 33. Considerant

The straightforward denial of property in the objects of nature is expounded with the most awareness by Considerant,[31] roughly in the following manner:

Everything that nature grants is a common good, belongs to all people undividedly (**pro indiviso**), and no single person can have separate property in it in preference to another. Nor can one generation in preference to another. On the other hand, what man produces through his labor is his creation, is not granted as such by nature, and is therefore his *own* for himself and for his heirs. Those currently possessionless[32] can therefore claim the soil of the earth, the landed property, from the possessors, for they have the same right to it. But this only pertains to the soil itself, thus as it was originally by nature, not what the present owners or their ancestors have made of the soil through their labor, its improvement, thus not the soil in its present increased value. This is where the difficulty arises: if the present landholders maintain their exclusive possession, it is an injustice to the possessionless, because the latter are deprived of a gift of nature; on the other hand, if they have to share their landholding with the latter, it is an injustice to the possessors because it means that their labor and that of their ancestors, i.e., their actual property, is taken away from them. The rectification is then the *guarantee of labor*. Because the soil can no longer be kept separate from the utilization of the soil, the possessors should keep the soil but guarantee the others an income in exchange for labor, i.e., employment and wages. This is compensation to them for their claim to the bounty of nature, the soil, the more so as the soil never nourishes without work, and, if it could be restored to its original condition and given to them according to their share, they would also have the labor of hunting, fishing, fruit gathering.

At first glance, this more moderate doctrine seems quite obvious, as if it hit the center of truth and strikes the right balance between the old social order and

---

[31]See the start of Stein's *Socialism and Communism*, p. 205. Considerant is entirely the pupil of Fourier; cf. his *Destinée Sociale*.

[32] ["Besitzlosen" – this word is commonly translated as "dispossessed", but the literal translation is possession (Besitz) + less (losen). "Dispossessed" implies previous possession that is subsequently removed, and thus introduces a value judgment that is not in the original, for "possessionless" makes no statement about previous possession.]

the new Communist system. But it, too, completely falls apart under closer examination.

According to its own principles, it cannot be carried out at all without admitting the bankruptcy of justice. For the just claim of the possessionless cannot be determined according to it: how much is the value of the original land, how much is its improvement through labor? How much do the current possessors have to give up for what they stole from the rest through consumption of common property (e.g., wood)? Conversely, how much is owed to the present possessionless, since they themselves or their ancestors may have had plenty and were spendthrift, through equality of consumption? And just compensation for the claim of the possessionless is likewise neither ascertainable nor grantable. The guarantee of labor, which only secures their meager subsistence, cannot be a substitute for withholding a share of the land, which would give them an object of labor and thus the possibility of acquiring similar independent property.

Furthermore, the doctrine is inconsistent. For if the gift of nature, namely the soil, is a common good, it was not for the present possessors and their ancestors to work it and appropriate the increase in value, as Proudhon rightly points out.

But all this impracticability and inconsistency is based on the fact that the basic idea itself – the separation of natural gifts and human labor – is untenable. These two factors of wealth are inextricably linked. All human labor has the gift of nature either as raw material or as reward. If it were so that the gifts of nature belong to man in common for all time, man's labor could find no raw material, for no one can work for his own appropriation from what is common, and it could find no reward, for what is common could be not provided as a reward to anyone who accepts and benefits from the labor. Conversely, if appropriation through human labor is to be permissible, then appropriation of the natural objects themselves must necessarily be permissible from the outset. And that the gifts of the earth, other than sun and air, require the mediation of human labor to serve for subsistence, is a proof that they are destined to be property.

Finally, from the outset it is an arbitrary prerequisite to declare ownership of the gifts of nature to be inadmissible. Considerant and those who stand by his standpoint have not even attempted to provide a proof for this; Proudhon alone attempted it, but failed to produce it.

§. 34. The True Rationale: Antipathy to God's Dispensation

The true motivation for the denial of property by Communism and Socialism, either in general or at least regarding the gifts of nature, does not lie in the weak reasoning of Proudhon and the like but goes much deeper, to a frame of mind, namely *antipathy to God's dispensation*. In fact man does not desire to receive anything from God's Providence and does not wish to recognize what one's neighbor receives through God's Providence. Nature appears to be a <63> storehouse of goods not from God as Lord distributing them but simply from men, with the one man being as much lord over them as the other, and with the totality of man, society, distributing them in terms of equality.

It is God who allots to each man his portion, his particular talent and his particular acquisition; upon this is based specific property for every person, as stated above (§. 24). If property is not based on this, only *arbitrariness* and *coincidence* remains: arbitrariness, that the one person takes possession and wishes to maintain it for himself, caprice, that the one person has the opportunity to take possession before the other. However, neither arbitrariness nor caprice can justify an advantage in the goods of the earth, to which in fact all men by nature must turn for their support. For this reason, when the Providence of God is not recognized as the legal ground of all property, the hunter or fisherman must surrender his prey: game and fish are by nature there for everyone; the rich harvest or the fruitful herd must be thrown in for the general use, and even the special gift by which the one has a sharper eye or a steadier hand extends him no right to them, because it is a means of supporting everyone. Communism therefore was justified in objecting against legal philosophy from Grotius up until Hegel, that property in the end is founded merely on the will of man, and it is justified over against current society because the latter, like Communism, is ready to free itself from God. But to be consistent the Providence of God must be resisted just as strongly with regard to peoples as to individual persons. If the proletariat in France were right to claim their original portion from the rich, so are the Laplanders justified in laying a claim against the French people, that they be pushed no further back into that unfruitful region while the French reside on the banks of the gleaming, flowing Loire, given that nature and the earth were given for all equally.

<64> As is the case with all efforts at all times to achieve a community of goods, the error of Communism therefore consists in general in the denial of

the ethical meaning of property and the illusion regarding the ethical value of the community of goods, but in particular it consists – and this is its innermost distinguishing characteristic – in the non-recognition of the leading of God in the distribution of goods. This latter point is the godlessness of Communism and at the same time the way in which it violates law: because that which through God's leading becomes a man's, is his most holy right.

Chapter 3: Real Rights and Personal Rights

§. 35. The Twofold Rights of Property*

<65> With the character of property* as unconditional entitlement to an external object established, the law of property* divides itself into two classes of rights: *real rights* and *personal rights* [dingliche und persönliche Rechte].[33]

In accordance with that character, the real right [das Recht auf die Sache] must of necessity be prosecutable against anyone who withholds it from the possessor, whether honest or dishonest, whether obtained against consideration or not [lukrativen oder onerosen] – **actio in rem**; the personal right, on the other hand, is just as necessarily prosecutable, but against the specific person who is obligated – **actio in personam**. If performance is a pure act or payment, it is self-evident that no third party is obligated to it. But even where performance consists in providing or relinquishing specific things, it is not the thing directly but its provision that is the object of the right, and therefore it is not the possessor of the thing who can be held to it but only the one obligated to performance. This is the strict implementation of Roman law, which Kant [34] for that reason considers to be the only possible one philosophically. **<66>**

§. 36. Satisfaction as Principle of Property

The legal structure may however also proceed predominantly simply from the other principle of property*, satisfaction, and thus realize retributive justice or equity rather than protective justice. For the relation of a person to an object (material thing [Sache]) is not something unconditional and thus not a standard to weigh all further events and acts, but the reverse, the events are treated at every moment in and for themselves and only thereafter is the relation of the participants to the thing determined. It is not who has the right to the thing but who, under these conditions taken together, has merited the more preferential treatment which is what is decisive to such an approach. It views whether some-

---

[33]Here in the law of property*, in accordance with its particular nature (§. 29), is precisely the area within which the diversity of objects of entitlement is a chief determining principle for legal norms.

[34]*Doctrine of Law,* p. 103.

one truthfully or insincerely, fairly or unfairly, cautiously or less cautiously has acted in the event in question, whether one's condition was affected by the insincerity of another, for example whether the honest buyer or pledgee merits protection rather than the incautious owner, whether the one who orders merchandise at an earlier period is to be favored before the one who orders later but who is nevertheless put in possession by the seller without taking that obligation into account, and the like. The withholding of a thing is in this case an injustice not simply because it belongs to another; everything depends on the event as to how one came upon the thing in question, and only thereby is settled to whom it belongs; and vice versa, things owed to us by another may be claimed from a third party according to the event by which the latter came to acquire it. In this manner real rights are absorbed through events among third parties, and personal rights are prosecuted in the manner of real rights. In fact, if consistently implemented the distinction between real rights and personal rights entirely disappears, because the concept of an un- <67> conditional right to an object itself disappears; all is resolved into a continuous allocation of objects in accordance with passing events and acts.[35]

§. 37. Control as Principle of Property

This viewpoint – which we should like to call the pure *utility principle* – possessed a significant power in ancient legal systems prior to the Roman. Certainly it was nowhere exclusively implemented, the principle of secure control being

[35]In this fashion a legal system is conceivable in which the actual concept of property, the right to a material thing, is entirely lacking as a positive one [ein positiver] and is only indirectly protected through prohibitions of actions which in themselves are illegal, as for example one who secretly appropriates a material thing, one who illegally sells it, one who finds it and does not announce the fact, etc., would have to restore it to the one who until then had it. In this manner property is protected through mere claims [Forderungen]. An institution of this sort in our legal system is **possessio** [possession], and thus the fruitless attempt to allot a place for it in the classification of real and personal rights. The **bonae fidei possessio** is certainly a real right, but one which in its further development is subject to that viewpoint of events and thus relativity, as for example that the one who earlier received something from the same originator [Autor] has priority over the one currently possessing it, from which as well the reservation of the praetor to himself decide in the case of conflict.

too deeply grounded in the essence of the law of property*.[36] The Roman legal system, in accordance with its character of unconditional entitlement regarding an object, brought the distinc- <68> tion between real and personal rights to clear consciousness and fixed implementation; it makes up the face as it were of the Roman law of property*. It alone guarantees the security of rights which we have characterized as the ethical idea of property*. Furthermore, it alone can be harmoniously carried out, while the contrary way, because of the vagueness of its principles, always leads to conflicts both between various claims independent of each other and various equally relevant considerations. The Roman law also has institutions based in part on the former point of view, but, at least in its original shape, it had in certain degree separated them from the legal system proper, based on magistrates' protection, for instance the **actio publiciana** and in a certain sense as well the **possessio** as a protection in things relatively dependent on personal events, and vice versa the **actio ad exhibendum, quod metus causa, Pauliana** as the prosecution of claims to obligation against third-party, usually underhand, possessors of the thing in question.

Germanic law, although equally based on secure entitlement, nevertheless did not implement this distinction to this level of consistency. The Germanistic concept of "Gewehre" often has the character of *relativity*. Regarding movables, my priority ahead of the third-party possessor depends on the manner in which I lost possession of the thing, whether against my will or in accordance thereof, in which case my incautious confidence comes at my own expense; regarding immovables it depends on whether I myself am still in possession, whether I have been so for a year and a day, whether my opponent or his testator was present at the time of the transfer to me, whether he was absent or present during the established time period when I acquired the preference, or, as the case may

[36]So for example according to the lawbook of the Manu, the sale or donation not made by the true owner is not valid as sale or donation (§. 299, in Hüttner, p. 279), although under conditions the one demanding reinstatement [der Vindikant] must reimburse half the selling price (cf. Schönemann, p. 490), when not the thing itself. However, according to Attic law (Heffter), the mortgagee has priority over the true owner and the honest possessor retains the thing when its originator [Autor] pleads for him against the owner. In this manner, that viewpoint obviously emerges here. Even the form of contested inheritance [Diadikasie] for such cases is an outgrowth of it.

be, whom did the same liege lord first enfeoff. Even if these determinations are connected with procedural arrangements [prozessualischen Einrichtungen], this **<69>** nevertheless at the least demonstrates a lack of the concept of absolute entitlement. For this reason, even now in the wake of the reception of the Roman law individual modifications and exceptions have been made in the fixed foundation of the Roman distinction between real and personal rights, which are appropriate in this detail and restriction, although in general and as a principle of the entire legal system – which is what the judge must implement absent exceptional determinations – the Roman unconditionality of entitlement deserves the preference.[37]

[37]For example "Hand muss Hand wahren" [only the direct acquirer of property might be held responsible]; determinations regarding public auctions; determination that the first buyer has priority over the second, to whom it was conveyed, when the latter knew of the initial purchase; purchase does not nullify tenancy, apart from judicial sale; the owner, when he demands the surrender of his property [wenn er vindicirt], must reimburse the purchase price or the amount of debt to the buyer or the pawnbroker; and the like. Such determinations, which are found in German local laws and municipal statutes, and in particular in our Prussian civil code, are as *separate determinations* more or less appropriate. Should one however desire to treat the here underlying notions as the *principle of legislation*, which with new legislative regulations and judicial decisions determines new cases, it would in the end threaten the security of property. In this sense, for example, the determinations of the Prussian civil code already in the case of unclear clauses are often expanded there, such that even the *statutory* lien of the landlord extends also to such introduced properties which are the property not of the tenant but of a third party.

§. 38. The Unity of Real and Personal Rights

Real rights and personal rights nevertheless also have a *deeper unity*. This is founded on the one hand on the general purpose of property*, satisfaction, which is the purpose of both, hence noncompliance on the part of the defendant in itself could not lead to a verdict of compensation, it first re- <70> quired special "Sponsionen," and vice versa, only the person of the debtor was liable for personal obligations, not his goods. The law of pledge, however, the most decisive manifestation of the transition between personal and real rights, was lacking to the Romans, who first learned of the true law of pledge (**hypotheca**) from the Greeks; the **pignus** of the older law had the effect of pledge only de facto, the **fiducia** only indirectly. In the later development of the Roman law and even more decisively in Germanic law, unity came to the fore. The latter in particular contains legal relations in accordance with which a real right, i.e., a property* claim attached to a thing, is exercised and completed in personal performance, and just for this reason, on the other hand, a real right is inseparably joined to the duty of personal performance – *services in kind* [Reallasten].[38]

---

[38]The payable performance is thus a personal claim; it does not pass to the successor as past due, but it can be made into a real claim through entry of title in the real estate register [Ingrossation]. To subsume the relation under a Roman type of action [Klagegattung], as for instance under the **actiones in rem scriptae**, as has been attempted, is therefore impossible. That rights of this character for the most part have sprung from public law is not relevant here; after all, they have acquired a property*-legal character.

Chapter 4: The Law of Material Things [Sachenrecht]

§. 39. Property in Things: Full and Partial

<71> The character of property* as free control and disposal requires a legal institution by which the person has *total power* over a thing. Fragmentation allowing the one to do this, the other to do that with the same thing, does not answer to it; rather, the thing must serve one person fully and completely as the object of his will, so that he freely disposes over it. This total power [Gesammtbefugniß] is *property.*

The purpose of property* further requires that every satisfaction be vouchsafed, even such legal institutions in which particular powers are detached from the total power of property and transferred to someone other than the owner, equally as an immediate and unconditional right to the thing, as a real right, especially the following:

1. The value of a piece of land often depends on certain provisions [Gewährungen] on the part of neighboring property [Nachbargutes] (forbearances or allowances for undertakings), and therefore in order to secure or increase this value, place must be made for the right to this undertaking in terms of the law of material things – *easements* or *praedial servitudes.*

2. Familial succession or the wish of the testator requires that the use of a thing or property be maintained for someone <72> (for example the widow) for that person's lifetime without the thing or the property being removed from the actual heir forever; for this reason the use of all or certain usages must be made available without being able to create the right of disposal in the manner of real rights – *usufruct* or *personal servitudes.* This is the motive upon which the institution of personal servitudes is based, which once formed are also extended entirely naturally through a contractual arrangement either for a shorter period or for life.[39]

---

[39]Real and personal servitudes have no inner affinity. Their summation under the single concept of servitudes in Roman law is based on pure historical grounds, that originally they were the only **jura in re** known to the civil law. What is common between them,

3. The security of the creditor and therefore also the credit of the borrower requires that the former in future must be able to count on the satisfaction through things that at present belong to the debtor – for this reason the right of possible alienation of a thing in order to cover a debt must be able to be arranged in terms of real rights – *lien* [Pfandrecht], etc. In accordance with the above, however, these rights are not independent, so that the object lies in the middle, between the one <73> with more and the one with less powers; they are restrictions, burdens on property – *real rights in material things owned by another* [dingliche Rechte an fremder Sache].

Finally, the exceptional nature of landed property, the yield of which is based on a dual factor, land and labor, the former of which moreover in the Germanic legal system often is granted by a higher authority, a representative of public power, entails peculiar legal relations:

1. a distribution of rights to each in accordance with their various contributions, be it in the form of a real right to a thing owned by another, *perpetual lease* [Emphyteuse], be it as truly *shared property*, the latter however not as a direct fragmentation of property right but rather as an organic relation among the participants;

---

attachment to a certain subject, in the former case the plot of land, in the latter the person, from which follows the nontransferability of the same, is in itself already hardly significant given the essential dissimilarity between land and person, and has even fewer other juridical consequences. Outside of the maxims valid for all **jura in re aliena** (e.g., **in faciendo consist. nequit – res propria nemini servit.**) they have nothing in common. So for example the **civiliter uti**, the **causa continua** etc. of real servitudes do not apply to personal servitudes, nor do the bailment and encumbrance of personal servitudes apply to real servitudes; the manner of origin and production, the treatment of possession and prescription is entirely different for each according to the necessity of the matter. Usufruct has much more in common with emphyteusis than with the **jus viae**, **actus**, **ne luminibus**, etc. It is by no means any inner ground by which these heterogenous rights are grouped over against the other **jura in re** as a common concept.

2. rights to land and soil, realized in a tax [Abgabe] on the possessor – *services in kind.*[40]

§. 40. Components of Property Rights

Property therefore is the right (the legal authority) over a thing in *its totality*. It is however for this reason the *general* and *complete* right to the thing, that is, it contains every power not specially removed, while on the contrary restricted rights have no authority other than what is expressly provided; and presumption contends for the unrestricted character of property. Furthermore, it is the *original* and *independent* right to the thing, while <74> other real rights assume property and an owner which restrict them. Finally, it is an *exclusive* right to the thing, while many other real rights held by various entitled persons may exist in the same thing independently of each other, for example praedial servitudes.

The powers contained in property, in accordance with both motives of the law of property* (§. 29), are of a dual form: rights of use and of disposal. The former involves use and usufruct, the latter concerns changes in the thing, in its substance or in its legal relation. However, because satisfaction is the initial motive of property*, the right of disposal, as was rightly emphasized by Hegel, cannot exist when all use is removed from it (**nuda proprietatis**). In fact, use should only be removed in restricted degree, namely either in restricted extent (for example praedial servitudes) or restricted duration (for example personal servitudes).

§. 41. Forms of Joint Ownership

Both natural organic bonds between persons and those artificially formed for a purpose, even if it be for the purpose of property* itself (marriage, agnation, community, common family property [Ganerbschaft], joint stock corporation) also exercise, by means of their power over persons, a power over those persons' position with regard to the thing, and thereby effectuate a joint right held by these persons to the thing, in determinate shapes. This was properly appreciated by Germanic law, and from it stems a series of institutions of this character, for

[40]Thus the *real purpose* [reale Bestimmung] of property* is to vouchsafe every satisfaction, from which arises the system of real rights, not, as Hegel constructs it, the *logical categories* of general (value) and particular (determinate thing) and the like. The former is only the proper principle of its construction.

which the Germanists developed the concept of "*shared property*" [Gesammteigentums]. The innermost meaning of this concept is that it is owed to people, to individuals, not however in their isolation as in Roman property but in their <75> organic unity; this had as a consequence that both, the organic bond (the community) and the individual, are vested with rights. It is hereby opposed on the one hand to the Roman doctrine of the legal person, which entitles merely the whole (bond, unity), and on the other hand to the Roman doctrine of joint property which entitles merely the individual. In it, the right-bearers are entitled to the property only jointly, not separately, and thus are not entitled to a determinate proportion over which they have unrestricted disposal. This is even true of community of goods in marriage, which comes closest to Roman joint property. But the participants have a direct part as individuals in the right; the latter does not belong to a legal person constructed from the participants only to be entirely separated from them; and therefore they may, in accordance with their specific relation, have individual powers of property as a separate independent right, as for example the shareholder having the right to sell his shares. In what manner the right of the whole is related to the right of the individual depends on the specific nature of each of these organic bonds. It is everywhere a specific individual articulation of the institution. For this reason no practical consequences for individual institutions can be derived from the mere concept of shared property; the practical significance of the concept as a general one consists much more in the negative sense of exclusion of principles regarding Roman joint property and property of the legal person.

Even so, the German-legal concept of *divided property*, which is not to be derived from the mere relation to the object, is based rather in the higher organic relation of persons, whom the object can serve in that relation as well as it can in their isolation. The Romanizing dismantling of this concept into property with **jus in re aliena** – with actual ownership ascribed either to the over- or under- <76> proprietor – would destroy the unity and innermost principle of this legal institution, it being based in the legal relation between the persons, which often first determines the property relation. For example, fealty or subjection, be it only for own collection of levies, or dismissal [Privation] which nevertheless rules out the devolution of usufruct to the owner [Konsolidation], etc., cannot possibly be construed from a **dominium** with **jus in re**. Nor can **dominium directum** be conceived as a mere political overarching power, because its consequences are too significantly private-legal and pecuniary for that. The capacity of the law of property* to be determined by such higher personal bonds is generally an advantage of Germanic law. Whether precisely *these* personal bonds will continue to exist in the future is another question, the answer to which it is not here the place to give.

§. 42. The Acquisition of Property

The *acquisition* of property everywhere presupposes the will of the acquirer, the *property intent*, property* being an affair [Sache] of freedom. However, this will alone does not yet yield property; there must first be a *ground of acquisition*, that is the effectuation of a specific relation to the object, be it direct, be it indirect through other people, through which the preference is gained ahead of others with the same will. The various sorts of such grounds of acquisition are based on the notion that things [Sachen] have the purpose of serving the human race, that is the peoples, as a whole for their preservation and satisfaction, and yet have the purpose of entitling individuals to specific rights, precisely in accordance with their actions and destinies. In line with this, property is primevally derived partly from the community and partly from the deeds of acquisition of individ-
<77> uals; and from then on it is partly the circulation of that property, partly the acquisition of new property which perpetually takes place, with the former however only occurring through acts or legal relations of persons. From this is derived the following system of grounds of acquisition:

§. 43. Original Acquisition

Acquisition of property is of two main sorts: *original* and *derivative* acquisition, that is, independent founding of property merely through an act or procedure of the acquirer, and derivation of the same from the rights of a former owner. The latter in terms of its concept always refers to the former.

Original acquisition is of three forms: *absolute, extinctive,* and *accessory* acquisition.

1. *Absolute* acquisition is that in which, beginning entirely anew, an ownerless object is first brought into private ownership. Landed property by its nature – it being a continuum and it being the basis of communal satisfaction – is based as a rule on *distribution by the community – assignation, enfeoffment,* etc. Movables, however, by their nature – in which such considerations do not apply – are

based on *individual appropriation* in accordance with the principle of freedom, which is valid for property*.[41]

This consists above all in gaining physical power over the object – *occupation.* It answers to the nature of property as the right of corporeal control over an object that self-effected physical control form both its foundation and initial aspect, that through it the object be considered as shackled to the legal sphere of the person. This is because it de facto brings about **<78>** the condition which is elevated through law to the character of duration (Book II [*Principles of Law*], §. 5), which is property.[42] Mere will therefore is not enough for appropriation [Aneignung], nor is the objective identifiability of the same, since it does not bring about this condition; it is the achievement of the deed, the finished taking of possession, which does so. Whether then the mere *act* of *seizure* is sufficient or whether *continued* holding [Innehabung] and use is required (usucapion), in order for the thing to be viewed as being subjected to our physical power, is purely a positive establishment.[43] That the thing must be own- **<79>** erless is

---

[41] Now not even *fallow farmland* [Lehden] can be occupied by individuals.

[42] The ethical effect of law is therefore none other than the conferring of the permanence corresponding to spiritual being, by means of the will and mutual recognition, to relations which man is incapable physically of attaining. One might also apply Kant's viewpoint here, that time and empirical conditions must be mentally abstracted away, more properly, that the human will be elevated over it, be master of it.

[43] For example, in what degree is it possible to occupy landed property in the case of its not being publicly assigned? I can traverse unending amounts of land and put up signs, of which I perhaps cannot cultivate or truly manage the hundredth part. That the act of taking possession must protect me from ejection [Dejektion] stands to reason but it is not yet property. On the other hand, shall the mere act of seizure be sufficient for me to be able to demand surrender [daß ich vindiciren könne] when through accident another and then a third party [ein Anderer und ein Dritter] come into possession, for me to acquire an enduring and absolutely actionable [unbedingt verfolgbares] right – shall not much more an enduring use (**usucapio** of one year or such like) be required through which the material thing is assimilated to my condition, in a certain sense gradually permeated by the atmosphere of my right [meines Rechts], the true basis of my personal existence? This appears to be the oldest meaning of **usucapio** in the **res mancipi**, that

based in the concept of taking possession as a form of absolute acquisition – its entire meaning refers to this situation. Ownerlessness is however for that reason only a precondition, not the ground of acquisition. Given the equal possibility of such appropriation for all, the taking of possession is ever a form of *priority*, and therefore the acquisition of property through the taking of possession is based on a dual ground: the recognition of the person and his act, which is the principle of all priority (§. 4), and the purpose of the institution of property, by virtue of which it not only lends mere preference in factual conditions but gives an enduring right.

Beyond taking of possession, the appropriation of movables consists further in *manufacture* (**specificatio**). The self-production of an object is by eternal law the truest and most absolute ground of property. Although manufacture is not production in the fullest sense, since it presupposes a material, it is nevertheless so in relation to the object [Sache] in this shape or form, to this sort [Species]. Where therefore the earlier shape cannot be recovered, or beyond that where the form is the essential thing,[44] manufacture can rightly hold as the production of a new thing the property of which is due the maker, and the former thing, and therefore likewise the property in it held by another, as having expired. For this reason, manufacture is not yet extinctive acquisition since the original prop-

---

from the beginning it could come to be considered strict property, with the effect of vindication, not through occupation but only through continued possession. The Germanic seizure of three days is based on the same idea while also on the idea of publicness [Oeffentlichkeit], the relationship to the whole, that the independent right is acquired at the conveyance only after a year and a day. Could this not at least be evidence that no legal decision can be derived immediately from law-ideas ("natural law"), since the natural-law theory precisely here tends to present the matter in such a manner that the Roman **rei vindicatio** follows imperatively from the seizure of an abandoned thing according to a command of reason.

[44]The Roman criterion, whether the thing can be put back in its former shape, is too external to be adequate in itself; for example, a great sculptor having molded a statue using someone else's clay would have to leave it to the owner of the clay. The consideration as to whether the main value consists in the form had naturally still to arise, analogous to the maxim regarding accession.

erty is not abrogated as such and directly (legally) but only directly (factually) through the expiration of the thing.

2. Extinctive *acquisition* is that which, in relation to already existing property of another, proceeds not as its continu- <80> ation but its abrogation. It consists in *adverse possession* (usucapion in its contemporary meaning). Just as when possession is obtained it has the power to grant property in an ownerless thing, so with its continuation, in accordance with the principle of prescription (Book II [*Principles of Law*], §. 38), does it have the power to liquidate existing property; but only – in accordance to the ethical principle of legislation – when possession is *reasonable*, be it merely inner reasonable awareness (**bona fides**) which is required, be it an outward occurrence justifying it (**justa causa**), and regardless of whether reasonable awareness (lack of awareness of ownership on the part of another) is required only at the moment of gaining possession or more strictly until the period of adverse possession ends.

3. *Accessory* acquisition is the acquisition of a thing through its connection with another with which we already have a legal relation, be it by way of *outward accrual* (**accessio, alluvio**, etc.) or inward *organic generation* (acquisition of fruits). Here it is the *connection* to the primary thing, and our legal relation to it, upon which the acquisition is grounded, according to various considerations depending on the two main forms.[45]

Occupation is to be considered the primeval origin of all property at most to the degree that the people from whom the allocation of landed property proceeds, itself occupied that land.[46] But the property of individuals had its initial origin pre- <81> dominantly in the distribution by the community, in that the

[45]In the former case, the owner of the primary thing [Hauptsache] is to acquire the accessory thing [Nebensache] by reason of inseparability. In the latter case, the separation of the accessory thing (fruit) from the primary thing is what nature is after, and therefore here it is precisely someone other than the owner of the primary thing (**bona fide** possessor, beneficiary) who acquires, albeit by virtue of his relation to the owner.

[46]This is only occupation vis-à-vis other peoples. By contrast, that the conquered Samnitic land fell to the Roman state and not to the conquering soldiers, and that English lands fell to King William I and not to the barons who fought with him, is not based on the principle of occupation but on the relation between state or sovereign and individual.

acquisition of land, this cornerstone of all possession, as a rule proceeds from it. The subjective isolating natural law theory (even Hegel) ignores this and constructs all property upon the foundation of self-appropriation by individuals, contrary to history as well as to the idea. In general, occupation, regardless of the significant place it takes in legal philosophy due to its absolute origin, nevertheless in real life is an extremely rare and furthermore usually impure application; for the occupation of game, of fish, etc., usually depends on preconditions (authorization for hunting, fishing, etc.). The connectedness with which peoples and generations expand across the world of things, and in which in fact the spiritual existence of the human race consists, precisely entails that there was no room for such an absolute isolated act. Now that society has grown old, property as a rule is based on bequeathal, and where it is to arise in already existing things (not in those which first must be manufactured), it does so not through absolute beginning but through the liquidation of previous property, through usucapion. According to true doctrine, property must in the final analysis be derived from authority, not from acting on one's own [Eigenmacht] (§. 26) and must be construed in its continuity, by which it passes through the generations as a general condition of property*, not as an isolated, newly initiated acquisition of individuals.

§. 44. Derivative Acquisition

Derivative acquisition, as derivation from the rights of a former owner, has the character of being conditioned by the property of predecessors. It is based either on higher personal bonds to them – and thus is the consequence of a representa- **<82>** tion of their person, whether the first acquirer or the last possessor (e.g., succession, **dos, arrogatio**) – or on the act of conveyance of the object in question.

The requirement of taking possession is not essential to derivative acquisition in the way in which it is for initial appropriation. In fact, with acquisition through representation it would be positively unnatural, in that here the right, by virtue of solidarity with the predecessor, is continued *as one's own*. But even with acquisition through conveyance it is not absolutely necessary, because one acquires power over the thing by means of the will of the other person. So, for example, according to the French law code property in movable things is acquired through mere contract; this makes it impossible for it to be sold dishonestly to a third party prior to realized physical transfer [erfolgter Tradition].

Roman law, by contrast, here too requires *physical transfer*. Herein is contained an extremely pointed expression of the inner significance of property, to wit, that lawful power over a thing can be initiated in no other way than through acquisition of the physical thing. For this it provides yet a great advantage. Namely, it is appropriate to properly appointed legislation that the moment of transfer of property be precisely designated, and this cannot more appropriately occur than through conveyance. With immovable things, either public recognition of conveyance or at least public pronouncement of the same is customarily required in the public interest. Here public registration and the like designates the transfer, making corporeal delivery a superfluous requirement.

Chapter 5: Possession

§. 45. The Nature of Possession

<83> The factual situation of power over the thing, exercised with the intention of ownership but without property having been established, does not extend any right to the thing; nevertheless, like property it serves the general purpose of property*: human satisfaction through things by means of free power over them (by means of their subjection to the will). For that reason it is appropriate that legal protection be granted it, only of another sort than property, namely not security in the *thing itself* and therefore against anyone who *withholds the thing*, but only security of the *factual situation*, and thus only against those who *abrogate this situation* (through their *positive act)*. This is our institution of *possession*. Its intention is not to protect the person against violence but to *conserve the factual situation towards things*.

With its violation, possession therefore vouchsafes not mere claims for compensation (**actio injuriarum**) but a claim to non-interference with or return of the thing. But it secures these only against those acts the form and manner of which endanger the *security of the factual situation* towards the thing,[47] namely, against forcible or clandestine **<84>** seizure or the attempt thereto. These are the specific violations of possession.[48] Possession therefore is only secured against *certain forms* of damage, namely those directly, physically caused by another (this alone is the disturbance of the factual situation), and thus always under the premise of a *positive* (active) injury (tort) on the other side (Book II [*Principles*

[47]This is what characterizes those actions as torts. Although their character as tort presupposes that they injure the *person* – not, as Puchta explained it, that the person is bodily harmed (this only being true in the case of forcible seizure), but that the will of the person to have the thing is violated – that character itself consists in the violation of the *factual situation towards the thing* acquired by the person. The former is the general basis of private tort, which therefore is also found in every other form of it, while the latter is the specific and positive basis for which reason they are torts.

[48]That the withholding of **precarium** in Roman law falls under the viewpoint of violation of possession rather than violation of contract is of a purely positive character and had good historical grounds.

of Law], §. 49) and is only *indirectly* secured by means of a claim on this violator (**actio in personam**). For this reason it is by no means an in itself neutral fact, obtaining legal significance only as a natural precondition to injurious actions; instead, in accordance with the above, it contains its legal significance within itself and only for this reason do those actions count as injurious. Upon this basis, its existence (acquisition, loss) likewise is not merely a matter of factual assessment but through legislation is joined to juristic criteria.

The institution of possession is therefore a *provisional* or *subsidiary arrangement* of the same life relation the actual intended and definite arrangement of which is the institution of property, to wit, the relation of men to things; but just because of this, it is not an arrangement like property which takes the view of the *right to the thing*, but which takes the view of the *mutual actions* of men, that the one not intentionally injure the other in his factual situation.[49] **<85>**

§. 46. Possession First Recognized by Roman Law

The extension of protection to possession as a special institution alongside property is therefore characteristic of the Roman law; because where a legal system recognizes the right to the thing not pure and simple but with regard to the actions of all participating persons and the events between them (see above, §. 36), property and possession merge into each other. Thus, even the Germanic Gewehre in movable things is such a cross between property and possession in that in it, as in Roman possession, legal help is only vouchsafed against positive unlawful privation (not against every form of withholding) of the thing, but even against the third-party possessor, as with Roman property. By contrast, in Roman law, in which property is recognized as the unconditional right to the thing, a second sphere is set apart for the relation to things according to that viewpoint.

---

[49]Compare above, §. 36. By the way, by no means does this explain the condition of the possessor (in subjective relation) to be provisional property (the possessory interdicts as provisional vindications), although the institution of possession (objectively as legislative arrangement) contains a provisional regulation for the same situation, the definitive regulation of which is property. Even less so, of course, is possession then a *presumptive* property. Legislation protects the factual situation not because it has the presumption of the law in its favor, but because as factual situation it merits conservation.

In Roman law, the protection of possession, at least in the more ancient period, also had a generically different character from that of property. The latter is based on recognition of unconditional subjective entitlement, the former, by contrast, on public order (by no means against violence and disturbance of the public peace, but for the maintenance of the factual situation to things as such), thus especially with the **ager publicus**, to which private entitlement was unthinkable. In the former case, the power of the ruling authorities serves private claims as superior force, so to speak; in the latter, the private claim first springs from the ruling authority.[50] **<86>**

§. 47. The Relation of Possession to Property

If the inner purpose of the protection of possession is as described – a provisional, subsidiary arrangement of the relation to things, the definitive and true arrangement of which is property – then possession must remain in a *constant relation to property*. Possession is to arrange these relations according to those factual considerations only in the case where legal considerations are lacking, and therefore must give way where such arise. Roman law (and even more, Roman theory) does not accord this relation its rightful importance.[51] It allows possession and property to run alongside each other without connection, in that, without regard for the institution's deeper origin and goal, it treats the claim to restitution on account of forcible or clandestine seizure merely as an

---

[50]As with all interdicts, the ones dealing with possession are based on the authority of the praetor: an accusation is made not because of the violation of a right but because something has been done contrary to the command of the praetor. The character of all **judicia imperio continentia**, to which they also belong, is no other than that their principle is the power of the ruling authorities [obrigkeitliche Gewalt] and not, as with the **judicia legitima**, recognized entitlement. Cf. my *Ancient Roman Law of Accusation* ["älteres römisches Klagenrecht"].

The protection of possession later was elevated [erstarkt] to a full-fledged private-legal institution. For this reason in our legal system protective measures regarding the factual situation in things have been added to the provisories [Provisorien – temporary rulings] which, as originally with **possessio**, are founded not on the right of the party but on the regard for and solicitude of the judge.

[51]**Nihil commune habet proprietas cum possessione** [property has nothing in common with possession], l. 12 §. 1 de adqu. vel amitt. poss. (41.2).

independent **obligatio ex delicto**, by which the right to the thing is not even taken into account. Only in one respect did the deeper motive of the matter assert itself in Roman law: the **interd. ret. poss.** was used as preparation in the property suit to establish the role of the defendant. <87>

By contrast, German procedural practice, partially derived from the canon law, reconstituted this connection. This is expressed in particular in:

1. Above all, that the incontrovertible defense [(liquide) Einrede] of property is sustained against the possessory action (interdict) [gegen die Besitzklage (Interdikt) Statt hat];

2. That **possessorium** and **petitorium** are treated not as procedures concerning entirely different things, the former a delictual obligation, the latter concerning property, but as procedures aiming at one final goal, thus that cumulation of the two takes place;

3. That the entire institution is extended to legal relations of the character of real rights other than property and in fact partly to those concerning which a similar formal injury as a rule virtually never occurs, but the purpose of which merely is the conservation of a provisional situation until the definitive legal inquiry.[52]

These and similar determinations are therefore not to be considered as disfigurements and misunderstandings of the Roman law but rather as natural advances and improvements of it. In no way is the Roman, independent development of both institutions – property in its thing-oriented, absolute character, possession in its only indirect protection by means of the **obligatio ex delicto** – thereby to be forfeited, but only finally reoriented to their common higher goal. The Roman <88> shape of the institution, first clarified by Savigny, and its formation in German practice up until that point are entirely divergent in terms of technical structure, the former based upon the opposition of property and delictual obligation, the latter on the opposition between **definitivum** and **provi-**

[52]One could also count among these, that in accordance with practice a better possession can be asserted to be in **possessorium**, i.e., not in consideration of a better possession from formal consideration of disturbance (**vi clam**, etc.) but from material grounds ("**possessor antiquior et titulata**"), like the leading procedurists (Bayer, Linde et al.) still presume; but this practice, as Savigny has shown, rests merely on a misunderstanding of canon law and should instead be abandoned.

sorium. Our legal-philosophical principle – the purpose (τέλος) of possession – demands that they nevertheless be united in such a manner that the motivating factor and the goal of this practice remain preserved, and the entire Roman technical apparatus be consciously inserted as medium, as the manner of achieving that goal, under the cited modifications which this goal entails.

§. 48. The Place of Possession in the Legal System

When classified according to the true systematic viewpoint, to wit, as *legal institution,* possession has its *position in the system* undoubtedly among *real rights.* Its purpose is the ordering of the relation to the thing. Should one however systematize in terms of that subordinate viewpoint of rights and the objects of those rights, then possession has no place in that system, or rather that classification, since it is no right to an object. For "right" in the sense of our legal system involves an unconditional protection, that is, one independent of the continuity of a factual condition, and "object of right" is accordingly an object (thing, performance) which is to be the entitled's pure and simple, all of which simply does not hold true for possession. For this reason, possession here only comes into consideration as factual precondition for **obligationes ex delicto** (interdicts).[53]
<89>

§. 49. Theories of Possession: Savigny, Thibaut, Gans, Puchta

Savigny clarified the obscurity over this doctrine which had reigned until he came along, and his "Law of Possession" is the model of a juristic monograph. The significance of possession originates in the fact that it is a factual relation which corresponds to property as legal relation, it is a protection against formal (i.e., positive) unlawful acts, it is therefore a juristically relevant and protected fact, not a right, etc.; these enlightening viewpoints were emphasized by him, and all of us therefore stand upon the foundation he laid. That Savigny treated

---

[53]Nor can I agree with Puchta regarding this doctrine from a systematic viewpoint. To wit, he describes possession as a "right to one's own will" or a "right to one's own person." The "rights to one's own person" in that case would be twofold: 1) the right of personality, 2) the right of possession. But possession, in that it has an *external object* and presumes an *act of acquisition*, cannot possibly hold as a mere right to one's own will or to one's own person and form a class together with honor and the like. Such would only be the general capacity to possess, not possession of a specific thing.

possession merely as the precondition for the **obligationes ex delicto** and not as an independent legal institution is the standpoint of the Roman law itself, which to elucidate faithfully in its own coherence was his task. The entire juristic formation of the Roman law of possession is thereby given, in classical, irreproachable completion. On the other hand, I cannot so unconditionally fall in with Savigny regarding the final motive of this formation. For the innermost relation of possession, that it is the same relation to the thing factually as property is legally, which precisely Savigny first clarified – he puts it at the pinnacle of his treatment only straightaway to give it up, in that he grants it no significance in itself but allows it to arise merely from the necessarily accompanying injury of the person. He thereby makes the inviolability of the person himself rather than the inviolability of his position with regard to the thing to be the foundation of the institution of possession. In spite of this, in his course on civil law Savigny, with sure legal-philo- <90> sophical insight, assigned possession its proper systematic position among real rights.

Thibaut rightly asserts that the maintenance of the provisional situation is the core of entire institution of possession, and that accordingly possession does not first gain significance through the interdict but vice versa, the latter only exists for the sake of the former. But firstly Thibaut hereby does not distinguish between the legislative or law-constructive motive and the juristic (technical) principle, and therefore rejects Savigny's unassailable disclosure of that principle; furthermore, Thibaut conceives the former, true motive in an unsuitable generality as protection of the provisional situation in general, the exercise of rights in general, without regard for the entirely specific nature of factual power over things (the analogy to property), and thus arrives at his misconceived systematic classification of possession within the General Part. From this so very generally conceived motive, nothing indeed can be gained for possession than what in similar manner holds for the provisionally existing marital status, for the defendant against a claim, etc., and precisely the characteristic effects of possession remain for him, as he himself admits, without explanation as something incidental, something positive.

It is exactly the truth of the Savignian doctrine which Gans combats, in that he asserts that possession is no less than "a decisive right,"[54] certainly unlawful

---

[54] Gans, *Foundation of Possession* [Grundlage des Besitzes], p. 33.

with respect to property, but this relativity holds true for all rights. Gans finds support for this assertion in the face of the undeniable factual nature of possession in the fact that every right is based on a fact, thus possession, in that it also enjoys legal protection, of necessity is **<91>** of the same nature as all other rights.[55] This however is an obvious confusion of the fact as being a transitory versus an immanent cause of rights. Every right requires a fact for its *origin*, e.g., property requires delivery, usucapion, etc., but once this has occurred, the right continues its own independent existence, even when the fact ceases. By contrast, possession requires the fact for its *continuance* as well; should the fact cease, so would its protection. From this viewpoint, it is not a right but merely a legally protected factual situation. Just for this reason, possession is likewise not merely lesser in terms of power or degree than property, not even a relative property ("inchoate property"); this would be appropriate to the **bonae fidei possessio**, but not to **possessio**, it rather being something entirely different in character. Just as untenable as this foundation of Gans's argumentation – that all rights are based upon a fact in the same way as possession – is the other foundation, that all rights stand in a relation of relativity one to another, like possession and property: "the significance of rights is always to be understood only in the relationship, not absolutely."[56] "In the way possession is unlawful against property, so is property against contract, contract against family, family against the state, the state against history." For the latter is neither true, nor does it apply to the relation between possession and property. Instead, property, contract, family, state are pure independent spheres, of which one cannot say that the one must yield to the other, must be "unlawful" against it, e.g., the family is just as holy as the state, and the state cannot dissolve family ties, etc.; by contrast, against property juristic possession is unlawful and void pure and simple. Beyond this, the **<92>** author's argumentation is moved by the truth that possession is an institution aimed at the relation to the thing in the same way as property, that "the will of the person, where it expresses itself in things, is a right," and thus the grounding of possession must be a direct and not an indirect one; but that is something

---

[55]"All legal concepts are however facts [Fakta]: I possess, have property, marry, inherit. These are facts, but there is a relation in them which one cannot deny the name of legal."

[56]*ibid.*, p. 38.

entirely different from "inchoate property" in the sense in which he applies it. Moreover, the practical goal of this polemic cannot be discerned.

Puchta's concept that possession *"derives"* its legal nature from the *"right of personality"* (i.e., that each ouster injures the will of the person) discloses an essential aspect of the legal-philosophical rationale of possession, although it does not exhaust it. Not only possession but no less property stems from the rights of personality, the recognition of the will, in the manner of the natural law teachers who actually deduce them solely from this. No less so contract. But the protection of possession, just as that of property, does not yet have its complete rationale and its specific formation in these rights of personality. It is not the ungrounded will of the person in and of itself which the law is to protect and has the vocation to protect, but the advantage gained from others under the favor of circumstances, the factual position with respect to the thing. That will is only the necessary precondition for this, which is no less the case for property, for the acquisition of the inheritance, etc. The will and its importance – as Puchta stresses – is the one side of the law-constructing principle, the other however is the significance of life relations in which the will is operative (compare §§. 1, 29, 56), in this case the situations towards things.

Therefore Savigny finds the basis of the protection of possession in the inviolability of the *body* of the person, Puchta in the inviolability of the *will*, I by contrast directly in the invio- **<93>** lability of their *factually existing relations to the thing.* Just as adverse possession and the gradual legitimacy of usurped thrones have one and the same principle (Savigny), just so do the protection of juristic possession and the esteem for de facto governments have one and the same principle, and if the latter did not exist, the former could not either. Juristic possession serves the same purpose (satisfaction through things) in unentitled fashion that property serves in entitled fashion; de facto government serves the same purpose (maintenance of public order) in unentitled fashion that legitimate governments serve in entitled fashion. In both cases, although the *subjects* have no title, the *objective relation* (the use of things, the maintenance of order) is justified and is something that should exist. Therefore subjects without title are protected or respected, as the case may be, as long as they are not confronted with an entitled subject.

Chapter 6: Obligation and Contract

§. 50. Personal Rights: Property in the Acts of Others

<95> Performances [Leistungen] by other people serve the needs of our existence just as much as does the possession of things, and the activity of personality in freely giving shape to the way of life, which requires property in things, therefore also requires the same power of free disposal and the same enduring secure right over that other means of existence. This enduring secure right is *obligation* (**obligatio**) in contradistinction to merely factual, momentary performance (**datio**). Obligation serves a dual purpose, that of meeting needs for which things are not appropriate (services, works), but beyond that, securing things for the future by means of the human will. The significance of obligation is not so much to make possible services or the communication of things – this can be achieved by mere factual performance – but instead to secure the future, partly by making possible a present performance or communication (**commodatum, mutuum**) without damage and hazard, and partly through which the future possession of an object is secured in a manner often not afforded even by continuous possession. For example, when I deposit an object or lend an amount, this might well secure the thing much better than if I held onto it. Herein lies an intellectualization of property*.

Obligation consequently is one's right to another's performance bearing some property* value, be it delivery of an ob- <96> ject, be it pure act. It is of a totally different character than the true rights of the person (family, class, corporation rights etc.), which have as their object dependence or commitment among the persons themselves, with an ethical and not merely pecuniary significance. Performance of the most intellectual [geistigsten] kind can also be the object of obligation (for example tutelage, education, artistic performance), albeit only to the degree that they permit a wage and money-equivalent in accordance with general estimation and practice. That which cannot in any way be considered an acquisition and something with money value (for example to be elected mayor, to be taken on as confessor) cannot be an object of obligation.

Because the individual performance of a person cannot be separated from his entire personality, an overriding question facing law and justice is the relation between the enforceability of the former and the freedom of the latter.

Purely personal actions (such as services) cannot be made perpetual objects of obligation because they then become a personal dependence of the person. Purely personal actions furthermore cannot be coerced to the degree that they alter the total personal position in life of the obligee (e.g., a singer having to keep an engagement after having decided to give up singing as a career). The Romans therefore only handed down sentences in terms of general money value even for obligations entailing the provision of specific objects. Lastly, the person of the debtor should not be treated as an object of collateral for a performance of a pecuniary sort, as in the older Roman law, which allowed for the sale or the cutting into pieces of the debtor. *Imprisonment for debt* is not justified on the ground that the person himself is collateral for the performance, but on the ground that imprisonment in general is the means of the ruling authority to hold people to the fulfillment of their **<97>** obligations, both public and private. Neither therefore does it rest on contract, as something which cannot take place due to the inalienable right of freedom, but on protection by the ruling authority. Therefore the abolition of imprisonment for debt is an injustice against the creditor, the denial of government help, and, because it destroys personal credit, an injustice against all those in need of credit. However, this must have regulation and limits – eternal imprisonment for failure of performance to the creditor is unjustified because the person himself is not likewise a subsidiary object of obligation. By contrast, the property* of the debtor stands unconditionally as guarantee for these performances of pecuniary value.

§. 51. The Forms of Obligation

The many specific kinds [Species] of obligation derive from the multiplicity of needs of reciprocal grant or regarding the mutual assurance of future provision, as for example the transfer of objects as property or for use, hire of services, exchange, etc. They are the ways developed in common life by which one person can be made liable to another. But in order for these obligations to exist between specific persons there must be a specific ground, an event (**causa**) between them. In every such event, both the persons of creditor and debtor are designated[57]

[57]The **actiones quod met. caus., ad exhib., de glande legenda**, actions of injury [Noxalklagen] therefore are not true **obligationes** but pure **actiones**, the **debitor** not being designated once and for all through the *event* but determined and fixed only through

and the content of **<98>** the obligation more closely specified. It is then likewise characteristic that the nature of the obligation, the principles of its treatment, are determined by the grounds of its origin (obligations of contract, tort, alimony, legacy); property on the other hand is always the same regardless of its origin, whether it be through occupation, usucapion or whatever.

§. 52. Origin and Goals of Obligations

All obligations have the goal of establishing a communication of property* *either originally, or as a substitute* for previously caused damages, the former in consequence of actions and events which in the view of the parties or in accordance with their own nature have as their purpose the foundation of a legal relation (*transaction* [Geschäft] in the widest sense), the latter in consequence of a *debt* owed by the obligee. Accordingly, one may distinguish between two main forms of obligation, *transaction* obligations and *tort* obligations, which then are subject to a generically different treatment.[58]

The origin of obligations, which, in accordance with the above, likewise determines the treatment of the same and thus its classification, is however more specifically the following. In accordance with the general dual principle of all legal origin (Book II [*Principles of Law*], §. 37), this is based partly on the *freedom of the parties involved*, partly on the *given specific relations* among them. The former has the priority, because the sphere of property* is characterized by freedom. Obligations arise from freedom either **<99>** through contract or injury, the former obligating fulfillment, the latter damages (Book II [*Principles of Law*], §. 49). The given relations which in accordance with the purpose of life conditions generate an obligation are manifold in accordance with the nature of these relations, for which reason the Romans summarized them under the

---

the **lit. cont**. The extra-judicial refusal of restitution therefore does not here justify a substitute action, grounds no **mora**, etc., there are only **actiones** and not **obligationes**. Furthermore, the determinate person of creditor belongs to the essence of an obligation. The **cessio actionum** is an expansion, not the abolition of this principle. An exception to this is our obligations au porteur, which however is an institution of public-legal character.

[58]The claim for damages arising from a contract is a transaction obligation; it is not meant to restore damages caused but to fulfill that which was promised of an original distribution, its value or interest, as the case may be.

designation "**ex variis causarum figuris**" [from a variety of reasons]. Nevertheless, these main classes may be distinguished among them:

1. Some arise from the purpose of property* transactions, similar to contractual obligations. The need to secure a return or substitute through agreement also creates an obligation immediately, apart from agreement, in cases in which such is actually not possible or is customarily omitted due to prevailing opinion and expectation. Here belong most of the Roman law's "quasi-contracts," e.g., **negotiorum gestio**, claims for restitution [Kondiktionen], etc.[59]

2. Some arise in the purpose of other institutions, namely familial and successional relations, in order to realize claims arising from these, as for example endowment, alimentary obligations, **actio tutelae**, legacy, etc.

3. Some are merely for the purpose of protecting other rights, namely property rights, and thus are more **actiones** than **obligationes**, for example **ad exhibidendum, damni infecti cautio, de glande legenda, de arbor. caedendis**, etc. <100>

§. 53. Obligation not Limited to Contract

The most significant ground of origin of obligations, derived purely from the purpose of property* transactions, is *contract.*

Misled by this, legal philosophers, in particular Kant and Hegel, viewed contract rather than obligation as the other aspect of property* over against property, in contradiction both to legal practice and true relations. Certainly, contract is the form of origin of obligation κατ' ἐξοχήν [par excellence], because origin through contract has its root purely in the purpose of property* transactions, and thus in obligation itself; nevertheless, it is not the only ground of its origin. Obligation is not merely to serve voluntary property* transactions but also the fulfillment of familial bonds, successional relations, settlement of property claims and the like, and, what is more decisive, contract in turn is not restricted to obligations but also forms the basis of other legal bonds. It is only the abstraction by which the bare relationship of will is accentuated, that the one will is bound to the other, without consideration of the object (whether for a performance of pecuniary value, for a future marriage, for a relationship of

[59]In similar manner, the duty to provide compensation is sometimes, out of equity for that which was damaged, extended to such to which, strictly speaking, violation ought not be imputed – "quasidelict," which then are treated analogously to tort obligations.

protection such as fealty, for a goal respecting the law of nations, etc.) from which stems such a complete identification of contract with obligation.

§. 54. The Nature of Contract

Contract is a mutual stated agreement among specific persons regarding a legal relationship to be founded amongst themselves.

Contract in the broadest sense is of *two different forms.* It is either a mere means of founding legal relations which immediately afterward separate from contract to continue an existence <101> in accordance with their own requirements and laws, for example marriage, **pactum hypothecae**, physical delivery, ratification of the state constitution. Or it contains the legal relation in itself and continues to be the latter's cause and source (substance), so that complete fulfillment continuously proceeds only in pursuance of the agreement and according to the standard it sets. To this pertain above all contracts of obligation [Forderungsverträge], but not these alone: others do as well, for example, in some respects engagement to be married, then contracts in the law of nations (e.g., alliance). For example, spouses require of each other faithfulness to vows, support, shared lifestyle, not because of agreement made in concluding the marriage but because of marriage itself; the property owner does not lay claim to an object because of physical delivery but because it is his property; on the other hand, the buyer, the renter, the principal lodges a claim because of a contract and in accordance with it.[60] In the former case contract is the transitory cause, in the latter case the immanent cause. The former are contractual *acts,* the latter contractual *relations,* that is to say, the former arise through contract (agreement) without themselves being contracts.[61]

---

[60]In this manner, the North American opposition understood the Union to be a treaty and thus dissoluble; but the principle was pushed through that although the foundation of the Union was a treaty, currently the Union is no treaty but rather a fundamental determinant [Grundbestimmung] of the North American state constitution.

[61]So is the divergence dispelled between Hegel, *Natural Law* [Naturr. – a.k.a. *Philosophy of Law*], §. 75, and Savigny, *Pand.* [a.k.a. *System of Modern Roman Law*], Book III, p. 307, concerning whether marriage is a contract. The determinations regarding consensus (error, condition) for which reason Savigny aims to establish the quality of contract certainly have their application in the *solemnization* of the marriage, which is a

<102> In the former class, the act of agreement and fulfillment coincide in a single moment; for example, marriage is likewise fulfilled through consent, because further fulfillments, as already noted, are based not on consent but in marriage itself, just as the lien is already extended with the closing of the **pactum hypothecae**. By contrast, in the latter class future fulfillment, which can be required only through contract, is what is in view; this brings up the question regarding legal obligation to fulfillment following a change of will in the meantime – the weightiest problem faced by early "natural law."

§. 55. Contract as the Expression of Freedom and Faithfulness

Freedom lies in the *essence of the person*, providing on the one hand the possibility of devotion, disposal, on the other enlargement; therefore *immutability* lies also in that essence, in accordance with which the disposal now willed is also willed in all its consequences, taking them into account with the same certainty as with something already present. From this is derived the possibility not only of immediate grant (**datio**) but for agreement in a bond of will in accordance with which it is granted in future. This agreement is *contract*, that is, promise and acceptance as one element, and the immutability through which the arisen confidence (faith) in the future is fulfilled is *faithfulness* [Treue] (**fides**), that original characteristic of personality. Contract is based on freedom and faithfulness, but *its binding character is faithfulness.*[62] Faithfulness is the ethical <103> idea of all contractual bonds, both legal and moral.

---

contractual act, but with regard to marriage itself, which is no contract, they have this only in restricted measure.

[62]Should one, as do most natural-law teachers since Kant, e.g. Gros (*Textbook of Natural Law* [Lehrbuch des Naturrechts]), derive the obligatory nature of contract [Vertrag] simply from freedom ("the possibility of any causality"), then one can deduce the possibility of present conveyance and performance but not future commitment. The latter lies not in freedom but in immutability and faithfulness, as Kant himself rightly recognizes. At any rate, however, *freedom* in its true significance and *faithfulness* are concepts which mutually postulate each other, namely the divergent and indissoluble attributes of personality. Therefore it is *not freedom but personality* from which *contracts* are to be deduced. The claim that faithfulness is a mere moral and not legal concept is one of those fundamental errors of abstract natural law, denuding law of ethical ideas (cf. Book II [*Principles of Law*], §. 6).

Contract is therefore the means by which free beings by their wills and this certain immutability establish a bond between themselves that in itself and in terms of necessity would not otherwise exist between them. This contractual bond is essentially different from the bond of love: its commitment does not arise through one's making the well-being of another a goal of his own, but simply through the immutability of one's own will, the demonstration of the arisen faith. The former is a giving up of separate purposes and interests, the persons themselves becoming as one; the latter premises the preservation of the complete separation of purposes and interests, and exists because of this separate existence.

§. 56. Contract More than Mere Mutual Willingness

When in this manner contract fully freely and absolutely originally establishes a bond of obligation for those engaging in it, it still requires for this a basis in the makeup of the bond whereby it of itself and in general serves a higher order and necessity. This is therefore the point at which merely moral contracts diverge from those that are legally binding. For a contract to be binding only morally, it should serve an ethical, in which case a rational goal. Neither the unethical nor the purposeless contract has any moral obligation. For a contract to be fully binding legally, it must serve a legal goal, <104> that is, its content must have a relation that forms a necessary component of common life and thus the legal order, for example marriage, obligation in its various types, purchase, exchange, rent. The union of wills is therefore certainly the actual binding factor (by virtue of faithfulness) but even so it is only binding under the precondition of that content. Therefore, obligations in particular are by no means the mere product of human freedom and union of wills; they are already delineated spheres in the order of common life, the union of wills being only the means for particular persons to engage in these, albeit – because, being property* relations, they belong to the sphere of freedom – certainly also determining them more precisely in terms of content. The purpose of property* transactions require that such exist and requires that they exist only in accordance with the will of the parties involved; for this reason contract is the means for establishing them, and vice versa, the contract having them as content is legally binding. That the union of wills alone does not establish legal obligation is confirmed hereby, that a contract which does not have such a relation as its object is likewise not legally binding,[63] and inversely, obligations may also arise apart from contract simply in accordance with the need of property* transactions when persons are indicated for them in some other fashion, e.g. **condictio indebiti, negot. gestio.**

Accordingly the binding force of contract, in accordance with the idea of private law as a whole (see above, §. 1), is based on two aspects: the essence of the person (freedom and faithfulness) and the purpose (τέλος) of the bonds it is to establish. The former is the subjective and therefore also the formal aspect, the latter the objective aspect. Kant brought the **<105>** subjective aspect, freedom and faithfulness, into view.[64] Kant however did not express his entire philosophical viewpoint in a positive manner, as from the will, which, unchangeable in time, wills the same then as now, but in a negative manner, requiring the elimination of the interim and the act of fulfillment (the "empirical conditions"), and viewing that which is granted as "presently," that is, as timelessly acquired. But then the entire natural law theory, in accordance with its viewpoints, leaves completely out of consideration the objective aspect, the higher order of the institution in which contract intervenes, that it serves as means, which alone distinguishes the legally binding contract from the merely morally binding, entirely analogously to how in the case of property that theory only considers the power of the ("subjective") will and not the ("objective") purpose of the same unto satisfaction.[65] **<106>**

---

[63]For example, a teacher or artist convinces another who obtains a commission to refuse it with the promise that he too will refuse the next commission offered himself. This, in particular when no pecuniary interest is involved, is not a legally binding contract even though *the act* of agreement has all the criteria of a contract.

[64]*Doctrine of Law*, p. 100. He believes that he is deducing from freedom what in fact he deduces from faithfulness.

[65]The *canon law's* arrangement regarding contracts engaged *under oath* is based on an error similar to that of the natural-law theory. The canon law as well attached the power effectuating collective obligation only to the subjective elements – the *agreement of the parties*, here strengthened by the oath – which in actuality is likewise located in the objective elements – the *suitability* [Qualifikation] *of the transaction* – in that it of necessity must depend on them. Roman law, by contrast, had the proper principle that a shortcoming in the objective elements, which are the precondition of all effectiveness,

§. 57. Contracts are Classified According to Purpose

Obligations derived from contracts are distinguished into various classes in accordance with their *content*, the purpose (τέλος) they are to serve. Every other distinction, even that according to the viewpoint of unilaterality as opposed to reciprocity, is more or less externally formal. Accordingly, the following main classes manifest themselves as natural relations with similar legal consequences:

1. Contracts consisting in *unilateral performance:* stipulation of performances, forbearances, endowment and the like. They are the simplest affairs, they contain the least degree of obligation (no **culpa levis**); in fact, because they comprise pure forfeiture, the question arises as to whether they are meant to be serious and binding, and to what degree they are allowable.

2. Contracts consisting in the *surrender of a thing against its return:* **commodatum**, **precarium**, **depositum**, **mutuum** and all the Roman innominate contracts comprising the relinquishment of a thing (in **genere** or **specie**) against its future return. Here also belong contracts in which a thing is given on certain grounds or for certain goals, subject to return should the ground prove unfounded or the goal not be attained, and such an obligation is constituted – subject to conditions – by the surrender even when there is no contract, merely due to the inner requirement of the transaction (claims for restitution [Kondiktionen]).

In accordance with their nature these contracts and transactions are in a certain sense real contracts; they comprise the surrender of a thing, this constitutes them, prior to this the obligation cannot exist. The contract through which a **mutuum**, **depositum**, etc., is given differs completely and <107> concerns an entirely different commercial need; the commitment of the receiver to return is not derived from the **pactum de mutuo dando** but always follows solely from the **mutuum** itself, the surrender of money in prospect of its return.

Surrender also forms an essential component of the transaction when the object of the right is to receive back. For this reason it has the character of re-

---

cannot be rectified by the mere strengthening of the subjective elements contained in the oath.

ciprocity, usually the **actio contraria**,[66] although with the more secure commitment, thus granting of **culpa levis**, usually only on one side.

3. Contracts comprising the *exchange of performances and grants:* purchase, exchange, rent, and everything that takes place in the four forms (*do ut des,* etc. – for example insurance contracts), if the same thing is not to be returned otherwise.

These contracts are essentially reciprocal, commitment beginning simultaneously on both sides. In this case the question therefore arises firstly as to who is to begin the performance, then the **exceptio non adimpleti contractus**, and finally the consideration as to whether involuntary hindrance on the one side frees the other side from having to do his part – both sides gain here, since as a rule both practice **culpa levis**.

4. Contracts comprising a *business relation*: **mandatum** and **societas**, each in accordance with its various forms.

What is particular to these is that their content is not from the outset established by specific performances; instead it is interpersonal relations that do so, because often no preset performances are established as a specific object. And one entirely characteristic consideration arises in this case, the legal relation to *third parties,* in that the nature of a business relation entails <108> the one standing surety for another, the one acquiring for another.

The need to conduct business allows the obligation to arise even without an order – **negotiorum gestio**.

The requirement arising from common danger also founds a social relation (to save oneself by incurring losses [jettisoning cargo to avoid shipwreck], but then to share the damages equally) without contract – **lex Rhodia de jactu** (treated by the Romans, quite inappropriately, as a modification of lease).

5. *Contracts of chance* [Glücksvertrage]: games, gambling. The character of these is that no true need exists for them in commerce; the main question in their case therefore is to what degree they are obligatory at all.

6. Contracts that serve an already existing obligation, either to confirm, to secure, or to modify it – *accessory* contracts: **constitutum**, pledge, novation.

---

[66]That the **mutuum** forms an exception to this lies not so much in the kind of binding force as in the object, to wit, the abstract sum through which and to which no damage can occur.

These deal with the requisite of the preceding obligation and the relation to it of newly arising ones.[67]

§. 58. Kant's Classification

The Roman system of contract is based on the special requirements of their actionability in accordance with Roman law and therefore possesses no general truth, and in particular is totally inappropriate for our **<109>** current situation. Kant[68] substituted for this a philosophical system in which contracts are either:

1. *Endowment* contracts (under which the interest-free loan, the **commodatum**, the **depositum**), or
2. *Exchange* contracts (purchase, exchange, authorization [Mandat], etc.), or finally
3. *Completion* [Vervollständigungs-] contracts (pledge, surety).

This system also found favor with Hegel.[69] In terms of both of their fundamental concepts this is certainly correct, but it has the fault that in its implementation it is erected merely on the form of performance (the **datio**) rather than on the form of obligation (the **obligatio**) and therefore is viewed in terms of the unilateral or bilateral character of the *benefit* rather than of the *legal bond;* and in general the diversity of obligation, both among the contracting parties and vis-à-vis third parties (for example, between purchase and partnership), which juristically is precisely of the most significance, does not take its proper place in this system.

---

[67]In this systematization of contracts, Pfordten (*Treatises from the Laws of the Pandects* [Abhandl. aus dem Pandektenrechte], p. 302) has already followed me regarding Roman law, and in greater detail. Proceeding from Pfordten, this system has gone over to Koch's account of the Prussian law of obligation.

[68]*Doctrine of Law*, p. 120.

[69]*Philosophy of Law*, §. 80.

PART THREE: THE FAMILY

Introduction

§. 59. The Nature of the Family

<110> The family serves the general natural purpose of *maintaining the race* [Gattung]. It fulfills this in such a way that man receives the satisfaction of the bonds of descent and love, and that the human race (or [bez.] the people) as a whole maintains the *unity of essence* which enables it to build a spiritual personal kingdom (Book I [*Philosophical Foundations*], §. 24). In consequence of the creatureliness of man and the material basis of his existence, this extension indeed takes place as mere procreation, hence man here participates in the general arrangement of nature: the race unfolds in both of the sexes, and procreation is linked to their physical complement and union. Solely by virtue of the personality of man, these relationships, which in the lower reaches of creation only form momentary passing acts, with him becoming enduring bonds permeating all of existence. The complement of the sexes becomes a bond of imperishable full personal devotion, becomes *marriage;* procreation becomes an enduring bond between parents and children, namely *upbringing,* this being the free communication of one's own human essence in accordance with its ethical spiritual side, just as procreation is the natural communication of the same in accordance with the mere natural side. As such, in this spiritual ethi- <112> cal character, they are the *institution of the family.* As the bond of descent and therefore essential unity, the family is however the sphere of love in eminent degree – because love (the self feeling and willing in another) everywhere has as its foundation the unity of substance – and is, because it founds the same unity of essence for the human race, the primeval source and archetype of love for neighbor.

Consequently the family is firstly a bond of corporeal unity (union of the sexes – descent), but this corporeal unity is the bearer of a higher spiritual unity, firstly of *love,* then of *vocation* on behalf of the purpose of the family, each with differing specific determinacy (married love, respect for elders, etc.) for the different members according to the nature of the organic bond.

§. 60. The Relations of Family

Family relations are therefore initially these two: marriage and the bond between parents and children, namely *authority of upbringing.* Joined to these, however, is *inheritance*, the succession in the property* of the deceased, as that which stems from the family, the continuation of personality and the love based on it being the foundation of all transmission of property*. Furthermore, artificial imitations of the bonds of the natural family also make their appearance, *guardianship* as a substitute for paternal protection and, as the case may be [bez.], paternal upbringing, and the *servant relation* as a substitute for the subsistence grounded in one's own family on the one hand, and as an extension of one of the goals of the family, namely external satisfaction through the provision of aid by the members, on the other. These also lack the sanctity of the family bond proper. **<113>**

§. 61. The Uniqueness of the Family Relation

The family stands out among all institutions of the legal order by its *moral character*,[70] while according to its entire being it is the inner union and devotion of specific persons. Simply through the moral motive of its members it already has an objective existence as an enduring organic bond prior to any law (that is, prior to any formation by the whole) and its legal formation likewise has the idea of personal devotion as its determining principle, in the same way that other institutions have the idea of freedom, justice and the like. *Love* is here *graphically displayed.* Under other circumstances love affects the requirement of individual acts; here it affects the construction, the shape of relations, for example the community of station [Standesgemeinschaft] of the spouses, the indissolubility of

---

[70]Even in morality [Moral] (subjective ethical behavior [subjektiven Sittlichkeit]), it distinguishes itself as an exceptionally sanctified relation. The basis for this is simply that the family has such a great significance in the natural economy; and then that the bond to which one owes existence, the primordial bond, is the innermost source of all that is ethical – *piety*. This is the supreme virtue, firstly piety towards the Creator, then towards our physical procreator. All ethical behavior is based on piety, and when separated from this it is no longer true ethical behavior.

the marriage bond.[71] Precisely because of this, however, the family is by no means a *mere* moral relation, with only *limited* influence on the law, but is in its entirety no less a legal institution in its own right; it is the task of the community to maintain it in its ethical shape, and its same ethical idea, the idea which determines the life of the members in it, that is, the moral requirement, also determines its shape in the common life, that is, its legal order; however, the latter does not realize this idea in its <114> full content but only in its most external (negative) contours (Book II [*Principles of Law*], §. 6).

§. 62. The Public Character of the Family

The family is the center of human existence, the bond of individual life and common life, as it constitutes the complete satisfaction of the individual while also being the means by which the race, and thus the community, civil and religious, arises, both corporeally and ethically-spiritually (through upbringing). For this reason state and church intervene here in a twofold manner: not merely, in accordance with the above, to maintain the *ethical form of the family* within the common condition, but also for the sake of their *own civil and ecclesiastical interests.* Thus for example the restrictions on marriage between close relations, the prohibition of arbitrary divorce, the duty to provide material support, are maintained because they are in accordance with marriage in its ethical requirement; but when the state links marriage to evidence of livelihood, to the approval of one's military commander, in that case it is not considerations of the ethical order of marriage that are at question but purely civil ones. The family therefore indeed is a private-legal institution and as such is based on the principle of individual freedom, but it is everywhere likewise permeated with standards of public interest (**publici juris**), that is, both good mores (**boni mores**) and civil and ecclesiastical considerations, which restrict individual freedom.

§. 63. The Characteristics of the Family

Accordingly, the characteristics of the law of the family are as follows:
<115>

---

[71]Therefore the objection to the indissolubility of marriage, that it is merely morally and not legally commanded by reason or Christ, is inadmissible; for in the case of the family it is precisely the moral principle which is simultaneously the objectively form-giving principle also determining law.

1. It contains not only rights but above all *an ethical and organic shape,* and thus order, necessity; for example, the impermissibility of certain marriages or divorce, the requirement of a shared life, etc.

2. The rights contained in it have the *person* as their object, that is, the inner, enduring dependence which fills life, and not things or isolated performances. Only in consequence of this personal dependence do material [sächliche] claims (**dos, peculium**) and individual benefits (alimony, endowment) arise.

3. These rights are as a rule *reciprocal,* not unilateral, in which the one party is the subject, the other is the object, as in the case of obligation.

4. These rights are always likewise *duties,* even in juridical perspective, and thus as a rule are not disposable or alienable even in the case of mutual consent.

5. The law of the family, because of the family's concrete [plastisch] organic character, not only entails the rights and duties of family members but also a *common legal position* in the state, for example station, legal domicile, etc. Accordingly, family bonds, marriage and filiation, must also be established in public general terms; they should not, like property* claims, apply against one opponent [Gegner] and not another, or in one country and not another.[72]

§. 64. The Shortcomings of the Natural-Law Concept

The earlier natural law theory, rendered incapable by its subjective standpoint of comprehending an organic relationship such as is exemplified in the family, degraded this institu- <116> tion to the lowest level. According to Kant, marriage is a contract for the mutual exclusive use of sexual functions, while with Fichte, unrestricted sexual intermingling can legally take place. With Gros, from the standpoint of the law of reason marriage can be engaged for a limited or unlimited time, while polygamy and marriage with close relations is not to be ruled out. It is one of the most significant services to legal philosophy that Hegel brought the true significance of the family as an organic ethical institution to bear in that field.

[72] Already on these grounds the son of the Duke of Sussex, by way of a marriage declared null and void in England, was also denied the right of succession regarding Hannover.

Chapter 1: Marriage

§. 65. The Marriage Bond

<117> The essence of marriage is the *complementarity of the sexes.* The difference between the sexes, and their union as the origin of all new life, is a general law of physical nature. What significance this law has is not a problem of ethics but of natural philosophy.[73] So much is certain, that the sexes are the expression of two general principles of nature, a spiritual generative principle and a material receptive principle. The essence of human marriage, however, is the elevation of these principles and their bond in the *character of the personal.*

Natural *principles* here become personified inasmuch as gender difference is not merely a difference of physical constitution but also of ethical spiritual

---

[73]Compare Schelling, *On the Relation of the Real and the Ideal in Nature*, Hegel, *Encyclopedia,* Pt. I, §§. 220, 221, pt. II, §§. 367, 368. But who is of the opinion that the mystery of the sexes and procreation is revealed through these and similar expositions? I withdraw (and did so already in the second edition) my own deduction of marriage drawn in the first edition [*The Philosophy of Law According to the Historical Perspective: Volume II: Christian Doctrine of Law and State*]. Certainly the sense that was imputed to the incautious expression on p. 244 is not there; the entire conception is not any the less erroneous for that reason, since I placed in God Himself what only belongs to the creation. [Here is the passage in question: Private law comprehends these relationships: mutual recognition of personality, property*, and family. In them together man's god-like nature is fully revealed. For man's personality is the image of the divine, man's property* corresponds to the creation, family to God's eternal begetting. Together they form the kingdom of man. These relationships have their purpose and their fulfillment in themselves, they are not there, as the most recent philosophical school teaches, to serve the state, to be subsumed in it. God wills man and his well-being and perfection for man's sake, not for His own sake. But just as man should and can only be blessed and perfect when enveloped and fulfilled by God, so private law is encompassed and permeated by public law. State and church give him his sanction, they give him his norms, they finally give him guarantee and real protection. And the beginning of all private law, personality and legal capacity, have a place in public law, just as its conclusion and end, legal prosecution, returns to public law].

determinateness, through which in particular the gender characteristic of the woman becomes a specific virtue (modesty, maternal love, etc.) and the union of the sexes at the same time becomes a mutual impulse and support <118> of ethical spiritual essence. The *bond itself* however becomes personified in that it is elevated from the mere union of sexual functions into the union of persons for which the former only serves as substrate, thus into a bond not of mere momentary complementarity but of the persons concerned immutably becoming as one in feeling, knowledge, and will, into a *living union*.[74]

Marriage is therefore a bond of love, however *love of a specific sort*, namely complementarity, and so has as its final ground the insufficiency of one's own existence and therefore mutual need, physical and spiritual. Furthermore, it is for this reason not a primarily ethical relation but a *natural relation elevated into the ethical*, which for that reason has natural functions as its necessary basis. It is the transfiguration of nature, the culmination of the physical process of creation, just as the church, as the bond between Christ and the congregation out of which spiritual life springs, is the transfiguration of spiritual relations.

Accordingly, marriage is necessarily *monogamy*. Polygamy does not allow for such mutual devotion, such a thorough union of persons. As such, it is contrary to the essence of marriage and the right of the wife. In it, the husband cannot entirely devote himself to any of the wives, nor can the wife devote herself entirely to the husband, in that she cannot make his love for the other women into her own. Polygamy belongs to that stage of nature in which the full character of personality is lacking, and where on the other hand fertility is the main goal. Man sank back into this stage; "from the beginning it was not so." It therefore has no climatic justification, for the highest ethical relations of man cannot depend on climate; it only has world-historical license during earlier periods, in accordance with the leading of Provi- <119> dence. But precisely because of this, once true ethics is revealed it can no longer be regarded as having such. Justifiably did the church, upon converting polygamous peoples, always insist that the husband only maintain the first woman he married and separate from the others.

---

[74]Regarding the climax of nature with respect to the physical process of procreation, see Steffens, *Anthropology*, Vol. 2, pp. 214, 222, 234.

§. 66. The Elements of Marriage

Accordingly, the purpose (τέλος) of marriage is the *complete personal union* of both spouses upon the foundation of sexual union, to which procreation is linked. It therefore has a goal outside of itself, the begetting of children; but its first and sole independent goal lies in itself, the union of the spouses. Therefore the sterile marriage is no less binding and sanctified than the fertile one. The contrary viewpoint, which only recognizes the begetting of children as a positive goal and attributes to marriage itself only a negative goal, to guard against fornication, does not attribute to marriage its full right and ignores its positive goal, the life union of the spouses.[75] This may also be related to the exaggerated preference attached to celibacy, even apart from the spiritual order.

The juristic concept of marriage is the union of both sexes in a *complete life and legal community.* Accordingly, marriage is:

1. *Sexual community* (**conjunctio maris et feminae**). This is an essential aspect of marriage, although by virtue of the ethical nature of man it is only the *basis*, not the actual *content* of the same. For this reason, its later cessation (**imponentia superveniens**) does not impair the marriage, and even in the case of <120> its absence from the start, the consent of the spouses establishes a valid marriage, only without the effect of indissolubility marriage otherwise has; this latter might be termed a *naturally incomplete* marriage. Where however the union of sexes is lacking not only in individual instances but is impossible by general natural laws, there cannot and should not be a marriage.[76]

2. *Life community* (**consortium omnis vitae**), that is, the community of livelihood, household, domicile, sharing in prosperity and adversity. The ethical

---

[75]Extremely precisely expressed, e.g., *Tancred.*, Wund. edition, p. 61: "**Omne matrimonium aut causa suscipiendi prolis aut causa incontinentiae fit**" [Every marriage is either for the purpose of bearing children or for the purpose of incontinence]. This of course is based on isolated biblical texts, but these do not have the intention of comprehensively expressing the essence of marriage.

[76]This is the basis for the prohibition on the marriage of eunuchs. Roman law (Justinian, *Digest,* 23.3.39.1, de jure dot., also compare 1.7.9, J. de adopt.) understands it according to its logical aspect: the concept of marriage is lacking in it; canon law (Bull. magn. II. 634) does so according to its ethical aspect: sexual union without the natural purpose of marriage is sin and offense.

nature of human marriage only exists in this full life community. It therefore may not by way of exception (for a specific marriage) be forsaken, be relinquished by contract as with the physical basis, otherwise the concept of marriage is abolished.

3. *Legal community* (**juris communicatio**), that is, the community of rank, class, legal domicile, bequest to children. This legal community can by way of exception be lacking in important relations. So for example in our unequal marriage (misalliance, morganatic marriage). One may characterize this as a *civil incomplete marriage.*[77]

Marriage thus has a natural, an ethical, and a civil element. **<121>**

§. 67. The Role of Consent

As a bond of personal union, marriage can only be effected by the persons to be joined together, through their act of union, "consent." The motive behind this action (physical attraction, paternal authority, considerations of rank, personal attraction) is the business of subjective morality. Even so, part of the concept and legal order of marriage is that it is validly solemnized only through *free consent*. For all that, however, marriage itself is still *by no means a contract*, in that it stands, not under the spouses, but over them; it has a norm, content, and binding power not through them but through its own ethical nature, and since this is not based on their will, it cannot be abolished by them either. Not only the ethical but also the legal effects of marriage – common domicile, mutual aid, etc. – are far from being the effects of contract. They also undeniably come about according to the nature of marriage. Even the consent (consensus) upon which the *solemnization* of marriage is based is distinguished from other contracts in that it does not comprise individual provision under protection of separate interests but nothing less than a complete devotion of the person (see above, §. 54). By all means is the marriage ceremony subject to the juristic principles regarding consent (e.g., invalidity of coerced consent, etc.); but these

[77] Morganatic marriage etc. is falsely picked out (already from J. H. Böhmer onward) nearly universally as an example of **matrimonium ratum sed non legitimum** [see n. 89]. But it is just as much **legitimum**. Such an example is instead formed by marriage without parental consent in accordance with Roman Catholic canon law. Morganatic marriage is only **civiliter imperfectum**. In the same manner, one may designate *mixed marriage* as an *ecclesiastical incomplete* marriage.

principles nevertheless are essentially modified in consideration of the special nature of *this* consent and the nature of marriage itself (e.g., restricted effect of error, impermissibility of conditions, determination of time, etc.).

§. 68. The Role of Religion

Marriage is primarily and on the whole an *ethical* and *civil* <122> relation, not a religious one.[78] For it serves the purpose of maintaining humanity in itself to give it completed shape, not to bind men to God (Book I [*Philosophical Foundations*], §§. 24 and 25). To this end it stands primarily and on the whole under the ordering power of the state and not the church. For all that, it has no less a relation to religion and the church, and that is a dual one, a truly religious or *ritual* and a *dogmatic.*

1. Marriage has *firstly* a *religious*, i.e., *ritual character.*

Already the miracle of procreation embedded in nature produces the consciousness of the proximity and love of God to the creature, which explains the idolatry in pagan cults. In human marriage, the ethical miracle of full personal union of spouses is erected on the foundation of this natural miracle, which in Christian doctrine is even referred to as the symbol of the bond between Christ and the church. This, as true ethical union, as union in pure love, standing over natural inclination and its mutability, can however go on in no other manner than in the innermost focal point of human personality, in the bond with God, i.e., only owing to the spouses joining with each other in God and He with them in immediate proximity. Here, where that which is ethical involves the person himself and his entire devotion as a person, appears its inseparability from that which is religious (Book I [*Philosophical Foundations*], §. 24). This proximity of God and the human need for God's blessing are therefore that which lends marriage its religious character. Pursuant to this, it is also to be solemnized by <123> the church and under its blessing and not through the spouses alone or merely

---

[78] The description of marriage as a "*civil* relationship" has absolutely nothing in common with its description as a "*contractual* relationship." The civil order, and in particular the ethical order upon which it is based, entails requirements regarding the will and the agreement of parties in the same degree as does the religious order. This is quite often confused, however, especially by Catholic writers, who then oppose the *contractual* character instead of the *civil* character to the ecclesiastical character of marriage (the sacrament).

by the civil ruling authority (civil marriage). With a mere civil marriage, then, no religious sentiment is actually assuaged or satisfied, and already from the first ages of Christianity the ecclesiastical union was considered to be a requirement of a true marriage ceremony.

For all that, however, marriage is still not in any way a *sacrament*. For it is not the means of bringing the spouses closer to God, to augment their religiosity, thus not a *means for the benefit of religion*, but vice versa, religion (the bond with God) is here the means to fulfilling and transfiguring the human relation. The divergence of the two churches here is based admittedly in the first place on a discrepancy of the concepts one attaches to the word "sacrament." The Catholics label as sacrament every visible relation to which an invisible divine grace attaches, while the Protestants only label those institutions sacraments which serve as signs and seals of the redemption purposes of the new covenant. To this degree it is only a verbal dispute. But the combination of marriage with baptism and the Lord's Supper indicates that in consequence of that concept marriage is conceived not as a *human relation in need of grace* and assured of grace, but is itself a *means of grace*, is conceived as a relation aimed at religion and redemption.[79] This conception has significant practical consequences. One of these is the strengthening of the indissolubility, without exception, of the bond; for indissolubility by all means exists entirely independently of the concept of the sacrament, is based upon entirely different biblical texts and even is historically more ancient, but <124> it is confirmed by it, in that a sacrament as indelible sign (**signum indelebile**) may sometimes be repeated but cannot be abolished. A further consequence is the maintenance of marriages which otherwise would have to be considered null and void (e.g., by error regarding the pregnancy of the bride). Finally however and mainly, the claim to *exclusive jurisdiction of the church* regarding the *validity* of the marriage is based primarily on this conception. For if marriage truly is a means of grace in this sense, like baptism and the Lord's Supper, it is entirely in accordance herewith that only the church and by

[79] In this therefore the opposition between Protestant and Catholic doctrine by no means consists in Protestants only recognizing "the *natural* sanctity and divine *consecration* of the married state," as Walter (*Textbook of Canon Law*, §. 288) represents it. The *divine foundation* of marriage is also taught by Protestants.

no means the state can judge and determine regarding the requirements and the existence, that is, the efficacy of it.

2. *Secondly*, marriage also has a *dogmatic character*.

Marriage is the primeval relation of human existence, more ancient than any civil order, even more ancient according to our Christian faith than the limitations of the earthly condition, that is to say, established by God in paradise. But from the beginning it had inviolable divinely sanctioned laws. Now that man finds himself outside of God, consciousness of these commands is yet maintained only in the church, as the conserver of the immediate divine revelation.[80] For this reason, although the church in the Christian state is not the lawgiver regarding marriage such that the legal arrangement must issue from it and be validated in civil life by its authority – this is the affair of the state – even so, what the church attests to be such unchangeable divine law (**jus divinum**) and maintains as such within its ambit, is the insuperable norm and limit for the legislation of the Christian state.

Besides, beyond these laws as divinely attested it certainly befits the church that it, by virtue of its power of educa- **<125>** tion, itself issues directives regarding the validity and permissibility of marriage. But that which the church in this latter capacity, and thus according to its own human insight, arranges (e.g., the **forma Tridentini**) it cannot proclaim as an inviolable rule vis-à-vis the state. Accordingly, the state should not declare valid those marriages which the church by **jus divinum** (dogmatically) declares invalid, but in its legislation it may ignore hindrances that it considers dispensable (e.g., the fourth degree of consanguinity); concessions which the church in its judgment wishes to make and in general may make, the state may unconditionally require of the church (e.g., allowance of the Tridentine form, unconditional provision of assistance or proclamation, etc., regarding mixed marriages). All of this it may do lawfully. Whether it acts wisely in this is another question, which can only be answered in each individual case.

Conversely, the church may not refuse the arrangements regarding the validity of marriage made by the state from ethical and civil considerations where

---

[80]It is true that the church itself in this regard diverges or vacillates within itself. But the essential ethical form of marriage is everywhere preserved in it, and is nowhere to be found outside of it.

they do not conflict with that divine law. As everyone knows, a great dispute is taking place in the Catholic church regarding this issue. The Curia does not concede any effect regarding ecclesiastical validity to regulations concerning the validity of marriage established by the secular ruling authority (e.g., requirement of parental or governmental/royal consent), since marriage, it being a sacrament, comes only under its jurisdiction. A more moderate party (Gallican) vindicates the right of the state to establish such regulations with ecclesiastical effect on the grounds that the civil contract indirectly is material for the sacrament, because where the civil contract is invalid (which the Curia does not dispute) the sacrament likewise does not extend.[81] In favor of the Curia, **<126>** this has been countered especially by Walter, that "the substance of the sacrament is the *natural* and not the civil contract," thus in judgment of the sacrament the positive arrangements of the state cannot receive any consideration. This argumentation, upon which the entire decision in the final analysis depends, evidently presupposes the principle that everywhere where the natural elements of the marriage contract, consent and in any case consummation, are present, and a divine prohibition does not exist, there the sacrament irrefutably steps in. But this principle refutes the Curia's own proceedings, in that *it itself issues human-positive arrangements* apart from which those natural elements would have no effect, thus especially the entire Tridentine form (**parochus ordinarius, duo testes**). If it is no divine commandment that each naturally concluded marriage of necessity be a sacrament, but rather the church can in human wisdom, for the sake of praiseworthy order, establish conditions of sacraments, such as the

[81]Most clearly in Héricourt, *The Ecclesiastical Laws of France,* P. III c. 5 art. 2: "Comme le sacrement de mariage a pour fondement le consentement mutuel des parties — — — ce contrat est en même temps civil et spirituel. D'où il faut conclure, que les souverains peuvent mettre des empêchements au mariage, non pas en donnant atteinte directement au sacrement; mais en déclarant nul le contrat civil, *sans lequel il ne peut y avoir de sacrement*" [As the sacrament of marriage is founded on the mutual consent of the parties, this contract is both civil and spiritual. From this it must be concluded that sovereigns can impede marriage, not by directly undermining the sacrament, but by declaring the civil contract null and void, without which there can be no sacrament]. In the same manner in Theiner: "Variae doctor. cathol. opinion. de jure statuend. etc." in extensive implementation, and in many others.

presence of two witnesses, then there is no ground why it should not concede this to the state as well.[82] Instead, therefore, the material of the sacrament is the natural and *at the same time ethically permissible* marriage contract. Ethically permissible it is <127> not, however, where a well-proportioned civil or ecclesiastical regulation runs counter to it.[83]

Where however, as in the German Lutheran countries, church government is joined with the state power in the princes, thus where a separate church order is lacking, just for that reason the church there is to be accorded a concurrency with the state, at least if the state wishes to answer to its Christian character. Even at the present time, where Protestant marriage laws no longer form part of the church order but are promulgated in the civil code, they nonetheless ought to be enacted with the prior attestation of the church (approval of the synods, consistories, faculties, and the like). Should in the meantime the prevailing condition of public mores and opinion demand some other arrangement, then it ought to be possible for the church to make a statement for itself regarding which marriages it attests to be permissible or otherwise in accordance with the divine Word, and in no way may an unconditional sanction be required from the church, viz. [bez.] its servants, for mere state laws. The prince, in our consti-

---

[82]Already prior to the Council of Trent, the church in this respect could be opposed in its extension of the prohibition of marriage to degrees not divinely prohibited. Should the church through such a positive arrangement hinder the admittance of the sacrament, where after all the natural contract of marriage was present and no divine law opposed, why could not the state do this as well, through positive arrangement, e.g., that parental consent be required?

[83] According to the confession of the early church, marriage concluded by sons [Haussöhne] or slaves without the consent of the father or master was not a marriage but a "**fornicatio**," therefore also no sacrament; should not the same hold true for marriages concluded by subjects against the laws of their ruling authority? However, neither the state nor the church should lightly establish such requirements which do not lie in general natural ethical principles but are of a mere positive-legal character (e.g., approval of a superior for someone in the military, of the sovereign for members of princely households), as disuniting impediments to marriage. They should restrict positive-legal disuniting impediments to marriage primarily to the form of public composition, through which in fact all other considerations most certainly can be preserved.

tution the organ also of the church for its binding statements and regulations, currently issues no statements and regulations anymore as organ of the church; for this he must have consulted the church itself (consistories, synods, etc.); instead, <128> he issues these merely as legislator of the state. Thus, in this matter the church in actuality has had its mouth shut; it has been made impossible for it to issue any regulation, in fact any guidance for its members.

In the same manner as with legislation and on the same grounds, *jurisdiction* over affairs of marriage is primarily and with legal effect a matter for the state. The consequence of the sacrament concept certainly leads to the conclusion that only the church can judge regarding the invalidity of marriage or divorce. But the true nature of marriage as a likewise religious relation does not remove it from civil jurisdiction but only requires that this religious dimension be protected. One such concerns the religious influence on the spouses, in the antecedent spiritual admonition and attempt at reconciliation; another concerns the ecclesiastical soundness of the verdict in the mixed courts: consistories, contemporary Württemberg marriage courts, etc. With respect to this latter, the Christian or [bez.] denominational [konfessionelle] confession of the judge can serve if need be as sufficient guarantee, when for the rest the laws themselves agree with the doctrine of the church. Beyond this, the church's disciplinary maintenance of the religious commandments regarding marriage and pastoral influence and discipline can never be taken away by the jurisdiction of the state. It is only the *legal* consequence which must be enforced by the secular jurisdiction. However, it comports with the sanctity of the marriage bond and the dignity of the publicly recognized church for the state to vest ecclesiastical courts with its authority to this end.

§. 69. The Role of the Civil Order

As long as the church was persecuted by the state, conflict over legislation regarding marriage did not yet arise. <129> Both institutions pursued their separate paths. The secular power, as is self-evident, had no regard for the church, and the church maintained in its sphere its ethical commands regarding marriage without concern for secular legislation, through ecclesiastical means, penance and excommunication. Even after the Byzantine empire assumed the Christian confession, no essential change took place in this, as would have been expected. The clear awareness regarding the connection of state and church was lacking, the malleability for shaping the national condition as yet lacked the

Christian principle. It therefore took quite some time before the Christian principles of marriage passed into *legislation* in any degree at all; the church strove after this, and rightly so, but without success.[84] So for example divorce by mutual agreement and by reason of barrenness of the wife were only abolished by Justinian in a later ordinance, and divorce for imprisonment not at all. The legislative *authority* in marriage matters was however simply and indisputably vested in the emperor. Even the ordinances of Theodosius and Justinian, who bore true Christian sentiment, were issued through pure imperial omnipotence and discretion, apart from any cooperation of the church.

By contrast, in the Western kingdoms the Roman church asserted legislation and jurisdiction over marriage, and that by divine authorization. Not merely the principles, which it attested as divine regulations, but also its own human arbitrary ordinances had unconditional validity, and conversely the secular power issued no command regarding the validity of mar- **<130>** riage. But more than this: the entire legal order and civil validity of the bond of marriage rested exclusively and immediately on its *authority;* the secular ruling authority had no share in this but was simply directed to maintain and execute by means of its external power (**brachium saeculare**) what the church established or judicially decided.

The resistance of the Reformers was directed against this as well as against the content of then-existing ecclesiastical legislation. It is by no means the divine order for the church to have exclusive jurisdiction over affairs of marriage; the secular ruling authority has jurisdiction just as well, and in fact the latter has the duty to issue marriage statutes when the church proceeds against God's Word and Christian freedom, as was actually the case regarding divorce, spiritual kinship,[85] etc. It never came into the Reformers' minds, however, to proclaim marriage to be purely a secular affair, standing only under civil considerations and

---

[84]Here belongs in particular the decision of the African synod (c. 4. C. 32 qu. 7). The "**in qua causa legem imperialem petendam promulgari**" [an imperial law was requested to be promulgated in which case] could not possibly have the meaning, as Eichhorn (*Ecclesiastical Law*, p. 299) states it, of getting the imperial law to recognize ecclesiastical penance, because that would not have occurred to the synod, but rather the meaning of getting the ecclesiastical law of marriage to be sanctioned civilly.

[85][Marriage hindrance centering on the godparent relationship.]

not under religious commands, or that the testimony of the church regarding divine laws of marriage is not a binding norm for the legislation of the state, or that jurisdiction is more appropriately exercised by the secular than the spiritual authority. In fact, the contrary is emphatically the case.[86] To state expressly that there is an immutable commandment of God for marriage would not have occurred to them, since at that time it was self-evident; but in all their discussions and even in their exhortations to the princes to act against Catholic statutes, they actually invoke a divine command. Thus, even when Luther in many of his private expressions declares marriage to be a "secular affair" the connection and the perspective thereof was for the clergy not to "govern" directly therein but for that which in <131> reality stands under human discretion (**humani juris**), and at the same time until then was largely conducted by the church, be left to the secular authorities or the mores of the country, such as, e.g., whether at nuptials one should attend services once or twice, how often public notice of the upcoming marriage is to be given.[87] On the other hand, Luther is far from leaving the decision as to whether the innocent party is free to remarry after divorce, or whether one may "repudiate his wife due to leprosy or bad breath," to the discretion of the secular ruling authority separated from the church. Rather, in this regard he himself gave inviolable ecclesiastical testimonial.[88] Regarding marriage courts, however, the Reformers spoke the same principle under all conditions, that they should be ecclesiastical and not secular courts, and held the consistories to be the most expedient. Thus the sense of the Reformers is neither

---

[86] Compare my *The Church Constitution According to the Doctrine and Law of Protestants*, 1st ed., p. 74.

[87] Luther's *Complete Writings,* X. 854. "The saying goes, 'as many countries, as many customs.' Thus, since the marriage ceremony and the married state are a *secular affair*, our ministers and sextons have nothing in that regard to order or *govern*, but to leave to each city and country its usage and custom as they are. Some bring the bride twice to the church, both in the evening and in the morning, some only once, some announce and invite from the pulpit two or three weeks prior. I allow the lords and councils to create and make such-like as they wish, it is none of my concern. But if it is desired of us that we bless them before the church or in the church, or pray over them, or marry them, we are obligated to do that."

[88] Luther's *Complete Writings,* X. 797.

to separate the content of marriage law from the doctrines of faith and testimonies of the church, nor to exclude ecclesiastical cooperation in its arrangement and upholding, but only the restoration of the state in that supreme and sole legal authority which befits it in that matter, and the freedom to make human praiseworthy ordinances beyond the divine commandments, which up until then the church had presumed to do. **<132>**

This intention is also confirmed by subsequent actual arrangement in Protestant countries, which undeniably springs from it. This is based on the connection of secular and ecclesiastical power in the person of the sovereign, which eliminated the conflict[89]; but even so, marriage was predominantly treated as an affair of the church, the confession of faith was considered its supreme guide, its arrangement was issued by the church government, effected in the church ordinances, not in the national statutes, thereby on the advice of the ecclesiastical organs since the consistories had jurisdiction.

Only since the time of Thomasius did the viewpoint gain ground, partly from misunderstanding the Reformers, that marriage is a secular matter and as such solely the responsibility of the civil ruling authority. A similar development has proceeded in the Catholic countries since the Josephine era.[90] Finally, the

---

[89]Accordingly, a division into **matrimonium ratum** [answering to ecclesiastical requirements] and **legitimum** [answering to secular legal provisions] formally is not possible. Nevertheless, materially it remains of importance. For example, there are now countless marriages which are **matrimonia legitima** and yet not **matrimonia rata** according to the principles of the Protestant church. Marriages which are not **matrimonia legitima** and yet **rata** do not exist because the Protestant church does not grant ecclesiastical sanction to a civilly inadmissible marriage. But the concept of a **matrimonium non legitimum** and yet **ratum** could become applicable in the case of the state not merely setting requirements for the validity of marriage but also mandating absolute prohibitions on marriage, in particular to the extent that they abolish those of Christian freedom as advocated by Protestants, for example, when marriage is declared by state law to be indissoluble in terms of the marriage bond even for Protestants, as was done in France, or marriage is denied to priests who have gone over to the Protestant church, etc. J. H. Böhmer and others therefore have no grounds for describing this distinction as something purely Catholic, which Protestants must abandon.

[90][A reference to the reign of Emperor Joseph of Austria (1780-1790).]

newer philosophic doctrine conceives of marriage as a purely civil relation, in fact as a mere contractual relation. Thus in recent times in many states the conversion has come not only in *formal* perspective, that the determinations regard- <133> ing the marriage bond form part of the civil code and fall under the jurisdiction of the civil courts – against which, under the modifications indicated in §. 68, nothing can be objected – but in *material* perspective as well, that legislation has been entirely detached from the Christian teaching regarding marriage.[91]

The three most recent major codes of law, the Austrian, Prussian and French, have the *formal* principle in common that legislation and jurisdiction in matrimonial matters emanate solely from the state. In their *material* principle, however, they are essentially different. The Austrian has the principle of the indissoluble *union* of church and state, i.e. of ecclesiastical and civil marriage, the other two equally, but to different degrees, that of *separation*, which is why the former is calculated for Catholics and contains a special arrangement for Protestants, whereas the latter are merely given as such for all subjects without any consideration of confession. The *Austrian civil code* vests all marriage legislation and jurisdiction exclusively in the sovereign and, in particular, in the secular courts. Indeed, it goes so far as to declare its civil legislation binding *in foro interno*, i.e. with regard to the sacrament, and therefore to compel the clergy to consecrate, dispense and so on. But for this it also follows Catholic dogma in its content, in such a way that it strictly complies with the provisions which the Roman Church declares to be a *jus divinum*, e.g. the non-dispensable degrees of kinship, indissolubility. On the other hand, it does not recognize the merely human orders of the Church as binding, abolishes, for example, the dispensable diriment impediments as well as in many cases the merely impedient impediments and itself sets requirements for the validity of the marriage (diriment impediments), e.g. consent of parents, guardians, military leaders. It thus subjects ecclesiastical ministers and authorities to secular jurisdiction, but never forces them to act contrary to the faith of the Church, because that which is the faith of the Church is its guide.

---

[91] [The following three paragraphs were not included in the first edition of this translation.]

The *Prussian civil code*, on the other hand, takes no account at all of the church in its content, and therefore contains a number of provisions that contradict the faith of Protestants no less than that of Catholics, e.g. divorce on the grounds of dislike or mutual consent, on the grounds of disgusting illness, etc. In contradiction to this, however, it makes the involvement of the church, the marriage ceremony, a condition of marriage. This leads to the alternative: either the clergy is forced to marry contrary to what it recognizes as a *divine* prohibition, which is violation of conscience, or the clergy is allowed to follow its conscience, in which case the code is illusory. In relation to Catholics, the latter has already been implemented by law. Obviously, however, this is not consistent with the fact that the state, through its code of law, allows Catholic subjects a number of marriages that are not permitted by the church, from the state's point of view guarantees them to a certain extent; on the other hand, by requiring the marriage ceremony while releasing the priest from the law, it renders them virtually impossible again. But the reprehensible thing lies in the former provision. If the Protestant clergy, as it can demand, were now also to be granted the same, which can hardly be withheld any longer, the entire legislation would be without effect.

The *French Code* consistently implements the separation of the secular and the spiritual which the Prussian Territorial Law contains only incompletely, and therefore does not, like the latter, arrive at that alternative. In the content of its provisions, it likewise takes no account of religious statutes (although it does not permit such arbitrary divorces as Prussian law); however, neither does it require marriage ceremonies, but allows marriage to be solemnized by the civil authorities – *civil marriage*.

This separation of the secular and the spiritual everywhere had the same defect: it placed a dichotomy between state and church, which were harmoniously to foster the human race, in that the state would sanction marriages which the members of one of the officially recognized churches solemnized under the faith and commandments of that church. It is the declaration of the profanation of marriage and therefore weakens, to the degree that it has an effect, the consciousness of marriage's sanctity and God-given ordinances. It leads to marriage legislation of lesser strictness and purity. The French civil code is still strict to a degree, in consequence of Catholic custom and the reaction against the previous period of general dissolution; but it is by no means derived from pure principles appropriate to the ethical essence of marriage; above all, the marriage statutes of the Prussian civil code run to the extreme opposite of strictness and purity. The expected advantage, that civil marriage would eliminate the conflict between church and state and thus a great deal of confusion, is only apparent. For the conflict then shifts to another area, between the church and its members, which excommunicates them in the absence of state intervention, and between the two confessions. This conflict would be much more appropriately and fundamentally eliminated if the civil legislation were brought into closer correspondence with the ecclesiastical, than when it is separated from it. The actual motivation behind civil marriage does not however lie in such **<134>** advantages, but simply in Christianity being recognized not as the public faith of the nation and the authoritative power in the state, but merely as a private conviction of individuals, and indeed here alone lies the decision for ecclesiastical or civil marriage. The civil solemnization of marriage (not civil marriage in general) is appropriate as an exception, to wit, in relation to sects which the state tolerates, but the clergy of which cannot be extended public authority to solemnize valid marriages.[92]

---

[92]Civil marriage as introduced in England by the legislation of William IV and Queen Victoria is something entirely different from civil marriage in the sense of the Continent. The occasion and goal there was only the liberation of dissenters from being forced to have their marriages solemnized by the state church. The civil character therefore extends only to the solemnization of marriage and not to the marriage laws and jurisdiction; these have retained their ancient Christian character, and even the civil solemnization of marriage does not consist in the marriage being solemnized through a civil act of a civil servant – this only takes place through the highest registering official (superintendent registrar) in London, who certainly is only seldom approached – but through dissenting clerics through religious rites answering to their congregation, albeit concluded in the presence of secular officials (registrars) along with two witnesses, and certified by them. Beyond this, the clerics of the state church and the religious communities which previously were hereto entitled (Jews and Quakers) do not even require civil participation, but as yet solemnize marriage merely through the religious act, in legally valid fashion. With regard to lists of marriages, as with those of baptisms (births) and deaths, the clergy of the state church, where they still draw up these lists, is required

§. 70. Restriction on Marriage: Near Relationship

The true restriction of marriage is *near relationship,* which general human sentiment testifies has a necessary ground in the ethical order. The point is to declare the following: <135>

Near relationship, in particular parental, and marriage are relationships separated by God in nature. As the physical bond is specific to each, so is the bond of love. They therefore cannot be mixed with each other. The primary ethical bonds can be amassed in infinity, e.g., love of neighbor, friendship, gratitude, teacher and student; but the natural organic relations with their specific significance are exclusive. The Old Testament puts it like this: "Thou shalt not sow your fields with two seeds, shalt not weave wool and linen together," etc., which expresses this thought symbolically: Thou shalt not move the boundaries set by God in nature. This is the meaning of our deep ethical revulsion (**horror naturae**) for incest.

Marriage, firstly considered for its own sake, is a bond of necessitous, fulfillment-seeking, yearning love (§. 59). Even aside from all physical aspects, which do in fact belong to its essence, it is, in its purest spiritual relationships, based on a need for completion, is only satisfied through reciprocation, and seeks the continuous effectuation thereof. By contrast, the parent-child relationship above all is a bond of elevated, solicitous love which is absolutely in no need (Godlike), on the one hand, and is of the most reverential awe on the other. This bond is completely destroyed and desecrated through the bond of equal need of fulfillment. Marriage between parents and children is therefore an absolute abomination.[93] But the bond between siblings is an *organic* bond of love *without need;* it has the organic purpose of *being* the family, of realizing its goal, not of *generating* the family, of being a means for it. The realized goal of the family is however a

---

to send them to the same supreme civil servant in London, and thus in this respect has been made into a subordinate civil servant. However, such lists are not, as is marriage, an ecclesiastical but a civil affair. Accordingly, marriage in England has retained its ecclesiastical character as it was, even in the most recent legislation; this legislation, in contrast with that on the Continent has a declaration of secularity and the greater relaxation of marriage laws neither as motive nor as consequence.

[93]Even the opinion that without her incest the human race would die out does not for that reason excuse Lot's daughter.

closed circle of those who are bound to each other in communal love for the parents, through equal, non-self-interested, **<136>** non-yearning love amongst each other.[94]

Another motive arises from the significance of marriage to the entirety of the human race, specifically the nation [bez. des Volks]. Within this relationship, marriage has the purpose of supplementing familial individualities [Familieindividualitäten], in so doing generating individualities and effecting a crossing of the human race. Therefore sexual love is already naturally contingent upon the attraction of a different familial individuality (Hegel), and marriage should go outside the family so as to expand the bond of love (Augustine). Accordingly, marriage within the family is an egotistical (narcissistic) involution of the same upon itself, similar to the connection of the same sex. Thus, since more families exist, the bonds separate themselves sharply: marriage as the means to establish the family, which must go outside of itself; the sibling bond as established family, the goal of which is to remain unmixed [unvermischt].

Accordingly, the actual original relationships of incest are those between parents and children and between siblings, each in turn in various manners and degrees.[95] From this point, however, extension takes place according to analogy, once to the relation of "**respectus parentelae**" (uncle and aunt), then to in-laws, since the closest **<137>** bonds, to wit, the bonds of piety, become common to the married couple. For in-laws in direct line, the prohibition on marriage is *unconditionally* based in the nature of the bond. But it is also *appropriate* for the collateral line of the first degree as well (marriage with a brother's widow, the

---

[94]The exception that we must suppose for the children of the first human pair is justified in that they represented not merely the family but at the same time the race. In that case, both aspects are pushed together in the bud, only later to come to separate development. Contrary to this, in terms of the natural order the relation between parents and children can never represent the race.

[95]Even one who rejects the revealed doctrine of the single progenitor of the human race at least cannot take away that, in the case of civilized people, sibling marriage by way of exception, at least between half-brothers and sisters, is recognized (e.g., Abraham, Cimon), but never marriage with parents. Once the race has been extended, both are certainly in the same way and absolutely reprehensible, albeit not in the same way in terms of the idea, thus from the beginning.

sister of the deceased wife), simply to foster the innocence and simplicity of the sibling bond among relatives by marriage. By contrast, that principle of full communication of bonds of mutual relationship derived from the becoming-one-flesh of the two spouses, and according to which the prohibition consequently extends itself everywhere as far as the relationship, even to the in-laws of the other spouses and again the in-law of a spouse previously deceased (relation of marriage of the "second" and "third kind") is to be rejected. Factually, the church has also abandoned this principle. Yet another extension exists for children of siblings in terms of the viewpoint of expanding the bond of love, thus not allowing the family to shut itself up in itself[96]; but further extension beyond children of siblings is exaggeration.

With these extensions, the institution of *dispensation* is appropriate, within limits and properly administered. The objection made to this, that a marriage is either immoral and therefore not amenable to dispensation, or it is not immoral and hence in no need of dispensation, is only apparent. In fact, in accordance with the former consideration it is often only *in general undesirable* for marriages to be contracted among such relatives, that they become customary, <138> without that particular marriage being *immoral in itself*, in fact in special cases it could even be desirable and good. Dispensation comes to the aid of such cases. Chiefly, however, the requirement of dispensation maintains the awareness that as general custom such marriages are not the proper social condition. Even so, dispensation is not to take place in relations of marriage of direct descent, nor perhaps, or at least only in the rarest cases, for marriage with one's aunt. Whether it is not more appropriate that many of these marriages subject to dispensation, e.g., among children of siblings, be made lawful, leaving it to

---

[96] The prohibition of marriage among children of siblings is falsely attributed to the *principle of enclosure* borrowed from rabbinical sources (**"vicinitas gradus prohibiti," "vallum et sepimentum legis divinae"** – Augustine, Melanchthon, Gerhard). It is based on the deeper and truer ground expressed by Augustine, for which reason these marriages were also objectionable to the Romans. Only the wider extension belongs to this, in no way grounded, principle of enclosure.

mores to keep them from becoming too frequent, cannot be subject to any unconditional rule, it depending on the sense of the times.[97] **<139>**

In our view, therefore, the prohibition of marriage has its basis in *the specific nature of the particular organic family ties*, parental and fraternal, and therefore extends only to them and to some equally specific ones which are analogous to them. The church in the Middle Ages, however, followed an essentially different

---

[97]With regard to the prohibition on marriage in general, the *Mosaic law* is by no means to be considered a *particular Jewish* law of God ("**lex positiva**"), as is usually the case in the Protestant church since Michaelis. For it is not concerned with ceremonies, but with an ethical relation; in particular, that the Jews should fall under stricter rules in this regard than Christians runs contrary to the entire relation of the Old and New Covenants, such as is shown e.g. in the command regarding divorce and polygamy. The early church therefore rightly recognized that these rules should rather be more strict than more lax, thus e.g. the prohibition of marriage among children of siblings, as already observed by the Romans. By contrast, the viewpoint held by the earlier Protestant church, and which was also maintained by Catholic theological faculties in Europe in the case of Henry VIII in opposition to the Pope, that the Mosaic law is an *indispensable* divine command, is erroneous. This is already shown in the dispensation of the Levirate marriage expressed in the law itself. In that the Old Testament does not know of dispensation, those relations which are absolutely illicit are left undistinguished from those which are not to constitute regular mores. The standpoint of the Catholic church in this is more true and free than the former rationalistic and the latter orthodox standpoints. For the rest, it is merely the prohibition on marriage with one's aunt and with the (not childless) widow of one's brother, which is the reason why one wishes to consider the Mosaic law as a mere Jewish law. But in those conditions of pure mores, these marriages did not exist as regular usage, in fact the former perhaps was entirely ruled out. It is no coincidence that the Mosaic law prohibits not in terms of descent and degree but according to particular ties. Marriage with one's aunt is less permissible than with one's uncle, because the relation of reverence is reversed; marriage with one's brother's widow is less permissible than with one's wife's sister, since in the latter case the woman already belonged to the man's family. This is because in marriage the wife enters into the family of the husband and not vice versa – a distinction which in ancient conditions (not only Jewish) certainly had greater significance, but which never entirely disappears. That Levirate marriage is a merely Jewish institution is self-evident.

view, misled by a misunderstanding of the Mosaic Law. It found the reason for the prohibition of marriage, without regard to the organization of the family and its particular vocational positions, to be *kinship* (consanguinity) *in general.* Accordingly, the prohibition of marriage has no limit other than that which is arbitrarily set for trivial reasons, such as the analogy of the seven ages of the world or the four humors in the human body. The boundless excess to which one has progressed is therefore not based on a merely quantitatively incorrect determination, but on an incorrect principle.[98]

In earlier times, one used to list a variety of grounds for the prohibition of incest, as for example Thomas Aquinas.[99] In more recent times, by contrast, the viewpoint (already listed by Aquinas) came to dominate, through the efforts of Michaelis, whereby the prohibition merely has the goal of hindering seduction which otherwise threatens among persons in such close contact. This goal, although certainly attained, cannot be the ground of the prohibition; a mere rule of prudence cannot bring about such a deep shudder. The concurrence of the prohibition of marriage with the allowance for unveiled encounters is certainly a poor argument that the former of necessity derived from the latter rather than the reverse. Even the Augustinian explanation from the viewpoint of expanding the bond of love[100] is insufficient in itself in that it, at least in its expression, is

---

[98] [This paragraph was not included in the first edition of this translation.]

[99] Aquinas, *Summa theolog.* 2.2. qu. 154, art. 9. A good critical exposition in particular with regard to more recent viewpoints is contained in the *Evangelical Church Gazette* [Evangelische Kirchenzeitung], June 1840.

[100] "Habita est ratio rectissima caritatis, ut hominibus, quibus esset utilis atque honesta concordia, diversarum necessitudinum vinculis necterentur, nec unus in una multas haberet, sed singulae spargerentar in singulos" [The demands of charity are most perfectly satisfied by men uniting together in the bonds that the various ties of friendship require, so that they may live together in a useful and becoming amity; nor should one man have many relationships in one, but each should have one – in *De Civitate Dei,* ch. XV, 16]; furthermore the **multiplicatio amicorum** being disregarded. The *Evangelical Church Gazette* cited above maintains this to be the true explanation, for the reason that it justifies so conclusively the exception of the *first* siblings. Even so, in return it includes the shortcoming that according to it Lot's daughters – under the condition of the error that they alone were left – acted entirely properly.

only based on considerations of expediency. In that it completely abstracts from the specificity of the family tie, it leads logically to unlimited extension, as forthwith took place.

In that regard, Hegel[101] rightly postulated an absolute **<140>** ground, although he unjustifiably looks for this merely in the fact that marriage as the free devotion of both sexes should not be concluded in already familiar (naturally identical) circles, but calls for various mutually unfamiliar individualities which then first join with each other into a community. According to this explanation, marriage between mother and son is only reprehensible because each lacks the charm of novelty. The horror of incest is however not so much or not merely a feeling that it does not do marriage justice but rather that it violates bonds of relation and piety. Much more appropriate is therefore the ground proposed by Aquinas as primary, and lately by Nitzsch, as the actual ground, that man owes his parents (and in consequence those initially descending from those parents) reverence, that this reverence is contrary to fleshly commingling, which always entails a certain shame ("turpitudo"). But this ground is not completely understood should one merely recognize in it the physical expression of marriage, which one then characterizes as shame, and not rather the innermost essence of marriage, the incompatibility with the parental bond, etc. **<141>**

---

[101]*Philosophy of Law*, §. 168: "In that, furthermore, this in itself limitless peculiar personality is of both sexes from whose *free devotion* marriage is derived, it therefore must not be concluded within already naturally identical, self-known and familiar circles, in which individuals do not have a personality peculiar to themselves over against each other, but from separated families and originally distinct personality. Marriage among blood relatives is therefore contrary to the concept by which marriage is an *ethical act of freedom*, not a connection of immediate naturalness and its urge." Then: "confidentiality, acquaintance, the custom of shared action is not to come before marriage but is only to be found in it, which has that much higher value the richer it is and the more depth it has." There is furthermore something disconcerting in the fact that Hegel contrasts marriage as an ethical relation, merely because of its *voluntary* union, with kinship as a mere *natural urge*. One might just as well reverse this, and contrast kinship as mere ethical relation to marriage as a natural (because of its ongoing physical basis) relation.

§. 71. The Place of Property in Marriage

In accordance with freedom of disposition, which is the general principle of property*, goods relations among married couples are subject to contractual establishment across a broad sphere. These however find their limit in the fundamental purpose of the family. The law therefore only has to express which forms it recognizes and which, in cases of doubt, are natural.

Marriage has the purpose of uniting the spouses in complete life community, but it does not at all thereby eliminate independent personality. Accordingly, joint property* is to serve the marriage (i.e., to feed the family, raise the children, etc.) in common, and thus to come under the administration of the husband, providing security to the wife where necessary, but in no way coalescing into an undifferentiated mass. A community of use and appropriation, not of rights, is to come about. This is to extend beyond death, so that the surviving members, in particular the wife, is granted an inheritance or in any case a usufruct in greater or lesser extension depending on concurrent interests. German laws are determined by these proper principles.

Accordingly, the *marital community of goods* is by no means founded in the essence of marriage, even though it would seem so at first sight. Its justification instead lies in the requirements of certain estates, in particular the industrial and trading classes, in which property* is also the foundation of the trade, the contracting of debt is part of the regular livelihood, and both spouses customarily take part in the expansion of property* (acquisition) through capital or labor. It is therefore an institution answering only to these classes and not at all in general. By contrast, the *Roman dotal system* is <142> not natural in this matter in that it only applies a portion of the property* of the wife to the marriage (**ad matrimonii onera ferenda**), while the remainder of her property is assigned, as it were, to separate enjoyment outside the marriage.

§. 72. Divorce[102]

In accordance with its purpose as the complete personal union of the spouses, marriage is *indissoluble.* A sexual connection with prior intent of dissolution or

---

[102]Compare *Regarding the Current Shape of Marriage Law* (2nd edition, Berlin, 1842) [author: Otto von Gerlach], my speech concerning the Dobenek motion to restrict

with a condition thereto thus no longer falls under the concept of marriage. But neither may subsequent change of will and sentiment grant entitlement to dissolution, if marriage is to retain its ethical form. *Adultery* forms an exception. For it is not merely the absolute violation of the ethical bond of marriage but it also abolishes marriage's physical basis, sexual union (i.e., exclusive bondedness) among the spouses, and hence is factually and fully the destruction of the marriage. It is then the specific and therefore sole ground of divorce, declared as such in Christ's statement (Matthew 5, etc.). Accordingly, the objection made in recent times from a philosophical standpoint in the Protestant church (Klee), that adultery cannot be generically distinguished from other violations of marriage, is unfounded. The seal of nature is dissolved by adultery, under which the spouses to that point were agreed as "one flesh," which is true of no other violation. The Protestant church is also not the only one to treat that biblical statement regarding adultery as a unicum; the Catholic church like- **<143>** wise restricts the lifetime separation, which divorce represents for it, to the case of adultery, and only allows temporary separation for other violations, such as malicious desertion, attempt on the life of a spouse.[103]

If it is the true form of marriage and thus the goal of civilized, especially Christian peoples, that likewise in the legal order divorce occur only because of

divorce in the Bavarian parliamentary hearings [Ständeverhandlungen] of 1837 (supplementary volume, XII, p. 181); Puchta regarding the Prussian draft of a divorce law in *Leaflets for Questions of the Day* (I), Berlin 1843; Savigny, *Representation of the Reform Undertaken in the Prussian Divorce Laws*, Berlin 1844.

[103]That adultery by the wife entitled the husband to divorce but not vice versa is a viewpoint that asserted itself already in the early church. Nor did Justinian (nov. 117) recognize adultery by the husband as in and of itself sufficient grounds for divorce (**repudium**) for the wife, but only when joined with scandal (the husband maintains the concubine in the house or is encountered with her in public multiple times in the same city); the French civil code followed this. Even though adultery by the wife in itself degrades her much more than that by the husband does him, and beyond this renders uncertain relations of descent, still according to Christian acknowledgement adultery by the husband is likewise an absolute violation of the marriage bond, and the sexes stand equally entitled vis-à-vis each other, so that it is not justifiable to legally bind the wife to the marriage after the husband has broken it.

adultery, then the existing condition of mores, which cannot endure such strictness, nevertheless justifies *analogous extensions* of this ground of divorce, to wit, to other *far-reaching fault on the part of the other*, especially where this concerns the marriage bond itself. This is the situation in later Protestant consistorial practice. The older practice allowed no other ground for divorce than adultery and malicious desertion – which it also considered to be a biblical ground – in particular it did not allow serious abuse, lunacy, crime, etc.[104] Since the age of Thomasius and Stryck, however, this was expanded, and beyond these J. H. Böhmer attested as sufficient grounds the refusal of marital duty, intentional sterilization, attempt on the life of a spouse, and lifetime imprisonment or exile. The same standpoint dominates Justinian's legislation (Novel 117). It appears to us to correspond to the contemporary condition for civil legislation. **<144>**

A determinate boundary in terms of this viewpoint cannot be discerned. *Serious fault* however always remains the *insuperable precondition.*[105] Whether the church can agree to analogous extension of the biblical grounds for divorce and such forms of remarriage in the case of divorce is a question belonging to positive theology. The conception of marriage and adultery given here speaks against it, as does the authority of the church itself precisely in the times of deepest Christian earnestness. All the same, to grant such an expansion, not of course as a sanction but nevertheless as an allowance, does not require the church to evoke the separation of civil and ecclesiastical marriage, and it might perhaps thereby preserve the sanctity of the commandment through a form of marriage ceremony which announces the ideas that such a marriage is based not on complete endorsement but only on allowance, as was expressed in the older Protestant church upon every remarriage of the innocent party, even where it occurred due to adultery. And in such cases there was never any coercion put on the clergyman who refused to recognize a divorce on any other grounds than the biblical one. The church government has no authority to do that.

---

[104] Carpzov, *jurispr. consist.* def. 202. Lauterb. *colleg.* I. 24. tit. 2. §. 21.

[105] The decision of the Council of State as reported (p. 57) in the *Representation* cited earlier [n. 102], that "the judge is to determine whether the marriage relation has been broken in no lesser degree by the *offense* than through adultery or malicious abandonment," aptly expresses the principle.

By contrast, altogether contrary to the ethical essence of marriage is divorce due to *unilateral or mutual dissatisfaction, "insuperable enmity," "estrangement of minds,"* when such is not motivated by serious fault on the part of the other party but derived from other grounds (decline in attraction, change in natural affinity, discovered imperfections or even trivial faults in the other spouse, conflicting habits, needs, hobbies, etc.) <145> and above all, divorce from mere *mutual agreement.* No less in conflict with the ethical essence of marriage is divorce due to *accident without fault* by the other spouse, such as due to revolting disease, later impotence, etc. These are the two classes of grounds of divorce to be rejected out of hand.[106] With the first, one places the caprice of the spouses or their arbitrary feeling above the ethical bond of marriage, while with the second one sanctions the violation of its supreme requirement, to bear mishaps in common.[107] A marriage that one wishes to uphold only as long as the feeling of affection continues, and one in which in misfortune one abandons one's spouse, is certainly not a true marriage. This is what newer legislation more or less has come to, motivated in part by the inappropriate exclusive foundation of the principle of individual freedom, which came about partly through misapprehended humanity, partly through the looser ethical outlook of the times and the preeminence of outward considerations such as expanding the population. The French civil code only contains one of these categories, that of mutual consent

---

[106]The classification of grounds of marriage: fault [Schuld] – mutual dissatisfaction – unhappiness of one party, and the implementation that only the former but not the two latter are admissible according to ethical principles, form the main content of my speech of 1837 cited above. The same form the principles of the *Representation* of 1844 [n. 102]. For an impartial judgment, this may perhaps be trivial but by no means doubtful. Thus even Wiese (*Textbook of Ecclesiastical Law*, III. 315), who in other things is among the laxest, accepts that only "deliberate violation of the duty of marriage" justifies divorce. Even so, neither my speech in Bavaria in 1837 nor the *Representation* in Prussia of 1844 was able to bring about a change in legislation.

[107]Not only did Luther (Walch X. 724, 797) agitate against such divorce; Kant did so as well (*Doctrine of Law*, p. 110), expressing himself thusly: "Should incapacity only occur afterward, that right can lose nothing through this *innocent coincidence.*" Even in the deliberations of the French Council of State under Napoleon, these three classes of grounds for divorce introduced by the law of 1792 found no single defender.

(consentement mutuel), and although this does not <146> correspond to the essence of marriage in principle, nevertheless in terms of result it is without disadvantage due to the gigantic hindrances this places in the way of such divorce. Add to this that the French civil code does not contain most of the grounds of divorce of Protestant consistorial practice, so that mutual consent often only serves in place of material grounds which are obnoxious to judicial treatment. Finally, the French civil code enjoins both parties from remarrying for three years, so that divorce cannot be used as a mere means of satisfying an other-directed inclination. The Prussian civil code, by contrast, introduced both categories, in great extension and without provisos.

Accordingly, if divorce is not otherwise justified than by serious fault, so then is punishment also necessarily visited on the guilty party by the ethical community, state or church, enough so that the blameworthiness is actually attested, that remarriage at least for a specific period be prohibited to him as the one showing himself unworthy of marriage. Divorce can never be considered as a mere episode, as an event for which no one is responsible. If guilt adheres to both parties, then divorce is ruled out altogether; for it is merely a favor to and an entitlement of the innocent party. Thus the church, in consideration of the grounds of marriage which it alone permits, maintains that adultery conducted by both sides cancels each other out, and divorce is not granted. The same must then also hold true when legislation establishes the extension of this ground of divorce to other serious fault, where guilt much more often emerges on both sides.

§. 73. Principle of Marriage: Personal Satisfaction or Higher Order?

Such seriousness regarding grounds for divorce is advis- <147> able even merely from consideration of results. For even lax legislation, if it otherwise does not wish to sink to the level of complete abandonment of the marriage bond, is incapable of coming to the aid of every unhappy marriage. Now on the other hand, it is by means of these fixed principles that the sanctity of the marriage bond in public sentiment is preserved which otherwise is destroyed by the spectacle of facile divorce, and even in individual marriages contentment is often strengthened vis-à-vis temptations brought on by the prospect of arbitrary separation and remarriage. Regarding the latter consideration, the question is whether the number of marriages is greater which, in themselves unhappy, avail themselves of lax marriage laws, or whether the number of these marriages, in themselves happy or at least curable, become unhappy only because of lax marriage laws? The question is whether in fact "insuperable enmity" is not in the majority of cases much rather an unresisted other-directed affection? More decisive however than the consequence is the principle itself. An ethical polity cannot allow the sanctioning of divorce or remarriage which is in conflict with the essence of marriage in order thereby at the cost of mores to provide its members relief for or improvement of its natural well-being. Instead, it has the obligation to register its own, i.e., the national, the state, the ecclesiastical, ethical valuation of marriage in its laws and in the order of the public condition (Book II [*Principles of Law*], §. 6).

Above all, this is confirmed or rather only brought to clear consciousness through the Christian principle. *Christ's statement* regarding divorce is of course *not* a direct *law for the external legal condition* of the state or even of the church, but only for conscience. This is already clear from the preceding parallel statements, which obviously only concern moral relations. Even so, it is a *disclosure of the ethical idea* of the institution of marriage, and this is the principle of legal formation in <148> all life relations including this one.[108] From this follows that civil legislation is not to espouse this statement verbatim and in its fullest extent, i.e., merely to implement it, but nevertheless that it must stand on the same basis as it, that it not follow a principle which deviates from it. There is therefore a stricter and a milder implementation of the Christian principle of divorce for civil legislation, both appropriate according to prevailing conditions, the more so because in this matter, legislation does not have the vocation of making known a confession but much rather of exercising an educational power, for which it must of necessity adhere to the given prerequisites. But the Christian state should never put the public legal ordering of divorce under another principle and restrict it to the mere morality of the individual.

In consequence, the *ethical* and the *Christian* principles for divorce (or, as many express it, the "human ethical" and the "divine holy" marriage), which in recent times are set in opposition to each other, not only are not oppositions but in terms of results not even distinctions. There is no ethical principle for marriage apart from the Christian and no positive Christian apart from the ethical. Christianity herein represents mores [Sitte] over against bad customs [Unsitte]

---

[108]Compare Book II [*Principles of Law*], §. 6, and §. 61 above.

precisely world-historically [weltgeschichtlich]. In the entire pagan world, and even in Judaism, marriage in fact was viewed predominantly as a mere *tie of inclination*, especially on the part of the man, and therefore divorce was arbitrary[109]; by contrast, the **<149>** Christian church considered it predominantly as an *ethical bond*, the obligating power of which does not depend on inclination and life satisfaction and can only be dissolved by the most serious blame of the other part. This notion is yet common to both the strictest Roman Catholic discipline and the laxest more recent Protestant praxis, but it is this which is the ethical notion of marriage. It is therefore obviously a regression to pre-Christian bad customs when now once again a widespread viewpoint regarding the *spouses' happiness in life* is made into the absolute principle for divorce. According to it, divorce shall take place where one spouse or both find themselves to be entirely mistaken in their hopes of satisfaction in life even without any serious, yea perhaps without any, blame at all from the one side or the other. The same spouses, reasonable, well-meaning, good-natured, yet leading with each other an intolerable marriage, in that they do not match with each other – these same spouses will be able to swap and establish two happy marriages, why then chain them to each other? Perhaps only a few consciously go so far, but unconsciously it is this manner of viewing things which underlies opposition to that severity of the divorce laws, and the entire opposition of opinions is, reduced to its innermost core, none other than the question whether the *life satisfaction* of the spouses forms the sole and single principle or whether above anything else it will be the *ethical form of marriage* that forms this principle. No compromise is possible

---

[109]Polygamous peoples actually do not come into consideration here at all, in that the husband, for which it is intended, does not have a need for divorce, despite which among these peoples the husband often is entitled to a license of repudiation. With respect to monogamous peoples, the Attic law permitted the arbitrary repudiation of the wife, arbitrary abandonment of the husband, just as the Roman law in unrestricted fashion permitted not only divorce by mutual agreement but, already early on, the unilateral abolition of marriage (**repudium**). The latter did have disadvantages when it occurred without any legally recognized ground; but the sundering of the marriage always followed. Where in that age a restriction on divorce is found, it is based not on the ethical essence of marriage but only on the treatment of the wife as mere thing or on an agnatic or political interest, or a mere ceremony of religion.

with the former viewpoint; such would rest on a stricter or milder interpretation, but yielding here would be tantamount to abandoning the Christian viewpoint altogether on this <150> point. One in that case would have to admit that he postulates not the good but the pleasurable as the principle of social order.

The rationale, finally, that in the case of estrangement of minds the marriage bond as bond of love is already abolished and therefore that divorce is only the legal expression of an existing fact, is based on the confusion of *natural* and *ethical love.* The former is located in sentiment and therefore is mutable, arbitrary, while the latter is located in the will and ought not change; the former is a form of luck [ein Schicksal] that strikes people, the latter is an act which depends on their freedom. It is however precisely the essence of marriage to elevate the bond of mere sentiment into the ethical bond of the will. Marriage certainly has sentiment as its basis, for which reason sentiment is decisive in contracting marriage. In this regard, the notion from Roman law is entirely true, that with regard to engagement not only is an action for entering into marriage denied but even one regarding damages or stipulated punishment, in order to keep any extraneous motivation from having an effect. But once the marriage is concluded, the ethical tie can no longer depend on sentiment. Hegel in particular gave occasion to this rationale, albeit not in accordance with his own deeper conception of marriage.[110] Besides, should one assume <151> this, then one should, marriage

[110]In his *Philosophy of Law* (§. 176), Hegel states: "In that marriage is firstly the immediate ethical idea, with its objective reality in the intimacy of subjective sentiment and feeling, therein lies the initial contingency of its existence. As little as any compulsion can take place regarding contracting marriage, so little does there otherwise exist a merely legal positive band that can hold the subjects together where conflicting and hostile sentiments and actions have arisen. Nevertheless, a third ethical authority is required which maintains the right of marriage, the ethical substantiality, against the mere opinion of such feeling and against the arbitrariness of mere temporary sentiment and the like, distinguishing this from total alienation and first confirming the latter and only in that case able to dissolve the marriage. Addendum: since marriage is based on *subjective arbitrary feeling*, it can be dissolved.... Marriage *ought* of course to be indissoluble, but it does not get any farther than *ought*.... Should a total alienation take place, such as through adultery, then the religious authority should permit divorce." It is

being a bond of *reciprocal love*, also recognized *unilateral alienation* as a ground of divorce, in fact as entirely permissible, entailing no disadvantage. Thus one logically proceeds from this rationale to the mutual right of arbitrary repudiation.[111] Even more than this, when feeling is decisive, no one can function as judge except the spouses themselves, and therefore only a judicial announcement of the divorce need take place, not a judicial decision. When Hegel makes the requirement of "an ethical authority which maintains the right of marriage against the contingency of mere temporary sentiment, distinguishing the latter from total alienation, and only in the case of the latter allowing the marriage to be dissolved," it must be taken into account hereby that the judge in himself has no means and no standard for these subjective feelings, but that they can only be made objectively recognizable through something like the path taken by the French civil code, to wit, through great and lasting difficulties.

Out of this mingling of feeling and will, pathological **<152>** and actual or ethical love, has at last emerged the complete reversal of ethical judgment as asserted by the disciples of Hegel's school in innumerable dailies and leaflets. The claim here made is that the principle followed by the church of all confessions and to this point likewise predominantly by the nations of Europe, whereby marriage, apart from the case of serious fault, is to be maintained even in the

---

precisely the opposite which follows from §. 164, however, wherein the essence of marriage is established in "consciousness gathering itself from its naturalness and subjectivity to notions of the substantial, and rather than reserving to itself contingency and arbitrariness, removing the connection to this arbitrariness and yielding to the substantial, obligating itself to the Penates."

[111]The fact that the Prussian civil code allows a childless married couple to divorce by mutual assent, while not allowing unilateral renouncement apart from injury by the guilty party, is based on the fact that in accordance with the subjective standpoint of science during that time, marriage was considered to be an arbitrary contractual relation among the spouses. Since the time of Schelling and Hegel this conception has found scarcely any scientific defender. The same is true of the motive behind this legislative determination which only now has become known through the above-cited *Representation* [n. 102]: the interest of the population. The consequences to which the Prussian code in accordance with "its private-legal principle" must lead have been laid out by Puchta *op. cit.* in the most incisive manner.

case of estrangement of minds, is itself the unethical character of legislation; ethical character, on the other hand, is when a marriage that no longer maintains what it should, is no entire unification of life, no picture of true marriage, should instead be dissolved in order to open the possibility of an ethically complete matrimonial state through another marriage. This theory does not consider that the estrangement of minds is no mere event but an act and a fault [Schuld]. It does not consider that marriage depends on every person *for himself* to make it ever more into an ethical one, should it not in its full picture answer to the ethical idea of marriage, and that only this, and this likewise imperatively, is required of him. Above all, it does not consider, and this is the headquarters of the error, that the *existing marriage* is a *higher given bond* over the spouses. For in accordance with this, all ethical demands are only viewed merely with respect to this given marriage, into which one has entered, not however the idea of marriage in general, to be totally fulfilled in this or that marriage, and that the dissolution of this marriage is quite simply the violation of an ethical bond which gains no justification through the beautiful harmony of a second connection; how harmoniously did not most of the French kings live with their mistresses! It is the same doctrine proposed by "Young Germany" without sophistry and appearance of mores: to maintain oneself bound to an existing marriage is foolishness, but where the innermost individualities have recognized themselves as belonging together, there the sexual union should, yea shall **<153>** follow, and the existing ethical bond, this priestly ceremonial, is unjustified over against it.

In accordance with the same principle to recognize no *given bond* as binding, it is the ethical demand of the father to separate from his son when he yields him worries rather than joy, to consider him totally as no longer being his son; the ethical demand of the people through uprising to separate from its king when it believes it can no longer lead a complete state life with him; the ethical demand of people to be able to separate from their bodies through suicide when these yield no satisfaction and no vigor, in fact nothing but temptations. That which is ethical is everywhere the given ethical bond recognized as being higher, standing above, while that which is unethical is that which can be dissolved arbitrarily in order to seek another, that which the person lacking strength of will and self-denial hopes to fulfill merely by virtue of natural feeling and desire. If man did not have any ethical entitlement to leave such a marriage, then it is certainly not the legislation which allows and sanctions it which is ethical, but that which does not allow such offence. The former therefore is instead based on this principle: spouses having violating the duty of marriage and ascended to a condition of hatred and irreconcilability are to be considered by the state to be a finished and immutable event (fait accompli); it grants the seal of approval; it empowers the spouses to add the highest violation to their previous violations of the marriage bond, namely to break that bond and to enter into a new marriage. Now then, as the discussion hitherto makes clear, we are far from the standpoint that legislation is always to require perfect ethical behavior of the citizen, for which reason civil laws are justified in allowing divorce in broader extension than is allowable for the mature Christian conscience. But this is ever only the exception, and that which legislation acknowledges and ought to acknowledge only as **<154>** a lack of perfect ethical behavior can never be passed off as its ethical principle.

Chapter 2: Concerning Mixed Marriages

§. 74. Difference of Religion

<155> *Difference of religion* must hold as a public and separative hindrance to marriage in Christian legislation. This means that no marriage between Christians and adherents of other religions (Jews, Mohamedans, pagans, members of deistic and pantheistic sects) is to exist. Not that the union of sexes among such in itself would be no true marriage, as in the case of incest. This is refuted already by the fact that when one of two non-Christian spouses becomes a Christian and the other does not, their marriage remains as valid as it was before regardless of the now-arisen difference in religion, and the church reluctantly rejects the notion of dissolution of such a marriage (**crimina in baptismo solvuntur, non conjugia**). Nevertheless, it is sin for a Christian to contract such a marriage since in marriage full religious union and mutual religious cultivation is to be sought, and the Christian who contracts such a marriage renounces this highest goal of marriage; which is why the Apostle Paul considers such a conclusion of marriage from the viewpoint that the Christian who enters into it, does so in the hope of converting the other party, and since there is no guarantee of this, he forbids it. Furthermore, it is an offence for the Christian community when such a marriage is entered into and thereby the Christian faith is treated as secondary matter. Finally it is part of the ruling authorities' concern for the public welfare not to allow marriages which are incapable <156> of fulfilling the highest, holiest purpose of marriage. On these grounds the church and the Christian state have the right and the command to prohibit such marriages and to nullify those which nevertheless have been contracted.

All of this presumes that Christianity alone is true in faith and mores, and that it is so in opposition to the other religions. From the viewpoint of the religion of reason, however, by which the things that Christianity holds in common with the other religions is the truth, and those which are particular to it are superstition, myth, and human addition, one therefore must just as consistently approve marriages among proponents of different religions, in fact even promote them in order for the immateriality of the difference among the religions to become manifest and establish itself ever more in the public consciousness. In the question regarding the permissibility of marriage between Christian and

Jew, etc., it emerges, as with the question regarding civil marriage, and even more so, that the answer only lies in the principal decision whether the Christian revelation is the truth or not, whether it is the exclusive truth or not. But the external result also confirms the truth of faith in this regard, while such marriages require not a higher unified religion but only irreligion, and the spouses in such marriages lack any power of adaptation and agreement in the succession and conflict of natural urges.

§. 75. Difference in Christian Confession

Something entirely different than the difference of religion is the difference of *confession*, marriages between Catholics and Protestants, in common parlance *mixed marriages.*[112] Here **<157>** is faith in the same revelation, the same acts of God, the same documents of the Good News; it is only the understanding of this revelation which differs, and even for this understanding the great interpretation which is contained in the three ecumenical creeds is held in common. Between Catholic and Protestant, of course, an essential divergence of religious and ethical conception exists, but no diametrical opposition as in the other case. What is common is infinitely more significant than what separates. Spouses here may be in agreement in the bond to the Redeemer, so that the highest goal of marriage need not remain unfulfilled. For this reason such a marriage cannot be considered sin as such, not simply an offence, not unconditionally a hindrance to an actual Christian marriage. On the other hand, mutual attraction and mutual satisfaction of individuality (to be distinguished from mere sensual love) is an essential aspect of marriage in accordance with God's ordinance – one marries a person and not a dogmatics – and therefore here can be of importance, where there is no absence of religious community but only a lesser degree thereof, at least for those who do not have a special external or internal vocation in the church. There are therefore examples of mixed marriage of which one can say with confidence that they were entered into according to God's will. In fact, from the standpoint that one's own confession is not the only and the perfect church and the other mere error and apostasy, one may find, albeit not commonly, a mitigation of confessional stridency and a fostering of general Christian unity.

---

[112]Compare my treatment of the issue in Harless's *Journal for Protestantism and Church* [Zeitschrift für Protestantismus und Kirche], January 1st, 1839.

This notwithstanding, it must be recognized that mixed marriages are subject to great difficulties and dangers when conducted not merely for human satisfaction but to be pleasing to God, and the above-mentioned favorable result is not <158> the rule but the exception; which moreover must become even more seldom the more the Catholic church, which of course in terms of dogma has not yet given up the Protestant church, likewise in life asserts the absolute rejection of that church to the utmost extent. And correspondingly, the intrusion of its clergy with regard to the education of children in a pitched battle rips the family apart.

Therefore, the church has neither ground nor right – the state even less so – to *declare* such marriages *null and void*.[113] The church, including the Protestant church, should however in general *advise* its members *against* them. Whether the church should be involved in such a marriage or *take part in its solemnization* is determined variously according to the standpoints of each confession, whether in fact it is simply living faith in Christ which holds as the condition of salvation or, beyond that, obedience to the determinate ecclesiastical authority derived immediately from God as well. In accordance with its strict concept, therefore, the Catholic church cannot allow participation in a truly mixed marriage and does not allow it. It makes the condition that the function of the family, the upbringing of children, is to be purely Catholic, and does not anticipate a religious bond of the Catholic part with the Protestant but instead only the guarantee of the former against such a bond. In that case it is no mixed marriage. The Protestant church on the contrary may concede a truly mixed marriage and participate in it, but even so the upbringing of children is for it the decisive thing as well.

§. 76. Upbringing of Children

<159> The religious upbringing of children can have no influence on the validity of the mixed marriage, while such a marriage can only be judged in accordance with itself and with the question of whether the spouses can remain in a religious community. But the attitude of the spouses in regard to upbringing is subject to the judgment and, as the case may be, the disciplinary action of the

---

[113]For the Eastern church, of course, the Irullanum declared marriage with heretics to be null and void (ἀκυρὸν τὸν γάμον); but the heretics here intended also stood outside the ecumenical creeds.

church at every moment in the marriage, and at the moment of the marriage's inception it is likewise a sign of what spirit the marriage will have, and the attitude of the church regarding its solemnization rightly is determined by it.[114]

The Catholic Church (in countries of mixed population) behaves towards mixed marriages, if sufficient guarantees are given for the Catholic education of children, just as it does towards purely Catholic marriages,[115] but where these guarantees are lacking, it either refuses this cooperation, or, as an extreme concession, grants it such that no approval of the Church is expressed. It allows only the passive assistance of the clergy, not the active joining and blessing, it performs the vows without mentioning the a-catholic faith of the other party in order to avoid offense, and it issues dimissorials remarking impediment to marriage on the grounds of heresy. This is the full rigor of the ecclesiastical principle, and deserves not censure but recognition.

The Protestant Church, from the strictly dogmatic (orthodox) standpoint of an earlier period, when it elevated correct dogma almost to the condition of salvation in a similar way to the Catholic Church's obedience to legitimate church authority, had to behave in a similar way, and did so.[116] But with the greater inwardness that it permanently gained during the pietistic period, it must also make the demand on the Protestant part of the family that it withhold from

---

[114] [The following paragraphs along with §§. 77–79 were not included in the first edition of this translation.]

[115] The fact that even in this case only passive assistance is granted and the marriage is to be solemnized outside the church building is only a recent and as yet still isolated arrangement, which is not even logical. For since no civil law requires the Catholic Church in any way to bring about such marriages, the alternative is only either not to solemnize them at all, or, if it does so, not to degrade a sacred act (sacrament).

[116] The Lutheran Church followed entirely the same principles as the Catholic Church, (Carpzov. jurispr. consist. lib. II. def. 6. Gerhard de conjugio §. 378. Quenstett syst. theol. pars iv. c. 14. qu. 4). The Reformed Church in France declared mixed marriages to be absolutely illicit (**illicitum**), namely it obliged the parents to warn their children, if they wished to enter into such marriages, and to lodge a protest against the marriage itself and to demonstrate this to the consistory; only if they fulfilled this obligation might they participate in the resulting marriage through endowment, etc. (la discipline des églises réformées en France chap. 13. art. 4).

none of its children the pure and certain teaching of the way of salvation as the church has recognized it; but if that Protestant part nevertheless concedes to the marriage partner of the other part the children of his or her sex, it can at least condone this and solemnize and bless the marriage itself.[117] For it permits mixed marriages not only in the (negative) view that the Protestant part is not deceived or at best wins over the Catholic part, but in the (positive) hope that even with continuing confessional difference a true Christian communion in the living inner faith, which stands above the ecclesiastical regulations, may be achieved, as it regards so many truly awakened Catholics who are nevertheless faithful to their church as its own. But it can also place this same hope in the outwardly shared education of children, that the inner power of faith will create unity. The consent of the Catholic spouse to the division can, however, be taken as a sign that this interiority has room in the marriage, and it is in this, not in the transaction over the children, that the justification lies of that indulgence in the God-ordained division of the nation itself.[118] On the other hand, if all the children are designated for the Catholic Church, this is conversely a sign that in this marriage it is precisely not the interior sense but rather the Catholic emphasis on the hierarchical union that predominates, and therein lies the most decisive expression of the contempt or even indifference of the Protestant part towards its church. Such a marriage cannot therefore be consecrated by the Protestant church, in particular while that church has emerged from a state of apathy and indifference and has become imbued once again with the profession with which it is familiar, nor allow such demeanor by its members to go unpunished.[119] Moreover, it itself assumes the responsibility if they consider the

---

[117] [The division of children according to sex was part of the legal arrangement of those times. Stahl discusses such an arrangement below, p. 136.]

[118] The fact that this consent may also have arisen out of indifferentism does not stand in the way, otherwise most purely Catholic or purely Protestant marriages could not be blessed.

[119] The sanctions of the church can only consist in exclusion from godparenthood and from ecclesiastical offices, etc., but not in exclusion from the Lord's Supper. The Protestant church can only allow this to occur for what is in itself and under all circumstances a sin against God. Only the sworn promise to alienate the children from his

renunciation of the Protestant education of their children to be permissible and harmless, just as the current recklessness of Protestant husbands has not the slightest reason or excuse[120] in the lax and indifferent behavior of the Protestant

---

church justifies exclusion of someone from the Lord's Supper, because this really is absolutely sin.

[120] Another view here is that in the case in which the Protestant party gives up nothing of what the law allows him, he is not to be blamed, and therefore the church is not to give any sign of disapproval but is to consecrate the marriage. Accordingly, in Prussia, for example, and elsewhere where the same law applies, it would have to be insisted that the Protestant bridegroom should not withdraw any of his children from the Protestant church, otherwise he should be denied the blessing, whereas the Protestant bride should not be asked to do anything at all, and should be granted the blessing regardless of the fact that she alienates her entire offspring from the church, unless she expressly promises what already applies according to the law. This view does not seem tenable to me. The church cannot make its demands on its members according to chance, whether the civil laws determine things one way or another; that is not the religious standard of marriage. This would mean that the Protestant Church in a country in which it is marginalized and the children of mixed marriages all become Catholic, would nevertheless have to approve of these marriages and cooperate for them. But it also leads to a double grievance under equal legislation such as that of Prussia. On the one hand, if the church does not address all children unconditionally like the Catholic Church does, it is unjust to proceed against the Protestant bridegroom who believes he must encumber his bride with the children of her sex. On the other hand, the Protestant bride who enters into a mixed marriage under such a law is not free from the accusation of indifference to her church if she has not somehow assured herself of her bridegroom's intentions, and would thereby be strengthened in such indifference. That the woman, as the serving part, has no responsibility, would be an oriental and pre-Christian idea, and according to it she should also have no responsibility in those countries where the laws determine the division according to sex, if she leaves the religion of all children to the man. The church can only have an autonomous standard, independent of civil legislation. Either it must insist on all children everywhere, as was the older strict practice, or it will see to the relinquishment of children of the opposite sex. There is no third option. Only the former strictness is completely consistent. But even the latter leniency has a principle,

Church itself. It goes without saying that in a matter that depends so much on the innermost state of the souls of the personalities involved, both pastoral and ecclesiastical-disciplinary behavior must be adapted with great freedom and breadth to the considerations of the particular case.

§. 77. Contracts Regarding Religious Upbringing

It is proper for the church to make *contracts* for the future education of children a condition of its cooperation, where the civil laws attach judicial effect to such contracts; for to the church they are then as much as an immediate grant of rights over the children. But if this effect is not attached to the contracts, they give no security against changed convictions, and it is objectionable to impose on the legal conscience of the promisor what ought to be against his religious conscience. The church then has no other unimpeachable means than to carefully investigate the *present* disposition and intention of the betrothed, and to demand declarations on this from both parts, which are then only of an assertory, not promissory nature, in which it therefore imposes on the other part only present veracity, but not future action against present conviction.

Under all circumstances, however, it is reprehensible for the church of the other part to demand or accept an *oath-bound promise* that the education of the children into its faith will be permitted or even left unhindered. Such an oath is a sin for the one who swears it as well as for the one who demands it. For even if the person swearing has no conscience at present about allowing his children to be brought up in a creed other than his own, the positive truth of which is in any case not certain to him, since he does not himself convert to it, he

---

it is a completely different kind of Catholicism, to which the Protestant part joins, depending on whether the Catholic part agrees to the division or not. The attachment to the respective civil legislation has neither principle nor consequence. The result that, if the religion of the father is decisive everywhere, parity will emerge on the whole, may only be a subordinate consideration. The concern of the church is not primarily the overall result for the expansion of its domain, but the particular marriage, and in this the first thing is the Protestant husband, his dutiful behavior and the securing of his salvation, and only afterward the children to be expected in the future.

The civil legislation is not violated or thwarted by the procedure of the church recommended here, since where one church refuses cooperation, the other certainly grants it.

nevertheless necessarily lives in uncertainty and in his own awareness of uncertainty as to whether or not he will have a conscience about it in the future. But it is indisputably sacrilege and sin to promise on oath that of which one is and must be doubtful as to whether it is lawful in his time to do it, to take God as surety for that which one may recognize as contrary to his commandment. If the Catholic swears to make his children Catholic, and the Protestant to make them Protestant, this is only an affirmation on oath of a recognized duty. But if the Catholic swears to let his children become Protestants, and vice versa, or the Jew swears to let his children become Christians, he swears by God to do what he is not allowed to do according to his belief in God, and therefore commits a sin by the oath itself, apart from its fulfillment or non-fulfillment. This does not change even if the church to which the oath is made really is the true God-ordained church. For the oath depends not only on the nature of the matter, but also on the consciousness of the person swearing. Whoever swears assertorically to a true fact, but in the opinion that it is false or in doubt about it, commits perjury. In the same way, anyone who promises his children on oath to the true church when he himself does not believe in its truth is committing perjury. What does not come from faith is sin. Now, should it not be a sin to swear one's children to a church when one's own confession is contrary to it? For the same reason such an oath, if it has really been taken, is not binding; for the oath against one's own duty is not binding according to a principle that is undisputed in the church,[121] and the church to which the person swearing belongs is authorized and called upon to declare it void.

§. 78. The State and Recognition of Mixed Marriages

The state has no reason to promote mixed marriages, since religious indifferentism also shakes its foundation, but it does have an interest, in a mixed population, in the existence of the possibility of intermarriage, as a condition of uniform patriotic sentiment; it must therefore secure this possibility if a church ever wished to frustrate it for its own purpose (e.g. by refusing to grant dimissorials).

The following principle applies to the right of the state against the church in this respect: it can demand everything from the church that the church does not regard as contrary to God's commandment (**divina institutio**) according to its

---

[121] C. 22. qu. 4. – C. 2. 33. X. de jurejur.

own doctrine and practice, even if it would like to refuse such by virtue of merely human ecclesiastical considerations (see above pp. 97f.).

Thus the state can absolutely demand from the Roman Catholic Church passive assistance, proclamation and dimissorialia in the forms customary for this case, and the omission of censures. For it is clear from its own practice that it can grant all this without violating divine order, and if it does so in some places (e. g. for Bavaria in the instructional letter **litteris jam inde** 1834) only in the event of the threat of even greater evil and offense to the "detriment of religion" (that is, the conversion of the Catholic part), hence in its interest, the state can demand that it grant such unconditionally, out of respect for civil order and out of consideration for the state, which gives it protection and care and public authority, and which is concerned with keeping the peace between the confessions. The state can also prohibit one church from making contractual promises to the members of the other and binding them contrary to the commandments of their church, but it would be more advisable for it not to concern itself with this and only to reject the legal effectiveness of such promises. But the state cannot and should not allow one church to accept such promises from the members of the other *under oath*, and it is entitled to punish this through penalties imposed on the clergy, since it has the right and duty to prevent the seduction of its subjects into acts that are immoral and sinful under all circumstances.

On the other hand, the state is not entitled to impose on the Catholic Church any act of approval and ecclesiastical consecration for such marriages, such as the blessing, the dimissorialia without mention of the impediment, or the blessing of the woman who has given birth. Nor can it forbid the most precise investigation of the present intention with regard to the upbringing of the child, both with regard to its member ("bridal examination") and with regard to the other party.

§. 79. Principles of State Recognition

For its own (civil) regulations on the religious upbringing of children from mixed marriages, the state must observe the following principles if (as in Germany) the confessions have equal rights:

1. *The concordant will and joint disposition of the two spouses* must first and foremost determine the religion of the children at every moment until they become independent. A legal provision which determines the religion of the children even against the common will of the parents would be contrary to the right

of the parents, but it would also be contrary to the religious promotion of the children, since the question as to which of the two spouses predominates in the religious sense, and to which confession the particular marriage as a whole leans, is so decisive for this. The church, however, has no right to oppose this. For the church has no direct right to the children against the educational authority of the parents, but only a right to the parents belonging to it, that they bring their children to it. This right must, however, be protected by the state for the publicly recognized church; if both parents belong to the same church, the state may not allow them to alienate their children from it, for example, by letting Roman Catholic parents allow their children to become German-Catholic. Only in the case of mixed marriages does this right of the two churches cancel each other out; for parental authority, which is always an inseparable whole, here stands under neither confession entirely.

2. On the other hand, *contracts between parents* concerning the religion of their children, i.e., promises which are binding for the future, even if one party has in the meantime changed his mind, must be declared inadmissible and invalid. The religion and religious upbringing of children is not the subject of a contract, it is not something disposable; it is an ethical duty and profession, and cannot be disposed of or contracted over. Parents always remain subject to the dictates of their conscience and cannot pretend to disregard such at any time when it becomes clear to them. As little as one can make a contract about one's own religion, just as little can one make a contract about that of one's children.

The legal arrangement itself – which thus occurs if and insofar as the spouses do not jointly decide otherwise – can be either that the children follow the father or that they are divided according to sex. In favor of the former is the natural and legal principle of paternal authority and the preference for uniformity of religious upbringing. In favor of the latter is the fact that, according to the Christian position, the woman nevertheless retains her independent personality under the authority of the man, which is why in the decision on the means of religious and moral education she must be subordinate to him everywhere, but in the decision on the highest end itself, on the choice of religion, she should not be excluded; furthermore, that if all the children follow the father, the mother occupies an isolated, alienated position in the family likewise for her person; finally, that since the permission of mixed marriage rests in general on the hope of a reconciliation of the confessional opposition between the spouses through intimate religiousness and family love, this very reconciliation must also be possible between the children with different religious upbringing, while on the other hand the awareness of this opposition is stimulated in the children even without this, through the mother's differing religion.

Both arrangements are therefore permissible, and it cannot be said of either of them that it is the appropriate one and that the other is not. Such an unconditional judgment is not possible here for two reasons: First, because the mixed marriage always remains an inharmonious relationship, and for this reason a harmonious solution of it is not possible everywhere, but rather, according to one side or the other, disagreements must always arise; second, because the legal arrangement in this case should only ever be subsidiary, if the spouses do not decide otherwise according to their particular confessional temperature, and there are no fundamentally unconditional necessities for merely subsidiary arrangements. In the case of an irenic position of the churches themselves, the division according to sex is certainly the more appropriate, but the more sharply opposition and polemics emerge, the more it will come to pass that every mixed marriage must throw itself completely and unconditionally into the arms of one church, in which case the provision that this is subsidiary to that of the man will prove its worth. But the result will then be that only the man's church will be involved, and that the woman herself will often follow suit. In short, given the severe opposition of the churches, mixed marriage is in fact no longer possible, and every mixed marriage will merge into an unmixed one.

Chapter 3: Paternal Power

§. 80. The Purpose of the Parent-Child Relationship

<161> The purpose (τέλος) of relationships between parents and children is the upbringing of the latter into full human existence, into spiritual and civil independence; no less as well, however, is this purpose the satisfaction for the parents to have a natural bond and attachment to their children; and eventually, beyond upbringing, the enduring bond of love and piety, respectively, for each.

§. 81. The Nature of Paternal Power

Until the child achieves independence, the relationship has an organic activity, that is, a continuous action (function), which differs for each member, focusing on one and the same goal, namely this self-same independence. This goal entails on the one hand parental duties: alimentation, education in accordance with station, daughter's trousseau, and the like, and on the other hand parental rights. The latter are firstly *protection and representation* outwardly, in particular in court (the Germanic *mundium)*, then the *power of upbringing*. These together are the concept of *paternal power*. The power of upbringing extends across all relations of life: choice of calling, religion, marriage. To what degree children have a choice in these areas differs according to the object and the age of the children. The power of upbringing certainly has as one of its <162> essential aspects the furthering of the child towards attaining the goal, although as the entire bond is also to serve the satisfaction of the parents, so does it no less include a rule over the children for their own benefit, namely disposal over their services and labors.

This thought, grounded in the essence of the matter, certainly also underlay Roman paternal power, although in line with the spirit of the whole Roman law it is the right of the father as such which forms the leading principle of legal formation and not the protection and upbringing of children, for which in the final analysis this right chiefly exists. For this reason guardianship, the main aspect of which is protection, had no analogy in Roman law, while according to Germanic law paternal authority and guardianship are entirely homogeneous (Rudorff).

§. 82. The Duration of Paternal Power

Paternal power ends with the independence of the child, which is its main goal. For this, however, full independence is required, to wit, both inner spiritual independence, i.e., maturity (coming of age), and external civil independence, i.e., the ability to maintain oneself (one's own household). This is emancipation according to German law. Roman emancipation is not suitable to the twofold perspective of the purpose of paternal power, in that in itself this power lasts a lifetime, and in that it can be dissolved through caprice prior to the attainment of independence.

The organic action of the bond ends with the independence of the child, but the ethical bond of love and piety continues to exist.[122] This generates not only moral claims but also <163> legal ones, albeit, in accordance with the general character of law (Book II [*Principles of Law*], §. 6), only of a negative content. This includes the hindrance of certain disrespectful or uncharitable actions (for example legal charges, incriminating testimony, etc.), the obligation to mutual alimentation in extreme need, and the like. Mostly, however, this bond expresses itself in *the law of succession*.

§. 83. Concerning the Property* of Children

A similar principle as with that of spouses holds with regard to the property* of children. As long as the paternal power lasts, and so the children have their existence dependently simply in the family, then their property* as well, should they have any, should serve the family just as do their personal performances, in that they resort under the administration and usufruct of the father. But this restriction ends with attained independence (emancipation), and with respect to this they at that point should already be capable of acquiring separate property*. Neither the ancient Roman incapacity of children to acquire nor the later Roman-legal ongoing partial usufruct of the father even after emancipation are appropriate.

---

[122] This is the deeper meaning of the Attic institution that the paternal power lasts for life but that the son actually becomes independent at the age of twenty, by being entered in the civil register. The latter in Athens depended on political maturity, as in Germanic law it depended on private-legal maturity.

§. 84. Concerning Adoption

A lack of children on the one side and a lack of means for upbringing and of an estate on the other leads to artificial reproduction, that strangers enter in the relation of physical parents – *adoption*. It is the substitute for the parental bond. The Romans one-sidedly treated it as a means for parental <164> power, even though it is the latter which is a means. It therefore ought not exceed the requirement of such a substitute, to wit, it is permissible only to the childless, and the natural bond is not be dissolved.[123]

§. 85. The Natural-Law Explanation of the Parent-Child Relationship

This relationship confronted the older natural law theory most peculiarly with the difficulty, in fact the impossibility, of deducing it as legally binding, it definitely being given by nature and not grounded by human will, thus ruling out the application of the presumed contract, this school's ever-ready way out of difficulty. Therefore already Grotius[124] found that in strictness it should not be accounted among legal relationships, while Thomasius in his later separation of law and morality decisively and logically ascribed the relationship between parents and children simply to the latter.[125] Kant[126] attempted to derive the legal nature of this relation from the fact that, because one brings a person arbitrarily into existence without his consent (!), one is also legally obligated to provide conditions satisfying to him. Should one agree with this line of argumentation, then parents would be obliged to provide alimentation and the like while children would not be obliged to submit to parental authority in case they were more content without it.

§. 86. Concerning Guardianship and the Servant Relationship

<165> *Guardianship* is a substitute for paternal power. It therefore naturally entails protection and upbringing. The power of upbringing is here lesser, in that with respect to the preference for the natural bond the share of the mother

---

[123]Regarding the obligations stemming from paternity out of wedlock, see my *Parliamentary Speeches*, January 17th and February 4th 1854.

[124]*De Jure Belli*, Book II, ch. 7, §. 4.

[125]*Institutions of Divine Jurisprudence*, Book III, ch. 4.

[126]*Doctrine of Law*, pp. 113, 114.

expands, and even the inclination of the already mature child (e.g., to enter into a vocation) has more weight for a guardian than a father. Protection on the other hand is more significant in that the inherited property* is the chief consideration. On the whole, the position of the guardian is less a right, like the father's, than a function, and in the end terminates in mere claims to property*. Guardianship is however for that reason by no means a mere requirement of *administration* (**negotiorum gestio**). Apart from any personal and educational influence on the ward, the necessity that the ward must recognize this administration and representation is in itself a bond of enduring personal dependence which is foreign to claims-relations. Should one rather wish to consider guardianship as a public office, there is no grounds to dispute this. It would be more in accordance with nature, however, to consider it as a familial bond, at least in our legal condition, where the guardian also participates in upbringing, and therefore the relationship in terms of its content supplies everything that nature made the task of the familial, i.e., the paternal power.

Just so is the servant relationship a sort of family relationship and no mere obligation of contracted service (**locatio operarum**). For it does not concern individual isolated services but a continuum of them, having as substrate a certain life community, a household community. For this reason it has the aspect of domestic power over and above that of obligated contracted service. Hence the servant (according to our law) stands in his entire conduct of life in a certain dependence upon mastership, and the latter in a certain responsibility [Haftung] for the ser- <166> vant, and there are e.g. many remarks which in other contexts could be construed as injurious but which regarding servants are not treated as such. Such dependence upon a strange family, to which one does not belong as an actual member through the unity of blood, is of course a relation that does not correspond to the prototype of the fulfilled human condition. Nevertheless, it is simply ineradicably grounded in earthly conditions (Book I [*Philosophical Foundations*], §. 46) just as is the distinction between wealth and poverty, from which it in the final analysis is derived. It therefore is not eliminated when one ignores it, i.e., when it is conceived not as a dependency but as a contract relation, so that when the agreed performances take place the servant stands on a fully equal level with the master. For in fact the dependency nevertheless remains since the servant in need of food must ultimately submit to the master, and the only disadvantage is that both parties regard each other only as a means for their convenience and their preservation, who are inwardly committed to nothing but what has been promised. In this manner mastership is arranged badly, while even worse, the servant is abandoned. The latter is furthermore exposed to greater temptation of immorality which inheres in a lesser, in itself unelevated status, by virtue of the greater license stemming from the dissolution of the bond. The ennobling of this relation does not consist in its being dissolved into a mere claim relation but in its approximation to the familial bond. This can only be accomplished through custom, not legislation; but the latter at least ought not destroy the precondition of such custom, which is the legal recognition of domestic power and responsibility. On the other hand, the stricter boundaries of domestic power, the supervision of its use by the ruling authorities, and the complete freedom to dissolve the bond are the guarantees of the personal freedom of the servant, which recent times of course <167> did not discover but, rightly, have asserted more strictly.

Chapter 4: Freedom of Instruction

§. 87. The Right of Fathers and the State in Instruction

<169> It is the right of the father and the core of paternal power (§. 81) to determine the upbringing and instruction of children. The state cannot remove this right and usurp it. But for its part the state has a vocation and right to direct [leiten] upbringing and instruction. The upbringing and instruction of the children is incumbent upon the father; but it is incumbent on the state to ensure pure mores and higher intellectual culture [Bildung] for the nation. Therefore upbringing and instruction are the outgrowth of both paternal power and state power, the former for individual upbringing, the latter for national education. In particular, however, to the degree that it concerns training for public office, the setting of conditions and thus the regulation of instruction are an affair of state.

Accordingly, the state has the right:

1. Generally to require a certain degree of education [Bildung] – elementary instruction – and to this end to prescribe that all children either attend the popular school or receive an education equal to the popular school.

2. Of all who maintain schools or otherwise wish to undertake instruction as gainful employment – not merely as tutor in support of a single head of household –to require above all certain moral guarantees, then also certain public tests and certificates of ability as to whether they meet that general <170> standard of popular instruction.

3. To require attendance at public institutions (gymnasia, universities) for state offices and in order to practice as physician, lawyer, etc.

This has been the customary arrangement up until the most recent times, and is so even to this day.

§. 88. The Contemporary Demand for Freedom of Instruction

This arrangement is now opposed by the demand for *freedom of instruction.* By this is intended *firstly* that anyone, regardless of any examination or authorization, is allowed to impart instruction and to set up an educational institution, and therefore that anyone is allowed to run such an institution; *secondly*, that only *a final examination* be required of state offices and practice as attorney or physician, not attendance at any public institution, that, as the saying goes, the state only inquire after the knowledge, not after the source of the knowledge.

In Belgium this freedom of instruction has been fundamentally and fully realized.[127] It has thus become the poster image for the same. In France in the final years of the July monarchy, it was vigorously demanded (by the Catholic party) (since it was also promised there in the constitution). It was claimed here as an inalienable right on the basis of the title of individual freedom, and mainly the title of paternal power, in that only the father can decide to whom he entrusts his children. But the demand for freedom of instruction in fact is not justified, and least of all for these titles.

The right of each and every father to determine the instruction and upbringing of his children does not preclude the state from exercising the right to protect the entire population from teachers without ability or moral guarantees, as little as does the right of every man to decide about his body preclude the state from prohibiting quacks from practicing medicine. The specific decision therein always remains with the father, but the state circumscribes the circumference by excluding that which, in terms of the public consideration, is impermissible. The <171> comparison made in the debates that the state should not apply preventive measures to instruction as little as it does to the press, and only intervene when a school gives offense, does not apply. For even admitting the absolute

---

[127] Article 17 of the Belgian Charter states: "l'enseignement est libre, touts mesure préventive est interdite, la répression des délits n'est réglée que par la loi" [teaching is free, all preventive measures are prohibited, the repression of offenses is regulated only by law]. According to Belgian legislation, practice as a lawyer or doctor is conditional on the scientific degree of doctor or licentiate, but all degrees for philosophy, letters, law and medicine depend only on an examination, not on study at an institution. The law of higher education determines "toute personne peut se présenter aux examens et obtenir des grades sans distinction du temps, du lieu ou de la manière dont elle a fait ses études" [anyone can take the exams and obtain grades regardless of time, place or how they studied]. This examination is not consigned to a state school even for obtaining degrees, so that there is no indirect obligation to attend, but special examination commissions are set up as juries (in Brussels) for this purpose. Each of them is composed of seven persons, two of whom are designated by the Chamber of Deputies, two by the Senate (upper house) and three by the government.

impermissibility of preventive measures for the press, the press remains the activity and vocation of individuals even when acting in the public square; by contrast, the education and instruction of the nation is an activity and vocation of the state itself. Even though in ancient states they were the exclusive vocation of the state, and even though nowadays, in the spirit of the Christian-German peoples, the first place in this comes to the father, that vocation of the state is still not entirely absorbed.

Above all, the right of individual freedom cannot be asserted against the requirement of attendance at specified educational institutions as a precondition for civil service on the grounds that the provenance of knowledge is of no concern to the state. For although with regard to specific individuals, each considered in his own right, the place at which he obtained his knowledge may be a matter of indifference, it is not so with regard to the level of education of the applicants taken collectively. This collective result depends upon the educational institutions. The mere final examination is no substitute for attendance there, since the standard for all examinations must necessarily be established in accordance with the candidates themselves, and the general avoidance of truly appropriate public educational institutions would therefore lower the standard itself, which it is the concern of the state to maintain at its level. To what degree freedom here recommends itself on educational grounds is an entirely different question; it cannot be required on legal grounds.

Freedom of education in this rationale is just as revolu- <172> tionary as the declaration of the rights of man. It destroys higher order and leading in favor of unlimited freedom of individuals; in its consequences it leads to the state having to tolerate even God-denying institutions of instruction, in the same way that it cannot do anything about a God-denying tutor.

§. 89. Religion and Freedom of Instruction

The deeper motivation from which the demand for freedom of instruction has sprung is however by no means individual freedom or the inviolability of the paternal power but instead the effort to detach education from the state and turn it over to the clergy. This undoubtedly was the intent and apparently the result of freedom of instruction in Belgium. It was likewise the sole object of the desire for it in France. Through this freedom the effort was made for the clergy and the orders to be able to open schools for elementary and gymnasial instruction apart from any interference by the state, and for attendance in these schools not to be disadvantageous in future application for civil office, so that Catholics might send their children to these schools without hindrance. In a word, what was desired was *ecclesiastical popular instruction in emancipation from the state.*

There is much stronger basis in truth in this real motivation than in that asserted one. The *religious conscience of the father* and the *vocation to instruct of the church* have their well-founded right vis-à-vis the state, and the appeal to this ground is a great deal more proper than to that of the right of individual freedom and paternal power. The state has the right to have every father subordinate his view regarding the method of upbringing and instruction and regarding the ability of specific teachers to the goal of national instruction; but it has no right to have the father subordinate his religious faith itself to that goal. <173> Such exclusive and unrestricted power of the state over education is something out of the ancient world, and the deeper life of the Germanic peoples opposes this, as do the divine commands of the Christian faith which stand elevated over the state. No less does the state-recognized church have a right to a share of popular instruction. Certainly, it is not its right either directly or indirectly, through the freedom of the head of household, to direct instruction and the institutions established for it, to determine the standard and form of intellectual cultivation. It does have the right to have an effect on the institutions of learning to the degree that the students do not become alienated from it but rather become more closely connected to it. For institutions of learning are also of necessity institutions of upbringing; every lesson educates, and the system of teaching to which students are subjected cannot be without influence on their religious sentiment. This is not restricted to religious instruction; other studies, e.g., in history and natural science, exert a religious influence; that influence is exerted mostly by the personality of the teacher. Therefore, when the state school is dechristianized or set into opposition with the relevant recognized confession, then its monopoly or authoritative power is no longer justified, neither in direct manner in the state school, nor even in indirect manner in the institutions of education for state offices. For in that case the law of conscience is in effect; one cannot coerce a father to submit his child to an influence antagonistic to his religion, and the right of the church to conduct its educational vocation separated from the state is no less valid.

By contrast, it is a transgression when the church fundamentally and therefore generally (or at least where divergences with the state power exist, which can never be entirely removed) calls for national education on its own, separated and even emancipated from the state, as, e.g., in Germany where freedom of <174> education is demanded more openly and consistently, not in general but only for the church, that the episcopal people's or secondary schools not be supervised by the state, that examinations of teachers not be required for them, since the church itself provides the moral and scientific guarantees here. Education as such, the cultivation of intelligence and knowledge, is not however the vocation of the church but of the state, and even upbringing, the cultivation of sentiment [Gesinnung], has an aspect which the state cannot leave to the church alone. A care is entrusted to the state for the sake of loyalty and national patriotism, and for recognition of civil considerations and peace among the confessions, which the church could not possibly provide; and by no means does education by the church in itself offer the guarantee that it will not establish a sentiment in which those duties appear, not independent and unconditional, but subordinated to the power and disposition of the ecclesiastical authority, the guarantee, thus, that it will not instill the principles of Boniface VIII and Bellarmine.[128]

The task is therefore to maintain the school on the Christian and, depending on circumstances, the specific confessional foundations, and to accord the church the fullest, most effective share in this, without giving up the solid grip of the state for positive guidance of instruction and the supervision of religious influences. No objection of oppressed conscience and no pursuit of emancipation which opposes this is grounded. When however the state establishes a system of education detached from or even in contradiction to the religious-ecclesiastical foundations, there it is well-grounded, according to the degree of contradiction, to assert the inde- <175> pendence of the religious conscience of the father and the educational vocation of the church, right up to the demand for freedom of instruction.

---

[128]See my lectures on *Protestantism as a Political Principle*, p. 51, and *Catholic Refutations*, a statement accompanying the fourth edition thereof, p. 19.

Chapter 5: Inheritance

§. 90. Significance of the Right of Succession

<177> The law of succession is a consequence of the family bond, in particular the parental bond. The latter has by nature the purpose (τέλος) of imparting the fullness of existence and therefore also satisfaction to the children, and in them to have the furtherance of one's own personality and therefore also of property*. It is only because of the children that the right of succession even exists, even when it is extended to other natural relations.

In accordance with this – its natural goal as the furtherance of personality – inheritance is not an immediate admission (acquisition of property) to the *objects* of property*, arising from grounds of the law of property*, but by means of a bond among the persons, admission to the entire *sphere* of property* *rights* of the testator. The total content of this sphere (rights and liabilities [Verbindlichkeiten]) therefore retains its relation continuously to the testator and thereby its juristic unity (**successio universalis**), a unity which precedes that of the individual objects, not one which, as with the **universitas facti**, first arises with their accumulation, and thus also is valid even where only one object ("**res licet minima**") is extant.[129]<178>

For the entire human race, however, the *order* and *continuity* by which it holds property* in the succession of generations lies in this familial succession (and the testamentary succession which imitates it), by means of which it uninterruptedly governs property* as the substrate of consciousness and will and preserves both the legal spheres of persons respecting property* and, through these, the continuity of the generations.

---

[129]German succession as well, although rightly characterized as **successio singularis** vis-à-vis Roman succession, is not this in the strictest sense; since entry into the inheritance occurs only via a connection to the testator (whether the first acquirer or the last possessor is irrelevant here), not directly (as e.g. in the case of purchase); and insofar as the heir is not liable to creditors of the testator, namely regarding the inherited immovable property [Gut], this is not because he is a singular successor but because the testator could not encumber the immovable property with debt.

§. 91. Forms of Succession

Accordingly, the succession of children – and, by analogy, relatives in general – on the one hand is the necessary consequence of the familial bond, the purpose inherent in parental property* itself. But according to the *self-causation of the person,* particularly with respect to property, which the parents do not lose, it presents itself on the other hand as *the consequence of the act of the parents*, as a gift and impartation, albeit therefore as a *duty* of parents in this respect as well. Hence it is not an "admission to the particular possession of in-itself common property*,"[130] as if the right already previously existed and the other recipients or exercisers had been removed, but is truly succession, the new acquisition of a propertied estate [eines Vermögens], and therefore on the one hand determined by the will of the parents, as will be shown presently, and on the other hand dependent upon the will of the children (right of acceptance or **<179>** renunciation).

To this aspect is joined the freedom of disposition of the testator – *testamentary succession.*

When, that is, succession is likewise a consequence of the testator's act, then he is also entitled in greater or lesser degree to specify it in terms of content. Hence he may:

1. give to his natural heirs by means of a special declaration of will that which was already due them by virtue of the bond, in doing so declaring it outwardly and publicly as a work of his will,

2. more closely determine in detail this legally necessary succession, e.g., arrangement regarding inheritance portions,

3. impose legacies and other obligations on the heirs (the legacies are valid not by virtue of a disposal over the objects of property*, since the testator does not have this, but by virtue of the family-like power over the heirs, for which reason: where there is no heir, there is no legacy),

4. disinherit them for debt (this as well is only the consequence of the fact that succession is a work of the act of the testator; were however succession only

---

[130] Hegel, *Philosophy of Law*, §. 178. This expression is too broad regardless of the truth of the thought Hegel thereby intends to express. It is applicable at best to the **successio ex pacto et providentia majorum**, and even in this case one inherits not from the last possessor but from the first acquirer, and it is upon that act that the succession rests.

"admission to in-itself common property*," then disinheritance would be impermissible even with the most extreme debt, as little as it is permissible for the father to punish the children by taking *their* property),

5. finally, bequeath the estate purely in accordance with his own will, construct entirely artificial bonds of inheritance, be it for the entire estate where no natural necessity exists, be it only for a portion of the same. **<180>**

§. 92. Testate Succession

Accordingly, the inner purpose of parental property*, viz., to be left to the children, is the only ground not merely of the remaining intestate succession but also of testamentary succession. There would be no testament without intestate succession, the former being partly the more specific determination, partly the surrogate, of the latter. The character of the testament is therefore not free disposition over property, since this ought not extend beyond life, but the free imitation of the natural familial bond, analogous to adoption.[131]

Testamentary succession therefore is restricted by natural limitations, particularly in the children; it can only be implemented to the degree that these do not exist or are not excessively restricted.

The right of the last will and testament was not entirely lacking with any people but rather occupied an extremely secondary position after the right of intestate heirs, in particular the children; so e.g. in Attic law, which did not authorize a testament where no children existed. Roman law first brought testamentary freedom to decisive and independent, not mere subsidiary, validity, but to the degree that it violated the natural bonds, to wit, bound to legal forms but unrestricted in terms of content. Later development moderated this, in particular through the **querela inofficiosi** borrowed from the Greeks, and the principle of an obligatory portion. The latter is still too slight in Roman law, to wit, measuring a third to a half. The Prussian civil code rightly sets this amount higher, while beyond that the French **<181>** code guarantees the children half to three-fourths of what would be their intestate portion.

---

[131]This is demonstrated most clearly in the Attic law, which knows no other form of bequeathal to **extraneos** than through adoption by means of testament, so that the testament must necessarily include the adoption of the heir. See Gans, *Universal-Historical Development of the Law of Succession* [universalhistor. Entwickelung des Erbrechts], I, p. 315.

§. 93. Intestate Succession

Because the bond between parents and children is the origin of all right of intestate succession, the solidarity of those descending from one procreator is the natural principle of the *order of succession* with him and among themselves. Accordingly, the Germanic *parentela principle* appears to be the natural and intimate one before mere proximity of degree, although in the same clan [Sippe] this would be the Roman *principle of representation.*

Regarding intestate succession the viewpoint has ruled from earliest times that the estate [Vermögen] remains within the male line as the superior sex. As such, in Athens the complete exclusion of daughters alongside sons and the institution of the epikleros,[132] in Rome the exclusion, not of course of the daughter, but of those descending from the daughters (the cognates), and the Germanic preference for the male line in the succession to the patrimony. Since through Christianity, however, the female sex has been elevated to an essentially equal position, it is in general owed the same entitlement, in the way that later Ro- <182> man law developed it. Only regarding landed property, particularly the landed nobility where such exists, is a preference for the male line justifiable in respect to the civil and political position of the family which it includes and which is represented by that property. Here therefore the female line is maintained by the male: through the agnates, the husband, the jointure. On the other hand, if the estate comprises movables, the female sex would have no security against poor administration by the male sex given such an arrangement. Additionally, that arrangement assumes that marriages largely are concluded within the same station. It is from the civil and political significance of landed property

---

[132] ["*epikleros* (fem. adj. acting as noun), *epiklerote* (abstract noun): An *epikleros* was the daughter of a man who died leaving no male heir; she was not his heiress, but possession of his estate went together with her hand in marriage." S. C. Todd, selections by Michael de Brauw, "A Glossary of Athenian Legal Terms," in Adriaan Lanni, ed., "Athenian Law in its Democratic Context" (*Center for Hellenic Studies On-line Discussion Series*). Republished in C.W. Blackwell, ed., *Dēmos: Classical Athenian Democracy* (A. Mahoney and R. Scaife, edd., *The Stoa: a consortium for electronic publication in the humanities* [www.stoa.org]), edition of March 16, 2003. Contact: cwb@stoa.org.]

that the institution of inalienability and beyond that of indivisibility spring. This can be treated appropriately in the doctrine of the estates [Ständen].[133]

§. 94. Recognition of Inheritance

Since inheritance is an expression of the familial bond, in fact to that degree is itself the familial bond expressing itself in the working of property*, not only is its recognition essential by the individuals from whom one wishes the factual performance, but a general public recognition of the heir as well. Just as fatherhood or marriage naturally cannot be recognized by one disputant and denied by another but must either exist in the same way for everyone or not, so also inheritance (§. 63). The Athenian institution is based on such a notion: if an inheritance was to be settled, everyone with a claim came before the Archon, who ascertained the heirs among them, and when they were recognized, it was <183> public, in front of all. By contrast, the Romans allowed the inheritance to be fought over among the disputants in isolation, and in the various proceedings which in this manner arose the judges chanced to come to various decisions, with one-half of a testament remaining in force, the other half overturned, producing intestate succession. This is an abuse. The Roman institution nevertheless is based on the no-less true concept that the right of inheritance ought not be ascertained by the ruling authorities (administratively) but must remain open to every claimant for legal action. Even so, the two notions are in no way irreconcilable.

Furthermore, the action regarding inheritance is not to be considered a mere **actio in rem**, i.e., a suit against the totality of property [Sachen], but analogously to family actions, as a **praejudicium** which nevertheless likewise contains its realization in individual performances and restitutions. Considered in this light, the entire treatment is quite simple; the matter initially present itself in this manner to an impartial person, while the Roman jurists' conception of the action as a mere **actio in rem** leads to the unnatural expression that one must consider the **debitor hereditarius** to be a **quasi juris possessor** and the like. A double component, the right to the **successio** and the right to the **hereditas**,

---

[133] The Mosaic law, which exists here as everywhere as a divine prototype, does not establish indivisibility and the exclusion of the later-born, but does establish by means of the Jubilee year the inalienability and maintenance of landed property in the same family, which otherwise can naturally only be determined according to the male line.

accordingly cannot be distinguished. Instead, although the inheritance is precisely a bond for the sake of the propertied estate [das Vermögen], the manifold effects are given in itself, which are united by it as its cause. In technical treatment, therefore, one ever only has to apply the principle: when the bond is recognized by the opposing party or by means of evidence is forced to do so,[134] and he <184> himself cannot find support in a special right, then everything that was the testator's must become the plaintiff's: his real rights, his claims, *but also his factual advantages*, to the degree that they have a legal relation and were lost through the inheritance, e.g., the possession of a thing which the testator detained merely as **depositum**. All of this must be able to be achieved through the action of inheritance, since all of this is only the consequence of recognizing the bond of succession. Should one consider it as an **actio in rem**, then the inclusion of such a merely detained thing cannot be justified, while on the contrary it is entirely natural when considered as a **praejudicium**; for the thing belongs together with the estate of the testator in the broadest sense, it belongs to his pecuniary situation, and therefore must also become the representative of his person. Through the inclusion of such things in the whole, the heir in no way receives more property* than the testator had, he only receives *ways of pursuing his rights* which the testator did not have; and this is appropriate and necessary, since he must factually first obtain possession of the property* that the testator already had. If this is considered to be peculiar, then it must be considered so above all because the heir had the **hereditas petitio** at all, to which not even the testator himself was entitled.

§. 95. Natural-Law Theory of Succession

Earlier natural-law theory conceived of testamentary succession as the product of property, thus the completely free disposition of the testator over what belongs to him, with intestate succession viewed as a presumptive testament. So Grotius[135] and all his followers, and likewise the civilians up <185> until most recent times. Just so on the other hand did Kant conceive of succession as

---

[134]Throughout nearly the entire history of literature one considered it noteworthy that the action of inheritance also runs against the **pro possessore** possessor; but were it not admissible here, then it could not hold against the **pro herede** possessor, in that the latter is a **pro possessore** possessor when the petitioner presents his evidence.

[135]Grotius, *De Jure Belli et Pac.*, Book II, ch. 7 §. 10.

acquisition of property through contract.[136] This conception would find its refutation, if it needed another, in the fact that disposition over property beyond one's lifetime is left unexplained, that the transfer of liabilities in no way can be derived from it, etc. Hegel was the first to conceive succession in its proper significance as the result of the familial bond, and thus intestate succession as the original form.[137] But Hegel's conception, as already noted, needs to be developed in more detail in that this substantial bond likewise includes both the will and the act of the testator, and therefore the latter aspect, to a certain degree and under certain circumstances, is made into its own independent principle of succession. Only in this manner can testamentary succession be understood at all, and it moderates Hegel's exaggerated aversion to testaments. The St. Simonian denial of the law of inheritance is based on the concept, like the more moderated denial of property described above (§. 33), that one can only have property in what he has acquired through his own labor. It is however illogical that despite this the St. Simonians always allow property to exist, even in that which is the mere gift of nature.

---

[136]Kant, *Doctrine of Law*, p. 134.

[137]In the area of positive legal science this happened contemporaneously through others, e.g. Savigny.

APPENDIX: REGARDING THE VALUE OF ROMAN PRIVATE LAW

§. 96. Greatness and Shortcoming of Roman Law

<187> It is a true and now widespread insight that Roman law first and foremost *realized the idea of law* in world history.[138] The significance of this statement is, as we already discussed (Book II [*Principles of Law*], §. 17), a dual one in accordance with the nature of law: the realization of law in both the objective and the subjective sense. Both the pure exclusive validity of positive legal norms without admixture of moral or political motives and the unconditional recognition and preservation of acquired rights is the great character trait which distinguishes the Romans from previous peoples. The struggle to preserve a form of the state considered to be divine was, at least in later times, foreign to them; the struggle to produce an ideal form of state was from the beginning foreign to them. The inviolability of the legal order and of acquired rights are the ground motive of their public condition. This in fact is <188> the origin of the conscious and implemented separation of personal and real rights which we must consider to be the true foundation of a secure private-legal condition (§. 37).

The concept of entitlement (law in the subjective sense, acquired rights) nevertheless manifests itself in a one-sided conceptualization with the Romans, namely as *simple pure entitlement, unpermeated and unmitigated by any duty and higher determining necessity*. Not that the Romans, as with the current natural-law and revolution theory, assumed abstract content-less human rights or that they only attributed to citizens mere rights and no duties: it is everywhere

---

[138]This insight, induced by the great historical investigations of our time, was first expressed with clarity and specificity by Hegel. The earlier period (Herder, Johannes Müller) is far behind him. Despite this, I by no means subscribe to Hegel's further exposition regarding the Roman world epoch. Nor can I find its eternal significance, like Hegel does, in the fact that the opposition of both aspects, the substantial (objective) and the subjective, were expressed in the two classes and their struggle, nor can I find Hegel's ethical verdict regarding the Romans in opposition to the Greeks to be true and justified. Even so, this is not the place to enter further into this discussion.

specific, concrete, established rights as they derive from the nature of the legal institution, the vocation of various positions in life, the purpose of commerce. But measure and restriction in the use of these rights, their dependence on a counter-performance, on the fulfillment of a duty, as likewise ought to proceed from the nature of the legal institution, is unamenable to the Roman conception; the duties exist as an entirely separate matter, beside and outside the rights. In the Roman conception, *law* is a *sphere of the completely absolute (sovereign) action.*

§. 97. One-Sided Focus on Bare Entitlement

This character trait is already often manifest in its *public law*. The consul had the right stemming from the nature of his office to accept votes; viewing this in terms of the described spirit as a right, he might arbitrarily refuse to accept the votes for this person or that. By virtue of their vocation, the senators have the right to vote in extensive speeches, in consequence of which, in accordance with the Roman conception, it is their right before addressing the matter at hand, "to speak about what they wished, as long as they wished." The Decemviri had as supreme ruling authority the right to call new elec- **<189>** toral assemblies and therefore might, as was their right, also decline to do so, by which it came about that they remained in office beyond the lawful term. Even the supremely important institution of censorship as an ethical court of judgment arose only in this manner. In establishing the office of censor, no one thought of an ethical court, but instead the long-omitted wealth estimate and the classification in classes according to this estimate. The estimate was however from then on the right and therefore as everywhere else the pure right of the censors, who therefore in accordance with the free exercise of their right placed anyone in the class they wished, and they would place those who badly managed their farm or poorly groomed their horse, etc., in the poorest class, made them into Aerarii, as they, from a motive of revenge, did to Mamercus Aemilius without any grounds for doing so. The offices were not without any obligation; they were subject to accusation afterward; but the content of the right itself, the manner of its exercise, was not predetermined by this obligation, for which reason any manner of exercise was valid and could not be hindered. It is also to be considered a consequence of this conception that in the case of a violation against one of the Roman classes, the accused would be judged not by those of his own estate (as according to the Germanic principle), nor by an unbiased third-party court, but precisely by the penultimate estate [vorletzten Stande].

In the area of the *law of material things* [Sachenrechts] this principle can manifest itself less obtrusively since property [Eigenthum] by its very nature is a free right, unalloyed by obligation, over a mere passive object. Even so, a closer inspection reveals that here as well peculiar traits are not lacking. Landed property may not be subjected to any tax on earnings; taxes were levied on property in general, and landed property was included in the assize, but a duty on a specific piece of <**190**> land as such and especially on a specific yield from that land (tithes), as found among other peoples earlier and later, is contrary to the Roman concept (Niebuhr). Likewise, the right of the property-owner is not affected by his obligation as debtor; he is liable to the creditor only in his person, not in his material things. Likewise there are no land taxes [Reallasten], ground rents [Grundrenten], etc., because property would thereby be conditioned by fulfillment of a liability. Precisely from this stems the overly strict implementation of the rule "**servitus in faciendo consistere nequit**" [servitudes do not impose positive acts]. Therefore everywhere the right of property-owners as such cannot be accompanied by an obligation, cannot be dependent upon its fulfillment. Furthermore, there is in the ancient civil law no real right to another's thing that would be dependent upon payment of a deposit, like the later **ager vectigalis** and the manifold relations of this sort which from the beginning were developed by the Germanic law. Both ancient institutions of the category of real and personal servitudes, leaving aside their heterogeneity in other respects, have this in common in contrast with later ones, that they are bare unconditioned rights. Finally, there are no real rights limited by time, which thus contain a restriction in themselves, no property which can cease **ex nunc**, no right to another's thing that is not at least for life. The temporal usufruct is, as is the **habitatio**, expressly explained as being more of a factual than a legal nature.[139] The latter admittedly had yet further a general ground in the nature of the case. **<191>**

---

[139]It also has to do with the fact that usufruct bequeathed to a minor son as legate, thus acquired from the father, depends not upon the life of the son but of the father. To wit, the entitled must have an unrestricted right. For this reason, though, the actual usufruct must be dissolved with **capitis deminutio**, although not the mere factual, temporal usufruct (Justinian, Digest, 4.6.20, de cap. minut.).

The *law of obligation*, on the other hand, took shape entirely in consequence of this principle of pure entitlement. Upon it, namely, is based the actionability of contracts. It is the notion: the only fully justiciable contracts are those which engender a pure unconditioned right, not a right depending on a counterliability [Gegenverbindlichkeit]. The stipulation is such a one: its innermost significance consisted in engendering absolutely unilateral claims, for even when a counter-stipulation is possible, the consequence is only the existence of two entirely independent claims, not a tie of mutual obligation. In the same manner the written contract [Literatkontrakt] only left room for a unilateral claim to a determinate sum of money, since every counter-debt is settled ipso jure. But real contracts [der Realkontrakt] with their peculiar determinations also originate from this. As long as no party has performed, as for instance in an exchange contract, the right is thoroughly permeated by a liability and conditioned by it; anyone asserting a claim had to recognize that counter-performance could only be demanded on the condition of one's own performance; this is not the Roman way of law. But for the one who has fulfilled his obligation, he is no longer liable for anything, he now has a pure entitlement, legal proceedings are therefore now open to him. The consequence of this, however, is the **jus poenitendi**. Since the one who has performed is the pure beneficiary, is completely free of obligation and only as such can be dealt with, he must have the choice either to demand back his own performance or the other. Apart from this he is treated as obligant as well. But there is no injustice in this, in that while the recipient can withdraw [pönitiren] up until the moment of acceptance, can refuse acceptance, therefore it is no less fair that the seller can withdraw up until the counterperformance takes place. Now these four contracts, which are indispensable in daily life and **<192>** can only exist as reciprocal, form an exception: they have as it were the **privilegium** in the Roman legal system. In this as well, by the way, that basic concept is not without influence on the determination as to what degree a counterperformance must be paid should the performance prove impossible by force of circumstances [bei kasueller Unmöglichkeit].

Just so is this character trait the key to the Roman law of the family. That the family here in a manner of speaking maintained itself in patriarchal independence and solidarity, while the power of the father maintained the highest jurisdiction, the right over life and liberty to some extent even to the exclusion of the power of the state, and that what is acquired by the children becomes part of the communal family estate [Familienvermögen] administered by the father, all of this had nothing strange about it, in fact belongs to the period when entitlement of individuals was as yet undeveloped. What is strange is that the position of the father could be asserted entirely arbitrarily, without any higher moderation and duty, that the father, according to his wish, without any restriction by the state, could condemn his son to death or sell him, that he during his lifetime could dispose arbitrarily of the property* acquired by the family, and in similar manner arbitrarily determine succession. It is however no different from senators speaking about whatever they wish as long as they wish, and the wealth estimator putting whoever he wished into the Aerarii. Paternal power therefore by no means is a form of property, which is how one occasionally has sought to solve this phenomenon, but rather familial power, in itself natural for that time, which however was conceived exclusively as mere entitlement unpermeated and undiminished by obligation and therefore certainly gaining a great resemblance to real rights. This also corresponds with the scientific systematic conception of the Roman jurists. They treat the law of the family not as a system of organized rela- <193> tions, marriage, parental relations, etc., but as a system of powers: **potestas**, **manus**, **mancipium**, therefore even guardianship as a **potestas in capite libero**, and marriage, to the degree that it itself does not contain a power (**manus**), as a mere form of acquisition of paternal power.

§. 98. Eternal Value of Roman Law: Steadfastness

We must view the steadfastness [Unverbrüchlichkeit] of positive law, and the steadfastness of entitlement with the implementation attached to it, as eternal legal truth; and in this regard the Romans were rightly characterized as the classical universal-historical people of the law, similar to the Greeks regarding art and the Jews regarding religion. Against this, the concept of pure entitlement incapable of suffering any admixture of duty is by no means a true principle of law, but instead the one-sidedness and imperfection of the Roman condition. Those gruff hearts and inflexibilities which originally sprang from the same source were of course mitigated, even elevated, by later development, but the lack inherent in it from the beginning still remained, *the lack, to wit, of a positive principle of organic formation*, i.e., human life relations taking shape from their higher concepts, as a whole overarching the participants, and in accordance with this allotting those rights and duties in determinate measure and mutual dependence. Germanic law is determined by such a principle. Its institutions, such as shared property, divided property, property reserved for parental use [Altentheil], caretaker administration of the estate [Interimswirthschaft], law of marital property (with or without community of goods) and the like are therefore unassimilable to the Roman standpoint, and regardless of how one judges the value of many of these institutions taken individually, the principle itself, to be able to evoke such and **<194>** similar institutions, is the true one, and in this regard Germanic law stands higher than Roman. With us, then, the Roman law, in accordance with an inner necessity, largely occupied the sphere in which man stands vis-à-vis man without organic connection; where however such a connection existed, particularly with peculiar positions of station, German law has asserted itself.

§. 99. Eternal Value of Roman Law: System in Terms of the Nature of the Case

In still yet another sense does Roman law represent eternal legal truth besides the steadfastness of positive law and the steadfastness of entitlement. Favored by that radical standpoint, Roman legal science in its prime was able to bring the entire content of private-legal relations, particularly regarding property*, regarding relations of possession and transaction, to clear consciousness and to capture it (to stamp it [marquiren]) in accordance with all its aspects. That is to say, what sorts of dealings or legal relations are possible, how they relate to each other, and what decision follows for them on the condition of the determinate legal principles given in their law. Let this serve as an example of what I mean: the distinction of eviction [Entwährung] on the basis of a ground preceding a contract versus a ground succeeding it, the distinction between **impedimentum naturale** (objective hindrance) and **facultas dandi** (subjective incapacity) in the doctrine of **casus**, determinations regarding **mora** according to which no **culpa** is assumed but nevertheless a hindrance of that sort (not the incapacity of the debtor) exempts from the consequences, the fixed limits of various transactions (purchase, deposit, rental) and the demonstration of consequences lying in the nature of each, the development of various estimates regarding compensation in suits of property and other such institutions, delinea- **<195>** tion of considerations and motives regarding property line revisions (**finium regundorum**), etc., etc. To that degree Roman law is *raison écrit* [written reason], i.e., not a *codex of natural law* but a *codex of the nature of the case.* To wit, this development of relations and their decision is, as a rule, the proper one per se, to the degree that the legal principle itself (thus, in the first example, the bindingness of contract according to the content of consensus, etc.) is proper. On the other hand, where the Roman legal principle is false or one-sided, the entire development is of course useless and cannot serve as the standard for other times and conditions, and to the degree that our condition has new peculiar legal principles (law of marital property, agrarian law, etc.), to that degree can the development of the connections given in those life relations not be expected from the Romans but is to be achieved by our own jurisprudence, for which however that Roman development at the least serves as a pattern and example. The distinction between that which itself is a legal principle and that which is the unfolding of the natural material for the principle, i.e., that which is the nature of the case (Book II [*Principles of Law*], §. 13), clears the way for judgment regarding Roman law which even with the fullest recognition of its value is nevertheless free of all preferential treatment and is fully compatible with the highest esteem and cultivation of Germanic legal elements. For instance, I am, as my exposition of the relevant material everywhere indicates, far from recognizing the Roman law of obligation (to the degree that it is constructed on the basis of restricted actionability), Roman regulations regarding the law of marital property (dowry system, exclusion by relatives of spouses from all inheritance) or paternal power, etc., as *true legal* (ethical) *principles*, although on the other hand I recognize the treatment of the law of obligation (eviction [Eviktion], **<196> casus, mora, culpa**, Aedilian edict, etc.) as the *true revealed nature of the case.*

This revelation of the nature of the case is however something entirely different and deeper than the *mere intellectual consistency* [Verstandeskonsequenz] emphasized by Hegel as the only and in fact quite equivocal advantage of Roman law. The Romans' intellectual consistency is of course also an indispensable medium for applying legal principles to the matters of life in a proper and harmonious manner, for which reason it generally is likewise an example for all jurisprudence, even though it occasionally, especially in the system of **strictum jus**, breaks loose from actual needs of life and borders on hair-splitting. It is only through this consistency that the Romans were able to complete their law as an implemented system, closed in itself, although with the parts calibrated in terms of each other. But this mere consistency in itself would not have assured Roman legal science of its universal-historical power, were it not supported by the energetic concrete observance and valuation of life relations and commercial connections. The nature of the case (i.e., the connections and requirements inherent in factual life relations) stands in profound relation to the law-ideas themselves (Book I [*Philosophical Foundations*], §. 5); in fact, it is none other than the *purpose* (τέλος) *of life relations* which we have assigned as the principle of legal philosophy, only in subordinate fashion, that is to say it does not refer to the *highest final* goal, thus the actual ethical ideas of the institution, but, assuming this to be given in positive law, to the *intermediate* goals. The Roman jurists therefore are the most complete legal philosophers in this sphere, although for the highest sphere, the profoundest ethical and social principles of law, they are not that in the least.

Should one consider the value of Roman law to lie in the complete exposition of law-ideas rather than in the complete <197> exposition of the nature of the case, then one runs the risk of harming national legal development to its benefit. On the other hand, should one consider that value to lie in logical consistency, systematic completion, antique simplicity, that which is commonly understood as the scientific exemplariness of Roman law, thus only the *formal* aspect of the method of treatment, one thereby fails to appreciate that Roman law also contains a plethora of outstanding *material* decisions just as true for our conditions as for Roman. At this point it is idle to ask whether nevertheless it would have been more felicitous if Roman law had not formally been received in Germany but had only served as a pattern for free imitation. This having happened, we do not wish to rejoice in its possession merely as a legal-scientific *strength* but also as a legal-scientific *treasure*, and this will not keep the life-appreciation of the nation and the present, wherever such is established, from being brought to validity and authentication in the law. An ejection of Roman legal material from our life is as little possible as it is desirable. Just as the English people grew from Romans and Germans into a single people, its speech grew from a twofold stock into one speech; in a similar manner our law in Germany will always bear the imprint of its double descent in itself, and when in accordance with Dahlmann's true remark that mixtures of peoples [Völkermischungen] of that sort by no means tend to yield the worst products, why should the same not hold true for mixtures of law? The task, however, to assign to each its proper and beneficial portion and to promote their inner unification in legal consciousness as well as legal conditions, cannot be solved in the area of general reflection but only for each legal institution in accordance with its particular requirement. An undeniable fact is that we have entered a period in which, to a degree which has not been seen earlier, the legal profession [Juristenstand] is filled with the **<198>** knowledge of German law and in consequence as well with its spirit and the measure of its judgment. That hereby the German element must ever more attain the greater extension coming to it is a surely inevitable consequence and one of the best hopes of the national condition (Bluntschli). The proponents of the doctrine which first brought the coherence of law and people and thereby the national significance of law to scientific consciousness cannot and will not greet this other than with joy, and work for its fulfillment each according to vocation and gift. *Historical* direction and *national* direction are so little in contradiction that they much rather mutually condition each other, and when the one combats the other, it only misunderstands itself.

WORKS CITED BY STAHL

Acts, Book of. Cited on page 46.

Aquinas, St. Thomas. *Summa theologiae.* Various editions. Cited on page 139.

Aristotle, *Politics.* Various editions. Cited on page 45.

Bull. magn. [further information unavailable]. Cited on page 120.

Carpzov, Benedict. *Jurisprudentia ecclesiastica seu consistorialis....* 1649 and many editions thereafter. Cited on page 143.

Considerant, V. *Destinée Sociale.* Paris: Phalange, 1837–1844. Cited on page 62.

Eichhorn, Karl Friedrich. *Principles of the the Ecclesiastical Law of the Catholic and Protestant Religious Party in Germany* [Grundsätze des Kirchenrechts der katholischen und der evangelischen Religionspartei in Deutschland]. Göttingen: Vandenhoeck und Ruprecht, 1831–1833. Cited on page 129.

Gans, Eduard. *Foundation of Possession* [Ueber die Grundlage des Besitzes: eine Duplik]. Berlin: Veit, 1839. Cited on page 90.

—. *Universal-Historical Development of the Law of Succession* [Das Erbrecht in weltgeschichtlicher Entwicklung: eine Abhandlung der Universalrechtsgeschichte]. Berlin: 1824. Cited on page 180.

Gerlach, Otto von. *Regarding the Current Shape of Marriage Law* [Ueber die heutige Gestalt des Eherechts]. Second edition. Berlin: Oehmigke, 1842. Cited on page 142.

Gros, Karl Heinrich. *Textbook of Philosophical Legal Science or of Natural Law* [Lehrbuch der philosophischen Rechtswissenschaft oder des Naturrechts]. Stuttgart: 1829. Cited on page 103.

Grotius, Hugo. *De Jure Belli et Pacis* [The Law of War and Peace]. 1625. Cited on page 34, 164, 185.

Harless, Gottlieb Christoph Adolf von (ed.). *Journal for Protestantism and Church* [Zeitschrift für Protestantismus und Kirche]. Erlangen: A. Deichert. Cited on page 156.

Hegel, G. W. F. *Encyclopedia of Philosophical Sciences* [Encyklopädie der philosophischen Wissenschaften]. Unspecified edition. Cited on page 117.

—. *Lectures on the Philosophy of History* [Vorlesungen über die Geschichte der Philosophie]. Aalten: WordBridge Publishing, 2011 [1833]. Cited on page 28.

—. *Philosophy of Law* [Grundlinien der Philosophie des Rechts]. Berlin: Nicolaische Buchhandlung, 1821. Cited on pages 5, 11, 57, 101, 109, 139, 150, 178.

d'Hericourt du Vatier, Louis. *The Ecclesiastical Laws of France* [Les Lois Ecclesiastiques de France]. Paris: 1721. Cited on page 125.

Hüttner, Johann Christian. Translation of William Jones, *Institutes of Hindu law; or, the Ordinances of Menu, according to the gloss of Cullúca: comprising the Indian system of duties, religious and civil* [1796]. Weimar, 1797. Cited on page 67.

Kant, Immanuel. *Metaphysical Elements of the Doctrine of Law* [Metaphysische anfangsgründe der Rechtslehre]. Königsberg: bey Friedrich Nicolovius, 1797. Cited on page 25, 65, 104, 105 109, 145, 164, 185.

Koch, Christian Friedrich. *Das Recht der Forderungen nach gemeinem und nach preußischem Rechte* [The Law of Obligations according to the Common and the Prussian Law], 3 volumes. Breslau: 1836–1843. Cited on page 108.

Justinian, *Corpus Iuris Civilis,* Novel 117. Cited on page 143.

Justinian, *Digest,* 4.6.20, de cap. minut. Cited on page 191.

—, l. 12 §. 1 de adqu. vel amitt. poss. (41.2). Cited on page 86.

—, *Digest,* l. 39. §. 1, de jure dot., j. de adopt. Cited on page 120.

Lauterbach, Wolfgang Adam. *Collegium Pandectarum theoretico-practicum.* 3 volumes. Tubingae: 1714–25. Cited on page 143.

Luther, Martin. *Complete Writings* [Sämtliche Schriften], vol. X. Edited by Johann Georg Walch. Halle: 1739–1753. Cited on pages 131, 145.

Pfordten, Ludwig Karl von der. *Treatises from the Laws of the Pandects* [Abhandlungen aus dem Pandektenrechte]. Erlangen: 1840. Cited on page 108.

Plato. *The Laws.* Various editions. Cited on page 50.

Proudhon, Pierre Joseph. *What is Property?* [Qu'est-ce que la propriété?]. Nouvelle éd. Paris: Marpon-Flammarion, 1841. Cited on page 61.

Puchta, Georg Friedrich. *Leaflets for Questions of the Day* [Fliegende Blätter: Beiträge zu den Fragen des Tages], I. Berlin: 1843. Cited on pages 142, 151.

Savigny, Friedrich Carl von. *Representation of the Reform Undertaken in the Prussian Divorce Laws* [Darstellung der in den Preußischen Gesetzen über die Ehescheidung unternommenen Reform]. Berlin: Veit, 1844. Cited on pages 142, 144, 145, 151.

—. *The Right of Possession* [Das Recht des Besitzes : Eine civilistische Abhandlung]. Gießen : Heyer, 1806. Cited on page 89.

—. *System of the Modern Roman Law* [Pand., a.k.a. System des heutigen Römischen Rechts]. Leipzig : Veit, 1840. Cited on page 101.

Schelling, Friedrich Wilhelm Joseph von. *On the Relation of the Real and the Ideal in Nature* [Ueber das Verhältniß des Realen und Idealen in der Natur, oder

Entwicklung der ersten Grundsätze der Naturphilosophie an den Principien der Schwere und des Lichts]. Hamburg: Perthes, 1806. Cited on page 117.

Stahl, F. J. *Ancient Roman Law of Accusation* [Ueber das ältere Römische Klagenrecht]. München: 1827. Cited on page 86.

—. *The Catholic Refutations* [Die katholischen Widerlegungen: eine Begleitungsschrift zur 4. Aufl. meiner Vorträge über den Protestantismus als politisches Princip]. Berlin: 1854. Cited on page 174.

—. *The Church Constitution According to the Doctrine and Law of Protestants* [Die Kirchenverfassung nach Lehre und Recht der Protestanten]. Erlangen: T. Bläsing, 1840. Cited on page 130.

—. *The Philosophy of Law According to the Historical Perspective: Volume II: Christian Doctrine of Law and State* (Heidelberg: J. C. B. Mohr, 1833). Cited on p. 117.

—. *The Philosophy of Law: Volume I: The History of Legal Philosophy* [Die Philosophie des Rechts: Bd. 1: Geschichte der Rechtsphilosophie]. Third Edition. Heidelberg: Mohr, 1854. Cited on pages 28, 57; second edition, pp. 10, 11.

—. *The Philosophy of Law: Volume II: The Doctrine of Law and State on the Basis of the Christian World-View* [Rechts- und Staatslehre auf der Grundlage christlicher Weltanschauung]. Third edition. Heidelberg : Mohr, 1854. Cited on the following pages:

Book I [*Philosophical Foundations*]: 3, 13, 14, 19, 21, 108, 111, 119, 122, 166, 190, 191, 197

Book II [*Principles of Law*]: 4, 6, 8, 34, 36, 37, 49, 53, 78, 80, 84, 98, 99, 103, 106, 111, 114, 144, 145, 147, 148, 159, 162, 163, 181, 187, 196

Book IV [*Doctrine of State & the Principles of State Law*]: 51, 59

—. *Protestantism as a Political Principle* [Der Protestantismus als politisches Princip]. Second unrevised edition. Berlin: Schultze, 1853. Cited on page 174.

—. *Parliamentary Speeches* [Parlamentarische Reden]. Ed. J. P. M. Treuherz. Berlin: Verlag von Hermann Hollstein, 1856. Cited on p. 164.

—. *Seventeen Parliamentary Speeches and Three Lectures* [Siebzehn parlamentarische Reden und drei Vorträge]. Berlin: Hertz, 1862. Cited on p. 17.

—. *Speeches* [Reden]. Berlin: Hertz, 1850. Cited on p. 32.

Steffens, Heinrich. *Anthropology* [Anthropologie]. Breslau: Josef Max, 1822. Cited on page 118.

Stein, Lorenz von. *Socialism and Communism in Contemporary France* [Der Socialismus und Communismus des heutigen Frankreichs]. Leipzig: Wigand, 1842. Cited on page 62.

Tancred., ed. Wund. [further information unavailable]. Cited on page 119.

Theiner, Johannes A.: Variae doctorum catholicorum opiniones de jure statuendi impedimenta matrimonium dirimentia: dissertatio canonica. Breslau: 1824. Cited on page 126

Thomasius, Christian. *Institutions of Divine Jurisprudence, in which the Foundations of Natural Law are Clearly Demonstrated According to the Principles of the Illustrious Pufendorf* [Institutionum jurisprudentiae divinae libri tres : in quibus fundamenta juris naturalis secundum hypotheses illustris Pufendorffii perspicus demonstrantur ... Editio septima porioribus multo correctior, ... acc. Halae Magdeburgicae]: Salfeld, 1730. Cited on page 164.

Walter, *Archiv für das Kriminalrecht*, vol. IV [further information unavailable]. Cited on page 8.

Walter, Ferdinand. *Textbook of Canon Law* [Lehrbuch des Kirchenrechts: aus den älteren und neueren Quellen bearbeitet]. Second edition (many other editions available). Bonn: Marcus, Büschler, 1823. Cited on page 123.

Wiese, Georg Walter Vincent von. *Textbook of Ecclesiastical Law* [Handbuch des gemeinen in Teutschland üblichen Kirchenrechts als Commentar über seine Grundsätze desselben]. Vol. III. Leipzig: 1804. Cited on page 145.

ROMAN LEGAL TERMS

N.B.: Many of these terms may be referenced in William Smith, *A Dictionary of Greek and Roman Antiquities.*[140]

[140] URL: https://tinyurl.com/48au6euy

INDEX

N.B.: The page numbers below refer to the numbering of the original edition.

www.ingramcontent.com/pod-product-compliance
Ingram Content Group UK Ltd.
Pitfield, Milton Keynes, MK11 3LW, UK
UKHW020033121026
15625UKWH00060B/731/J

9 789076 660820